How Parties Win: Shaping the Irish Political Arena

In recent decades, Ireland's three major political parties have maintained over 80 percent of the vote in the face of rapidly shifting social cleavages, political values, and controversial issues, not by giving voice to particular interest groups or reacting to issues of the day, but by attempting to transform interests and issues to their own advantage.

Sean D. McGraw employs a richly textured case study of major parties in the Republic of Ireland to engage the broader comparative argument that political parties actively shape which choices are available to the electorate and—just as importantly—which are not. His longitudinal and mixed-method study relies on a variety of sources, including public opinion surveys, political party manifestos, expert surveys, content analysis of media coverage, the author's own survey of nearly two-thirds of Irish parliamentarians in both 2010 and 2012, and interviews conducted over six years.

Additionally, McGraw offers a novel way for understanding how party leaders select, and at times purposefully sideline, pressing political and social issues in order to preserve their competitive advantage. By relegating divisive issues to extraparliamentary institutions, such as referenda or national wage bargaining systems, major parties mitigate the effects of changing environments and undermine the appeal of minor parties.

Sean D. McGraw is Assistant Professor of Political Science at the University of Notre Dame, where he is a Fellow in the Helen Kellogg Institute for International Studies, the Institute for Educational Initiatives, the Keough-Naughton Institute for Irish Studies, and the Nanovic Institute for European Studies.

HOW PARTIES WIN

Shaping the Irish Political Arena

Sean D. McGraw

University of Michigan Press
Ann Arbor

Published in the United States of America by the
University of Michigan Press
Manufactured in the United States of America
⊗ Printed on acid-free paper

2018   2017   2016   2015   4   3   2   1

A CIP catalog record for this book is available from the British Library.

Library of Congress Cataloging-in-Publication Data

McGraw, Sean D.
    How parties win : shaping the Irish political arena / Sean D. McGraw.
        pages   cm
    Includes bibliographical references and index.
        ISBN 978-0-472-11950-9 (hardcover : alk. paper) — ISBN 978-0-472-03612-7
    (pbk. : alk. paper) — ISBN 978-0-472-12081-9 (e-book)
        1. Political parties—Ireland.   2. Ireland—Politics and government.   I. Title.
    JN1571.M45   2014
    324.2417—dc23

                                                            2014039444

For my mom and dad, who taught me,
by their quiet and selfless example,
to love, which is really all that matters in life

Contents

Acknowledgments

I fell in love with the land of my ancestors on my first visit there in 1990 and have been returning ever since. Ireland is now a second home for me, and I am grateful to the dozens of friends there who have welcomed me into their homes and lives over the past two decades. The Fitzgeralds, the Keoghs, and the O'Connors have become like family to me. I am particularly grateful to the generous team at the University of Notre Dame's Keough-Naughton Centre in Dublin, led by the brilliant and steadfast Kevin Whelan; his wife, Anne Kearney; and the abiding and ebullient Lisa Caulfield and her husband, Paul Sinnott. Without their insights, generosity, hospitality, and tireless support, this book simply would not have been possible. I can never thank Providence enough for bringing into my life Don and Mickie Keough and Martin, Carmel, Fergal, and Rachael Naughton, along with their families. Their friendship has been the treasure of a lifetime.

My intellectual life in Ireland has been richly supported by the extraordinary faculties at several superb Irish universities, especially those at the Geary Institute at University College Dublin and the Political Science Department at Trinity College Dublin. Individual scholars such as Michael Gallagher, Richard Sinnott, David Farrell, Jane Suiter, Gail McElroy, Ken Benoit, Liam Weeks, Eoin O'Malley, Muiris MacCarthaigh, Elaine Byrne, John Coakley, Gary Murphy, Theresa Reidy, Sean Donnelly, and Will Phelan all shared their expertise freely with me and enhanced my outlook of Irish and comparative politics. Niamh Hardiman, Michael Marsh, and Ken Carty have been my patient tutors of the nuances of Irish politics. Their vast collective knowledge and penetrating questions, as well as their willingness to comment on drafts of this book, have been invaluable to me. Though I am forever indebted to them, the limitations of the analysis provided by this book are mine alone. I am deeply appreciative of Brendan Tuohy, a valued friend, for introducing me to many of Ireland's political, economic, social, and cultural leaders. I owe a profound intellectual debt to the late Peter Mair. His insights into political parties in Ireland and in advanced democracies more broadly have framed my own study of parties.

Over the past ten years, I have been fortunate to interview hundreds of politicians and civil servants at every level of Irish politics. Their openness and willingness to share experiences with me, as well as allowing me to observe them on the campaign trail in their constituencies, has been an education in itself. With support from the Helen Kellogg Institute for International Studies at the University of Notre Dame, I was able to conduct two parliamentary surveys in Ireland, in 2010 and 2012. Notre Dame graduates Mikey Moses and Joey DiPiero—with the help of Joe Stranix, Patrick McCormack, Alison Cudworth, and others—helped conduct face-to-face interviews with nearly two-thirds of the Dáil. For their helpfulness in introducing me to their colleagues, I thank individual politicians from several parties: my long-time friend Mark Daly from Fianna Fáil; Barry Ward, Brendan Griffin, and Taoiseach Enda Kenny from Fine Gael; Ruairí Quinn from the Labour Party; Michael McDowell from the Progressive Democrats; John Gormley from the Green Party; and Aengus Ó Snodaigh from Sinn Féin.

I have deeply appreciated the intellectual community at the Minda de Gunzburg Center for European Studies at Harvard University and the Harvard Government Department. I enjoyed and profited greatly from my time at Harvard, both as a graduate student and, more recently, as a visiting scholar at the Center for European Studies, in 2013, where I learned a lot from my officemate Conor O'Dwyer. With enduring gratitude, I thank the members of my dissertation committee: Peter Hall, Robert Putnam, and Grzegorz Ekiert. Their intellectual prowess and generosity of spirit are simply unsurpassed. In particular, Peter has read and commented on more drafts of this book than I am sure he would like to remember, but he graciously pushed and supported me at every turn. In addition, several others at Harvard were influential in my intellectual formation, including Daniel Ziblatt, Torben Iversen, and Steve Levitsky. The friends I formed in graduate school, along with their growing families, continue to enrich my life and inform thoughtfully the way I look at the world, especially Jason Lakin, Paul Bodnar, Meg Rithmire, Nirmala Ravishankar, and Eric Lomazoff.

My colleagues and mentors at the Kellogg Institute and the Department of Political Science at the University of Notre Dame have nurtured my vocation to higher education since my days as an undergraduate. The Kellogg Institute has provided me an intellectual home as a guest scholar on various occasions, and my time there has been a defining factor in my intellectual life. With a grateful heart, I thank the late and incomparable Guillermo O'Donnell and the indefatigably brilliant Scott Mainwaring for their advice and counsel as both teachers and friends. Samuel Valenzuela, Andy Gould, Dave Campbell, Sebastian Rosato, Patrick Griffin, Bill Evans, Jaimie Bleck, Sarah Daly, Guillermo Trejo, John Deak, Michael Coppedge, Michael Desch, Ruth Abbey, Declan Kiberd, Jim Smyth, Phillip Munoz, Lauren Faulkner, and Monika Nalepa also provided thoughtful guidance and support. My colleagues and friends in the Keough-Naughton Institute for Irish Studies, under the tenacious leadership of Chris Fox, and the Nanovic Institute for European Studies, led by the gracious and creative Jim McAdams, have been more than generous in their friendship and support. My life-giving friends Sarah Kreps and Gustavo Flores Macias from Cornell have greatly improved my scholarship over the years, with their penetrating questions and comments on various drafts of this book. The mentor of all mentors, David Collier from Berkeley, has also been a constant source of probing questions and keen insights from the outset of my scholarly career.

In the collection and analysis of the rich and multidimensional sets of data employed by this analysis, I was greatly assisted by three incredibly talented younger scholars: Nicolas Somma (Pontificia Universidad Católica de Chile), Robert Brathwaite (James Madison College at Michigan State University), and Ben Mainwaring (Fulbright scholar at the University of Essex). In particular, Ben helped me enhance how I used the data from my parliamentary surveys and the comparative cases to enrich my overall argument. His questions, insights, and editorial comments were essential, and he will no doubt leave his own mark on comparative politics in the years ahead. In addition, Drew Clary, David Murphy, and Connor Hayes have provided invaluable support for my empirical analyses over the years.

The research for this study was supported by grants from the Fulbright U.S. Scholar Program, the Minda de Gunzburg Center for European Studies at Harvard University, and the Kellogg Institute and the Institute for Scholarship in the Liberal Arts at the University of Notre Dame. Though acknowledging the support received from these institutions, I bear sole responsibility for any shortcomings. Part of the material in chapter 4 originally appeared in "Managing Change: Party Competition in the New Ireland," *Irish Political Studies* 23, no. 4 (2008): 627–48, published by Taylor and

Francis (www.tandfonline.com). A word of gratitude goes to the team at the University of Michigan Press, especially to Melody Herr and Kevin Rennells, for their insights, generosity of time and spirit, promptness, professionalism, and kindness. I am also grateful to Les Harris for his invaluable assistance in creating a thoughtful and useful index.

Over the course of years during which I have written his book, I have been greatly blessed with supportive faith communities, including Our Lady Help of Christians Parish and Trinity Catholic High School in Newton, the Weston Jesuit Community in Cambridge, the Marist Priests Community in Dublin, and the St. Ignatius Jesuit Community in Dublin. Frs. Tom Stegman, SJ, and Brian Daley, SJ, have been valued spiritual companions over the years. The Alliance for Catholic Education (ACE) Advocates communities in Boston, Dublin, and South Bend have always been a great source of encouragement and inspiration. I especially thank my soul mates Kelly and Anand Surapaneni, as well as Kathleen and Dean Celio/Mazzone and Anthony and Molly Zavignin/McMahon, for keeping me going. The Mannings, the Donninos, the Fennells, the Spillmans, Michael Redding, Erik Goldschmidt, and so many others in the ACE Boston community were also lifelines for me. I thank tireless servants John O'Malley and Elaine Mahon in Dublin and our partners in Irish Catholic education throughout the country. At Notre Dame, I thank the extended ACE and Institute for Educational Initiatives communities for sharing the mission to help underserved children everywhere flourish fully. The Rosato and Hoyt clans have been a sturdy shelter of friendship for me at Notre Dame; their homes and families have become my own (and a source of great night prayers as well). Friends and mentors like Patty O'Hara, Scott Malpass, and Mike Seamon have taught me about commitment and fidelity, and I am grateful for their witness. In Boston, I was invited to become a member of Gary and Diane Kaneb's extended family, whose friendship and love I treasure. Along the way, beloved friends and their families have shared their homes with me as writing havens, particularly Colleen Ryan, Francis and Kathleen Rooney, Andy and Joan McKenna, Karen and Vic DeSantis, Mary Ann and Jack Remick, Rick and Megan Hernandez, Tom and Margaret Larkin, and Beth, Terry, Bev, Tom, and Debbie Scully. The Kalbas, Silk, Raleigh, Smith, Keegan, Shannon, and Zurcher families have stuck with me for over two decades, and their love and support have been essential.

I would not have the passion for teaching and research that defines my life and ministry were it not for my family, particularly my mom and dad. I cannot thank them enough for their vibrant witness and for the ways in which their example has shaped my life, as well as the lives of my loving siblings Patty, Mike, and Patrick—who provided constructive feedback at every stage of writing—and my best friend and twin, Shannon. I am also blessed with another family, the Congregation of Holy Cross. I am grateful that my community and the studies committee led by Bill Miscamble have supported me with the time and resources to pursue my dream to become a student of politics, a teacher, and a priest. I am forever grateful for the friendship and support of the great Holy Cross priests Nate Wills, Richard Warner, Bob Dowd, Dan Groody, Kevin Russeau, Tom Doyle, Jim McDonald, and John Jenkins.

Finally, I thank two people who have become an unending source of life and friendship for me, Tim Scully and Lou Del Fra. There is no idea, word, or even dream that they have not heard and read (and even, at times, reread) during these last twenty years of friendship and brotherhood. Their unconditional love has freed me to become most fully who I am in ways that I did not know were possible. Their commitment to serving Catholic schools and the Gospel through Holy Cross, Notre Dame, and the Alliance for Catholic Education has led me to live more fully. I thank them for sharing with me themselves, their families, and their ministry.

ONE

How Parties Win

A Telling Case Study

How do political parties achieve and then retain electoral predominance within a fully competitive party system? Major parties, defined as parties that persistently gain at least 15 percent of the total vote and remain a viable coalition partner in government, occur in just over half of the cases in a recent study of forty-seven democracies from around the world in the period from 1945 to 2006. The subject of *How Parties Win* is why and, perhaps even more important, how some major parties succeed electorally over time while others decline or disappear altogether.

It is often simply assumed that major parties will continue to experience electoral success—even over long periods—once they become major parties. As a result, the precise mechanisms by which parties actively reconstitute themselves and their linkages with the electorate are undertheorized. Previous explanations, especially those that focus on sociological, partisanship, and formal institutional explanations, ultimately fail to satisfy. These arguments view parties principally as dependent variables, reflections of larger, more fixed elements within society. Though they have proven useful in explaining the foundations of party systems, they insufficiently account for how major parties continue to survive. These arguments fail to explain fully how major parties endure long after the social realities that originally underpinned the cleavage structure disappear, after the collective identities of key social groups and political parties fragment and their shared interests dissipate, or after the organizations supporting these social divisions decay. Thus, such approaches fail to provide an adequate explanation of precisely how major parties maintain their electoral predominance, especially during periods of dramatic social, economic, and cultural change.

In this study, political parties are viewed principally as agents—as independent, rather than dependent, variables. Parties seek to shape how societal interests are translated into the political arena; they are not merely reflections of social realities or expressions of deep-seated social demands. Rather, parties constantly shape interests in a myriad of ways, employing multiple strategies within the ideological, institutional, and organizational arenas. Since no single strategy is sufficient in itself for understanding how major parties maintain their electoral success, my analysis improves on previous studies by using a diachronic multidimensional approach. In addition to integrating how parties proactively seek to shape electoral outcomes as a result of the choices they make on these multiple dimensions of competition, I offer a novel construct for understanding how party leaders select and sometimes purposefully sideline pressing political and social issues to preserve their electoral advantage. When major parties displace controversial and divisive issues to extraparliamentary institutions—such as referenda, national systems of wage bargaining, quangos, tribunals, and courts—they mitigate the effects of changing environments and dampen the ability of minor parties to alter the overall nature of electoral competition. This successful displacement of issues affects, in turn, the range of strategies on the ideological and organizational dimensions that parties can choose from to preserve their electoral predominance. Ultimately, because the long-term electoral success of major parties can create the impression of electoral immobility and quiescence, even the perception of "freezing" within the electoral market, we need to uncover political entrepreneurs' activity in shaping the political arena, which is often feverish but otherwise hidden from view.

The three established political parties of the Republic of Ireland—the parties and party leaders that comprise the principal empirical focus of this book—provide a crucial case for assessing how major parties achieve and retain electoral predominance. On average, these parties have managed to grab and maintain their hold of over 80 percent of the total vote, in the face of dramatic social, economic, cultural, and political change. The underlying cleavage structure in Ireland, the political value system, and the issues dimensions relevant for elections have experienced sharp change. Dramatic shifts have also occurred in the demographic composition of the electorate, as Ireland has transitioned from one of the poorest to one of the wealthiest European countries in less than a generation. Additionally, changes in Ireland's political institutions, such as membership in the European Union (hereinafter EU), North-South relations and institutions, and the national system of wage bargaining, have altered how politics in Ireland is conducted. Each of these potential sources of change has been visibly present in recent decades, yet the party system has outwardly experienced more stability than change in electoral outcomes, which previous theories cannot fully explain.

In the face of these unprecedented changes in Irish society over the last several decades, Ireland's three historic parties have maintained their electoral predominance by employing mutually reinforcing strategies within the ideological, institutional, and organizational domains. An underlying narrative of this study describes how political parties compete in a dramatically modernizing social, economic, and political context. However, somewhat paradoxically, I show herein that the meta-trends of organizational centralization and professionalization, the institutional displacement of controversial issues, and the centripetal character of ideological competition are the very factors that have reinforced the long-standing character of Irish party politics. Rather than rationalizing patterns of party competition, these trends have deepened the clientelistic and personalistic approaches that contribute to politics as usual in Ireland. My multidimensional approach to understanding how Ireland's major parties behave holds important lessons for the behavior of major parties in other contexts. How major parties in Ireland shape the demands of the electorate, constrain the political arena, and circumscribe the degrees of freedom enjoyed by competing parties has great relevance for understanding party behavior in other cases.

In this chapter, I provide a broad analysis of the comparative data concerning the electoral predominance of major parties and a brief overview of competing explanations for this predominance over the long term. I also present my argument that parties and party leaders are best viewed as agents whose choices, made along multiple dimensions, continually and dynamically shape the political offerings available to voters. Through this study, we will see how Ireland represents a telling case for understanding the processes of party endurance and adaptation more broadly by employing a multidimensional and longitudinal perspective.

Major Party Survival in Comparative Perspective

Comparative research on how major parties survive and maintain their electoral supremacy over long periods has been less than robust, perhaps because of a perception that most major parties in competitive party systems survive over the longer term. However, a review of the data reveals that major parties do not, in fact, automatically preserve their electoral predominance over time. Electoral results from forty-seven countries that experienced at least four consecutive democratic elections by 2006 demonstrate greater variation in the electoral success of major parties than one might expect. It is far from inevitable that major parties, once established within a system, will sustain their electoral stronghold.

Consider the evidence presented in table 1.1.[1] For the purposes of this analysis, a party is identified as "major" if it secured 15 percent or more of the vote in parliamentary elections and as "minor" if it gained more than 1 percent but less than 15 percent of the vote. Parties were included if they were "major" in 1945 or when a regime initiated democratic elections, if after 1945. I did not include parties that became major after 1980, because the goal was to observe the ability of major parties to survive over the longer term. To capture the variation in potential electoral trends, I offer four summary categories: the designation "always major" represents a party that secured 15 percent or more of the vote in every election; "major-minor (now major)" denotes a party that dipped below 15 percent of the vote in at least one election but recaptured enough votes to be a major party in the most recent election; "major-minor (now minor)" is a major party that has dipped below 15 percent of the vote and remained there; and "dissolved" indicates a major party that no longer exists. Roughly half of all major parties (56 percent) from across the regions successfully maintained their status as major parties in every election. Another 33 percent of major parties experienced mixed electoral success and were minor parties in at least one election. A considerable percentage of major parties in Europe (28 percent) and Latin America (25 percent) have experienced declining elec-

TABLE 1.1. Major Party Electoral Success, 1945–2012

	Europe	Latin America	Asia-Pacific	North America	Total number of Parties
Always major	22	6	6	3	37
Major-minor (now major)	5	2	0	1	8
Major-minor (now minor)	11	3	1	0	15
Dissolved	2	1	2	1	6
Total number of parties	40	12	9	5	66

Note: See the appendix for a list of the parties counted in this table.

toral fortunes and are no longer identified as major parties, based on their most recent electoral results. Finally, 9 percent of major parties in this set of countries have disappeared altogether.[2]

As recent scholarship has demonstrated, some major parties experience serious decline or disappear, as is evidenced by the Conservatives in Canada or some of the early Japanese parties. Disillusionment, anger, weak partisan identities, and large-scale perception of incompetence led to rapid decline of major parties and the collapse of democratic regimes in Venezuela, Bolivia, and Colombia.[3] Italy presents a paradigmatic case of the rupture of a party system in a long-established democracy. There, the Christian Democratic Party (DC) collapsed, and the Communist Party (PCI) dissolved, beginning a tortuous decade-long process of reconstitution into a vastly different leftist party. The failure of leaders within Italy's predominant parties, especially the DC, to adapt effectively to a dramatically changed global ideological environment (by either rearticulating their own programmatic appeals or reestablishing links to groups within civil society) contributed powerfully to their demise. This failure, combined with a large-scale reliance on state institutions and resources for the distribution of patronage to its supporters, led to eventual collapse of these major parties.

Among the major parties that have preserved their electoral predominance, there are no clear-cut patterns in terms of which types of parties tend to succeed. For example, historical legacies, ideological background, organizational structures, and institutional frameworks fail to explain fully the variation in electoral outcomes for major parties in these cases. Patterns of longer-term electoral survival of major parties from different ideological backgrounds are mostly mixed. In Europe alone, left-leaning Social Democratic parties have fared the best, with twelve of sixteen of these founding parties always maintaining their major party status, compared to only seven of sixteen center-right parties. Centrist parties have experienced the most erratic results. Of the eleven major center parties that existed since their country's first election, only three have managed to never drop below the 15 percent threshold.[4] Although left-leaning parties have been able to rely on greater numbers of core supporters to maintain their major party status, there was an overall shift to the right in the 1990s and the first decade of the twenty-first century, a trend that has benefited center-right and right-leaning parties in the last two decades. Nevertheless, we must be cautious of overstating the importance of ideology in determining these results. Parties not only reflect social realities but also shape them, which means we must be careful not to place too much weight on overall trends on the demand side of politics. In addition, party strategies on other dimensions can influence the ability of parties to adapt their programmatic positions to attract votes. That a party's choices on one dimension affect their available options on another dimension reinforces the imperative to study the multidimensional strategies of party entrepreneurs from a longitudinal perspective.

The utility of employing an approach that takes account of party strategies on multiple dimensions over the longer term exists even in the United Kingdom and its former colonies, where major parties exhibit slightly higher rates of persistent electoral success than the average across all countries in the sample.[5] For example, there are fourteen "always major" parties among the eight countries with British roots (including the United Kingdom), which equates to an average of 1.75 "always major" parties per country. This compares to only 1.27 "always major" parties per country if we consider all the countries in the sample and to only 1.09 if we remove the British legacy countries. Six out of eight of these "always major" parties have succeeded in majoritarian electoral systems, which generally produce two parties with a higher percentage of votes and could contribute to the greater numbers of major parties that have predominated over the long term. However, care must be exercised so that we do not attribute too much weight to electoral systems in explaining the electoral predominance of major parties. Not only have major parties in the United States, Canada, and the United Kingdom undergone dramatic shifts, even morphing and merging to become virtually new parties, but we also observe persistent major party domination in proportional representation systems.

These British-influenced countries have also likely benefited from a longer historical experience of democracy and therefore have deeper partisan identities and organizational advantages than major parties that emerged more recently. Nevertheless, again, we must be cautious not to overstate these advantages. Mainwaring and Zoco's analysis of electoral results in forty-seven countries leads them to conclude that competitive regimes inaugurated in earlier periods have much lower electoral volatility than regimes inaugurated more recently, even controlling for other factors. They argue that the political parties in regimes formed prior to 1945 and even pre-1978 effectively incorporated citizens into the political system and established strong attachments and long-lasting identities between parties and voters that later-forming regimes lacked.[6] In many of the post-1978 regimes, weaker attachments between parties and voters have led to disillusionment of large segments of society with parties and politics as a whole. As previously mentioned, this had serious negative consequences for democratic survival in less-established democracies such as Venezuela,

Bolivia, and Colombia. Such developments reaffirm the vital role that parties perform in incorporating citizens into the political system and developing the deep partisan identities essential for stable democracies.

Critically for our purposes, all-encompassing parties that engender long-lasting identities among their supporters—the very factor that distinguishes stable from volatile regimes—no longer appear to be present even within stable democratic regimes. Extensive evidence suggests that even in consolidated party systems, major parties are no longer all-encompassing, are less effective in incorporating citizens into the political system, and engender much weaker attachments and partisan identities among the electorate.[7] Even so, in many of these regimes, established major parties remain electorally dominant, and there is broad electoral stability, which suggests that parties are surviving for very different reasons than they did when they established their electoral supremacy. Therefore, we must turn our attention to identifying the precise ways in which successful major parties have survived in radically altered environments.

The fundamental argument of this book is that successful major parties shape how societal interests are translated into politics; they do not merely respond to changes on the demand side of politics. To overcome limitations of previous explanations of how and why major parties have been able to survive electorally over long periods despite dramatic social changes, I argue that political parties are best studied as actors that proactively seek to frame social change, rather than merely being shaped by it. Our understanding of political parties is limited if we view them as principally reflections of underlying sociological realities, as subject to a given set of electoral arrangements, or as a reflex of enduring political cultures and norms. The choices of party leaders and the strategies they adopt matter decisively for explaining why and how parties survive. By focusing on the strategic choices of party leaders to shape the political arena, I will underscore the specific ways in which major parties and party leaders select critical political and social issues, sometimes purposefully sidelining issues, to preserve their electoral predominance.

Competing Explanations

Demand-Side Theories

The electoral predominance of major parties has been explained primarily by two different types of arguments, one focusing on the demand side of the political equation and on how parties reflect social and institutional realities, the other concentrating on the supply side of politics and the various ways in which parties seek to shape how societal interests are represented within the political arena. In the types of arguments that underscore the importance of the demand side, voter interests are influenced by deep-seated social realities and cleavages, partisan identity, economic conditions, and formal institutions such as electoral systems. Successful major parties most closely reflect and respond to what voters want. In essence, these types of explanations generally argue that once the founding set of parties has secured the support of the electorate, "new entrants" have difficulty successfully displacing established parties. The argument continues that these "founding" political parties are able to reinforce traditional divisions and thereby "freeze" the electoral landscape during the period of initial electoral mobilization, which allows them to capture the enduring loyalty of voters. A certain path dependency ensues, making it difficult for major parties to lose their privileged place in consolidated party systems.

These demand-side arguments have proven useful in explaining the electoral predominance of major parties in some periods but not in others. For example, sociological explanations are often insufficient because they view parties largely as reflections of the salient social cleavages at the time of the initial mobilization of the electorate, which cannot account for how the major parties attract voters in an era when the initial cleavage structure has lost its salience or when strong partisan identities wane. In addition, not all cleavages are "generative"; that is, not all become crystallized in a political party.[8] Before cleavages take shape in the form of new political institutions, such as a political party, political elites must select and translate or "politicize" them. Party leaders make pivotal decisions about whether and how to compete over cleavages. Economic explanations are also insufficient to explain party predominance through different eras. Although economic factors certainly influence voter choices, major parties have maintained their electoral success in periods of penury and plenty, and not all cases of severe economic crisis have led to major party decline or collapse. Similarly, a reliance on electoral rules for an explanation underappreciates their contingent nature and the ways in which party leaders have employed various strategies to produce varied electoral outcomes. Electoral rules cannot adequately account for countries, like Ireland, in which smaller parties and independents experience considerable electoral success in the short term but prove unable to sustain themselves over the longer term. Their lack of success over the longer term implies that we must factor in how actors are interacting within the electoral system to produce these results.

As we shall see in later chapters, these types of arguments are useful in explaining major party survival in a specific era, but they are insufficient, in and of themselves, for explaining ongoing electoral success. In the Irish case, for example, these arguments help us to understand the early periods of Irish party competition, but they fail to explain the predominance of Ireland's three major parties in the period since the 1980s, when Irish society was utterly transformed and elections became more competitive. Chapter 2 will provide detailed evidence that highlights the insufficiency of these types of demand-side arguments, by demonstrating that major parties have maintained their electoral success in radically different social, economic, and political environments.

Another type of argument focuses primarily on the demand side of politics by employing spatial theories of party competition. The key insight here is that political parties modify their ideological positions to increase their electoral appeal in conjunction with changes in public opinion. The main driver in such arguments continues to be the social demands of the electorate, but greater emphasis is placed on the active ways in which parties respond to ever-changing demands among voters. Anthony Downs's scholarship represents an early version of this approach, assuming that voters have independent preferences and that parties merely respond to voters. Downs defined parties as teams of individuals that adopt ideologies as a means of achieving their office-seeking goals.[9] From this perspective, the most successful parties are those that are most responsive to shifts on the demand side of politics. Parties are vote-maximizing actors that respond to popular opinion by offering policy proposals that are attractive to large enough sectors of the electorate to win sufficient votes to gain office. Presumably, once major parties capture the support of particular sections of the electorate, they maintain this support over time. According to Downs's argument, the only way significant change occurs within a party system is if rapid changes in the distribution of voters happen, such as when suffrage is extended or when a major change occurs in popular citizen preferences.[10] Dramatically altered electoral environments create openings for new parties to emerge, which can adopt new, popular programmatic appeals without facing the mobility constraints of established parties.

However, not all major shifts in the distribution of voters have generated new parties, and more often than not, even when new parties do emerge, they fail to survive over the medium and longer term. For scholars such as Downs, the answer to this puzzle is that opportunistic leaders of established parties alter their parties' programmatic appeals to capitalize on positions that correspond to where large proportions of voters place themselves along the ideological spectrum. Successful major parties, therefore, alter their ideological positions because of challenges from minor emergent parties and maintain their predominance, while the minor parties tend to disappear. The continuing electoral success of major parties within this perspective ultimately rests on the capacity of their leaders to adapt their programmatic positions to maximize their electoral appeal. Following the Downsian approach, much research has focused on the shifts in the demand side of politics as the real driver for change and has overlooked the active role parties take to frame the parameters of ideological competition.

Supply-Side Theories

In addition to the electorate's demands for policies and material benefits, parties also offer a supply of policies and promises. From this perspective (an approach favored in this study), party leaders proactively shape the set of choices available to voters, rather than primarily responding to voter demands. The demand-side approaches previously described are useful, but the critical ability of party leaders to manage the supply of representation needs to be incorporated more fully into our understanding of how major parties adapt and survive electorally.

Recent supply-side research has begun to explain how parties adapt their strategies on ideological, institutional, and/or organizational dimensions in order to shape the contours of electoral competition and the choices available to the electorate. Many of these studies, however, have focused on party adaptation on one or two dimensions, without appreciating a broader perspective of the range of choices available to party leaders on multiple dimensions. Since party strategies on one dimension influence what is possible on other dimensions, studies that isolate key choices on a particular dimension often ignore or underappreciate the dynamic and often multidimensional character of party competition. The multiple ways in which parties manage the demands of the electorate in mutually reinforcing ways require greater attention.

Choices within the Ideological Dimension

There are several ways in which party leaders seek to shape how interests are translated into the political arena within the ideological domain. First, party leaders must decide on an appropriate combination for the programmatic and clientelistic linkages they offer the electorate. Factors such as levels of economic growth, intensity of party competition, and control over state resources interact to influence the set of incentives confronting parties as they seek to balance these different types of appeals.[11] Second, once party leaders choose to compete with other parties over ideological concerns, they must decide what issues to engage, which positions to take, and how much to emphasize them. A critical insight advanced by recent scholarship is that major parties not only shift their positions on issues but also alter the salience and ownership of issues based on whether they assume adversarial or accommodating policy positions. These choices can affect electoral fortunes for parties across the spectrum within a party system.[12] Finally, party leaders must choose who they are seeking to represent within the electoral process. Whether they choose to represent all voters, only those that share a defined set of ideological beliefs, or a party's own rank-and-file member interests can greatly impact how parties compete ideologically and how well they do in elections.[13]

Recent research has also advanced our understanding of how parties engage these various decisions on the ideological dimension, but further work is required. For example, it is unclear why ideological competition would take on a centripetal character in a modernizing country like Ireland despite a growing heterogeneity of views on a multitude of issues and an electoral system based on proportional representation. A fuller understanding of ideological competition requires taking into account the choices party leaders have made to displace issues. As the Irish case will illustrate, issues are regularly displaced as party leaders recur to extraparliamentary institutions such as referenda, national systems of wage bargaining, and quasi-autonomous state bodies (quangos). When party leaders choose to displace issues institutionally, they can affect the salience and ownership of issues, much like when they shift programmatic appeals. During electoral competition, these displacement strategies allow major parties to avoid exacerbating internal divisions over controversial issues, such as abortion, and to focus their energies on issues where they have a proven edge over minor parties. At the same time, these strategies also permit the major parties to claim that these contentious issues are being addressed within the political arena. This introduces another means by which major parties can buffer their electoral support as they deprive minor parties of opportunities to mobilize the electorate around salient issues in a rapidly changing social and political environment. By examining the institutional dimension in conjunction with programmatic appeals, this study both applies and extends recent scholarship on party competition on the ideological dimension.

Choices within the Institutional Dimension

Major parties have consistently enjoyed certain advantages over their minor party competitors. By exploring the choices parties make on the institutional dimension, the analysis in this book expands our understanding of how political parties take advantage of the state to preserve their electoral predominance. The argument set forth here underscores the importance of institutions because they provide party leaders with a powerful set of tools to advance their own agendas. I offer a different perspective than the classic "cartel party" thesis originally put forth by Katz and Mair. A key focus of their argument is the way in which major parties manipulate institutions to secure financial and material resources: for example, enacting favorable regulations that provide established parties with state funding for campaigns and free access to television broadcasts. Major parties in most advanced democracies, including Ireland, have sought to protect their electoral predominance in similar ways by securing monetary and material resources. However, party leaders have also employed institutions to secure ideological and symbolic resources and prevent challengers from utilizing these resources. In addition to examining how parties increasingly depend on the state to fund party organizations, to regulate campaigns, and to extend patronage, I demonstrate how established parties manage how issues are addressed in the political arena via an array of extraparliamentary state institutions.

Later chapters will demonstrate how even though party leaders in Ireland may not have intended to create a set of state institutions to relegate difficult issues from the electoral realm, these institutions, once created for other purposes, have been used by entrepreneurial party leaders to secure an electoral advantage. They have incrementally provided Ireland's major parties with institutional vehicles to creatively represent heterogeneous social interests and maintain internal party heterogeneity while handling complex policy issues and making decisions that privilege some groups over others. These institutions have simultaneously inhibited new parties and issues from successfully dividing the major parties. This ability to overcome the challenges of defection and threats from new entrants is a hallmark of cartel parties as they respond organizationally to a new electoral environment. Therefore, my approach identifies another means by which parties seek to affect the salience of issues. The institutional displacement of issues critically affects the range of strategies available to major and minor parties on the ideological and organizational dimensions. This, in turn, helps major parties retain their electoral support in radically different electoral environments.

Choices within the Organizational Dimension

The choices party leaders make within the organizational domain are directed toward effectively mobilizing the electorate to win elections. An important finding from recent studies is that the internal structures of parties greatly influence the capacity of parties to shape electoral competition to their advantage.[14] In particular, the balance between rank-and-file members, elected officials, and a party's headquarters are critical to understanding how parties select candidates and party leaders and decide on which policies to promote. Recent scholarship has emphasized how the internal autonomy and flexibility of party leaders vis-à-vis rank-and-file members affects the degree to which parties can adapt their strategies to changing social and electoral contexts.[15] Likewise, parties' internal heterogeneity affects their ability to adapt. When parties are comprised of internal constituencies that can be mobilized in favor of a programmatic shift, party leaders are less vulnerable when they choose to lead their parties in a new direction.[16] A greater appreciation of these internal structures and processes has enhanced our understanding of how parties use organizational strategies to preserve their electoral edge. However, these studies also cannot sufficiently explain the electoral survival of major parties.

As we shall see in later chapters, organizational linkages are especially critical. The centripetal character of ideological competition and the institutional displacement of issues can contribute powerfully to prevent changes in society from altering the nature of electoral competition. To use the Irish case as an example, parties often evince very little programmatic differentiation during elections. As a result, personal appeals and organizational capacity are the primary mechanisms by which candidates and parties establish and maintain linkages with voters and distinguish themselves from one another among the electorate. Major parties coordinate their national and local efforts to maximize their organizational edge over minor parties and independents, thereby sustaining their electoral advantage over the longer term. I show that precisely the meta-organizational trends of centralization, professionalization, and other attendant modernizing political developments are, paradoxically, the very factors that have reinforced the long-standing, local character of Irish party politics. Whereas Kirchheimer saw electoral-professional and catchall parties as catalysts of modernization, these trends have deepened the clientelism and localism that contribute to politics as usual in Ireland. The capacity of that country's major parties to keep the locus of competition on the ability of candidates to deliver goods and services to the local constituency bolsters their electoral appeal over their minor party challengers. Thus, parties can affect the demands voters perceive as important by mounting certain kinds of activities within constituencies and balancing this with a coordinated effort at the national level to maximize their electoral outcomes.

The Cumulative Impact of Party Leader Choices

I contend that parties and party leaders do more to shape the demands of the electorate than previous studies acknowledge. Certainly, parties respond to the changing demands of the electorate, but they also condition the choices available to voters. This book, therefore, integrates the study of the supply and demand of representation within a political system by restoring a greater appreciation of how parties proactively shape electoral competition. Additionally, this analysis underscores the choices Ireland's major party leaders have made on ideological, institutional, and organizational dimensions in order to preserve their electoral predominance and thwart challenges from minor parties.

Like previous scholars, I analyze how major parties adapt their ideological positions and organizational structures to sustain effective linkages with voters, but my analysis also emphasizes the institutional dimension, which is necessary to understand how parties maintain their predominance over the longer term by shaping the choices available to the electorate. In the case of Ireland, major party leaders have repeatedly shifted their programmatic offerings over a series of elections, largely by adopting issues that have gained or could gain popularity within society to dampen the appeal of minor parties and independents. By shifting their programmatic offerings, the major parties greatly constrained ideological competition, leaving voters with little choice but to choose the candidates and parties best positioned to serve local interests—the established bailiwick of the major parties. The constant shifting of ideological positions by major parties has, over time, prevented minor parties from "owning" particular issues, and it has therefore helped the major parties sustain their longer-term electoral advantage. In the realm of Irish party organization, the growing centralization and professionalization undergone by the major parties has resulted in a consolidation of the organizational advantage they hold over minor parties and independents in terms of numbers of candidates and volunteers as well as financial resources.

Over time, smaller parties appear to have weakened under the financial and media-intensive demands that modern electoral politics imposes on party organizations.

Rather than primarily focusing on how parties increasingly depend on the state for financial resources, campaign regulation, and electoral rules (as some scholars suggest), I present specific evidence from the Irish case to reveal that established parties manage issues via an array of extraparliamentary state institutions to shape how changing societal interests are engaged politically in ways that preserve their electoral success.[17] Since the 1970s, precisely when the electoral marketplace was opening up and becoming increasingly competitive, these extraparliamentary state institutions removed contentious issues from parliamentary debate, fostered consensus among the electorate, and ultimately constrained the electoral arena. Including this institutional dimension helps deepen our appreciation of how political parties actively engage in selecting (or ignoring) the multitude of potential cleavages that exist in any given society, which, in turn, helps consolidate the remarkable electoral predominance of Ireland's major parties.

The adaptive capacity of party leadership acting strategically and simultaneously along these three dimensions has facilitated broad consensus within Irish politics. By stifling more contentious disputes within society and relegating controversial issues outside the electoral and parliamentary arenas, party leaders have constrained the political arena and consolidated their electoral predominance. A closer analysis of the recent period of rapid social, economic, and political change will show how Ireland's leading political entrepreneurs have employed these various mechanisms to channel and sometimes even manipulate the public will. Rather than giving voice to the many contending issues and social groups that have emerged as a result of Ireland's dramatic modernization and thereby risking a heightened intensity of interparty competition, the leaders of Ireland's major parties have sought to manage interests both within and outside the parliamentary and electoral arenas.

Ultimately, a central contention of the analysis in this book is that the longer-term electoral effectiveness enjoyed by major parties rests largely in dynamically and interactively appreciating the strategies they employ across these three dimensions. Party strategies within the ideological dimension often interact with organizational features of parties, which, in turn, can also be also influenced by what options party leaders choose to engage within the institutional domain. As the Irish case will illustrate, the centripetal nature of ideological competition in Ireland has been sustained over the long term largely because major parties have displaced to extra-parliamentary institutions the issues that could have otherwise restructured electoral competition and negatively affected their appeal among voters. In turn, organizational strategies have interacted with these ideological and institutional strategies, allowing party leaders to focus their attention on tactics that enable them to deliver goods and services to their constituents more effectively and then focus elections on their competency to deliver.

Ireland: A Telling Case

The study of strategic actions of Irish party leaders provides a useful case for understanding precisely how major parties survive over long periods despite dramatic changes in society. A useful case is not necessarily a "typical" case but a "telling" one, in which "the particular circumstances surrounding a case serve to make previously obscure theoretical relationships sufficiently apparent."[18] Party competition in Ireland provides a telling case for both empirical and theoretical reasons.

Few countries have been enmeshed in a dynamic and changing environment like the one that resulted from the unprecedented social, cultural, and economic transformations experienced by the Republic of Ireland from the late 1980s onward. Within a span of a generation, Ireland was catapulted from one of the poorest to one of the wealthiest countries in Europe and then, since 2008, into one of the most fiscally challenged countries once again. The economic boom of the 1990s and the first decade of the twenty-first century utterly transformed Irish society. The boom altered incomes, the nature of the workforce, levels of educational attainment, the structure of family life, the percentage of immigrants, and even where people lived. Significant shifts in attitudes and voter preferences among the electorate have occurred simultaneously as Irish society rapidly evolved. The sources for these shifts among the electorate include the historic achievement of peace in Northern Ireland; the attenuated role of the once-dominant Catholic Church and the attendant proliferation of contending moral views; the increased presence of immigrants of European and, increasingly, non-European provenance; the electorate's sharpened awareness of corruption among incumbent politicians; and Ireland's deepening integration into the European Union and the global economy. The social, cultural, and racial homogeneity that once characterized Ireland has become less prevalent, hollowing out the consensus that had eased the forging of the broad, cross-class appeals so vital for the major parties' longer-term success.

Despite this dramatically changing environment, Ireland's three historic parties—Fianna Fáil (Soldiers of Destiny), Fine Gael (Family of Gaels), and Labour—have successfully dominated elections for eighty years by averaging a combined 84 percent of the first-preference vote since 1927 and leading every single government. Although Labour does not consistently maintain the vote threshold of 15 percent necessary to be considered a major party at all times, I include it in this discussion of the other two major parties because it is the oldest party in Ireland and has been Fine Gael's most consistent coalition partner since 1948. Even the seismic shock of Fianna Fáil's thrashing at the polls in the 2011 general election did not fundamentally alter the long-standing predominance of these three historic parties. The success of Ireland's major parties is striking in the midst of the country's dramatic social transformation and the heightened electoral challenges from minor parties and independents. The original undergirding of the party system—namely, the legacy of the Irish Civil War and the traditional Catholic, peasant, and agrarian cultures—has subsided. Fueled partly by declining party attachment and increasing numbers of floating voters, elections have become increasingly hotly contested. Despite the potential for the emergence of new issues, cleavages, and parties, the historic parties have maintained their electoral predominance in a multitude of electoral contexts.

The degree and scope of Ireland's social change have eroded the utility of previous explanations for major party success. Ireland's historic Civil War partisan identities have waned, and the once traditional, agrarian and insular society has evolved into the one of the world's most globalized societies. Additionally, Ireland's electoral system of proportional representation by single transferable vote (PR-STV) is a necessary but insufficient explanation of electoral outcomes. PR-STV affords voters a high degree of choice, as they can rank their preferences among candidates from every party and independents when casting their vote in multimember constituencies. This facilitates an emphasis on personalistic and localist politics, while allowing parties to compete over programmatic differences as well. The major parties have benefited from this institutional arrangement (as will be discussed in chapter 2) mainly because members of larger parties who are elected to office are better positioned to respond to local concerns—a recognized priority for many Irish voters. Nevertheless, PR-STV is proportional and presents a relatively low threshold. Minor parties and independents have periodically emerged because they are strong advocates for neglected issues and constituency needs, and they have been rewarded electorally. However, a majority of these smaller parties and independents have failed to survive over the longer term. How major party leaders have been able to contain minor party challenges and maintain their electoral predominance in an era featuring hotly contested, more competitive elections and greater diversity of social, economic, and cultural attitudes within the electorate requires explanation beyond what institutional arguments about PR-STV can provide.

To study this phenomenon, cross-sectional analysis is insufficient. The longitudinal analysis employed here, which accounts for how parties compete in different electoral environments, is more useful for understanding the precise ways in which parties and party leaders both shape the choices available to the electorate and respond to evolving demands from the electorate. The inclusion of multiple sources of empirical evidence supports this approach. First, evidence from surveys and aggregate voting data establish how parties are adapting to changes in the views of the electorate and how this affects electoral competition. Next, to establish a more comprehensive picture of how party leaders shape the demand side, the analysis provides an exploration of the policy positions that parties offer, the choices of governments on the institutional dimension, and the ways in which party organizations have changed at both the local and national levels over time. This entails analysis of political party manifestos, expert surveys, and the content of media coverage during campaigns, as well as detailed electoral case studies and interviews of hundreds of individuals at the local and national levels, conducted over six years of field research in Ireland. Additionally, I personally designed and implemented face-to-face parliamentary surveys that focused on the specific strategies employed by each Irish TD (Teachta Dála, member of the lower house of the Irish parliament) during the 2007 and 2011 election campaigns. These interviews of over two-thirds of Irish parliamentarians in two very different electoral and social contexts allow us to test many of the theoretical arguments outlined in this study. The multiple methods approach that I have employed has augmented the causal inferences of this single-country case.

A close longitudinal analysis of a single-country case study contributes to the comparative study of political parties by identifying new causal mechanisms, which, in turn, clarify longer-term political processes and outcomes. Furthermore, this approach allows us to test and reformulate important theoretical arguments.[19] In this case, the analysis refocuses our attention on the vital role political parties perform in shaping electoral competition rather than merely responding to changes on the demand side. Concretely, this book underscores how the institutional displacement of controversial issues and the persistent emphasis on localist politics has helped Ireland's major parties preserve their electoral predominance in a rapidly changing society. The ability of party leaders to frame contentious issues in ways that both protect their interests and respond to vital concerns among the electorate represents a novel finding. The multidimensional approach employed here highlights how the choices that party leaders make interact, in dynamic and reinforcing ways, to help them maintain their electoral success. Ultimately, exploring key elements of both the demand and supply sides, at both the macro and micro levels in Irish elections, invites a similar approach to the study of parties and party systems in other countries. It remains to be seen what the cumulative impact of these party strategies will be on the quality of democracy over the longer term in Ireland, but this study offers initial insights into how we might think about such normative questions and how we might begin to consider what they mean for parties elsewhere.

Organization of the Analysis

In chapter 2 of this book, I describe the dynamic environment in which Irish parties have been competing since the 1970s, emphasizing how the main structural features of Irish society have experienced change. The chapter introduces the puzzle of how major parties survive electorally despite a reshuffling of the underlying cleavage structure and decided transformations in the social and political attitudes of Irish voters, set within a context of declining voter attachments. Chapter 2 also underscores a disconnect between the supply and demand sides of Irish politics. Curiously, the chapter emphasizes how salient issues among the electorate are not consistently translated into electoral or parliamentary debates and exert little effect on electoral outcomes.

Chapters 3–5 turn to explanation, exploring the multiple ways in which party leaders adapt to manage the sharp transformation that characterizes contemporary Ireland. Each chapter explains sequentially the choices Ireland's major party leaders make on one of three key strategical dimensions—institutional, ideological, and organizational—in order to preserve their electoral predominance.

Chapter 3 highlights the unusually flexible and ultimately centripetal character of ideological convictions held by the major parties. Detailed evidence from manifestos, expert surveys, and parliamentary surveys is marshaled to demonstrate how Ireland's major parties have constrained the electoral arena, thereby preventing minor parties from shifting the nature of electoral politics away from tried-and-true electoral tactics of focusing on competency of delivering goods and services at the local level.[20]

Chapter 4 examines the choices party leaders make to address key issues facing Irish society via extraparliamentary institutions within the Irish political system, including referenda, the national system of wage bargaining, quangos, tribunals, and courts. Ireland's major parties relegate issues that, if left for parties to compete over openly in elections, could generate unwanted contention, disrupt the entrenched advantage of historic parties, and advance the electoral interests of challenger parties. An analysis of key moments in the period since the 1980s provides insight into the tangible ways in which parties cleverly managed issues in these other institutional contexts in varied ways, depending on their overall electoral strategies.

Chapter 5 explores the changing features of party organizations, highlighting growing trends toward professionalization, bureaucratization, and centralization within national party organizations. Evidence from constituency-based case studies, hundreds of interviews, two parliamentary surveys, and analyses of internal party organization underscore intense modernization of politics at the national level, which, in turn, reinforces the tenacious localism in Irish politics. Major party leaders have masterfully navigated the PR-STV system as a result of the combined ideological, institutional, and organizational strategies they have employed to maximize their electoral outcomes.

In chapter 6, I discuss the critical reasons why these party strategies have worked in the Irish context and apply the lessons acquired from this case to a broader set of comparative cases. The sets of strategies adopted by major party leaders within the three domains discussed in this book can be observed in a variety of other contexts. For example, parties in Europe and Latin America employ referenda and national wage agreements, thereby displacing controversial issues to the extraparliamentary arena. Additionally, Irish major parties' reliance on persistent localism and clientelism in the face of modernization presents an interesting comparison with how major parties in other countries (e.g., Venezuela, Italy, and Japan) have employed similar strategies to maintain their electoral predominance.

I conclude the discussion in chapter 6 by exploring the implications that this study's findings have for the quality of democratic representation. In particular, I highlight the risks that political party leaders run in endlessly finessing the very issues important to the electorate as they seek to preserve their electoral success. The choices party leaders make to balance how they structure interests from above and represent interests from below greatly affect whether and how parties are able to maintain their vital linkages with voters and sustain their electoral success. At the same time, the impact of the practices discussed in this analysis on the quality of democracy is perhaps not strictly negative. After all, voters and constituents consistently exercise their own choices, returning to office, time after time, the very parties and party leaders who logroll the issues so effectively. This book ends by posing questions about the consequences of the cumulative effect of these multiple choices for the character of democratic representation.

TWO

Ireland's Political Arena

A Puzzling Mismatch of Supply and Demand

The study of Irish party competition, especially since the onset of sweeping social, economic, and political change, presents a puzzle. Despite seismic shifts, why have many of the salient political issues associated with these changes not been translated into the electoral arena? How and why have dramatic changes on the demand side of Irish politics not been mirrored by a similar degree of change on the supply side? Is it the case that social factors bear little impact on Irish electoral competition, or (more likely) have political parties somehow acted to mitigate the effect of these changes on partisan politics? Whereas some approaches emphasize parties as reflections of social interests, merely responding to shifts in public opinion, I argue that Ireland's major parties have framed issues strategically to serve their electoral interests. The Irish case provides keen insight into the ways in which political parties interact with society both to represent constantly evolving interests and to shape how these varied interests are addressed within the political arena. By highlighting this critical channeling function performed by Ireland's major parties, I seek to restore a fuller appreciation of the mediating role that parties play in democracies.

In this chapter, I first illustrate key changes on the demand side of Irish politics, including diversifying socioeconomic conditions; shifting religious and cultural practices, attitudes, and norms; and declining party attachments. A greater diversity of perspectives now exists on a growing number of salient issues within Irish society, some of which hold the potential to reshuffle electoral fortunes in the political arena. The original conditions that were believed to explain the electoral predominance of major parties no longer exist, which implies the need to look to other causes.

Second, I describe trends in Irish general elections, underscoring the remarkable constancy on the supply side. A more in-depth analysis of the content and nature of partisan appeals to the electorate will occur in later chapters. For now, I simply highlight that Irish elections have been characterized by noteworthy continuity over time, across regions, and among nearly every conceivable social group. The ongoing predominance of Ireland's major parties, despite the rise and fall of minor parties and independents, reinforces the insufficiency of pure formal institutional arguments that rely on Ireland's PR-STV electoral system to explain the trends we observe.

Finally, this chapter explores how these demand-side changes are and are not reflected within the electoral arena. Reviewing issues identified by voters as most important and models of voting choice reveals a critical disconnect between what matters to voters and what is actually competed over during elections. These findings confirm that parties shape how issues are engaged in the political sphere; they do not simply reflect social concerns. It is not that social demographics and programmatic concerns do not matter for Irish voters. Rather, party leaders have adapted their strategies on multiple dimensions to minimize the impact of these factors and to keep the focus of electoral competition on competence and the ability to deliver locally—the traditional bailiwick of Ireland's major parties.

The Dynamic Demand Side

Ireland's dramatic social, economic, and political transformation has turned virtually every aspect of Irish society on its head. As I will show throughout the remainder of this book, the puzzle Ireland presents is that the demand side of issues associated with the seismic shifts in Irish society has not been translated into the electoral arena. To prepare us to better understand how this has occurred, this section illustrates how the most important of these changes bring a growing diversity of experience and set of attitudes among voters on programmatic concerns and overall expectations of what parties and the state should be providing. It explores the extent to which these social changes have contributed to the opening up of the electoral marketplace that has occurred since the mid-1980s. This review reinforces the insufficiency of explanations primarily focused on the demand side, since the major parties have survived—even thrived—despite the waning of the social bases for major party support. The review also confirms our need to examine the precise ways in which parties shape how these dynamic social interests on the demand side become translated into electoral politics.

The Founding Cleavage and Historical Legacy

The nationalist cleavage was the basis for the initial formation and subsequent development of Ireland's party system, but it has grown less salient in the contemporary electoral arena. Unlike many other Western European party systems, the Irish party system emerged not from sharp social divisions such as class but, rather, as a result of a split emanating from within Sinn Féin ("We Ourselves") during the Civil War (1922–23). This split pitted those who favored the Anglo-Irish Treaty that established the twenty-six counties of the Irish Free State in the south and the six counties of Northern Ireland that remained part of the United Kingdom (Cumann na nGaedheal, which later became Fine Gael) against those who opposed the treaty (who later became Fianna Fáil). Historically, a significant proportion of voters were strongly attached to one of these two Civil War parties on the basis of this initial defining identity, making the votes of implacable party loyalists unavailable to party competition.[1] In addition, the Labour Party's failure to compete in the initial elections of 1918 is often cited as a key factor that has hindered its ability to attract supporters, because nationalist issues framed party competition and elections during the earliest phase.[2] These founding conditions have contributed to the cross-class nature of partisan ideological appeals and to the overall weakness of the Left in Irish electoral politics.

Later chapters will discuss in greater detail the broadly similar incentives that the three historic parties face as they seek to preserve their electoral predominance. To be succinct here, the nature of the party system's founding cleavage, the resulting narrow ideological divide, and the subsequent catchall character of all three parties have provided incentives to these three parties to compete in comparable ways. Fianna Fáil has dominated elections for extended periods, including leading government for all but nine of the forty-one years between 1932 and 1973. The sheer electoral success of Fianna Fáil during this period meant that Fianna Fáil strategies provided a virtual road map for other parties; it became "the way of doing politics." These largely imitative electoral strategies worked pretty well; Fine Gael and Labour have led every non-Fianna Fáil government since 1932. As the contemporary electoral environment has become more competitive and uncertain, the historic parties have adopted broadly similar strategies, thereby preventing smaller parties and independents from altering the overall dynamics of electoral competition that have ensured their success for decades.

The intractable challenges—over decades—associated with a permanent resolution to this founding divide have provided few electoral incentives to the historic parties. As the parties saw nothing but risk in adopting a strong stance on Northern Ireland, the issues posed by the North have been conspicuously absent as a decisive factor during general elections.[3] However, a majority of Irish voters have consistently and overwhelmingly expressed the view that Northern Ireland is an important issue for them during elections. For example, 58 percent of respondents in 1982 reported that Northern Ireland was a very or fairly important issue to them in the recent general election. There were similar results in 1989 (53 percent), 1991 (76 percent), and 2002 (68 percent).[4] During this period, the number of Irish citizens who believed that Northern Ireland was a critical issue was twice those who did not. Yet, somewhat contradictorily, when respondents were asked, in open-ended questions, to rank the most important issues in the same elections, Northern Ireland barely surfaced. In fact, between 1969 and 2011 (see table 2.2 later in this chapter), Northern Ireland has only twice been perceived as one of the most important issues (by 12 percent of respondents in 1973 and 13 percent in 1997). Surprisingly, even highly controversial and publicized events—such as the death of ten hunger strikers in Northern Ireland who were protesting their lack of recognition as political prisoners in 1980–81, the Anglo-Irish Agreement in 1985, or the cease-fire negotiations of the 1990s, all of which posed considerable challenges for politics in the Republic—failed to elevate Northern Ireland into a top election issue.[5]

The violence of the conflict in Northern Ireland known as the Troubles peaked in the early 1970s. Half of the 3,172 deaths due to political violence throughout the Troubles occurred between 1971 and 1976.[6] In contrast, the more contemporary period has been characterized by the cease-fires of the mid-1990s, the Good Friday Agreement of 1998, and the consolidation of a peace agreement with the implementation of the power-sharing government in 2007. As further time elapses from the Civil War and peace consolidates in Northern Ireland, one might expect to find declining support for Fianna Fáil and Fine Gael, especially among younger voters for whom the Troubles are but a distant memory and the Civil War is known only from history books.[7] Despite the obvious importance of the founding cleavage in shaping the Irish party system at its inception, how this original divide can continue to hold its grip requires explanation. The social realities that originally generated the cleavage structure have faded, the collective identities of key social groups and political parties have fragmented, shared interests have dissipated, and the organizations supporting these social divisions have experienced decay. This fluctuating environment invites a closer examination of the type of party-citizen linkages that the major parties have been able to sustain over the longer term in order to maintain their electoral support as the founding cleavage has waned.

Partisan Identity

Given the declining salience of the founding cleavage, it is not surprising that partisanship levels have dramatically declined. Since 1978, Irish parties have experienced a steady decline of voters who "feel close" to a particular party.[8] The percentage of voters in the Irish electorate reporting that they lack a close relationship with and are therefore "unattached" to any party has more than doubled, from 34 percent in 1978 to over 77 percent in 2011.[9] This development could presage real changes in party fortunes and, ultimately, a restructuring of long-standing patterns of party competition, because "attached" voters are obviously much more likely to vote for their party.[10] Among respondents that reported feeling close to Fianna Fáil, 81 percent voted for that party in 2007, and only 9 percent voted for other parties. The comparable figures for those feeling close to the two other historic parties were slightly lower: the percentage that voted for "their" party or other parties in 2007 were 76 percent and 7 percent for Fine Gael and 70 percent and 23 percent for Labour.[11] Declining party attachment and consistent electoral results suggest that parties have found other ways to maintain consistent support. If the weakening of party attachments continues to accelerate, parties may experience even more dramatic challenges to their electoral fortunes. If the major parties do not employ strategies to maintain their predominance, this rising uncertainty in the electoral marketplace opens the door to growing competition from new parties within the electoral arena.

Sociological Factors

Irish society has undergone a complete overhaul. Changed, in particular, are the very factors that many employ to explain the electoral dominance of major parties and the character of political competition—namely, Ireland's Catholic, peasant, and agrarian roots. These factors, Carty argues, consolidated traditional values, reinforced clientelism, entrenched local machines, and nurtured strong allegiances to particular candidates and parties.[12] Though these factors no longer dominate the Irish social and geographic landscapes, the heavy emphasis on localism persists, which has continued to benefit major parties over their minor party challengers. Ireland was once one of the most homogenous European societies, which made it easier to develop consensual policies that were applicable in virtually every locale. This homogeneity, too, has changed. Sources for the shifts include the attenuated role of the Catholic Church and the attendant proliferation of contending moral views; the increased presence of immigrants of European and, increasingly, non-European provenance; the sharpened awareness of public corruption among incumbent politicians; and Ireland's deepening integration into the EU and the global economy.

One of the most fundamental shifts in voter attitudes occurred as a result of the changing status of the Catholic Church in the cultural arena. The Irish, once a homogeneous, overwhelmingly Catholic and socially conservative people, have undergone profound change. The preamble to the 1937 Constitution is revealing: "In the name of the Most Holy Trinity, from Whom is all authority and to Whom, as our final end, all actions both of men and States must be referred, We the people of Ireland humbly acknowledging all our obligations to our Divine Lord, Jesus Christ . . ." Contrast these words with those of Ireland's ceremonial head of state President Mary McAleese seven decades later, when she identified contemporary Ireland as "neither Catholic nor Protestant, neither agnostic nor atheist, neither Islamic nor Jewish, but a welcoming homeland for people of all faiths and of none. It is a homeland indebted to a rich and complex Christian heritage and with a rich and complex multi-faith heritage already in the making."[13] McAleese's words are all the more striking given that she is openly and devotedly Catholic. More recently, Michael D. Higgins, who was elected president in 2011, incorporated a humanist reflection in addition to the normal prayers in his swearing-in ceremony. The Irish state also closed its embassy to the Holy See in 2011 in reaction to the Vatican's response to the sexual abuse crisis, further sidelining the Catholic Church within Irish politics.

Although most Irish citizens (87 percent) still identify themselves as Roman Catholic, the practice of Catholicism in contemporary Ireland has undergone dramatic change.[14] Religious practice, defined in terms of regular Mass attendance (i.e., attending religious services at least once a week or more), has fallen from 91 percent in 1974 to 83 percent in 1981, 65 percent in 1999, and 34 percent in 2012—with below 20 percent in 2012 among the young, the large working-class areas of Dublin, and other large urban concentrations.[15] Although, among advanced industrial democracies, Ireland continues to exhibit one of the highest levels of regular attendance at weekly religious services, regular religious practice has undergone a precipitous decline there in less than a generation.

Even though attendance at religious services has dropped off considerably, other indicators of religiosity, such as belief in God or an afterlife, have remained exceptionally strong among the Irish.[16] The central issue for many Irish Catholics pertains not to diminished core religious beliefs but, rather, to a bruising loss of confidence in the institutional Catholic Church. The highly publicized sexual abuse scandals in the 1990s and the subsequent inadequate response to the crisis on the part of church leaders in the 1980s and 1990s have steepened the decline of this historically strategic institutional actor. Confidence in the church has plummeted, from 51 percent in 1981 to 20 percent in 2008.[17] Disapproval of clergy influencing voting shot up from 26 percent in 1991 to 44 percent in 1999, and disapproval of the institutional church seeking to influence government decisions jumped from 28 percent in 1991 to 54 percent in 2008.[18] The numbers who reported that the church was providing adequate answers to moral problems and challenges of family life also collapsed, with less than one-third of those interviewed reporting that the church offered viable answers to key issues facing contemporary Ireland.

These shifts have been accompanied by attendant changes in attitudes toward religious and moral issues—notably abortion, divorce, and homosexuality, sources of anguished public debate throughout the 1980s and 1990s. Opinion polls and surveys reveal a stronger liberalizing trend when Irish citizens are asked for their views on divorce (legalized in 1996) or abortion (which remains virtually illegal, except, according to new legislation in 2013, in cases when the mother's health is in grave danger). For example, 64 percent of Irish respondents in 2006 believed that abortion was acceptable in some circumstances, a decisive change from the 1980s. Likewise, those who considered abortion always wrong or never justified has declined consistently over this period, falling from 82 percent in 1981 to 36 percent in 2006.[19] Unsurprisingly, younger age-groups consistently hold more liberal views toward abortion.[20] Among all age-groups under the age of sixty-five, an average decline of 40 to 50 percent occurred among those who thought abortion was always wrong. By contrast, those over sixty-five have remained, on average, 85 percent opposed to abortion in all circumstances.[21] Even greater shifts in public opinion have occurred in the last few years. A 2013 poll found that there was support for permitting abortion in particular circumstances: 84 percent would permit abortion when a woman's life is at risk, 79 percent when the fetus is not capable of surviving outside the womb, 78 percent in cases of rape or incest, and 70 percent when a woman's health is at risk. Traditional views grounded in Catholicism have not entirely disappeared, however, and abortion is a potentially divisive issue today: only 37 percent of citizens support legalizing abortion for cases when a woman simply deems it to be in her best interest.[22] Despite ongoing tensions, which provide parties with the potential for mobilizing different sectors of societies, abortion and other cultural issues have remained essentially sidelined during electoral competition. As we shall see in subsequent chapters, political parties have consistently found ways to avoid addressing these controversial issues head-on, at least until public opinion has shifted sufficiently to allow them to assume a populist position without jeopardizing their electoral chances.

Ireland's previously underdeveloped, agrarian, and peasant society has also changed—morphing, within one generation, into a highly developed, postindustrial society that ranks among the world's most globalized.[23] The economic boom of the 1990s and 2000s turned Irish society on its head: income levels doubled; educational access expanded by more than 500 percent for secondary and third levels; women in the workforce doubled; urban population increased from 40 to 60 percent; the island of perennial emigration metamorphosed to the point where 10 percent of the population was comprised of immigrants; and the long-term scourge of unemployment was reversed as the number in employment doubled—rising to over two million in 2006. In the downturn since 2008, unemployment has once again spiked, to 15 percent in 2010–12.[24] Income inequality has also widened since the 1990s, making Ireland one of the most unequal nations in the developed world.[25] Finally, Irish citizens are moving more frequently, which could further undermine the ties of localism that pervade Irish politics. Although 70 percent of Irish citizens still live within the county in which they were born, geographic mobility has been increasing since the early 1990s.[26]

These rapid and unpredictable transformations posed profound challenges to Irish society, relating to changes in family structure, women in the workforce, child care and education costs, the legalization of divorce, and social benefits for nontraditional families, among many other changes. Most important, the social and economic homogeneity that once characterized Ireland has become less prevalent, hollowing out the consensus that had made broad, cross-class appeals—so vital for the major parties' longer-term success—easier to forge. One might predict that these increasing disparities would generate a wider dispersion of attitudes toward competing economic and social policies, thus opening up the electoral market for ideologically driven left- or right-wing parties to capitalize on these differences. But the growing diversity of attitudes on issues has not led to dramatically altered electoral outcomes in Ireland. Major parties have continued to dominate electoral competition, thereby thwarting the ongoing rise of minor parties.

When partisan attachments were declining during Ireland's economic prosperity in the 1990s, the major parties maintained their electoral support. Conventional thinking would have Irish voters reward the main political parties for their effective stewardship of the Irish economy. High growth rates, low unemployment, low inflation, and a successful insertion into the global economy should then garner rich electoral harvests for Ireland's governing parties. Ireland's newfound wealth increased total government spending and made otherwise contentious policy trade-offs largely unnecessary. Additional resources also made it easier for candidates at the local level to "deliver the goods." Ireland's expanding economy, it could be argued, facilitated the integration of non-Irish individuals without exacerbating intense conflicts over jobs. Ireland's expanding economy and resultant job growth muted the agonizing immigration debate so glaringly present in other Western European countries. Ireland's economic success encouraged the peace process within Northern Ireland, enhancing dialogue with the promise of economic security. The implication is that had the dramatic shifts affecting the identity and lifestyle of Irish citizens described in this chapter occurred during a period of economic decline, established parties would have been held accountable by the electorate, with a potential reordering of the party system.

Although the expanding economy may have contributed to the electoral success of the major parties, economic conditions do not provide a sufficient explanation for the predominance of the established parties over the longer term—or even in the period of economic crisis between 2008 and 2011. The literature on "economic voting" generally links economic performance with the incumbent parties, as voters reward or punish these parties according to their assessment of how well the economy is doing either for them individually or the nation as whole.[27] The primary economic indicator that Mair used in an earlier analysis of economic voting was the percent change in the per capita disposable income (measured by taking total personal expenditures on consumer goods, services, and personal savings, calculated in constant prices). The only two elections between 1948 and 1987 where the incumbents increased their vote share (1965 and 1973) were also the only two when positive growth was registered in per capita personal disposable income. According to this analysis, incumbents do better when personal disposable income increases. The correlation between percent change in the electoral support for incumbent parties and percent change in the personal disposable income was .31, which suggests that 10 percent of the variance in the electoral record of incumbent governments is explained by levels of personal disposable income.[28]

However, in the period of rapid economic growth since 1987, major increases in economic well-being have coincided with increased electoral volatility. More recent data comparing the change in the vote share of governing parties with leading economic indicators (GDP growth, unemployment, and inflation) reveals that incumbent parties have consistently performed badly in elections irrespective of economic factors (see fig. 2.1). The 1987 and 2011 election results indicate that economic crisis dramatically undermined the electoral support of incumbent parties; however, no government won reelection between 1973 and 2002. The incumbent party or parties received a lower percentage of first-preference votes in sixteen of the nineteen elections between 1948 and 2011, with Fianna Fáil alone experiencing slight increases as an incumbent in 1965, 1973, and 2002. There is a clear and visible association between GDP growth and incumbent parties' electoral success (though there are too few cases to reliably analyze quantitatively), but incumbent parties have been punished by voters even in periods of strong economic growth, as in the elections of 1997 and 2007, when the incumbents lost votes despite GDP growth of 9.5 percent and 5.3 percent, respectively. This indicates that factors other than the economy drive Irish voters' behavior and loyalties, at least in times of economic prosperity.

Even in the few elections where Fianna Fáil experienced success as an incumbent, economic indicators were mixed. Economic growth was on the rise in 1973, unemployment was down, and inflation had increased by only 2.7 percent from the previous year. While growth was still positive in 2002, it was slower, inflation was unchanged, and unemployment was slightly higher. The Rainbow Coalition of the Fine Gael, Labour, and Democratic Left parties likewise suffered electoral defeat in 1997, even though GDP growth was over 9 percent, inflation was less than 2 percent, and unemployment, while still double-figured, was less than in many previous years. The link between the economy and unemployment has only limited explanatory power, especially because the critical economic indicators rarely have entirely positive or negative effects at any one time.

In sum, explanations for electoral outcomes based primarily on either

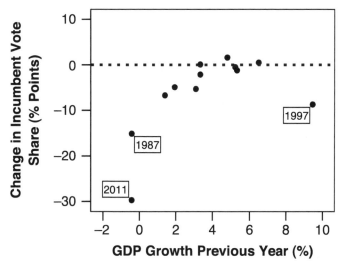

Fig. 2.1. Incumbents' Vote Share and GDP Growth, 1973–2011

single economic indicators or aggregate economic data ultimately provide an insufficient understanding of the long-term electoral predominance of Ireland's major parties. These parties have thrived through thick and thin. Most recently, the severe economic and financial crisis experienced in Ireland beginning in 2008 certainly influenced the crushing defeat of Fianna Fáil and the Greens in the 2011 election. Yet, it is unclear whether there will be longer-term ramifications for the party system, because Fianna Fáil appears to have bounced back from this historic defeat. This circumstance echoes a pattern where Irish incumbent parties have been punished by voters to some extent—both in good and bad economic times—but have rebounded with extraordinary consistency. As we shall see later in this book, economic crisis is generally a key factor in the decline or disappearance of major parties and in dramatic changes in party systems. However, not all economic crises lead to such decline or change. Therefore, we must look to the behaviors and practices of the parties themselves to gain a fuller picture of how these parties have preserved their preeminent place in Ireland's crowded electoral market in periods of economic plenty and penury.

Irish Attitudes on Specific Issues

There is a puzzling disconnect between the growing diversity of attitudes on the demand side of Irish politics and the relatively stable electoral outcomes on the supply side. The stable supply of outcomes have mitigated how dramatic changes in society have been translated—or not—into the electoral arena. To more fully appreciate this puzzle, I examine voter attitudes on key issues and relate them to voters' perceptions of where political parties stand on these same issues. Differences exist between voters' ideological positions, on the one hand, and parties' ideological positions, on the other—a surprising result that warrants further examination.

Spatial theories of electoral competition assume that voters are motivated by policies and that they choose the parties and candidates closest in proximity to their positions. In turn, these theories perceive parties as vote-maximizing actors that respond to popular opinion: they offer policy proposals attractive to sectors of the electorate that are large enough to help them win sufficient votes to gain office. According to this perspective, one might expect parties' ideological positions to reflect the beliefs of some specified voting constituency. Consequently, shifts in citizens' preferences would prompt corresponding shifts in parties' ideological positions.[29] In an electoral system like PR-STV, where parties can win seats with as little as 10 percent of the vote, we would expect opportunistic parties to cater to attitudinal blocs of 20 to 30 percent of the population. As will be shown in the following discussion, there are relatively clear noncentrist blocs in Irish public opinion that appear large enough to sustain parties on issues like the environment and abortion—yet parties are not taking up these positions.

To gain perspective on the range of attitudes that exists on the demand side of Irish politics—and the paucity of alternatives on the supply side—consider a snapshot of the distribution of voters and the perceived position of parties on salient issues taken from the 2007 Irish National Election Study (INES).[30] Figure 2.2 reveals where voters placed themselves and the parties on the issues and cleavages that undergird electoral competition in Ireland. It indicates the approximate percentage of voters who place themselves at every point on a ten-point ideological scale. This figure shows that the clear-cut consensus and narrow ideological spectrum that is often assumed among Irish voters does not exist on every issue. Nevertheless, voters perceive parties as taking centrist and sometimes indistinguishable positions. Voter attitudes on these six issues indicate that despite a high percentage of voters who place themselves in the center of the ideological spectrum, a considerable degree of dispersion among voter attitudes still exists on almost every issue and is enough to potentially sustain noncentrist political parties in many cases.

Although voter attitudes are dispersed on these issues, voters perceive the parties as having centrist positions. Figure 2.2 includes dashed lines to

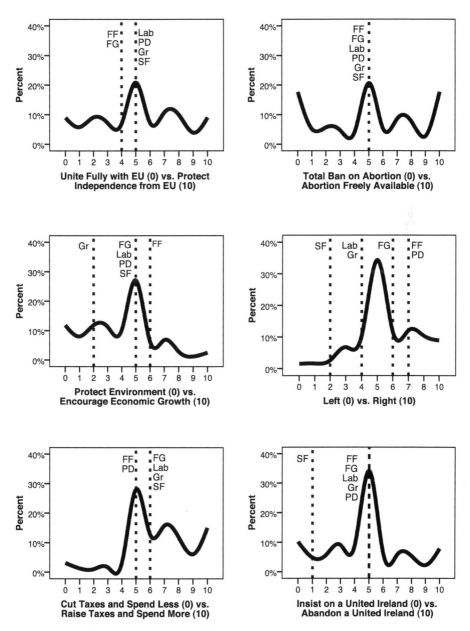

Fig. 2.2. Distribution of Voters' Self-Placement and Party Placement on Key Issues according to the 2007 INES

indicate the median position at which survey respondents placed parties' ideologies; most voters see Irish parties as having virtually indistinguishable centrist positions. Consider attitudes toward abortion: over 50 percent of the voters located themselves on the extremes of the spectrum, but the voters tended to perceive that all parties share identical, centrist positions on abortion. A similar dynamic exists with respect to attitudes toward the EU. A 2012 *Irish Times*/Ipsos MRBI survey found that 45 percent of respondents believed that integration had gone far enough, 16 percent felt that integration had gone too far, 37 percent believed that the process should continue, and only 2 percent had no opinion.[31] The dispersion of attitudes, with over a third of voters in 2007 holding more extreme positions, implies a lack of consensus on the issue. Yet a majority of Ireland's political parties have maintained their consistent and all-encompassing support in favor of EU policies, and voters perceive that differences between parties on this issue are small or nonexistent.

Attitudes toward the level of taxation and public service also reveal a disconnect between public opinion and parties' positions. Most of the parties in 2007 tilted to the right in terms of advocating tax cuts during this election. In fact, Labour—a party traditionally associated with the Irish center-left—was the first party out of the gate in promoting further tax cuts during the 2007 election campaign.

Emerging salient issues such as the environment and immigration similarly reveal a multiplicity of views among voters. Nearly 25 percent of voters place themselves in the center when deciding on whether protecting the environment or promoting economic growth is more important, but over 50 percent of voters reported a pro-environmental position. Although voters were skewed to pro-environment policies, the Green Party (with less than 5 percent of the popular vote) was the only party perceived by voters to share this position. Attitudes on immigration represent the most uneven results, as nearly 70 percent of voters agreed that there should be very strict limits on the number of immigrants permitted in Ireland. Though respondents were not asked to assess party positions on immigration, other sources suggest that parties avoided taking conspicuous positions on the issue. In the 2007 election, Irish parties generally agreed that integration and immigrants were important, but their efforts toward more effective integration were minimal. According to one study on immigration in Ireland, political parties were among "the least diverse, the least responsive, and the least capable of leading by example when it comes to representing the diversity of twenty-first century Irish society."[32]

The distribution of voters and party placement on the subject of Northern Ireland is noteworthy. Most voters placed themselves in the center of the spectrum on this issue. That voters also perceive all of the parties in the same location—even Fianna Fáil, the party with the historic emphasis on establishing a united Ireland—signals that the issue has been depoliticized in Irish politics. Data from other sources reveal that voters and parties continue to care about the Northern Ireland issue and may even mobilize around it and its symbols, but it rarely seems to influence vote choice. According to Lyons, support for a united Ireland has been relatively stable within Ireland but fluctuates depending on whether voters are asked about unification in principle or about specific policies. It is much easier to support and hope for an eventual united Ireland than to make choices about the precise roles and powers the UK, Irish, and Northern Ireland politicians and governments will exercise.[33] The high percentage of those in the center on this issue implies some combination of principled centrists who favor a unified Ireland and other voters who are less interested in the issue and therefore take a neutral stance. Meanwhile, increasingly professionalized party leaders might be reluctant to campaign on this issue because their ability to deliver results is simply very limited.

It is striking that voters have difficulty locating the political parties on these issue spectrums. Perhaps the most frequent response among the voters when asked to place parties on an ideological scale on these issues is "don't know," as table 2.1 illustrates. The lowest percentage of "don't knows" across all issues occur when parties have signature issues, such as environmentalism for the Greens (15.5 percent) and Northern Ireland for Sinn Féin (15.9 percent). Except for these instances, Fianna Fáil has the lowest percentage of "don't know" responses in every policy area, followed in order by Fine Gael, Labour, the Progressive Democrats, the Greens, and Sinn Féin. Voters are most unable to place parties on abortion, and the EU has the second-highest percentage of "don't knows" for every party. Later chapters will describe the strategies party leaders have employed on abortion and EU issues in order to produce these outcomes without jeopardiz-

TABLE 2.1. Percentage of Respondents Unable to Place Parties' Positions in 2007 INES

Variable	Fianna Fáil	Fine Gael	Labour	Progressive Democrats	Greens	Sinn Féin
Taxes and spending	19.0	22.6	25.9	28.6	30.5	39.3
Northern Ireland	17.8	21.3	28.5	29.9	35.5	15.9
Environmentalism	19.8	23.6	24.9	27.9	15.5	37.8
European Union	20.9	24.9	29.6	31.5	31.5	38.9
Left-right	23.1	24.2	25.6	26.4	27.2	29.8
Abortion	33.2	35.8	39.4	41.2	45.2	48.5

ing their support. Finally, voters appear worse at positioning Fianna Fáil and Fine Gael on a left-right spectrum than on most policy areas, whereas they are better at placing minor parties on a left-right spectrum than on many of the policy areas. The extent to which the major parties have strategically acted on multiple dimensions to facilitate these results will be analyzed in subsequent chapters.

As mentioned previously, Ireland's voters place all of the parties in one or two positions on the issue scales and most often in the centrist position. Interestingly, voters appear more likely to perceive no differences among the parties on issues most closely associated with the underlying cleavages that divide Irish society and that have been identified as the most critical issues for voters. Perceiving no differences, the voters place the parties in identical, centrist positions. For example, figure 2.2 reveals that voters locate all the parties in the center of the spectrum on abortion—a cleavage that pits religious/conservative citizens against secular/liberal ones and has been a source of great contention in Irish society since the 1980s. Voters perceive that only Sinn Féin has a unique position on Northern Ireland—the founding cleavage—whereas the other parties are all perceived to hold centrist positions on the issue. The voters also cluster the parties in a narrow ideological space on the EU and on taxation and spending issues, which are arguably the next two most critical issues dividing the Irish electorate. Decisions the parties make on these issues have considerable impact on the economic well-being of Irish citizens, and voters are divided on the policies, yet the voters perceive the parties as having similar positions. Voters perceive slightly greater differences among the parties on the environment, an issue that has attracted growing attention in public discourse. But the environment remains a relatively minor issue among both voters and parties.

Irish Perceptions of Left and Right

Although perceiving only minor differences among Ireland's political parties in terms of their ideological positions on the essential issues confronting society, voters appear to view parties differently from an overall left-right perspective. Rather than placing all of Ireland's parties in one, centrist position on the left-right spectrum (as they do on the various issue scales), voters in contemporary Ireland perceive the parties as representing four distinct locations on this spectrum (see fig. 2.2). As mentioned, research has found that left-right positioning is only weakly correlated with social attitudes in Ireland and is uncorrelated with economic issues. The left-right dimension has never really captured the most intense divides among Irish parties, nor has it been a particularly useful way of collapsing into one dimension the totality of issues over which parties compete. Irrespective of whether voters associate the left-right spectrum with religious/conservative and secular/progressive sets of issues or with economic issues, that voters perceive recognizable differences among the parties in terms of their overall ideological positions is striking given that this does not appear to be the case on specific issues. This implies that parties are behaving in ways that obscure their positions on specific issues without undercutting their broader left-right positioning in the eyes of voters.

Evidence from a regression analysis on vote choice in 2007 (discussed in detail later in this chapter) confirms that the position of voters on the left-right spectrum did not powerfully drive their decisions. The model shows that Fianna Fáil voters are, on average, substantially farther right on the spectrum than other parties' voters (as indicated via significant and substantive coefficients), but the intraparty variance in ideology is large relative to the interparty differences (as indicated via low R^2 values, ranging from .094 to .144). The average Fianna Fáil voter might be more conservative, but the left-right attitude is not a very good predictor of how that person will vote.

Other tests confirm that the differences between supporters of the same party are far greater than the differences between voters from different parties. An ANOVA (analysis of variance) test for interparty differences in ideology and policy attitudes show that only 1 to 2 percent of the variance in policy attitudes and 12 percent of the variance in left-right ideology is interparty. This confirms the cross-class and catchall nature of electoral support that Ireland's political parties have been able to sustain during the contemporary period of Ireland's dramatic social transformation. Again, marked differences exist among voters on virtually every issue, but this does not seem to affect which party a voter supports in elections. Therefore, we must reflect further on what explains the apparent disconnect between, on the one hand, the essential issues confronting Irish society and the dispersion of attitudes that exist among voters on the demand side and, on the other, how parties choose to compete over these issues and respond to voter concerns on the supply side.

The weak explanatory power of the terms *left* and *right* in political contexts in Ireland shows that they are "semantic containers" that respondents fill with their own meanings to make sense of a complex political world; they assume different and even contradictory meanings in different contexts and for different voters.[34] Repeated analyses of opinion polls taken between 1981 and 2007 reveal minimal relative change in individual self-placement on the left-right scale: Irish citizens consistently position themselves solidly at the center or center-right on the left-right continuum throughout the period. The similar placements over time mask the fact that perceptions of what it means to be on the left or right have changed significantly. Voters and parties alike have changed their attitudes and beliefs, but they have not altered their overall—relative—position on the ideological spectrum. Furthermore, that 15 to 20 percent of voters "don't know" where to place themselves on a left-right continuum reinforces the complexity of understanding this measure in the Irish context.

Given that successful political parties will shift ideological positions to match the evolving views of the electorate, it is not surprising that we observe similar patterns in terms of the relative placement of Ireland's political parties on the left-right scale. The longitudinal evidence suggests that a considerable percentage of Irish citizens place all the parties in the center of the ideological spectrum and consider Fianna Fáil and Fine Gael as occupying roughly the same ideological space. Additionally, a significant portion of the electorate is unable to decide where to place the parties at all. For example, 37 percent of respondents did not know where to align Irish parties on a left-right scale in one of the earliest polls that was conducted in 1976.[35] In that same poll, 8 percent of respondents perceived Fianna Fáil as slightly left of center, whereas another 13 percent perceived them to be "very right-wing." Similar differences in perception of where to place Fianna Fáil existed in 2007 as well. Fianna Fáil has long been lauded for its ability to be all things to all people, and the wide-ranging views of where the party is located on the left-right spectrum suggest either that the party's catchall appeal has been successful by being intentionally ambiguous in its policy appeals or that citizens have vastly different conceptions of what left and right mean. A more recent example confirms a similar pattern: 10 percent of respondents in the 2007 INES assigned Labour a value of 2 on a 10-point left-right scale, but 5 percent assigned it a value of 7 on the same scale.

It is important to reiterate the dynamic nature of party positions. Virtually all of the parties shifted their ideological positions throughout this period; however, their relative positions remained the same. These results reflect a widespread perception that the entire party system shifted to the right during the Celtic Tiger years, as consensus emerged over Ireland's low-tax regime and a variety of other social issues. By 2011, both Fianna Fáil and Fine Gael were perceived to have shifted further to the right because of their more explicit support of the requirements from the

EU, the International Monetary Fund (IMF), and the European Central Bank (ECB) to introduce significant austerity cuts in public spending. The overall ideological movement we observe implies a highly responsive set of parties that shifts its positions to maintain their appeals among a constantly changing electorate.

The fluid ideological positioning appears to have greatly reduced the ability of the minor parties to successfully market their policies among the electorate. The 2007 INES data reported that a considerable percentage of respondents recognized the "stated" programmatic positions of the smaller, more ideologically identifiable parties (the Greens, Sinn Féin, and the Progressive Democrats): 20 percent placed the Green Party on the left, 45 percent located Sinn Féin on the left, and 42 percent placed the Progressive Democrats on the right.[36] However, the number of respondents who did not know where to place these parties on a left-right continuum was between 25 and 30 percent, a much higher percentage than the 11 to 13 percent of respondents who were unable to place the major parties on the left-right scale. This is a remarkable result given that these challenger parties have generally sought to brand themselves with a more highly profiled ideological position than the three main political parties.

The number of Irish parties has doubled since 1973, but respondents still place two-thirds of the parties in the center and one-third of them (Sinn Féin and Labour) slightly on the left. Despite dramatic social changes and increased diversity of attitudes on an array of salient issues, voters continually support centrist positions offered by parties, because they perceive no other option. Successful parties must respond to the policy concerns of the changing Irish electorate to maintain their electoral support, but they are also framing issues in ways that mitigate the impact of the growing diversity within Ireland when it comes time to vote.

Ireland's Long-Standing Electoral Continuity

Although the demand side of Irish politics has experienced considerable change, the supply side has been much more stable—at least in terms of overall electoral results. It is instructive to understand the basic mechanics of PR-STV before we highlight longer-term electoral patterns. The PR-STV system allows voters to rank their preferences for as many candidates as are on the ballot within a constituency, and between three and five members of parliament are elected from Ireland's forty-three (changed to forty in 2012) multimember districts. This permits voters to support both candidates and parties, depending on how they want to rank their preferences. Although it is only necessary to place a "1" next to a single candidate to ensure a valid vote, a voter can also express lower preferences (i.e., 2, 3, 4, 5, etc.) for as many candidates as are slated in a given constituency. Should first-preference votes not be sufficient or necessary to get a preferred candidate elected, votes are "transferred" to the next preferred candidate. Even though one may award as many preferences as there are candidates, each voter still only has one vote, which may be transferred so as to minimize the number of "wasted" votes.[37] Each iteration of the vote count verifies how many candidates have successfully reached the quota necessary to elect candidates. If seats are still open, votes are augmented by combining the next-preference votes both of the surplus votes from any candidate who has successfully reached the quota and from the eliminated lowest vote getter. These combined votes are then transferred to the other candidates sequentially until the necessary number of candidates reaches the quota.[38] Over the years, the major parties have mastered the intricacies of this system, in several different contexts, to maintain their predominance. Later chapters will describe how Ireland's major parties have altered their strategies to take advantage of the incentives that PR-STV creates, albeit in constantly changing electoral contexts.

Ireland's three established parties—Fianna Fáil, Fine Gael, and Labour—have consistently won the most seats and votes in elections and have consistently dominated the formation of governments. Figure 2.3 illustrates this predominance of the Irish electoral landscape by the major parties over the span of almost a century. The major parties have proven adept at thwarting competition from over a dozen minor parties that have emerged and then disappeared throughout this period. This episodic appearance of minor parties reveals a pattern of fluctuations in Ireland between a system with two and a half parties (Fianna Fáil, Fine Gael, and the smaller Labour Party) and a multiparty system in which additional parties have entered parliament and formed government with either Fianna Fáil or Fine Gael.[39] Journalists and scholars alike characterized the electoral earthquake of 2011 as the "end of the affair."[40] A widely held view was that the 2011 election represented nothing less than a major realignment of Irish politics. But although Fianna Fáil then experienced a shellacking unlike any in its eighty-five year history, the more things appeared to change, the more developments during and after that critical election conform to longer-term patterns of party competition. The ongoing predominance of the three main parties taken together, albeit with different levels of individual support among these parties, is striking. Despite the electoral shock waves

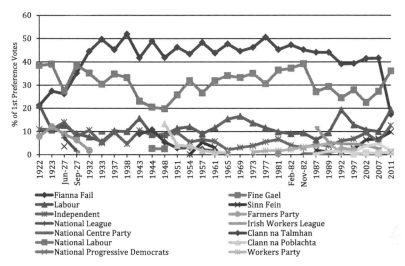

Fig. 2.3. Percentage of First-Preference Vote of Political Parties in Irish Elections,
1922–2011

delivered by the electorate in the 2011 election, the three historic parties
still received 73 percent of first-preference votes. Although this figure is
lower than the average of 84 percent since 1927, it is consistent with the
two previous elections in the twenty-first century, where the major parties
also received an average of 77 percent of the first-preference vote. As early
as 2013, there were initial signs that Fianna Fáil was not finished as a major
influence in Irish politics.

Furthermore, the persistence of long-standing patterns of coalition
arrangements after the 2011 election also signaled that the more things
changed, the more they remained the same. At that time, for the seventh
time since 1948 and marking a return to a familiar pattern, center-right
Fine Gael and center-left Labour formed a governing coalition to replace a
coalition led by Fianna Fáil. Since the founding of the Irish state, one of the
Civil War parties has always led the government. Despite Labour's 2011
campaign of "Gilmore for Taoiseach," Fine Gael was clearly in charge, and
Labour again assumed its accustomed minor position within government,
thereby lowering the prospects of a shift toward more sector-based patterns of competition. Among the ministries that Labour received in the
new coalition were the Department of Public Expenditure and Reform
and the Department of Social Protection, two departments whose budgets
were cut to the bone. These cuts most directly impacted the very voters

who were calling for more state-led left-leaning policies when they supported Labour. Whereas both poll losses over internal party divisions and uncertainty over future policy goals characterized Labour, Fine Gael kept its head down and tried to stay focused on controlling government decision making. Just as Fianna Fáil had done before, Fine Gael lobbed responsibility for unpopular decisions onto its coalition partners. The more pragmatic and ideologically flexible Civil War parties once again outmaneuvered Labour and the other minor parties. It is useful to take a closer look at Ireland's electoral trends over time, across space, and among different social sectors to appreciate the degree of their dominance.

Electoral Continuity across Time

A review of the electoral landscape over time underscores the ongoing electoral success of Ireland's major parties at a time when society was experiencing dramatic change. The electoral predominance of major parties challenges overly deterministic understandings of how sociological factors influence the supply and demand of representation in Irish politics, because major parties succeed in very different social contexts. In addition, the rise and fall of minor parties confirms that politics is far from static. The ability of the major parties to successfully respond to changes in society and challenges from minor parties reinforces the need to examine the role of strategic choices employed by Irish party leaders.

Until 2011, Fianna Fáil had been the most successful political party in terms of the percentage of seats won in parliament in postwar Europe. Since 1932, Fianna Fáil consistently received 40 to 50 percent of the first-preference vote, which is a remarkable feat even though the party's vote share declined to between 39 and 41 percent in the three general elections from 1997 to 2007.[41] The 2011 election measured a volatility level of 30 percent according to the Pedersen index—the third most volatile level ever in postwar Europe. In that election, Fianna Fáil experienced unprecedented defeat, with a first-preference vote share sinking to a mere 17 percent, a staggering decline by twenty-four percentage points since 2007.[42] This was Fianna Fáil's lowest vote share since the 1930s; the party's vote share had not dipped below 39 percent since 1932.[43]

During the same period, since 1932, Fine Gael fluctuated between 20 and 30 percent of the first-preference vote, while Labour averaged 10 percent. The Irish experience of a high degree of electoral continuity contrasts with Western European party systems, where voter volatility is greater, occurring generally within party blocs of similar ideological leanings.[44]

Although some degree of vote fluctuation has occurred among all Irish parties, Fianna Fáil had remained surprisingly immune to the vagaries of electoral fluctuation until the 2011 election.

When parties do perform poorly, they recover remarkably well. Fianna Fáil experienced a declining vote share in two successive elections only once (1982–87); Fine Gael has suffered consecutive losses only twice (1932–33 and 1938–48) and not since 1948; and Labour has done so on three occasions (1927–33, 1973–81, and 1997–2007). These parties have been highly resilient and adaptive to changing electoral environments. Even in the midst of more competitive multiparty elections and fluid coalitional dynamics, the historic parties have asserted their electoral hegemony. Despite a declining share of first-preference votes in the period of more competitive multiparty elections since the 1980s, the major parties maintained their dominance in the Dáil (the Irish parliament) in terms of their share of seats gained. Minor parties have been unable to breach this long-established pattern.

Until 2011, Fianna Fáil successfully offset its gradually declining vote share by optimizing Ireland's unusual electoral system. Although Fianna Fáil's vote share from its core party supporters shrank, it attracted lower-preference transfer votes from supporters of other parties. In the previous era of party competition in which it was Fianna Fáil versus the rest, supporters of smaller parties refused lower-preference votes to Fianna Fáil for fear of a single-party majority government: this concern has receded in recent general elections, given the emergence of multiparty coalition governments. Fianna Fáil's strategic choice to enter into multiparty governments since 1989 lowered the threat of transfers working against them. The party's seat bonus accordingly increased in the period before the 2011 election. The party's seats-to-vote ratio was 118 percent in 1997 and 2002 (averaging 108 percent since 1981) and 113 percent in 2007, before declining to a mere 69 percent in 2011, when the party gained ten seats fewer than merited by its 17.5 percent of the first-preference vote.[45] The party arguably ran too many candidates in the 2011 election campaign; their candidates split the vote in many constituencies, thereby reducing the numbers of seats they could have won given the percentage of vote they attracted.

The major parties' ability to attract lower-preference transfer votes has consistently been a crucial factor in shaping Irish electoral outcomes. A majority of voters cast their votes for candidates from more than one party, which means that candidates must rely on electoral support from beyond their own party faithful.[46] Successful candidates must balance their own personal support with a cross-party appeal strong enough to attract lower-preference votes. Only a minority of candidates in any given Irish general election is elected on first-preference votes alone: 19 percent (32/166) of elected TDs in 2007 and 12 percent (20/166) in 2011 won on the first count, thereby not requiring transfers from other candidates.[47] The overwhelming majority of candidates, therefore, require transfers to be elected: candidates must find ways to attract critically needed lower-preference votes. Despite the fierce intraparty competition that they may encounter, candidates from the major parties start with an electoral advantage, because they can generally expect that copartisan transfers and transfers from other parties and independents will increase their overall vote share.[48] The established parties' ability to attract both partisan and broader electoral support helped them secure higher reelection rates between 1927 and 1997: Fianna Fáil, 86 percent; Fine Gael, 81 percent; Labour, 79 percent; all other parties, 67 percent.[49] The strategic decision major parties make to attract partisan and cross-party lower-preference transfer votes has led to their higher reelection rates and, ultimately, their predominance over minor parties and independents.

Electoral Continuity across Regions

Overall electoral continuity exists across Ireland's different geographic regions as well, with some changes in recent years. Modernization has reshaped the Irish landscape by creating a new set of commuter regions and altering how rural and urban communities function. Since the 1990s, the principal divisions within the electorate have shifted from a relatively straightforward urban-rural divide into a more complex and variegated reality. Demographic transitions have repopulated previously declining rural areas, triggering the explosive growth of a significant commuter belt surrounding Dublin and some of the other large cities, as well as increasing levels of in-migration of people 25–44 years old into these commuter zones.[50] These trends pressurized the delivery of local services (transport, schools, child care, health care, retail, housing, etc.) and have posed challenges for government agencies and political parties to deal effectively with these emergent needs.

Despite these transformations, party support across Ireland's different geographic constituencies exhibits stubborn continuity. In fact, for more than six decades, since the Second World War, 75 percent of Irish electoral constituencies have supported the exact same ordering of parties in terms of their overall vote share. In all of these constituencies, Fianna Fáil consistently placed first, Fine Gael second, and Labour third or fourth, alternating places with either an independent or a candidate from a minor party.[51] Independents and minor parties have consistently enjoyed notable support, especially in urban areas, but they have been unable to break through the glass ceiling and to extend widespread support throughout the country. This pattern was shattered in the 2011 election: the order was reversed, as Fine Gael and Labour (and independents in several constituencies) dominated the top spots, and Fianna Fáil struggled for third or fourth along with Sinn Féin and an assortment of candidates from fringe parties and independents.

A closer look at the data suggests that political party competition across Ireland's varied geographic regions follows a predictable pattern: the more urban a constituency is, the more openly competitive it will be. Smaller, challenger parties usually garner more support among the urban electorate, whereas rural voters primarily rally around candidates from the established parties (and occasionally an independent). Given the remarkable degree of change in Ireland, I have included in my analysis a category for "commuter" regions, which designates those areas where significant percentages of the population commute to work in one of Ireland's larger cities (e.g., Dublin, Cork, Limerick, and Galway). In these commuter constituencies, the electoral results lay in between urban and rural constituencies; the three traditional parties remain strongest, but smaller parties enjoy episodic support.[52]

In urban areas, the Civil War parties have seen a consistent decline in their vote share, but they have generally retained first and second places in elections and show little signs of slipping into absolute irrelevance. Electoral results since 1973 serve as a useful starting point, because the 1973 election took place before many of the critical changes in Ireland that I analyze throughout this study. Before Fine Gael and Labour experienced a significant boost in 2011, all of Ireland's major parties experienced a declining vote share in urban areas between 1973 and 2007. Despite the declining share of urban votes, the results still reflect the general pattern we have already described: Fianna Fáil was first, with an average vote share in urban constituencies of 38 percent; Fine Gael was second, with 27 percent; and Labour was third, with 15 percent. Fine Gael's vote share fluctuated most, dropping from its peak of 40 percent in 1982 to its nadir of 17 percent in 2002, before rising to 30 percent in 2011. Up until 2007, Fianna Fáil and Labour have fared less poorly in urban areas, due at least partly to their larger share of the working-class vote. Labour surged to 25 percent in urban areas in 1992 under the leadership of Dick Spring, before returning to its pattern of lower levels of support in subsequent elections. That

Labour surpassed both Fianna Fáil and Fine Gael in number of seats in the 2009 local elections in Dublin foreshadowed the growing challenge confronting the two Civil War parties in urban areas. The 2011 election was particularly devastating for Fianna Fáil, whose vote share declined to 14 percent in Dublin, placing the party third in the capital city, trailing Fine Gael's 30 percent and Labour's 28 percent. After the death of former finance minister Brian Lenihan in 2011, Fianna Fáil no longer had any TDs in Dublin.

The minor parties have generally performed better in urban than in commuter and rural areas, in both vote share and seats. Minor parties have received an average of 20 percent of the vote share in urban areas, compared to 13 and 11 percent in commuter and rural areas, respectively. They averaged 13 percent of the seats in urban areas but only 3 and 4 percent of the seats in commuter and rural areas. Electoral support for any one of the minor parties remains subdued within each constituency, making it difficult for these smaller parties to attract enough votes to gain a seat. Even in the urban areas, the established parties dominate the number and percentage of overall seats won.

Minor parties appear to confront a glass ceiling, individually rarely breaching 10 percent of the vote in any given constituency. As a result, they are fortunate to win a single seat in any given constituency. Nearly two-thirds of the seats won by smaller parties in 2007 were in urban and commuter constituencies, with seven of twelve victories in urban areas. This pattern shifted slightly in 2011, when six of Sinn Féin's fourteen seats were in rural, border constituencies, where they benefited from the bitter backlash against Fianna Fáil. Even in 2011, however, nine of the nineteen seats won by minor parties were in urban constituencies.

While the smaller parties have begun to grow their share of votes in commuter constituencies, they succeeded in winning only one seat in 2007. Fianna Fáil performed slightly better within the commuter belt's constituencies in 2007 than they did nationally, receiving 47 percent of the first-preference vote in the commuter constituencies (41 percent nationally). By 2011, Fianna Fáil received only 18 percent of the first-preference vote in rural and commuter constituencies, compared to 14 percent in urban areas.

One might assume that with the increasing urbanization of the Irish population, it is merely a matter of time before most constituencies are characterized by the more open party competition experienced within urban constituencies. However, this outcome is by no means inevitable. Although parties experience a level of competition in commuter constituencies somewhere between rural and urban areas, Ireland's recent demographic trajectory projects a more complex and variegated reality. As rural areas experience repopulation and economic regeneration, with increased demand for delivery of services, it is unlikely that Irish politics will simply converge on the more competitive electoral dynamics of urban areas—unless, of course, minor parties and independents challenge the major parties by finding ways to compete with them both ideologically and organizationally throughout the country. As we shall repeatedly see throughout this book, the exceptional tenacity of localist politics in each type of geographic constituency results in a much more richly textured dynamic among Irish political parties, often resulting in dampened competition.

Electoral Continuity across Social Sectors

Ireland's historic parties have also maintained their electoral support across social classes. As mentioned earlier, the Irish party system emerged not from sharp social divisions such as class but, rather, as a result of a Civil War division. These civil war factions eventually took their seats as parties in the Dáil and channeled their intense rivalry into the electoral process, often inflaming Civil War rhetoric to deepen party identity.[53] According to one prominent Irish historian, "as other distinguishing features between the main parties became more difficult to discern, only memory continued to divide them. It may be that the image of the Civil War had to be burnished and polished, and the fires of hatred stoked, to foster the illusion that fundamental differences remained between the parties."[54]

The basis for early party competition centered on this founding political identity, and from the outset, parties generally lacked strong social bases apart from these inherited bellicose identities.[55] As a result, class-based politics, which predominated early Western European party systems, were absent in the early stages of the Irish case. The historic parties, long identified as "parties without social bases," have—over a long period—enjoyed the lion's share of support across every demographic group: class, occupation, rural/urban residence, age, gender, marital status, education, religious practice, and so on.[56]

To test these long-standing claims, I analyzed data from Ipsos MRBI opinion polls conducted between 1981 and 2006 (on record in the archives at the Geary Institute at University College Dublin). Based on these public opinion polls, the support for the major parties among each major demographic group has mirrored the overall support received by these parties in general elections.[57] Until the 2011 election, Fianna Fáil enjoyed the greatest share of support from among virtually every demographic group, with Fine Gael coming in second and Labour third, while independent candidates and the smaller parties trailed these three significantly.[58] Fianna Fáil had—over time—maintained its overall lead among voters in every category (including class), followed by Fine Gael, Labour, and the other parties, in corresponding descending order.[59] Sinn Féin and Labour generally elicited their greatest support among working-class voters, while the Progressive Democrats relied on higher support from middle-class voters. The 2011 election showed that the cross-class appeal of all the parties persisted. Not only did Fianna Fáil fall below Fine Gael and Labor, but support across most sociodemographic categories fell evenly to place Fianna Fáil in third and fourth place.

Fianna Fáil averaged 40 percent of support across age, gender, and marital status groups from the 1970s onward. Fine Gael peaked at 40 percent of support in the early 1980s and has since settled at around 20 percent of support among each social demographic category. Labour, similar to Fine Gael, has been most successful among single and younger voters (eighteen to thirty-four years old), but aside from these groups, Labour is consistently in third place, at around 10 percent of support across these social categories. The smaller parties have generally received between 5 and 10 percent of support across these demographic categories, with Sinn Féin being the exception that attracts greater support among both the youngest and the oldest voters, as well among males and single people. For each of these latter categories, Sinn Féin has increased its share since 2000.

In 2011, rather than Fianna Fáil leading in every demographic category (age, class, occupation, gender, education, residence, and religiosity), Fine Gael garnered the most support among all categories, followed by Labour and then Fianna Fáil and so on. Fianna Fáil's support fell between 23 and 28 percentage points among all types of voters, reflecting the cross-class nature of support for Irish parties.[60] The constancy of this dynamic reinforces historic levels of support for the two Civil War parties and prevents the minor parties—and, to a lesser extent, Labour—from capitalizing on more class-based appeals among the electorate. The longer this cross-class nature of party support survives, the more minor parties are enticed into making similar broad, catchall appeals to increase their vote share.

As highlighted earlier in this chapter, there have been considerable changes on the demand side of Irish politics. These changes could challenge the ability of the major parties to sustain cross-class support—a hallmark of Irish partisan politics from the outset. Since the late 1980s, a kaleidoscope of alliances have formed (and just as quickly dissolved) among political parties, depending on specific issues. Fianna Fáil, Fine Gael, and the Progressive Democrats shared similar beliefs on issues pertaining to the market and free enterprise; Fianna Fáil, Labour, and the Workers' Party coalesced around welfare and union issues; Labour, the Workers' Party, Progressive Democrats, and Fine Gael found agreement on broad social and cultural issues.[61] Thus, as issues change, the combinations of voters and parties that support these various positions have also evolved. These developments have made it more difficult for parties to cobble together broader, cross-class appeals among the electorate, but as we will see in the remaining chapters, Ireland's major parties have employed strategies to maintain their catchall appeal.

Electoral Continuity: Beyond a Formal Institutional Explanation

In general, electoral systems, which set the ground rules for party competition by determining factors such as constituency magnitude and threshold formulas, influence the number of effective electoral and legislative parties within a system, shape patterns of party competition and the types of programmatic and/or clientelistic appeals candidates and parties make, and facilitate certain types of government formation.[62] Ireland's electoral system is no exception. Ireland's PR-STV system is often attributed as a key factor in explaining both the longer-term electoral dominance of major parties and the persistence of localism in electoral competition. The conventional argument is that PR-STV creates a distinctive mixture of highly competitive, locally driven elections that emphasize clientelistic relationships, alongside relatively strong and stable party competition at the national level that benefits the established parties. The prevalence of intraparty competition inherent in PR-STV incentivizes copartisans to compete for votes by outdoing one another via strong constituency service. Furthermore, PR-STV is proportional, but only a quarter of Ireland's constituencies elect five TDs, which is the district magnitude that most accurately translates the percentage of votes into seats. That the remaining 75 percent of constituencies elect either three or four TDs benefits the larger parties.[63]

Despite the ways that PR-STV influences the nature of electoral competition and seems to benefit the larger parties, we must be careful not to overestimate the ways in which the electoral system itself explains the outcomes we observe. As we will see throughout this analysis, PR-STV powerfully shapes electoral behavior of parties and voters alike, but it is an insufficient explanation in important ways. First, although systems that use PR-STV have generally experienced major party dominance and longer-term electoral stability, the character of this dominance and stability looks quite different in the three countries that have used PR-STV. These variations suggest that a number of other factors influence the nature of competition in these different contexts. For example, the Irish party system has experienced periods of competition between both two and a half parties and multiple parties, whereas Malta and Australia manifest different patterns. Malta has had a two-party system since its independence in 1964, and Australia (which shifted to a list system for the Senate except in Tasmania) has had a two-block party system (Labor versus the Liberal-National Coalition), with very limited representation by smaller parties.[64] The nature of ideological competition and different degree of emphasis on clientelistic linkages also varies across these cases and influences how parties interact within the PR-STV parameters. Another difference is that when no candidates remain from one's preferred party, 99 percent of Maltese ballots are nontransferable. Maltese voters—in contrast to Ireland—do not give a lower-preference vote to a candidate from another party, even though this is permissible. In Ireland, nearly two-thirds of Irish voters vote for candidates from more than one party, which suggests a radically different type of competition among parties and voters.[65] These differences imply that PR-STV—and electoral systems more generally—cannot alone explain longer-term electoral outcomes.

The second weakness of a formal institutional argument relying on PR-STV is that this system cannot sufficiently explain variation in Irish election results. Ireland's major parties have consistently outperformed their challengers within this system. However, the numbers of independents and candidates from smaller parties has greatly fluctuated throughout Ireland's electoral history. Significant numbers of independents and candidates from smaller parties have taken advantage of the electoral system's low barrier to win seats in parliament throughout Ireland's history, which confirms that the electoral system is an important but insufficient explanation for major party dominance. That these smaller parties and independents have found it much more difficult to secure reelection and increase their vote in the longer term underscores the need to include other factors to explain how major parties respond to the challenge of minor parties once they establish their initial success.

Third, we often assume that the rules of the game are endogenously created by those actors in leadership roles at the founding of the system, which, in turn, facilitates the consolidation of such representation over time.[66] This is not the case in Ireland. One of the primary reasons why the PR-STV system was chosen in Ireland in 1918 was to ensure proportional representation for the Protestant minority and to limit the success of Sinn Féin.[67] Additionally, Fianna Fáil twice tried unsuccessfully to shift to a single-member plurality system, which implies that this was not their ideal electoral system. Ireland's major party leaders inherited this system and have learned how to work within the set of intraparty and interparty incentives to maximize their electoral outcomes, even in changing electoral environments.

Finally, Ireland's PR-STV cannot solely explain the emphasis on personalistic and localist politics. To begin with, Ireland possesses other institutional factors that, combined with PR-STV, strongly encourage localist politics. These include a long history of reliance on local politicians serving local needs, weak local governments that are financially dependent on the central government, and a byzantine, unresponsive, and archaic administrative architecture within the civil service that has long required specialist assistance to navigate.[68] The combination of these factors and Ireland's small size make it no wonder that close personal relationships between individuals and their members of parliament (TDs) dominate Irish politics. The average ratio of members of parliament to population in Ireland is 1:18,741, which is significantly smaller than the ratios that exist in Britain (1:45,000) or the United States (1:590,000).[69] These factors influence the nature of electoral politics in Ireland, even though much has changed in Ireland to weaken localist tendencies.

Later chapters will illustrate the multitude of ways in which major parties have employed strategies on the ideological, institutional, and organizational dimensions in different environments to maximize their vote within PR-STV and to retain localism at the heart of electoral politics. Personal connections and organizations designed to help elected representatives broker the delivery of goods and services from the state to the local constituency have been and continue to be the bread and butter of why major parties consistently outperform minor party candidates. The very fact that major party leaders have adapted how they seek to attract support and manage their vote share over time in different contexts confirms the intervening nature of this key institutional variable. In particular, the combination of major party leaders shifting their ideological positions and displacing potentially divisive issues to extraparliamentary institutions has helped preserve the salience of localistic politics within a much more globalized Irish society. All the more reason, then, that candidate selection and other organizational decisions remain pivotal to understanding how Ireland's major parties continue to survive in a highly competitive and evolving electoral environment.

Voter Motivations and Irish Elections:
A Disconnect between Supply and Demand

A careful analysis of what motivates voters when they actually cast their vote helps us more fully understand the disconnect that exists between supply and demand in Irish politics. First, there have been and continue to be salient issues among the electorate that have not been translated into electoral competition. Fundamental policies related to Northern Ireland, the EU, and growing divisions over moral issues have been absent during elections. Second, a greater diversity of attitudes on issues exists among voters, but these attitudes on a whole range of issues do not affect vote choice in general elections. Finally, Irish voters persistently base their vote on selecting candidates who will best serve the needs of the local constituency over and above programmatic proposals. These patterns underscore the critical role that major parties perform in setting the agenda during Irish elections and framing how interests are aggregated and translated into the political arena in ways that preserve their longer-term electoral success.

Most Important Issues in Irish Elections

Significant demographic shifts and changing mores over the past few decades created fertile ground for new issues and cleavages to affect political competition in Ireland. This section explores how these dramatic demand-side changes have been reflected—or not reflected—within the electoral process. Not surprisingly, economic concerns have consistently mattered most to voters, especially during times of economic distress and challenge. During the years of the Celtic Tiger economic boom, quality-of-life issues and demands for improved public services arose. However, essential issues related to Ireland's founding cleavage and other important divides have not informed voter choice in elections.

Evidence from the INES confirms a diversity of attitudes within the Irish electorate on salient issues. In fact, there may be as many as four or five critical dimensions that shape Irish electoral competition, including strong versus moderate nationalism, religious-conservative versus secular-liberal philosophies, left versus right politics, positions for and against European integration, and, perhaps, positions for and against environmentalism.[70] Marsh, Sinnott, Garry, and Kennedy conducted the most sophisticated analysis of Irish voters to date and concluded that there were really two main dimensions undergirding Irish electoral competition, one relating to the role of government and markets and the other relating to attitudes toward economic equality and the distribution of economic resources. For these scholars, the left-right self-placement is unrelated to either of these dimensions, being instead (weakly) related to the dimension of conservativism versus liberalism.[71]

When asked to identify the issues that were "most important" to them during elections, Irish voters since 1969 have consistently and most frequently identified "the economy" (the top three issues in each election are highlighted in table 2.2).[72] Throughout the entire period prior to the 1990s, Irish voters remained most concerned about double-digit inflation and unemployment. Only in 2002, with the economy booming, did unemployment fade from among the top ten issues cited by voters. (Inflation subsided as a critical election issue from the early 1980s onward.) Concern for the economy has remained high: the issue of "managing the economy" rose from fifth in importance in the 1997 election to third in 2002, 2007,

TABLE 2.2. Most Important Issues in Irish Elections, 1969–2011

Issues	1969	1973	1977	1981	1982	1982	1987	1989	1992	1997	2002	2007	2011
Inflation	28	28	40	27	19	16	5	0	5	0	0	0	0
Other	26	25	8	17	11	7	8	12	16	21	9	0	12
Education and welfare	25	25	9	4	2	4	4	0	0	9	8	15	1
Labour relations	24	0	0	0	0	0	0	0	0	0	0	0	0
Unemployment	20	11	30	48	46	45	59	30	53	39	0	0	6
Health	3	0	0	0	0	0	0	39	8	9	70	45	2
Northern Ireland	1	12	1	0	0	0	1	0	0	13	0	0	0
Tax	0	0	10	5	3	4	13	18	10	29	0	0	2
Crime / law and order	0	0	0	0	0	0	0	0	0	35	54	25	<1
Manage economy	0	0	0	0	0	0	0	0	0	14	22	23	18
Stable government	0	0	0	0	7	17	3	0	8	13	0	14	0
Cost of living	0	0	0	0	0	0	0	0	0	9	13	18	0
Less government spending	0	0	0	0	11	8	8	0	0	0	0	0	0
Drugs	0	0	0	0	0	0	0	0	0	20	8	0	0
Environment	0	0	0	0	0	0	0	0	0	0	8	13	0
Housing/mortgage	0	0	0	0	0	0	0	0	0	0	9	10	1
Abortion	0	0	0	0	0	0	0	0	0	0	12	0	0
Honesty and integrity	0	0	0	0	0	0	0	0	0	0	18	11	0
Specific local issue	0	0	0	0	0	0	0	0	0	9	10	10	2
Taoiseach	0	0	0	0	0	0	0	0	0	0	8	0	<1
Angry / let down	0	0	0	0	0	0	0	0	0	0	0	0	36
Economy	0	0	0	0	0	0	0	0	0	0	0	0	49

Note: Data for the perception of the most important issues is from several different sources, which is why there is minor variation in category titles. Each cell represents the percentage of respondents in election opinion polls and surveys that identified the respective issue as most important to them when deciding how to cast their vote. Data for 1969–92 is from Sinnott, *Irish Voters Decide*, 178. Data for 1997, 2002, 2007, and 2011 is from RTÉ exit polls. For more information on these results, see John Garry, Fiachra Kennedy, Michael Marsh, and Richard Sinnott, "What Decided the Election?" in *How Ireland Voted 2002*, ed. Michael Gallagher, Michael Marsh, and Paul Mitchel (Basingstoke, Hampshire: Palgrave MacMillan, 2003), 127.

and 2011. Since Ireland has joined the Economic and Monetary Union and adopted a single currency as part of its EU membership, wage agreements have been negotiated within the Social Partnership process, and managing the economy has been identified with fiscal policy, which explains why the significance of spending on health and social welfare has risen in recent elections.

An additional economic concern voters repeatedly rank within the top ten is taxation. The issue first surfaced in 1977, when Fianna Fáil campaigned on a highly populist appeal of abolishing local taxes and went on to secure one of that party's highest vote totals ever. Concern over taxation peaked in 1997, when 29 percent of voters identified high taxation as the single most pressing issue. Taxes were especially salient in the early years of the Celtic Tiger, between 1987 and 1997; the issue's visibility coincided with the emergence of the Progressive Democrats, who galvanized the Irish electoral scene with a call for drastic reductions in personal income taxes to reward personal initiative and risk taking.[73]

Historically, party identities and appeals within the Irish party system have not revolved around economic and class-based divisions, as they have in many Western European party systems. However, one might have expected that the changes that transformed Irish society would have made economic issues more central in defining competing party appeals. The potential to move politics away from long-standing Civil War identities and toward competing positions on economic issues appeared a real possibility. Yet, instead of an accentuation of differences among competing parties, we find growing party convergence around economic issues such as taxation and employment policy. The Civil War legacy may have waned, but the reliance of Fianna Fáil and Fine Gael on cross-class appeals in order to sustain their electoral predominance has consistently encouraged them to seek ways of maintaining consensual positions on salient issues among the electorate—especially during this period of social change. A broad political and social consensus emerged among the country's strategic political and social actors from the late 1980s. Differences between parties over economic policy making declined sharply, accompanied by a growing consensus that limited monetary and fiscal interference by the government were stimulating further economic growth beneficial to large sectors of Irish society. Increased integration into the EU and global markets, undertaken for Ireland's national economic well-being, was accompanied by a reduction of the scope of economic issues over which parties competed.[74] The result has been that economic issues have played a less prominent role in defining party competition than one might have expected.

With a far-reaching consensus cohering around economic policy, a measurable shift occurred in voter concern until 2007 with regard to health, crime / law and order, rising drug trafficking, the cost of living, and "new politics" themes, such as the environment and "integrity" in politics. Concern over adequate health care became the primary concern among Irish voters in three of the five elections between 1989 and 2007. Scrambling to compensate for decades of underinvestment in the 1970s and 1980s, successive governments invested record amounts in spending on health care. Despite these efforts, there is still widespread discontent with the lack of progress in reforming the system. One might argue that supply and demand are aligned in this particular case, given that both voters and parties are addressing issues of health care in recent elections. However, the combination of parties removing controversial issues from the electoral arena and assuming similar positions on other salient issues, such as health care, makes it difficult for voters to differentiate among the parties. Instead, voters end up plumping for the candidates and parties that look after their individual and local interests, which has perpetuated the success of the major parties.

Determinants of Voter Choice

Recent studies have sought to understand the determinants of voter choice in Ireland. Analyses of the INES suggest that most issues, even those with considerable salience among the public, exert a surprisingly minimal impact on voter choice. The most comprehensive review of the first INES in 2002 concluded that "[Irish] electoral competition is largely between parties that have little ideological or sociological identity" and that "support still owes more to long established loyalties than to any other factor."[75] Very little incentive exists for parties to present voters with a genuine choice between fundamentally opposed policies at the national level. Rather, voters place a premium on competence and effective governance.

To test these assessments of voter preferences in Ireland, I undertook a multivariate regression of the 2002, 2007, and 2011 INES data (complete details are available by request).[76] Given the smaller samples of minor party voters, I interpreted the results with a focus primarily on what distinguished voter choice for the three major parties, although most models included minor party voters as well. I constructed a variety of models to predict vote choice based on competing sets of variables: demographics, partisanship, ideology and policy attitudes, and perceptions of the government's performance (see table 2.3).

Party attachment remains the most substantial factor in shaping vote choice; but there are caveats. First, the majority of the electorate is not attached to any party, and partisan attachment cannot help explain the behavior of these voters. Second, the statistical significance of partisanship does not tell us where partisan identity comes from, although it is clearly somewhat independent from policy attitudes. Demographics, policy and ideological attitudes, and evaluations of previous performance all contribute somewhat to explaining variance in citizens' voting choices in Ireland. However, the explanatory power of these variables is relatively weak and inconsistent. The factors that explain vote choice for major and minor parties are not radically different, but because fewer voters support minor parties, it is more difficult to assess definitively what drives voting for minor parties.

Partisanship is the strongest predictor of vote choice tested in these models. Not surprisingly, voters who report feeling closest to a specific party are extremely likely to vote for that party. This is true for supporters of major and minor parties. For example, in a model excluding voters who are not attached to one of the major parties, partisanship yields a pseudo-R^2 value of over .50 in every case, indicating that it is an exceptionally good predictor of voting behavior. However, the predictive power of this variable is weakened by the very large number of "unattached" voters. In 2002, only 19 percent of the INES survey sample reported feeling close to one of the three major parties, and the number dropped to 9 percent in 2007 and rose slightly to 17 percent in 2011. Including minor parties does little to increase the number of voters reporting partisan attachment, raising it in each election to only 23 percent, 11 percent, and 21 percent, respectively.

Because partisan attachment is so low—77 percent of voters in 2011

TABLE 2.3. Summary of Models

	Nagelkerke pseudo-R^2 values		
	2002	2007	2011
Model A: Demographics	.184	.286	.232
Model B: Policy attitudes	.115	.185	.114
Model C: Retrospective evaluations[a]	.134/.088	.129/.079	—/.058
Model D: Left-right ideology	.094	.132	.144
Model E1: Partisanship (all voters)	.200	.185	.276
Model E2: Partisanship (partisan voters)	.611	.632	.777

[a]In the 2002 and 2007 INES, voters were asked about how well the government had performed in six areas (the economy, health services, housing, crime, the local economy, and job prospects). The first set of numbers is based on a model with all six of these variables. However, in the 2011 INES, voters were only asked about government performance on the economy and health services. The second set of numbers includes only these two variables, allowing for direct comparison between 2002, 2007, and 2011.

reported that they lack a close relationship with any party—the predictive power of partisanship to explain all voters' behavior is substantially lower. Nagelkerke pseudo-R^2 values between .185 and .276 indicate that partisanship is a good but not overpowering predictor of voting behavior. Therefore, the one factor with the most significant and consistent effect on vote choice in recent elections is becoming less relevant. In fact, even when voters do have partisan affiliations, this does not actually tell us why people are attached to the party. A variety of possibilities exist to explain voter loyalty, including shared ideological convictions with parties or party representation of class interests.

The second best predictor of vote choice in the regression analysis is demographics, which helps explain between 18 and 29 percent of voting behavior in Ireland. Minor differences in certain demographics can help us distinguish between supporters of Fianna Fáil, Fine Gael, Labour, or even the minor parties, but these differences are small and inconsistently significant. For example, differences in levels of education and urbanization distinguish between Fianna Fáil and Fine Gael voters, and levels of religiosity differentiate Fianna Fáil and Labour voters. In terms of levels of religiosity, voters who attend church a few times a year have a 1.77 to 2.20 higher odds of voting for Labour over Fianna Fáil compared to identical voters who attend church once a week.

Among minor parties, Green Party voters tend to be educated, urban, and secular; Progressive Democrat voters are also educated and urban and are more unlikely to be union members. Sinn Féin is the only substantial party whose supporters show a strong demographic pattern. Young, poor, and unemployed voters are more likely to support Sinn Féin than other voters do, which suggests that Sinn Féin plays a role as a protest party. Education, religiosity, employment status, and unionization have modest impacts on vote choice in at least two out of the three election cycles examined; other variables examined show either no statistically significant impact on vote choice or an impact that only surfaced in one of three election cycles studied. In short, demographics do have some influence on vote choice, but there is no sharp and consistent demographic dividing line: the differences of opinion within each demographic category seem to far exceed the differences of opinion that divide these demographic groups. This confirms the cross-class appeal of Irish parties and reinforces the conclusion that Irish political parties lack significant differences among them as regards their social bases of support.

Likewise, there were only modest divides between electoral supporters of the three major parties based on their policy attitudes. Statistical results indicate that these attitudes explain approximately 11 to 19 percent of the variance in Irish voters' voting behavior. Differences between the major parties were especially weak on the economic matters of tax levels, inequality, and business regulation, even as levels of inequality and wealth shifted dramatically in Ireland. Citizens who voted for Fianna Fáil, Fine Gael, and Labour showed distinct attitudes toward these three economic questions in the 2007 electoral cycle but not in the 2002 or 2011 cycles; this suggests that the divides between parties on these issues are ephemeral at best and might be no more than statistical artifacts. In all three election cycles, the traditional divide between Fianna Fáil and Fine Gael over Northern Ireland endures, but weakly. For example, voters who agreed that "the British Government should declare its intention to withdraw from Northern Ireland at a fixed date in the future" had 21 to 24 percent lower odds of supporting Fine Gael over Fianna Fáil than indifferent or unsure voters. The modesty of these differences may provide further evidence of the declining salience of the founding cleavage.

Divides over newer issues in the Irish political landscape appear to affect vote choice more than traditional Northern Ireland and economic divides, but their impact is still modest. Divisions regarding environmentalism distinguished Fianna Fáil voters from both Fine Gael and Labour in 2002 and 2007. Attitudes toward abortion also appear to modestly influence vote choice: the odds that voters with relatively progressive attitudes toward abortion would support Labour over Fianna Fáil in 2002 were 60 percent higher than the odds for voters whose attitudes on abortion were relatively more conservative. In 2011, the odds that the more progressive voters would support Labour over Fianna Fáil were 250 percent higher than the odds for other voters; yet differences did not materialize in 2007, suggesting that even this issue waxes and wanes in salience. Citizens who supported progressive immigration laws tended significantly to support Labour over Fianna Fáil in 2002 and 2007, but because the great majority of voters supported strict limits on immigration, this difference had little impact. Differences over policy positions do exist among the major parties, but the most substantial differences among them appear on issues that have emerged more as a result of social change rather than on longer-standing issues.

Minor parties are often associated with more distinctive policy positions, and the policy attitudes of minor party voters reveal slightly more distinct patterns. However, the small samples of minor party supporters make the analysis of these patterns less reliable. Green Party voters exhibited concern for economic and distributive issues that were not as apparent among major party supporters, in addition to support for the socially liberal policies also adopted by Labour. These voters generally believe that income is distributed unfairly, support regulating businesses, oppose public religion, and welcome open immigration. Curiously, although Green voters in 2002 and 2007 were more likely to accept higher taxes in exchange for protecting the environment, they did not do so in 2011, when their party was in government. Progressive Democrats represented similar patterns on the right: compared to the general electorate, they generally voted against taxation, opposed state regulation, and tended to avoid demanding British withdrawal from Northern Ireland. Sinn Féin voters predictably called for British withdrawal from Northern Ireland and viewed this issue as more salient than the other parties. They also leaned to the left on social issues.

If voting does not appear to be strongly determined by voters' positions on controversial policy issues, it also does not appear to be strongly determined by voters' perceptions of parties' competence and success in addressing various policy challenges. A model of voting choice based on voters' evaluation of conditions in Ireland since the previous election on five policy areas (national economy, local economy, health, housing, and crime) indicates that approximately 13 percent of variance in voting behavior can be attributed to retrospective evaluations.[77] As one would expect, those who thought conditions had worsened leading up to the 2011 election were far more likely to support opposition parties over Fianna Fáil and its coalition partner (the Greens) than were those who thought conditions had improved. This was true across issues. For example, compared with people who thought conditions had improved somewhat, people who thought housing, health, and economic conditions had worsened somewhat were between 28 and 101 percent more likely to vote for one of the two major opposition parties. Nevertheless, a great number of people with relatively positive perceptions of the past five years supported opposition parties, and many who had relatively negative perceptions supported government parties.

There were similar results for the minor parties. Respondents who believed the economy had improved were more likely to vote for the Progressive Democrats in 2002, and people who believed health services had improved were more likely to support them in 2007—largely because the Progressive Democrats were in government and played an important role in setting policy in these areas. Voters who were pessimistic about a variety of national conditions were more likely to back the Green Party and Sinn Féin during elections, pointing to these parties' role as extrasystem parties. However, this did not hold true for Green supporters in 2011, because the

Greens were so thoroughly tainted by their role in government during Ireland's economic collapse that they were uniformly deserted by voters.

This analysis of voting determinants confirms that differences exist among the supporters of Ireland's various parties in terms of their demographics, policy attitudes, retrospective evaluations of competency, and partisanship. However, the explanatory power of these variables is weak and inconsistent. Given the degree of modernization within Irish society, one might expect these factors to have assumed a greater influence in shaping how Irish voters cast their votes in the contemporary period. That they have not justifies taking a closer look to assess why the long-term patterns of electoral competition and outcomes persist. We have seen already, in chapter 1, that demand-side arguments relying on sociological, historical, cultural, and formal institutional variables are insufficient for explaining the predominance of Ireland's major parties in the contemporary period. Therefore, it makes sense to take a closer look at how the strategies employed by Ireland's major parties mitigated the impact that significant changes on the demand side have had on electoral competition.

The Motivations of Irish Voters

Issues do matter to Irish voters, as the previous discussion suggests; however, more relevant in terms of influencing vote choice is how voters perceive the competence of parties to govern at the national level and, very important, to deliver goods and services at the local level. Laver and Sergenti demonstrate that in an era when most candidates and parties adopt similar positions, the popular consensus on the relative ability of candidates to deliver on favored policies influences electoral outcomes significantly. In this type of valence politics, the parties that are perceived as being able to deliver survive, whereas lower valence parties tend to die.[78] In Ireland, the major parties have maintained an advantage because they have consistently been in the best position to form governing coalitions and hold key executive offices. As the next chapter will highlight, this dynamic exerts pressure on smaller parties to modify their programmatic positions, in order to attract support from larger sectors of the electorate and position themselves as likely coalition partners in a new government—where they might strengthen their ability to deliver as well. Unfortunately for minor parties, altering their ideological positions—over time—actually undermines their electoral support.[79] Moderating their original, more extreme programmatic positions to be viable coalition partners not only may cause smaller parties to lose support among their core voters but also makes them appear too similar to major parties. Being too similar to major parties and unlikely to deliver programmatic results, the minor parties also lose floating voters who fall back on the "tried-and-trusted" larger parties during elections.

The voting process in Ireland is another factor affecting the interaction of demand and supply in Irish politics. The PR-STV system provides voters with a considerable degree of choice in the ranking of candidates and parties. Thus, Irish voters can be candidate-centered or party-centered or can have mixed motives when voting. Given that candidates need to secure only five thousand to eight thousand votes to win a seat, the system allows voters to focus on specific candidates rather than on competing political parties, if they choose.[80] PR-STV also invites voters to weigh the relative merits of candidates versus parties, which entices some voters to value parties as most important. If one's party secures enough seats to enter government, they will be better positioned to serve their supporters' ideological and material interests. This electoral system provides voters with the ability to assess the balance between local and national issues in electoral campaigns, thereby generating both intraparty and interparty competition among candidates. This mixture of intra- and interparty competition creates multiple, often competing, incentives for parties and their candidates and gives voters plenty of choices to consider when casting their vote.

Pollsters and political scientists have found several ways to ask voters to identify what influences their vote choices. In 2002, for example, the INES asked respondents whether party or candidate was the most important factor in determining how they would cast their first-preference vote. The candidate was reported as more important by 62 percent of the respondents, almost double the 32 percent who reported that party was more important. Posing the counterfactual, INES asked whether the respondent would have voted for the same candidate if that candidate had stood under a different party label: 46 percent of the respondents said they would, 37 percent said they would not, and the remainder said "it depends."[81] The complexity of these results suggests that candidate and party factors both play a role for every voter and that the weighting of these factors can fluctuate for each voter as well.

Public opinion surveys have also asked voters to identify what influences their vote, based on more detailed criteria. As table 2.4 suggests, voters decide based on the following four criteria, in descending importance: (1) supporting a candidate who will look after local needs, (2) identifying with the policies advocated by the respective parties, (3) electing the Taoiseach (Irish prime minister), and (4) determining government ministers. Irrespective of methodology, surveys and exit polls conducted between

1977 and 2011 confirm that the most significant factor consistently shaping voter preference is the perception that the candidate will best serve the local needs (39 percent), followed by identifying with party policies (25 percent), electing the Taoiseach (16 percent), and, finally, determining government ministers (14 percent).[82] These results are similar to the overall averages generated by other polls. A large number of voters vote for a candidate who they believe will serve local constituency needs, such as providing better roads, keeping regional hospitals open, and assisting in gaining access to public services; these voters care less about a given candidate's alignment with party policies. Irish voters clearly expect their representative to deliver the goods, and the voters will penalize candidates who are perceived to be unlikely to deliver.

The 2011 INES data confirm the importance of serving local interests. In this study, the average voter reported that they would like TDs to allocate 46 percent of their time addressing local issues but that they only observe TDs devoting 40 percent of their time to local concerns.[83] This pattern, which holds for the three major parties and for Sinn Féin and the Socialists as well, is remarkably true across urban, commuter, and rural constituencies. Additionally, 73 percent of respondents in the 2011 INES identified "speaking up for the local area they represent" as the most important quality for TDs to exhibit, compared with 62 percent who valued TDs "speaking their own mind," 41 percent who appreciated TDs who "help individual voters sort out their problems," and only 30 percent who agreed that TDs should "be loyal to the party they represent."[84] Clearly,

TABLE 2.4. Voters' Perceptions of Most Important Voting Criteria, 1977–2011

	Constituency service	Party policies	Taoiseach	Government ministers
1977	46	21	8	18
1981	42	24	16	16
1982	35	27	20	17
1982	41	25	19	15
1987	38	29	15	18
1989	40	15	14	9
1992	37	21	—	—
1997	—	—	—	—
2002	37	25	—	—
2007	39	24	22	12
2011	37	41	12	7
Mean	39	25	16	14

Note: Data for 1977–92 were accumulated from opinion polls conducted during the respective elections (Sinnott, *Irish Voters Decide,* 169). The remaining data are from RTÉ exit polls (for the years 1997, 2007, and 2011) and the 2002 INES.

strong demand exists among voters for localized, parochial representation by their TDs.

That multiple surveys with varying methodological approaches arrive at similar results highlights the reliability of the finding that Irish voters highly value constituency service and concern for local issues. Furthermore, as later chapters of this book will demonstrate, even when policy positions do matter, they are often framed in ways to appeal to local concerns across the country. Party positions have proven flexible enough that they can be applied very differently by candidates from the same party depending on whether they are in rural Kerry or inner-city Dublin. This dynamic favors the larger catchall parties and weakens the ability of minor parties seeking to offer more succinct programmatic offerings to voters across the country.

Several analysts have argued that the election in 2011 should be considered a watershed because competing policy offerings between parties then dominated the campaign for the first time. For example, Farrell and Suiter suggest that the 2011 election was unusual because the parties launched policy position papers beyond their manifestos throughout the campaign. Media and independent experts in social media played a far more important role in scrutinizing party policies. The added emphasis on policy was accompanied by an uncharacteristically high percentage of voters who declared that policy positions were decisive in determining their vote: 41 percent, compared to an average of 24 percent since 1977.[85] Perhaps not surprisingly, given the disastrous state of the Irish economy at the time of the election, supporters of the opposition parties placed more emphasis on policies as critical for determining their vote in 2011, whereas government party loyalists understated the influence of policy. Fine Gael and Labour voters reported that their vote was determined more by party policies (45 and 48 percent, respectively) than by constituency service (29 and 32 percent, respectively), whereas 50 percent of Fianna Fáil supporters indicated that constituency service influenced their vote, compared to 27 percent who reported party policies as most important.[86] Overall, voter concerns over policy were higher than normal in the 2011 election.

This upsurge in identifying policy as decisive in influencing vote choice is important, but its significance should not be overstated. For starters, the strong emphasis on selecting candidates based on their ability to serve the needs of the local constituency remained high, at 37 percent, reflecting the continuing sway of localism. Furthermore, a great proportion of the increase among those who reported policy as significant was a result of the decline in voters identifying the Taoiseach or a set of ministers as the primary determinant of their vote, rather than a decrease among voters for whom constituency service was important. Given that widespread voter doubts persisted about the overall effectiveness of Enda Kenny (Fine Gael's leader), it is easy to understand how identifying the Taoiseach or a set of ministers declined in relevance in shaping voter preferences.

Another reason for exercising caution about the importance of policy offerings in the 2011 election is related to one of the central themes of this book, a theme that will be discussed in subsequent chapters: the centripetal character of ideological competition among Ireland's major parties. The political discourse of the 2011 campaign naturally focused on the economic crisis, and party leaders from across the spectrum bemoaned both the restricted policy options associated with the EU/IMF/ECB loan conditions and a lack of the resources required to tackle Ireland's growing social problems. As a result, a majority of the parties did not offer any significant alternatives to the tax cuts and spending restrictions, which were part of the November 2010 budget. An analysis of party manifestos and other policy documents from the 2011 election campaign reinforces the high degree of programmatic consensus among Irish political parties. RTÉ (Raidió Teilifís Éireann, Ireland's national public media organization) and a group of prospective voters examined the policy positions on ten specific issues and compared their results across the parties.[87] Consistent with the longer-term results that I will discuss in chapter 3, they found a remarkable programmatic consensus on the salient issues, especially among the major parties. Again, there were minor differences in tactics for achieving policy goals, but considerable overlap existed among the parties—especially between Fine Gael and Labour—on the policy goals themselves.

Whether this increase in the importance of policy positions among voters will continue in future Irish elections remains to be seen. However, even if policy motivations remain important to Irish voters, the impact that policy has on electoral outcomes may be minimal. As we have seen, policy attitudes and ideological positions have only a minor effect on Irish voters, who cast their votes for various candidates and parties. This dynamic helps bolster the electoral support of Ireland's major parties and weakens the longer-term viability of the minor parties.

In sum, this analysis of the demand side of Irish politics—namely, the interests and issues emerging from the Irish citizenry—portrays a voter who is increasingly unattached to a given party. Surveys and opinion polls have continually demonstrated that issues such as income inequality and wealth distribution, abortion, the EU, and the environment matter deeply to the Irish voter. Yet these issues that are increasingly salient among the electorate find little echo in the supply side of Irish parties. That emergent issues within the electorate have not resulted in opposing party appeals suggests that parties have acted strategically to suppress them. In the analysis to follow, I will argue that this is precisely the case and that previous studies of Irish elections have paid insufficient attention to the role parties have played in inhibiting demographic and attitudinal change from affecting electoral outcomes.

Conclusion

Although Irish society has experienced unprecedented change over recent decades, the Irish electoral landscape reflects remarkable continuity. This chapter has highlighted the dimensions of a transformed demand side of Irish politics, while contrasting it with aggregate continuity on the supply side. A puzzling disconnect appears between increasingly salient issues confronting the Irish public and those issues over which parties compete during general elections.

The searing modernization that Irish society has undergone in recent decades has resulted in significant changes in the demand side of Irish politics. The fundamental cleavage on which party competition was founded, the question of the North, has, for all intents and purposes, disappeared as a defining feature in Irish party competition. The most important strategic cultural actor in Irish society, the Roman Catholic Church, has all but vanished as a relevant political force in the country. As the role of the church has diminished, attitudes among Irish voters on potentially contentious moral issues (abortion, divorce, and homosexuality) have undergone profound change. The transformation of Ireland's economy has produced a more stratified and complex set of social actors and has sharpened inequality in a previously homogeneous social reality. Ireland's mobile and globalized society has also undermined traditional ties to local areas. In the face of this changing social reality, the number of unattached voters has grown significantly, and floating voters have become a majority of the electorate.

What accounts for this disconnect between a changing demand side and a more stable supply side? How have Ireland's major parties managed to insulate themselves from dramatic change on the demand side? What consequences does this troubling disconnect have for the quality of representative democracy in Ireland? The remaining chapters of this book seek to provide an answer to these questions.

The ability of the leading parties to win elections and to thwart the electoral challenges of minor parties and independents rests on understanding the role parties play in actively shaping and channeling the interests on the demand side of Irish politics. Only by more fully appreciating the role parties play as agents—and not as mere reflections of underlying sociological realities, as subject to a given set of electoral arrangements, or as captured by long-standing political cultures and norms—can we understand the puzzling inexpressive character of party competition in Ireland. Rather than viewing the heavy emphasis on localist politics that persists in Ireland as the natural outcome of deterministic and long-term legacies that give primacy to local matters, I argue that leaders of Ireland's major parties have sought to preserve localism because it has provided them a way to successfully structure political competition and to maintain their overall electoral hegemony. Therefore, the persistence of localist politics in a modernizing Ireland has been cultivated and sustained largely as a result of party leaders' strategies to prevent other forms of competition from taking over, especially at the national level. During the very period when dramatic social, economic, and cultural change within Irish society could have altered how parties compete, long-standing patterns of localist politics were perpetuated. As long as ideological differences among the parties remain constrained and as long as major parties control access to state resources, this emphasis on localism bolsters major parties' electoral advantage. To accomplish this shaping and channeling function and to reinforce their electoral hegemony, the leaders of the major parties employ three adaptive mechanisms: one in the realm of ideology, one in the institutional domain, and one in the organizational domain. The following three chapters will address each of these mechanisms respectively.

The adaptive ability of the leadership of the major parties on these multiple dimensions has consistently facilitated broad consensus within Irish politics. By stifling broader disputes within society and by parking difficult issues outside the electoral and parliamentary arenas, party leaders have constrained the political arena and consolidated their electoral predominance. A closer analysis will show how Ireland's leading political entrepreneurs have employed these various mechanisms during this period of rapid change in order to channel—even manipulate—the public will. Rather than allow the uncertainty of Ireland's changing society to disrupt entrenched patterns of party competition, the leaders of Ireland's major parties found mechanisms to manage emerging issues. These strategies, to which I now turn, have proven remarkably successful.

THREE

Shaping the Ideological Domain

In comparison to other Western European party systems, Ireland's ideological spectrum has always been perceived to be relatively narrow. When asked to specify the difference between Ireland's two largest parties, Fianna Fáil and Fine Gael, Sean Lemass, a former Fianna Fáil Taoiseach (1959–66), replied, "That is easy, we are in and they are out!"[1] This lack of perceived sharp ideological difference among the established parties is partly a legacy of the Civil War. The divisions created by the Civil War allowed the two historic parties to capitalize on long-standing loyalties, maintain an unusual ideological flexibility and cross-class constituent base, and select different policies depending on changing circumstances. Nevertheless, that voters still perceive only minor differences among Ireland's parties in terms of their ideological positions is surprising.

One would expect that the combination of dramatic changes in Irish society, the growing importance and diversity of programmatic concerns among the electorate, and the rise of minor parties promoting distinct ideological positions would have significantly altered the nature of ideological competition in Ireland—and it has. However, the major parties adopted strategies that have constrained the electoral arena at the very time when the electoral marketplace was expanding. Although ideological competition is sharper in recent times than at any other time in the Republic of Ireland's history, major party leaders have consistently adapted their parties' programmatic appeals largely as a response to challenges from minor parties. As we have seen in the foregoing analysis, the potential has existed within Ireland for new cleavages to gain salience. Parties must find ways to navigate divisions around left-right economic issues, social and moral issues, the EU, the environment, and immigration. Yet voters frequently lament that a lack of real party differences on critical issues leaves them little meaningful choice when casting their votes. How is this puzzle to be understood?

While marked differences among the parties on many issues continue to exist (especially between major and minor parties), established parties have continually shifted their programs to purposefully diminish voters' perceptions of policy differences between the parties, particularly during general elections. These ideological shifts have muted the distinctive electoral appeal of minor parties on key issues, weakening their electoral support over a series of elections. Major party leaders have combined this dazzling capacity to adapt programmatically and co-opt minor party issues with their ability to displace issues to extraparliamentary institutions (see chapter 4 for a discussion of this latter dynamic). Over the longer term, the historic parties' ability to combine programmatic shifts with strategic displacement of issues has preserved their predominance and prevented minor parties from dramatically altering the electoral landscape.

This chapter demonstrates that major parties have preserved their predominance largely by minimizing perceived ideological differences among parties, over time, on the most electorally salient issues. Differences among the parties do exist, but ideological competition must be understood dynamically: parties constantly shift their programmatic appeals to maintain broad electoral support and to mitigate any deleterious consequences of these differences. Any given distinction between the major parties and their challengers is likely to disappear within a few elections, as minor parties moderate their appeals and as major parties imitate or displace popular ideological challenges.

The distinction between major and minor parties is especially pertinent to the discussion in this chapter, because the different kinds of resources, structures, and goals of major and minor parties affect the strategies party leaders employ on the ideological dimension. Major parties benefit from their size and from long-standing loyalties among their supporters, and they are able to deliver material benefits and state resources to their constituents. The broad, cross-sector appeal of the major parties increases their ideological flexibility, which has served them well during periods of rapid social change when dependency on any one group is untenable. This broad, cross-sector appeal and unusual ideological flexibility have allowed the major parties to alter the emphasis they give to an issue or set of issues and to shift their positions without jeopardizing electoral support.[2] In this sense, Ireland's major parties resemble Laver and Sergenti's vote-seeking "hunter parties": they are always looking for new supporters and use policies instrumentally to attract voters.[3] Although the major parties have historical advantages, they have had to sustain their advantages by energetically responding to changes in society and to challenges from minor parties.

The choices faced by the leaders of Ireland's minor parties are, in some ways, the inverse of those faced by the leaders of the major parties. Minor parties lack the size, traditional support base, and access to government that the major parties have enjoyed. Ideologically, they have generally been founded to address issues that major parties were addressing insufficiently.[4] Irrespective of their foundation, Ireland's minor parties resemble what Laver and Sergenti refer to as policy-oriented "sticker parties" and democratically focused "aggregator parties." "Sticker parties" tend to maintain consistent ideological appeals and are usually less interested in changing their views to attract additional supporters. "Aggregator parties" rely on democratic procedures within their organizations to guarantee that the interests of their rank and file are represented. For these parties, shifting their programmatic positions on key issues can be quite difficult.[5] When survival thresholds are low, as is the case in Ireland, both of these party types are less likely to endure than vote-seeking "hunter parties."[6] In addition, given that Ireland's minor parties initially attracted support for offering alternate policies, they struggle to maintain their relevance and appeal if major parties co-opt the very alternatives that minor parties initially championed.

The Labour Party has a hybrid nature. Because it is the oldest party in Ireland, it is more like a major party in some ways: it has consistently played a key role in governing coalitions, and it has longer-term partisan ties. At the same time, however, it is similar to a minor party because it has averaged 10 percent of the vote and is usually considered more left-leaning than centrist in its programmatic offerings.[7] Nevertheless, Labour has catchall ideological tendencies and has behaved more in accordance with the vote-seeking, hunter mentality of the two major parties, even though it lacks the numbers to compete on their level.

To better understand the centripetal character of ideological competition and the strategies employed by the major parties to reinforce such competition, this chapter utilizes data collected from three principal sources: party manifestos, expert surveys, and two original surveys of Irish TDs. The analysis of party manifestos paints a picture of the evolving programmatic offerings of political parties. Rather than relying on external commentary, voter survey data, or even the actions of parties once in government, I examine manifestos because they represent the specific programs that parties emphasize as they compete in elections.[8] My analysis is rooted in Robertson's saliency theory, which argues that parties rarely confront each other directly on the same issues but, rather, emphasize different policy priorities.[9] In theory, parties place greater weight on certain issues or combinations of issues, based on both what matters to the electorate and where the party perceives they have enhanced traction with voters. A longitudinal analysis of data from the Comparative Manifestos Project can identify how much space parties allocate to different policy dimensions in each election and can show how parties alter their emphasis on key issues over a series of elections.[10] The degree to which parties emphasize or avoid issues in their manifestos can signal to voters how important an issue is to the parties; it can also affect whether rival parties are able to "own" a particular issue.[11] In an era when party leaders have left in the political arena few "positional issues" on which parties can take opposing sides, this approach helps explain how parties compete ideologically to affect the salience of issues. Clear patterns emerge that highlight distinctions between major and minor parties: how much they emphasize single issues and bundles of issues, as well as their overall policy agendas. By analyzing what parties accentuate in any one election and how these programs evolve over time, we can understand how major parties have responded to both public opinion and the threats of minor parties.

In addition to influencing the salience of issues, parties can also alter the content of their ideological appeals. Evidence from expert surveys and my two parliamentary surveys provides a more finely textured look at how parties and individual TDs take positions on salient issues. Chapters 1 and 2 of this book underscored the growing number of issues that concern voters and the potential for parties to mobilize around these issues. The issues that have dominated Irish politics over the past thirty years (and that are analyzed here) include Northern Ireland, religious and moral issues, the EU, immigration, the environment, taxes versus social spending, and corruption. Data from multiple sources reinforce the finding that although there are ideological differences among the parties, the major parties have successfully minimized these differences during elections.

In the remainder of this chapter, I first analyze contemporary interparty and intraparty ideological differences among Ireland's political parties, examining recent election studies and comparing voter and politician perceptions of party positions on key issues. Next, I turn to a longitudinal study of ideological competition, to demonstrate that while ideological differences may exist at any one time, these differences diminish over time as major parties shift their positions and manage voter perceptions. In this demonstration, I highlight two important related empirical trends. First, although minor parties have repeatedly emerged and gradually increased their electoral support, they have faltered or failed over the medium and longer term. Second, parties tend to converge ideologically over a number of elections. The next part of the chapter analyzes how and why this convergence occurs, underscoring parties' attempts to win votes and affect the salience of issues. The chapter concludes by discussing how the dynamic ideological competition among Irish parties shapes the electoral arena. Given the institutional displacement of issues and the centripetal character of ideological competition in Ireland, voters frequently distinguish between candidates and parties based on their ability to serve local interests. This dynamic reinforces the electoral advantage of major parties whose organizational outreach and relationship with the state allow them privileged access to the delivery of local services.

Ideological Differences in the Short Term

The transformation of Irish society in recent decades has increased the number of issues and the diversity of attitudes for Irish voters and parties alike. As discussed in chapter 2, however, the changes on the demand side of Irish politics do not appear to have been translated into the supply side, as voters still perceive rather narrow ideological differences among the parties on most issues. Using my parliamentary surveys and comparisons with voter attitudes from national election studies, this section of this chapter will establish that although differences among candidates and parties exist on a wide range of issues, these differences, both those between and those within parties, are generally not expressed during electoral competition or fully perceived by the electorate. Voters' perceptions here are surprising, given that voters are interested in policies. On average, a quarter of Irish voters identify party policies as the main factor for casting their vote, and this figure rose to 41 percent in the 2011 election. Knowledge of current affairs and political competition is almost a national sport in Ireland: INES data shows that three-quarters of citizens reported discussing politics with others before the 2002 and 2007 elections. Yet voters either perceive ideological similarity among parties on most issues or cannot identify where the parties stand. In either circumstance, policy positions do not appear to help voters distinguish between the parties during elections, despite a clear perception among politicians that parties possess distinctive and identifiable ideological profiles.

In this section, I first look at ideological differences between TDs and their constituents, to show that elites perceive a much greater degree of ideological differentiation than voters. Second, I look at interparty and intraparty differences among TDs on particular issues, to show that the large intraparty differences make it difficult for voters to differentiate parties. Third, I show how nonideological differences among TDs continue to endure and allow parties to contain ideologically heterogeneous elements. These three components of this examination describe the weakness of major parties' ideological appeals. Subsequent sections of this chapter then build on this discussion to show how major parties' ideological heterogeneity and indistinctness make it difficult for minor parties to challenge them.

Voter and TD Perceptions of Party Differences

Irish voters perceive much smaller distinctions between the ideological profiles of Irish parties than politicians do. Chapter 2 demonstrated that policy attitudes have little explanatory power in determining how people vote, and that voters perceive few differences among major parties' policy positions. Even on issues where TDs report important differences between parties, voters perceive parties as almost identical. This is true even when minor parties have made concerted efforts to "brand themselves" using distinctive policy appeals, such as opposing deeper European integration, as Sinn Féin and the Greens have done during referenda.

Figure 3.1 compares TDs' median placements of their party on key dimensions measured by my 2007 parliamentary survey with voters' median placements of these parties in the INES. Voters perceive only minor ideological differences among Ireland's major parties: the major parties' median perceived positions differ by one point or less on five of six issues. The only dimension on which voters identify large differences among the major parties is on the left-right spectrum, where the voters placed Labour at 4 and Fianna Fáil at 7. TDs recognize far greater differences between the parties and place the major parties more than one point apart on four of six issues: taxes and spending, left-right placement, the EU, and abortion. It is telling that TDs identify ideological differences between parties that voters do not perceive. Major party candidates either are not communicating these differences to voters or are consciously seeking to minimize them. Either way, this dynamic benefits major parties in the long run: the more

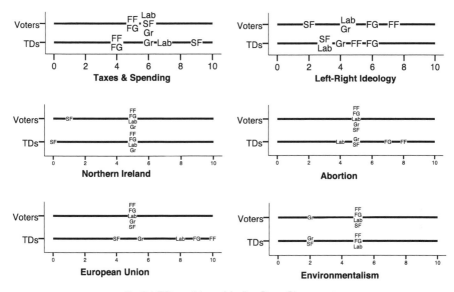

Fig. 3.1. TD and Voter Median Party Placement

consensus voters perceive among the parties, the less impact ideology will have on vote choice.

TDs are also aligned much more closely to their party's policy positions than voters are. To measure this, I examined the standard deviation of self-placement from party placement (among TDs and voters) for each policy issue, using data from the 2007 INES and a post-2007 TD survey.[12] Overall, TDs place themselves between 25 and 50 percent closer to their party than voters place themselves. On environmentalism, abortion, and the EU, voters are, on average, about twice as far from their parties as TDs are; for example, on a 10-point scale regarding European integration, voters are, on average, 2.66 points away from their party, while TDs are, approximately, 1.05 points away. In contrast, on "older" or more familiar issues, such as Northern Ireland, left-right positions, and taxing versus spending, TDs are only around 25 percent closer to their parties than voters are. This suggests that voters are more uncertain about where parties stand on the newer issues confronting Irish society. Although party elites may hold distinctive positions, they do not communicate these to voters.

This result is not surprising: comparative research shows that elites generally hold clearer ideological positions than the average voter. For example, Iversen's comparative study of twenty-seven European parties in the mid-1990s found that party elites usually have more extreme and clear left-right positions than their supporters.[13] More recent scholarship confirms that this is usually true because parties cater to the median voter, although niche parties may diverge less from their elites' sincere views, because they respond to their own median constituent rather than to the median undecided voter.[14]

Finally, Irish voters are often uncertain where parties stand on important issues. As discussed in chapter 2, the INES confirms that large proportions of the Irish electorate cannot place parties on ideological scales. This inability to identify parties' ideologies occurs although individual TDs and party leaders perceive important programmatic differences between parties. In the end, that the ideological differences politicians recognize among the parties are greater than the differences voters recognize says more about parties' strategies than about the sophistication or inclinations of Irish voters. To more fully understand why voters cannot make sense of the differences that do emerge between parties—especially when comparing major and minor parties—we must go beyond a cross-sectional analysis and adopt a longitudinal approach.

Voter and Party Attitudes on Issues

According to my parliamentary survey on the 2007 general election, TDs' attitudes on key issues varied substantially based on their party identification. In other words, TDs who place themselves to the left on an issue tend to belong to different parties than TDs who place themselves to the right on that issue. This finding contrasts with the result of the analysis of citizens' attitudes in chapter 2, which revealed that voters' attitudes on policies did not explain whether they were supporters of a particular party. A series of ANOVA tests to detect differences between voters' and TDs' policy preferences by party illustrate these findings (see table 3.1). The 2007 INES indicates that voters' positions on a left-right ideological scale are related to their party choices; voters' choices between all parties explain about 12 percent of the variance in voters' ideology. On specific issues, however, partisanship explains only a negligible proportion of the diversity in voters' attitudes. For example, party choice explained less than 3 percent of voters' disagreements regarding the future of Northern Ireland.

By contrast, party identity explains a great deal of the variance in TDs' attitudes. TDs' membership in a party accounts for 33 percent of the diversity in their attitudes toward the EU, 30 percent for left-right placement, 25 percent on abortion, 23 percent on taxes and spending, 18 percent on Northern Ireland, and even 14 percent on environmentalism. Party elites seem to perceive considerably greater policy differences on key issues between parties than voters do.

However, some of this apparent diversity occurs only because minor party TDs differ from major parties—not because major parties differ from each other. When we compare only supporters of the major parties, some perceived policy differences diminish. Interparty divisions between Fianna Fáil, Fine Gael, and Labour are most substantial in explaining TDs' left-right positions and views on abortion and have some power in explaining attitudes on taxes and spending and on Northern Ireland. Partisan divisions on these issues are less intense than when minor parties are included, but such divisions still account for about 14 percent of the variation in the attitudes of major party TDs toward taxes and spending and for about 9 percent of the variation on Northern Ireland. However, partisanship accounts for less than 5 percent of the disagreement between major party TDs on the EU and the environment; far more disagreement exists within each of the parties than between the parties. In short, minor parties offer distinctive programmatic positions as an alternative to the major parties, while major parties have relatively low levels of ideological cohesion that may make it difficult for them to develop strong ideological stances.

Not surprisingly, TDs' party identification also affects the reported positions of their parties. The 2007 parliamentary survey asked TDs to identify their parties' ideological positions. TDs from different parties tend to report that their parties have different stances, while TDs from the same party tend to report their party's stance similarly. Furthermore, the data support the view that individual TDs are less ideologically distinct than their party; the partisan divisions between individual TDs' attitudes are weaker than the divisions between parties' perceived stances based on the

TABLE 3.1. ANOVA Tests of Party Choice by TDs' Attitudes (R^2 Values)

	Among all parties		Among major parties	
	TDs	Voters	TDs	Voters
Left-right	.304*	.124	.273*	.104
Northern Ireland	.177*	.024	.094*	.001
Taxes and spending	.227*	.009	.158*	.000
European Union	.332*	.011	.036	.001
Environmentalism	.133*	.014	.047	.008
Abortion	.253*	.020	.249*	.005

Note: On left-right, $n = 101$ for all parties / 91 for major parties. Due to nonresponses, $n = 100/90$ on Northern Ireland and abortion, 102/91 on taxes and spending and the EU, 100/91 on environmentalism. Sample sizes should be roughly the same for all the data from my 2010 parliamentary survey.

*significant at $p = .05$.

findings of the ANOVA test. This suggests that individual TDs feel freer to adapt their ideological appeals to changing circumstances in their constituencies; they are not expected to strongly oppose the other party on every issue and will not stand out conspicuously from their own party colleagues if they take differing positions.

The complex ideological landscape of Irish political parties can also be seen visually. Figure 3.2 charts TDs' attitudes on six issues in 2007. The thick, vertical gray bars represent the middle 50 percent of the positions in each party (the interquartile range), with longer bars indicating greater disagreement within a party; the thin vertical lines represent the range of attitudes outside the party's middle 50 percent. The figure demonstrates how much overlap there is between various parties' positions. It is evident, for example, that policy divisions between the major parties are present on left-right placement and abortion, where Labour takes distinctly leftist stances compared to Fianna Fáil and Fine Gael. It is notable that the dispersion of TDs' attitudes within parties is greatest on abortion and the EU (especially for Fianna Fáil and Fine Gael); as we will see in chapter 4, the major parties have displaced these issues to referenda to allow for diverse attitudes without jeopardizing party unity. It is also clear that the divide between major parties on the European Union is very modest and that divisions between parties on this issue increase significantly when the Greens and Sinn Féin are included. In general, the three major parties have more dispersed positions than minor parties. The box plots point toward the same conclusion arrived at in the preceding discussion: there are clear interparty differences as well as significant intraparty differences on several key policy issues.

TDs' Ideology and Party Choice

While TDs discern important ideological and policy differences between Ireland's political parties (differences generally invisible to voters), TDs' partisanship is still only partially driven by these ideological and policy concerns. Civil War lineage still shapes TDs' loyalties, at least for the two largest parties. This can be seen in a series of bivariate, multinomial logistic regression models that predict TDs' party affiliations by using ideological and social variables measured in the 2007 parliamentary survey.[15]

Although left-right ideology has the strongest overall explanatory power in determining to which party a TD belongs (explaining about 30 percent of the differences between major parties), the explanatory power of Civil War ties is almost as strong. The stance taken by the family of a TD's father

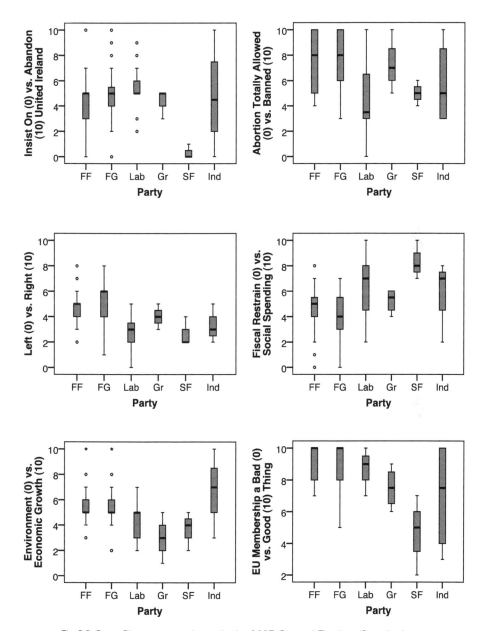

Fig. 3.2. Party Placements on Issues in the 2007 General Election. (Sample sizes were 746 for Northern Ireland; 583 for abortion; 730 for left/right; 678 for tax/spend; 705 for environment; and 679 for EU. These represent the number of respondents who were able to place all parties on the given scale; data from respondents who could not place all parties on that scale was not used.)

toward the 1921 Anglo-Irish Treaty establishing the Irish Free State explains approximately 28 percent of the variance in party membership among TDs. In multivariate multinomial logistic regressions, left-right attitudes are most important in discriminating between Fianna Fáil and Labour partisans, while Civil War ties are most important in discriminating between Fianna Fáil and Fine Gael partisans. For example, the odds of TDs supporting Fine Gael over Fianna Fáil are 96 percent lower when TDs' families (on their father's side) opposed the treaty than when their families supported the treaty. Neutral, mixed, or unknown family attitudes toward the treaty had no statistical impact on vote choice between Fine Gael and Fianna Fáil. These results fit with traditional interpretations of Irish political loyalty: strong Civil War ties split the two Civil War parties, while Labour's more ambiguous stance during the Civil War somewhat damaged voters' long-term loyalties to the party and forced it to rely on other appeals.

In predicting partisanship, TDs' Civil War ties seem to be mostly independent of their left-right ideology. A regression including both ideology and family ties explains 53 percent of the variance in TDs' party membership, far more than either variable can predict by itself. Linear regressions reveal that family ties do not predict, in a statistically significant manner, either a TD's ideology or a TD's attitudes toward Northern Ireland. Although TDs may inherit partisan loyalties based on their families' position in Ireland's historic cleavage, they do not appear to inherit policy attitudes. The continuing importance of Civil War loyalties in elites' partisan identity may be one reason why TDs with very different policy attitudes are still able to coexist in the same party.

Although family background remains critical to shaping partisan identification, it does not determine party positions on policy issues for these historic parties. This situation has left TDs from these parties remarkably free to adopt policy stances opportunistically, and they sometimes downplay differences with other parties and sometimes assume similar positions. The varied, ambiguous, and contradictory positions adopted by TDs from the same party make it more difficult for voters to clearly perceive and articulate differences between parties and to vote based on ideology and policy positions.

The Evanescent Character of Ireland's Minor Parties

A critical question for our analysis is why minor parties are not better able to communicate distinctive policy positions. Minor parties perceive them-

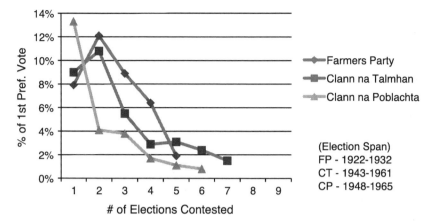

Fig. 3.3. Life Cycles of Early Minor Parties (1922–65). (Data from John Coakley, "The Rise and Fall of Minor Parties in Ireland," *Irish Political Studies* 25, no. 4 [2010]: 518.)

selves as ideologically distinct from the major parties and gain traction among voters, at least initially, because of programmatic appeals. Yet minor parties have found it difficult to sustain their distinctiveness over the longer term. Before turning to a detailed analysis of the timing, sequence, and substance of the ideological shifts that Ireland's major parties have undertaken in order to mitigate ideological differences, I will here review patterns of election results for minor parties. Despite initial and sporadic successes, minor parties generally falter after a series of elections. In an earlier period (1922–65), minor parties performed well in breakout elections but then steadily declined (see fig. 3.3). In the period since 1981, patterns are more varied: the Progressive Democrats (PDs) followed the earlier pattern; the Workers' Party and the Green Party experienced gradual increases in support before dramatically losing their backing; and Sinn Féin has steadily increased its first-preference vote through the 2011 election and experienced mixed results in subsequent polls after that election (see fig. 3.4).[16]

As noted previously, a great challenge for minor parties is that few candidates gain enough first-preference votes to win election under Ireland's PR-STV electoral system; most depend on lower-preference transfer votes from voters whose primary support is directed at other candidates. Candidates from the larger parties can easily attract lower-preference votes from copartisans and can count on their party's wide appeal. By contrast, minor parties typically run only one candidate per constituency and must rely on lower-preference votes from competing parties.

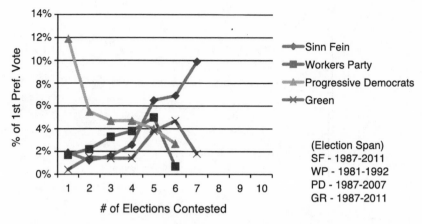

Fig. 3.4. Life Cycles of Contemporary Minor Parties (1981–2011). (Data from Coakley, "The Rise and Fall of Minor Parties in Ireland," 519.)

Candidates from minor parties therefore face a critical trade-off. On the one hand, each minor party can maintain consistent and distinctive policies, allowing it to maintain its appeal as a niche party and hold on to its rank and file. However, if the stances adopted by smaller parties gain broad support, larger parties can copy these policy appeals and co-opt minor parties' positions. Major parties can match the policies initially proposed by upstarts and can exceed minor parties' credibility in pledging to serve local needs and deliver on these policies in government. When larger parties absorb electorally successful policy positions, what benefit is there to vote for candidates from minor parties? If major parties can gain traction on the very issues that minor parties advance, the ability of the larger parties to deliver services once in government undermines the appeal of minor party candidates.

On the other hand, unless a strong geographic concentration of support exists within a constituency, smaller parties have an incentive to moderate their appeals to attract lower-preference votes from competing parties' supporters. Once minor parties dilute their distinctiveness, they risk undermining their initial appeal and the loyalty of the rank and file. Comparative evidence shows that voters punish minor parties more severely than major parties for watering down their programs, because distinctive programs were what attracted voters in the first place.[17]

This recurrent dynamic reinforces the centripetal character of ideological competition in Ireland. At first, when minor parties address issues or take positions ignored by the three main parties, they experience a flurry of electoral success. Next, within one to three elections, the smaller parties advance their issues onto the national agenda, but one result of their success is that they face stiffer competition from the larger parties, who have proven adept at co-opting just enough of the programmatic appeals to blunt minor parties' attractiveness. In turn, the electoral success of these minor parties prevents Fianna Fáil or Fine Gael from gaining a parliamentary majority and forces the major party into a governing coalition with smaller parties. Finally, in a government still dominated by Fianna Fáil or Fine Gael, the minor parties find it increasingly difficult to retain their distinctive ideological profile; without their "outsider" status, they are forced to compete with major parties in responding to local constituency needs. This is a game in which Fianna Fáil, above all, has been the acknowledged master.

As chapter 5, on organizational strategies, will illustrate, major parties relentlessly target constituencies where minor parties have succeeded, showering constituents with "goodies" and neutralizing contentious local issues that give minor parties their foothold. In subsequent elections, it is extremely difficult for minor party candidates to repeat their initial success. Major parties' ability to co-opt minor parties' popular policy positions while stressing their superior delivery provides them with an electoral advantage. Once successful, major parties then shift attention to more anemic issues like "government efficiency," where they are at less of a disadvantage.

In sum, within the context established by the embedded partisan legacy of the Civil War and its catchall parties, as well as the PR-STV electoral system, the major parties in Ireland enjoy an unusual degree of ideological flexibility that allows them to adapt their programmatic appeals opportunistically. An essential element of their strategy has been co-opting popular policy positions advanced by smaller parties to prevent these minor parties from "capturing" issues as their own. Over the longer term, this strategy has eroded the initial electoral success experienced by minor parties and has consolidated the electoral predominance of the historic parties.

Evidence for Convergence

As we have seen, a key challenge for minor parties over the medium and longer term is to maintain a distinctive ideological appeal while attracting enough votes to win seats. Although ideological differences have existed among Irish parties, these differences continually erode as major parties shift their programs to attract broader support. For the major parties, a deliberate strategy to encourage ideological convergence allows them to differentiate themselves by highlighting their ability to deliver goods and services to constituencies. Evidence from expert surveys conducted in the four elections between 1992 and 2007 confirms this pattern of centripetal ideological competition.[18] These surveys tap into the perceptions of a broad range of experts on Irish politics by asking respondents to locate parties on a scale of 1–20 on highly specific policy domains, including the ones discussed in this book.

Party Convergence, 1992–2007

Although persistent differences among parties remain, the dynamics of party competition leads parties, over time, to mitigate difference and heighten consensus. The findings in figure 3.5 highlight the centripetal nature of Irish party competition, whereby both major and minor parties converge on centrist positions on virtually every key issue. Consistent with my argument, there has been noticeable convergence on each of the policy issues over the four elections. In the earliest surveys I examine, the distance between party positions on a single issue ranged from nine to fourteen points, but this distance declined to between three and six points by the 2007 election. The smallest differences among parties by the 2007 election were on Northern Ireland (three points), moral issues (four points), and EU integration (four points), the three issues that have been strategically displaced to extraparliamentary institutions (see chapter 4). Experts' party placements on taxes and spending (six points) and on newer issues like immigration and the environment (five points each) were slightly farther apart.

The greatest shifts in party placement occurred on particular parties' core issues, indicating that minor parties have difficulty sustaining distinctive appeals built around a single policy issue. The Green Party moved from a score of 1.22 to 11.06 on environmental issues, their signature appeal, in the most dramatic shift for any party on any issue (9.98 points).[19] Experts perceived that the Greens had greatly moderated their support for protecting the environment at the cost of economic growth by the time they won six seats and entered government with Fianna Fáil in 2007. The second greatest swing in perceived position (8.99 points) was on Sinn Féin's policy on its signature issue, Northern Ireland. Sinn Féin shifted from staunch opposition to a British permanent presence in Northern Ireland (a score of 1.5) to recognizing, by 2007, the need to work with the British in the North (a score of 10.5).[20] As we have seen, minor parties risk their support

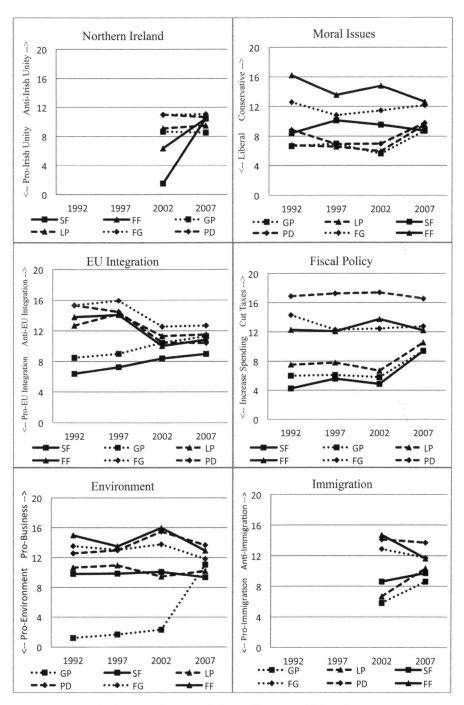

Fig. 3.5. Party Placement in Expert Surveys on Various Issues

if they converge on the positions held by other parties, especially on the issues for which they attracted attention. Why should voters vote for a minor party if the major parties offer similar policies and a better chance to shape outcomes once in government?

There were also significant shifts on taxation and spending issues and EU integration. By 2007, support for lower taxation was widespread. Although the spatial positioning of the major parties remained constant, with only a minor change for Fianna Fáil and Fine Gael, more move-ment occurred among the smaller left-wing parties. These parties were perceived as originally supporting higher taxes but then adopted more centrist positions by 2007: voters saw decades of growth and prosperity as driven by lower taxes, and the popular appeal of an extensive welfare regime shrank. For example, Sinn Féin experienced the greatest perceived change between 1992 and 2007 on taxation, shifting from a score of 4.24 to a score of 9.37; the Greens also shifted considerably, moving from 5.96 to 9.43; and Labour moved from 7.5 to 10.54. By contrast, the center-right parties did not move considerably. Fianna Fáil (12.3) and the PDs (16.6) remained constant over the four elections, and Fine Gael declined slightly from 14.29 to 12.77. Left-leaning minor parties were once again seen as moving the most and in a direction away from what originally attracted voters. It is one thing for catchall, ideologically flexible parties to shift their positions, but it is quite another for more policy-driven parties to do so.

On European integration, Fianna Fáil (with a score of 4.05), Fine Gael (3.38), and the PDs (4.85) were seen as shifting the most. All three par-ties were steadfast supporters of the EU, but reflecting growing concerns among the electorate, they appear to have moderated their stances to offset the surge in support for the Greens and Sinn Féin's anti-EU campaigning. The minor parties also seem to have moderated their stances toward the EU, even though these parties had gained much from their anti-EU posi-tions during referenda campaigns. As will be discussed in chapter 4, the dis-placement of debates over EU policy to referendum campaigns minimized the effect of this issue during general elections, which partly explains why the minor parties would moderate an otherwise effective means of raising their profile.

While some parties shifted more than others and while some issues saw more change, each of the parties in the study altered, to some degree, their perceived policy appeals on every issue. The average score for the amount of change across the issues was 2.50. The Greens (3.15), Sinn Féin (2.88), and Fianna Fáil (2.86) altered their positions slightly more than average; Fine Gael (2.19), Labour (2.12), and the PDs (1.80) changed their positions slightly less. It is striking that the Greens and Sinn Féin altered their positions the most and experienced the most significant increases in electoral support. However, these short-term electoral gains—made by moderating core party values—may have been Pyrrhic victories. They attracted votes in the short term but undermined their distinctive appeals over the medium term. On the opposite end of the spectrum, the PDs were perceived as altering their positions the least. In many ways, the PDs succeeded in shifting all parties toward their policy ideals, and they therefore did not need to change their appeals. Nevertheless, this ideological "victory" meant that the PDs were less relevant in the eyes of voters, because all parties shared their views. The PDs folded after the 2007 election. Once again, this demonstrates the considerable electoral challenges that minor parties face: maintaining ideological distinctiveness while competing with the major parties that offer broad, catchall appeals along with strong personalistic ties and a proven ability to serve local needs.

Convergence in the 2011 Election

Although there is no expert survey data for the 2011 election, the long-standing centripetal character of Ireland's ideological party competition appears to have persisted. The convergence of party positions on the most salient issues, especially when society was growing more demographically and attitudinally heterogeneous, illustrates once again how party leaders shift programmatic appeals to prevent new divisions from altering the overall pattern of Irish party competition.

The discourse of the 2011 campaign naturally focused on the economic crisis, and party leaders from the across the spectrum bemoaned the restricted policy options associated with the loan conditions of the EU, the IMF, and the ECB, as well as the lack of resources required to tackle Ireland's growing social problems. Most parties did not offer a significant alternative to the tax increases and spending cuts included in the November 2010 budget. An analysis of party manifestos and other policy documents from the 2011 campaign, conducted by television broadcaster RTÉ and a group of prospective voters, reveals the high degree of programmatic consensus among Irish parties on ten important issues.[21] There were minor differences over how to achieve policy goals, but there was considerable overlap, especially between Fine Gael and Labour, on the goals themselves.

According to a 2011 election study by Farrell and Suiter, parties disagreed substantially in only three areas: the role of the largely ineffectual Health Service Executive, which oversees health care in Ireland; the reintroduction of fees for tertiary education (abolished in 1994); and the appropriate balance between tax increases and spending cuts.[22] Fine Gael proposed a two-to-one ratio of cuts to taxes, while Labour advocated an even split. Within months of forming a new government, even these differences disappeared. For example, Labour's Minister of Education reversed the party's position and declared that it might be necessary to reintroduce third-level fees. Labour and Fine Gael essentially followed the austerity measures enacted by the previous government, led by Fianna Fáil.[23] Such policy reversals suggest that the intensity of the external demands from the EU and the severity of the scale of Ireland's fiscal crisis were such that the governing parties had no choice. Yet it also suggests that Ireland's major parties are adept at using external requirements as political cover in order to implement unpopular measures, especially if it means contradicting earlier positions. Regardless of party leaders' initial motives, their subsequent actions preserved the centripetal nature of party competition, making it more difficult for minor parties to make lasting electoral inroads.

TDs' own reports of their policy positions confirm that differences between the parties were extremely weak on issues related to fiscal austerity, the economic crisis, and the EU/IMF bailout. Independent, United Left Alliance (ULA), and Sinn Féin candidates were more likely than the major parties to endorse populist-leftist policies and to oppose the bailout, and Labour and Fianna Fáil candidates were slightly more supportive of these policies than Fine Gael candidates, but few consistent differences existed in TDs' attitudes toward the bailout. Most parties were internally divided about whether to support the bailout or instead endorse more populist economic policies: 60 percent of Fianna Fáil and Labour TDs supported "burning bondholders" and providing mortgage relief policies, while Fine Gael TDs offered support of 43 percent for mortgage relief and 36 percent for burning bondholders. This implies that substantial minorities in Fianna Fáil and Labour supported the Fine Gael government's policies and that substantial minorities in Fine Gael opposed their own administration's approach to the crisis. These internal divisions appear to overshadow strong contrasts between the parties.

When parties did shift in the 2011 election, they usually shifted in tandem with each other and toward the center, according to the Suiter and Farrell analysis.[24] The resulting party placements were close together, especially on left-right and tax-and-spend dimensions. Fine Gael and Labour's shift to the center allowed them to attract the median vote as well as to position themselves to enter a coalition with each other. Fianna Fáil, which remained more constant in its policy offering, was hamstrung and demoralized by its decisions in government and could not credibly distance itself from the vastly unpopular policies outlined in the EU/IMF/ECB deal. It moved to the right, but this move was partially a reaction to the disappearance of the Progressive Democrats. Sinn Féin shifted most in its policy positions since 2007 and defied the general movement toward the center. It adopted more left-leaning policies, especially on taxes and the minimum wage, and shed its more conservative stances on social issues to present itself as a party of the Left.[25] This seems to contradict the argument that parties must moderate their positions over time to be successful, except that Sinn Féin had already moderated its traditional platform based on Northern Ireland to a more generic leftist approach in an attempt to win votes. It coupled this moderation with populist economic policies to take advantage of the many disgruntled voters in 2011. Although policy positions enjoyed increased salience among voters in the 2011 elections, the major parties once again maintained their edge by fostering the centripetal character of ideological competition and preserving consensus on a broad range of issues.

Sustaining Ideological Flexibility as a Key Electoral Advantage of Major Parties

Manifesto data underscores the different policies that major and minor parties emphasize in Irish elections.[26] The main parties, Fianna Fáil and Fine Gael, and to a lesser extent Labour, follow a flexible, catchall approach. They adapt positions on a wide variety of potentially salient issues to appeal to a broad section of voters and co-opt upstart parties' programmatic appeals over a series of elections. In comparison, the minor parties display emphasis on a few issues. Ireland's rapid modernization since the early 1980s has given minor parties opportunities to engage new issues (e.g., the environment) or distinct ideological perspectives, either left (Workers' Party) or right (Progressive Democrats). Longer-term analyses of manifesto results, however, indicate that minor parties gradually watered down their positions in an attempt to attract moderate voters and address a broader array of issues. Modernization has increased the number of policy domains that voters expect parties to address, undermining the viability of single-issue campaigns.[27]

The increase in both the length of party manifestos and the number of issues in them likewise suggests that parties are confronting increasingly complex issues. The average number of quasi sentences in Irish party manifestos dramatically increased, growing from 222 in the 1970s to 323 in the 1980s, 720 in the 1990s, and 1,436 in the 2000s—increasing sixfold and surpassing the European average.[28] At the time the manifestos lengthened, minor parties were growing in electoral appeal and promoting distinctive sets of issues. These longer manifestos, which engaged more issues, were at least partly a strategic response by the major parties. Drawing minor parties into competition over a greater range of issues helped the major parties dilute minor parties' appeal among voters concerned with multiple issues. From 1981 to 2007, the mean number of issues addressed in the parties' manifestos increased from twenty-nine to forty-two. This trend was true for the three major parties (whose mean number of issues also increased from twenty-nine to forty-two) and for the smaller parties (the one minor party in 1981 included twenty-six issues in its manifesto, and the mean for all minor parties was forty in 2007). Initially, the proliferation of issues benefited the smaller parties with unique and popular positions. For example, new parties across Europe and within Ireland have focused on previously marginalized issues involving the environment, law and order, and the EU.[29]

As we have seen repeatedly, however, smaller parties gain attention by emphasizing unique issues but must trade off by neglecting other salient policy domains. Both the range and the complexity of issues emphasized by the major parties threaten to undermine the success of minor parties. Consequently, once minor parties gain sufficient visibility, they tend to expand their focus but then risk becoming less distinctive and thereby less appealing to voters. As a former leader of the PDs stated to his party conference, the small party must either remain "radical" or become "redundant."[30] The growing capacity and complexity of issue competition presents a quandary for the minor parties, stretching them programmatically and forcing them to adopt more catchall approaches to remain electorally viable—a strategy that ultimately plays to the strength of the major parties.

To measure the ideological approaches of Ireland's major and minor parties, I examine the percentage of its manifesto that a party devotes to the top issue or bundle of three issues in every campaign. These represent the highest-priority issue(s) for each party for each election between 1981 and 2007. Parties' original stances in 1981 provide a baseline from which to measure whether parties shifted focus away from their initial priorities, which can be used as an alternative measure of their programmatic flexibility or adaptability. Parties that advance many different top issues over the longer term are here identified as "catchall" or "ideologically flexible," whereas parties that maintain a consistent set of top issues are referred to as "programmatic" or "policy-oriented" parties. Although these measures are imperfect, they gauge the distinctiveness of parties' ideological offerings by testing whether major parties shift their top policy priorities depending on the electoral landscape while minor parties generally focus on the same package of policies over time.

Consider the major parties' ideological appeals since 1981. The data confirm that Fianna Fáil and Fine Gael both exhibit classic catchall, flexible ideological approaches.[31] On average, Fianna Fáil and Fine Gael each spent 15 percent of their respective manifestos on their most popular issue and changed their top three issues. The three issues that Fianna Fáil emphasized most heavily in 1981 comprised 46 percent of its manifesto that year, but these original three issues comprised, on average, only 25 percent of the party's manifestos from 1981 to 2007. Likewise, Fine Gael's original top three issues received 29 percent of the space in its 1981 manifesto, but these same issues took up less than 20 percent of the total space in Fine Gael's manifestos for the period.[32] The parties' top three issues change in response both to challenges from the other parties and to the changing interests of the electorate.

The fluid nature of Fianna Fáil's and Fine Gael's ideological appeals is even more striking when compared to the narrow, more consistent focus of Labour and the minor parties. One way to measure ideological flexibility is to examine whether a party consistently emphasizes the same issue in each election. The top issue continually changed for the larger parties: Fianna Fáil evinced seven different leading policy issues in their manifestos, and Fine Gael evinced six. By contrast, all of the other parties except the PDs put forward only one or two leading policy issues. Labour highlighted *Social Justice* and *Welfare State Expansion*. In the most recent elections, the Greens highlighted *Environmental Protection*, *Anti-Growth Economy* and *Welfare State Expansion*. Sinn Féin emphasized *Social Justice* and *Welfare State Expansion*; the Workers' Party, *Welfare State Expansion* and *Non-Economic Demographic Groups*; and the Democratic Left Party, *Social Justice*. Only the PDs, the only right-wing party, altered their top issue frequently, from *Economic Orthodoxy* (1987 and 1997) to *Welfare State Expansion* (1989 and 2007) to *Government and Administrative Efficiency* (1992) to *Technology and Infrastructure* (2002); all the minor parties of the Left maintained a more consistent emphasis on their primary concerns.

Nevertheless, over the medium and longer term, there is pressure, even for the minor parties, to dilute the attention devoted to their top three issues. The major parties varied the emphasis on their original top issue in the contemporary period, while the minor parties steadily decreased the space assigned to their highest policy concern. The Greens' focus on their top issue of *Environmental Protection* fell from 25 percent in 1989 to 8 percent in 2007, and the emphasis on their top three issues declined from 50 percent of their manifesto in 1989 to only 19 percent in 2007. The PDs reduced the emphasis on their top three issues from 42 percent in 1987 to 19 percent in 2007. Their original top issue of *Economic Orthodoxy* virtually disappeared from their manifesto in 2007, receiving only 1 percent of the manifesto's space then, compared to 12 percent in 1987. By 2007, even the more ideologically pure Workers' Party and Sinn Féin allotted 6 and 10 percent less, respectively, to their original top three issues.

The Democratic Left Party, which was led by former members of the Workers' Party, was the only party to increase emphasis on its original top priority, and it did so only for two elections. The party quickly merged with Labour after its 1997 election fiasco, and several of its leaders ascended to the leadership of the Labour Party. This merger demonstrates the trade-off between programmatic purity and winning office. The allure of office and the ability of the major parties to absorb minor party issues—or swallow parties altogether—once again combined to thwart minor parties. The parties that sought balance between programmatic goals and increasing electoral appeal did not abandon their policy priorities, but in de-emphasizing them, they began to increasingly resemble the other parties, thereby divesting themselves of their distinctive ideological appeal.

Another way to observe the ideological flexibility of the various parties is to observe the number of issues that make it into the parties' top three policy domains over time. This measure, which recognizes that a party may have more than one issue that is salient for them, shows whether a party emphasizes related or unrelated policy domains. Minor parties often promote several closely related policies within one policy domain, whereas major parties generally emphasize different policy domains in their top issues. For the entire period between 1948 and 2007, Fianna Fáil had twenty-two separate issues in its top three, Fine Gael had twenty-one, and Labour had nineteen. By contrast, the minor parties remained consistent in emphasizing only a handful of issues throughout the period (see fig. 3.6). The Progressive Democrats once again are the anomaly among the minor parties, because they advanced twelve different policy domains in their top three manifesto categories, in line with their strategy to take on the main parties at their own game and to play it more effectively. That the major parties and, to a lesser extent, the PDs were able to prioritize different bundles of issues over time demonstrates their programmatic flexibility. It is no coincidence that these ideologically flexible parties were able to

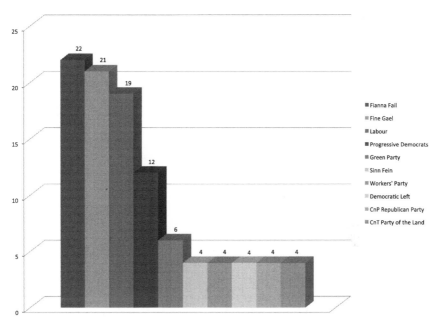

Fig. 3.6. Number of Issues in Parties' Top Three Manifesto Categories, 1948–2007

maintain their higher levels of electoral support over the period, while the more ideologically committed minor parties had difficulty sustaining their vote share after initial bursts of support.

Finally, major parties have sought to take advantage of their ideological flexibility and catchall appeals by emphasizing elements on both sides of divisive issues. For example, the stark transformation of religious and moral values in Ireland over the last thirty years has ushered in intense debate. The parties have sought to tread lightly in this debate and remain noncommittal, to avoid electoral quicksand. The manifesto data include two categories that capture party positions on this issue domain: *Traditional Morality Positive* and *Traditional Morality Negative*.[33] The larger parties display deep ambivalence on issues pertaining to morality, fluctuating between positive and negative positions and sometimes embracing contradictory positions in the same election. This "mugwumping"—espousing both sides simultaneously on a contentious moral issue—was pursued by all three major parties in the 1997 election: Fianna Fáil's total manifesto was 2.5 percent positive and 2 percent negative regarding traditional morality; Fine Gael's, 4.3 percent positive and 3 percent negative; Labour's, 0.8

percent positive and 2.4 percent negative. Given the even split among the electorate in the 1995 divorce referendum (50.3 percent in favor and 49.7 percent opposed), it is unsurprising that the major parties reached out to both sides simultaneously. Fianna Fáil and Fine Gael placed slightly more positive emphasis on traditional morality over the longer term. Labour adopted the opposite position, supporting more progressive social policies in six of the eight elections between 1981 and 2007 when "moral issues" were included in its manifestos.

The minor parties, which are generally perceived as more socially progressive than Fianna Fáil and Fine Gael, also de-emphasized contentious issues pertaining to moral values. The PDs were only slightly more socially conservative than the other minor parties on issues pertaining to morality in 1987, 1989, 1992, and 2007 but were slightly more progressive on these issues in 1997. Still, these issues never received more than 2 percent of the space within a PD manifesto. Over time, the Greens abandoned any mention whatsoever of moral issues, moving from devoting 4 percent of its manifesto to progressive social values in 1989 to not mentioning these concerns in 2002.[34] The other minor parties allocated less than 1 percent of their manifestos to moral issues, thereby ignoring a potential new source of electoral support during a period when society was becoming much more diverse in its attitudes on these issues.

The INES confirms that a significant percentage of voters report that abortion policies are important to them and yet a high percentage of respondents were unable to determine party positions on the issue. In 2002, 73 percent of respondents stated that abortion was very or fairly important to them, and 63 percent declared this to be the case in 2007. As noted in chapter 2, between one-third and one-half of respondents declared that they "did not know" where to place the political parties on the abortion policy scale. Strikingly, the parties associated with left-leaning positions on moral and religious matters (Labour, the Greens, Sinn Féin) were the very parties that INES respondents found most difficult to place on the policy spectrum. The minor parties and even Labour moderated their positions on moral issues, thereby reducing programmatic differences among the parties.

Voters' difficulty identifying party positions on abortion may reflect strategic ambiguity by parties. Table 3.2 shows citizens' attitudes toward abortion from the 2007 and 2011 INES, recoded into a three-category scale. Labour, the Greens, and Sinn Féin supporters were somewhat more likely to support legalizing abortion than supporters of other parties. However, every party except the Greens derived at least a quarter of its electoral support from voters who generally opposed abortion and another quarter from vot-

TABLE 3.2. Abortion Attitudes by Party

	Fianna Fáil		Fine Gael		Greens		Labour		Progressive Democrats		Sinn Féin		Independents		Total	
	2007	2011	2007	2011	2007	2011	2007	2011	2007	2011	2007	2011	2007	2011	2007	2011
Oppose	38	31	35	21	14	11	26	11	35	—	27	30	35	20	34	21
Neutral	27	36	34	38	32	56	34	47	29	—	29	35	29	37	30	39
Support	36	34	32	42	55	33	40	42	35	—	44	35	37	44	36	40

[a]A comparable question on Northern Ireland was not asked to voters in the 2011 INES.

ers who supported abortion. Any party that took a stronger stance on abortion could risk losing substantial support. By 2011, attitudes toward abortion in Ireland appear to have changed substantially; the total percentage of voters who opposed abortion dropped from around 33 percent to 21 percent. The proportion of Labour, Green, and Socialist voters opposed to abortion dropped below 15 percent, and the proportion of Fine Gael voters who opposed abortion fell from 35 percent to 20 percent. Fianna Fáil supporters, however, barely shifted their attitudes toward abortion. This suggests a rift that some left-leaning parties could use to mobilize supporters and draw contrasts with Fianna Fáil, although—as we have seen—the long-term prospects of such a strategy are weak. The long-term prospects for change in the patterns of ideological competition are weak because the major parties, Fianna Fáil and Fine Gael in particular, have continued to employ a flexible, catchall ideological approach. Rather than lose voters over specific issues, these parties are adept at co-opting issues, emphasizing them, or holding a deliberately ambiguous position to maintain their catchall appeal.

Minor Parties Case Studies

Given the electoral weakness of the minor parties over the medium and longer term, it is useful to examine the relationship between the choices these parties made on which policies to emphasize and their support in elections. Recall that major party leaders' decisions to avoid, accommodate, or assume an adversarial position on these issues also influences the electoral success of minor parties. As a result, a time lag often exists between, on the one hand, the rise of a new party and signature issues and, on the other, the major parties' decisions to increase emphasis or change positions on these issues. The interaction between these different types of parties over a series of elections highlights the dynamics in the preceding analysis.

The Workers' Party

The Workers' Party originated from a split with Sinn Féin in 1969 over the roles of militant republicanism and social radicalism and over whether to recognize parliaments in Belfast, Dublin, and London.[35] The party gradually increased its vote over several elections in the 1980s, from 2 percent in 1981 to its peak of 5 percent of the first-preference vote and seven seats in 1989. Yet by 1992, it received less than 1 percent of the vote and lost all its seats, while the Labour Party reemerged strongly. The Workers' Party's electoral trajectory is illustrative for several reasons.

First, the Workers' Party upheld well-defined ideological offerings, regularly highlighting *Welfare State Expansion, Non-Economic Demographic Groups* and *Social Justice* as its top three concerns. These issues accounted for half of its overall manifesto, leaving little space for other policy areas. The Workers' Party, like Clann na Talmhan before it, was essentially trying to raise awareness of the plight of its core constituency—in this case, labor.[36] It only moderated its emphasis on the original three highest priorities by nine percentage points over time.

Second, the Workers' Party illustrates issue co-optation by the major parties. Despite the sheer amount of energy the party expended on working-class concerns, virtually every other party ended up also addressing them. Therefore, even though the party only slightly moderated its emphasis on the original top three issues, other parties co-opted the same issues and undermined the party's electoral appeal. It took only one election cycle for Labour and, to a lesser extent, Fianna Fáil to react to the heightened attention—and electoral appeal—of the Workers' Party and virtually absorb the latter's concerns. Labour shifted the proportion of their manifesto spent on the top three issues of the Workers' Party from 24 percent in 1981 to 48 percent in the first 1982 election.[37] After the party disappeared, both the Democratic Left Party and Sinn Féin took up the mantle of these more left-leaning concerns. Although the smaller parties failed to parlay their policies into lasting electoral support, a broad consensus emerged on these issues.

Finally, the emergence of Social Partnership (SP) elevated the consensual role of unions (rather than their confrontational one) by including them in national wage agreements after 1987. In the end, the attractiveness of the more abrasive stance of the Workers' Party waned, and the party collapsed. Fianna Fáil had responded to key concerns among the electorate while displacing these issues from future electoral competition via Social Partnership. This allowed Fianna Fáil to focus on other issues in its election manifestos in an effort to maintain its broader electoral appeal. The combination of these factors illustrates that consistent policy approaches by minor parties can ultimately be undermined when major parties both co-opt these issues and displace them to extraparliamentary institutions.

The Progressive Democrats

The Progressive Democrats burst onto the electoral scene in 1987 with 12 percent of the first-preference vote, but their support steadily dissipated in each successive election, ultimately winning fewer than 2 percent in 2007. The party voted itself out of existence in 2008, deciding not to run candidates in any future local, European, or national elections. Despite their consistently declining votes, the PDs facilitated the consolidation of the coalition era of Irish politics. The PDs were the first party to enter a governing coalition with Fianna Fáil, in 1989. For sixteen of their twenty-one years of existence, the PDs joined Fianna Fáil in government. Their self-appointed "watchdog" role in governments dominated by Fianna Fáil at first bolstered but later undermined their electoral support. The PDs provide additional evidence of the predicament facing minor parties.

The leadership of the PDs, comprised of disillusioned former Fianna Fáil TDs and Fine Gael activists, adopted many of Fine Gael's economic priorities, so it is not surprising that the PDs offered few, if any, unique policies. However, the PDs sought to portray itself more as a modern, pro-business, right-of-center party. As the party with the most market-oriented economic policies, it is perhaps unexpected that the PDs shared more concerns with Labour in 1987 and the Greens in both 1997 and 2002 than it did with centrist Fianna Fáil and Fine Gael in these campaigns. Its highest-priority policy issues, such as *Welfare State Expansion, Social Group Interests* (e.g., farmers), *Environmental Protection,* and *Educational Expansion* allowed them to give a nod to centrist and left-leaning policy areas, but its emphasis on *Law and Order* and on *Free Enterprise Incentives* preserved its more rightist disposition. Given their attempt to disrupt the logic of Civil War politics, the PDs also sometimes emphasized such categories as *National Way of Life, Constitutional Negative,* and *Culture* to focus less on the rhetoric of nationalism and more on pragmatic policies to bring peace to Northern Ireland.

The PDs have largely been credited for shifting the ideological parameters of Irish politics. Widespread consensus emerged in the early 2000s over lower taxation coupled with incentives for the private sector as the best means to ensure Irish prosperity. This consensus created problems for the PDs in 2007. Bereft of substantive policy differences, Michael McDowell, the PD party leader at the time, found it difficult to counter opposition criticisms of him: "What could I do, it is very difficult to do negative politics. It was a peculiar election from that point of view. There was no point in me attacking the Fine Gael candidate; she was saying nothing that I disagreed with."[38] He did, however, try to set himself apart from parties of the Left with a witty mantra that he was "surrounded by the Left [Labour], the leftover [Greens], and the left behind [Sinn Féin]."[39] McDowell was not reelected, even though he had contributed significantly to Ireland's economic development, had facilitated peace in Northern Ireland by challenging Sinn Féin's criminality, and had prompted new legislation on citizenship. These high-profile achievements proved nugatory when it came to getting reelected.

As is highlighted by the example of the PDs generally and that of Michael McDowell in particular, staunch programmatic policy stands can be detrimental to political fortunes in Ireland, where voters also demand local delivery and strong personal ties. In the period leading up to the 2007 election, the Fianna Fáil–PD coalition enacted government policies toward doctors (consultant contracts) and lawyers (personal injury legislation) that significantly lowered the income of many middle-class professionals and produced a backlash among a core PD constituency.[40] The PDs' narrower support base, sustained largely by affluent professionals, was undermined by the policy decisions that the government led by Fianna Fáil made according to its estimation of the national interest. McDowell himself lost significant support among professionals in his Dublin South-East constituency.[41] Peter Cassells, former General Secretary of the Irish Congress of Trade Unions, argued that Taoiseach Bertie Ahern and Fianna Fáil manipulated the PDs into a coalition to support the most difficult decisions they thought needed to be made: Fianna Fáil then claimed that the PDs had forced them to do these unpopular things.[42]

It is telling that two of the most successful minor parties in Ireland's history, the Workers' Party and the Progressive Democrats, both emerged and disappeared in the period since the 1980s. Both sought—one from the left, one from the right—to shift party competition away from traditional nationalist politics toward politics that was more class-based. In one sense, these parties may have won the debate, because the major parties absorbed left-leaning policies in the 1980s and adopted right-leaning policies in the first decade of the twenty-first century. However, minor parties' transient success only encouraged the major parties to adopt their policies. Like a python, the major parties swallowed minor parties whole.

The Green Party

The Green Party was founded in 1981, won its first Dáil seat in 1989, and steadily increased its vote and seat shares, peaking in 2007 with 5 percent of the first-preference vote and six seats. It entered into government with Fianna Fáil after the 2007 election, but it was punished severely in the aftermath of Ireland's economic disaster in 2008 and lost all of its seats in the 2009 local elections and the 2011 parliamentary elections. The trajectory of the Greens highlights the challenge of electoral survival for minor parties when major parties co-opt their issues and make it necessary for the minor parties to moderate their distinctive stances to attract greater electoral support.

The three main parties have promoted environmental protection in their manifestos since the 1960s, because the environment critically influences Ireland's agriculture, fishing, and tourism industries. However, this emphasis increased in years when the Greens presented a more credible electoral threat. The three main parties have consistently allocated 1 to 3 percent of their manifestos to environmental protection, but they allocated additional attention in 1989 (Fianna Fáil allocated 8 percent, and FG allocated 11 percent), when the Greens won their first seat, and again in 1997 (Fianna Fáil allocated 7 percent; FG, 6 percent; and Labour, 6 percent), when the Greens fielded additional candidates.

Although Green Party issues were co-opted by major parties, the degree of the party's moderation over time is also noteworthy. As mentioned, the Greens decreased the percentage of their manifesto devoted to environmental protection from 25 percent in 1989 to just 8 percent in 2007. Furthermore, the Green Party apportioned 50 percent of their manifesto to their top three issues when they won their first seat in parliament in 1989, but this apportionment declined to only 19 percent in 2007, which is more in line with the percentage that the major parties allot to their key issues.[43] As figure 3.7 affirms, the subsequent convergence among all parties on environmental issues is due primarily to the Greens de-emphasizing their core issues, rather than to the other parties absorbing "Green" programmatic appeals. What is particularly striking is that although the major parties increased their emphasis on environmental protection, they made little effort to address other "Green" issues. Fianna Fáil increased its emphasis on these issues by 3 percent, Fine Gael by 6 percent before dropping down to 4 percent, and Labour by 5 percent. The major parties have proven adept at absorbing the more popular issues raised by minor parties (e.g., environmental protection) and leaving alone the less-appealing issues (e.g., antigrowth economic policies). This strategy of the major parties has further eroded smaller parties' ability to retain their initial electoral success.

Consistent with the conventional wisdom that pragmatists within the Green Party triumphed over more ideologically driven members, the Greens shifted their emphasis at the same time that they succeeded in elections in 2002 and 2007.[44] Not only did they reduce their focus on their core policy domains of *Environmental Protection* and *Anti-growth Economy* (ecological politics and sustainable development), but they also apportioned less space within their manifesto to negative attitudes toward the *EU* and *Traditional Morality*. These policy domains were key issues for early party

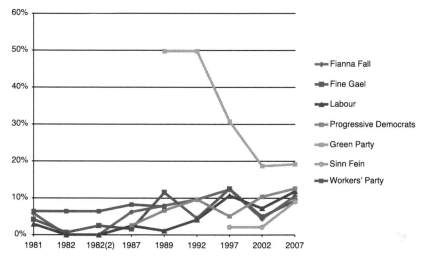

Fig. 3.7. Party Positions on the Green Party's Original Top Three Issues

loyalists, and the Greens' resolutely anti-EU stance was considered a crucial reason why the party tripled its number of TDs from two to six in 2002. Yet the Green Party reversed its longtime position on the EU and voted in favor of the Lisbon Treaty in 2008, revealing a deeper challenge for its strategic party positioning.

As the Greens' core programmatic concerns showed attrition, they increased their focus on popular policy domains such as *Social Justice* and *Welfare State Expansion* to compete with major parties on these issues. By doing so, they gained electoral traction in the short term but paid in the long run, for sacrificing the very ideological distinctiveness that gained them support in the first place—especially given the subsequent consensus that emerged around environmental issues.[45] The Greens' electoral collapse in the 2011 election, when they lost all six of their seats, had many causes. However, the Greens' governing coalition with Fianna Fáil and popular perceptions that they had compromised on too many of their core policy concerns certainly influenced this outcome, which is now familiar for a minor party.

A majority of Irish parties have become more supportive of environmental protection, which has muted its saliency during elections. Once again, if there are no real differences among parties on an issue, those issues are unlikely to shape voter preferences. The Greens gained electoral support because environmental protection was their principal priority; their attempts to address other issues and broaden their appeal led them to adopt positions identified with competing parties, such as promoting business interests and accepting lower taxes. According to INES results, voters never really identified the Greens as being distinctive on any of the other salient issues the party tried to engage. The sharp trade-offs faced by minor parties, driven by the gravitational pull to adopt the catchall strategies of the major parties, provide a constrained set of choices for minor parties.

Sinn Féin

Sinn Féin won its first seat in the Dáil in the contemporary period in 1997, after several elections in which it was shut out and secured only 1 percent of the first-preference vote. Since then, the party has steadily increased both the percentage of its first-preference votes and the number of seats it has won, peaking in the 2011 election with an all-time record of fourteen seats on 10 percent of the first-preference vote. Sinn Féin has remained unswerving in its emphasis on the same policy domains as evidenced by its manifestos, maintaining a more consistent ideological approach than the other minor parties. Since Ireland's economic meltdown in 2008, Sinn Féin has been the most outspoken opponent of austerity measures. As the only party that voted against the budget that paved the way for Ireland's EU/IMF/ECB loan late in 2010, Sinn Féin solidified its "opposition" status and was the only real "protest" option during the 2011 election.

Before concluding that Sinn Féin has cracked the minor party conundrum by remaining true to its core principles and will therefore avoid being swallowed up by Ireland's major parties, consider the following developments that may suggest otherwise. First, Sinn Féin has actually shifted its programmatic offerings in several ways. Sinn Féin's manifestos decreased their original emphasis on *Social Justice, Welfare State Expansion,* and *Farmers* by 9 percent between 1997 and 2007. In 2007, Sinn Féin struggled to maintain its left-wing and anti-EU policies, while simultaneously broadening its ideological appeal. The party's concession in 2007 over key corporate and individual tax policies revealed a willingness to modify core programmatic appeals to enhance its electoral attractiveness. According to one Sinn Féin candidate in a rural constituency, the reality of local competition dampened the party's more deeply held ideological aspirations. This candidate expressed disappointment at her party's national campaign because Sinn Féin changed its position on corporate and income taxation; she felt that the party was willing to dilute its principles excessively for political expediency. This candidate also complained that a willingness to enter a governing coalition with Fianna Fáil—even as a hypothetical case—watered down the party's more "pure" ideological appeal. If Sinn Féin were going to "get into bed with Fianna Fáil," she remarked, people might just as well go out and vote Fianna Fáil.[46]

Although this Sinn Féin candidate complained about the wishy-washy character of the national campaign, her own local campaign somewhat ironically focused more on improving roads and playgrounds than on advancing a principled, left-leaning economic agenda. Fianna Fáil's ability to position itself as the party that brought peace to Northern Ireland and economic prosperity to the Republic allowed it to mitigate Sinn Féin's popular support. Evidence from expert surveys also suggests that Sinn Féin had moderated its extreme republican views and holds virtually the same centrist positions as the other parties on Northern Ireland, that is, accepting a peaceful solution that necessarily entails an essential role for the British government. In this sense, Sinn Féin may not be as distinctive in terms of its ideological appeal as it likes to claim.

Sinn Féin's longer-term electoral prospects depend on whether voters truly share the party's ideological views. One could argue that much of Sinn Féin's electoral success in 2011 was due to the protest vote. INES data from 2007 and 2011 suggest that voters identify Sinn Féin on the overall left of the political spectrum but do not place Sinn Féin on the left on many issues and that they still perceive the party as very strong on Northern Ireland. Table 3.3, which compares INES results from 2007 and 2011 with identical questions on the TD surveys for the same elections, shows a persistent and unusually large gap between Sinn Féin voters and parliamentarians. Voters seem to consider Sinn Féin a centrist party with moderate positions on taxation and spending (average placement on a left-right scale was 4.5 in 2007 and 4.6 in 2011 and similarly centrist on taxation and spending issues). Sinn Féin TDs perceive their party as a leftist one and heavily favor higher taxation and spending: they placed themselves at 2.7 on a left-right scale in 2007 and at 2.4 in 2011. At least in 2007, voters also perceived Sinn Féin's position on Northern Ireland as more moderate than TDs did. Although voters identified Sinn Féin's position as more extreme than those positions of other parties (3.7 out of 10.0), this positioning is much less extreme than the 0.3 out of 10.0 position at which Sinn Féin TDs placed themselves on unification. This suggests that despite their best efforts, minor parties have difficulty shaking their initial reputation based on a single policy issue. This portrayal supports the view that voters in the last two elections have supported Sinn Féin more as a protest against the major parties or because of Sinn Féin's expanding organizational outreach and focus on delivering material benefits at the local level.

The challenges faced by Sinn Féin after the 2011 election echo a story that is now familiar. On the one hand, Sinn Féin represents a very different type of minor party. Their long-standing oppositional posture—both within and outside the electoral process—suggests that Sinn Féin may have what it takes to survive over the longer term. Similar to Fianna Fáil during the 1930s and 1940s, Sinn Féin established vibrant local organizations throughout the North and South in Ireland. Its ability to mobilize an even larger number of activists and volunteers during elections than can many of the major parties (see chapter 5) suggests that it may pose a credible electoral threat. Irish unification is a galvanizing electoral appeal for some, and Sinn Féin combines this passion with an uncommon effectiveness in meeting the concrete material needs of local constituents. Their success at winning seats on local councils and the national parliament allows Sinn Féin to coordinate between these two levels of government to deliver goods and services.

On the other hand, Sinn Féin faces a number of challenges. First, their clarion call to create a United Ireland is no longer as salient as it once was for many Irish citizens. The relative peace in Northern Ireland and the widespread recognition that any move toward a unified Ireland requires the consent of Northern Irish citizens and cooperation with the British government dampen the likelihood of unification in the foreseeable future. Recognizing this, the leaders of Sinn Féin have sought to establish the party as the authentic party of the Left. Again, although voters place Sinn Féin on the left of the political spectrum, Sinn Féin voters do not place themselves on the left on most left-right issues or on the overall left-right scale. Instead, Sinn Féin's recent electoral success appears to be related

TABLE 3.3. Perceptions of Sinn Féin Ideology

	2007		2011	
	TDs	Voters	TDs	Voters
Left-right	2.67	4.46	2.38	4.62
United Ireland	0.33	3.65	0.25	—[a]
Taxes and spending	8.33	6.15	7.88	5.28
European integration	4.67	6.84	5.25	4.10
Environmentalism	3.67	3.67	3.38	5.19
Abortion	5.00	5.69	5.79	5.19

[a]A comparable question on Northern Ireland was not asked to voters in the 2011 INES.

to the popularity of its protest against the major parties and to its organizational capacity to galvanize the local rank and file. Though the party benefited in 2011 from its populist positions, winning fourteen seats and enjoying a halo effect in polls after the election, its longer-term electoral trajectory is less certain.

The further Ireland moves from the financial collapse of 2008 and the original EU/IMF/ECB bailout, the more citizens have expected realistic proposals to advance Ireland's economy. Given Sinn Féin's experience in government in the North and their willingness to implement austerity measures, voters in the South suspect that Sinn Féin is only playing up an oppositional role and does not actually hold distinctive—or realistic—economic and social policies. As we have seen, once a minor party moderates its core ideological principles, it has difficulty sustaining its electoral appeal over the medium term. Sinn Féin appears to be headed in that direction. The party was already being asked in 2013 about its willingness to enter into coalition with one of the major parties, which demonstrates the trade-off it will face. Voters' demands that Sinn Féin develop more credible policies could alter the very nature of the party in the Republic of Ireland. Sinn Féin may be able to sustain itself electorally as a protest party over the medium term because of its deeply loyal base, but it will almost certainly face the dilemma confronted by all minor parties.

Thus, Sinn Féin's longer-term electoral challenge of maintaining a distinctive ideological appeal remains, especially following 2011, when most of Ireland's parties have shifted slightly left to address growing concerns over the effects of austerity. Ireland's major parties continue to possess an unusual degree of programmatic flexibility that allows them to co-opt a whole range of policies as their "highest priority" at any given time. This flexibility provides these major parties—over time—with an unusual capacity to absorb transient issues that can suddenly emerge in the context of an Ireland now in the throes of crisis.

Ideological and Clientelistic Linkages
and the Importance of Localism

An important by-product of the centripetal character of ideological competition and the institutional displacement of issues is the elevated importance of personalistic local ties. As we have seen throughout this chapter, ideological differences do exist within the electorate and among political parties, but these differences tend to shrink during elections. As a result, the distinguishing factor between candidates is often the brokerage ties that parties forge with voters in the constituency. Given that political parties generally establish links with voters via ideological appeals or material benefits, it makes sense that as ideological differences are minimized, voters turn to other, more personalistic ties with candidates and parties to determine how they will cast their vote.

Therefore, Irish politicians must establish a reliable reputation as an effective broker for the local constituency. A TD's brokerage role is multifaceted: TDs act as middle men, information providers, local promoters, and legislators.[47] What matters locally varies based on the constituency's sociodemographic and geographic conditions. Candidates must adapt their appeals to their respective constituency by demonstrating that they can meet the needs of their constituents. For example, in urban areas, candidates stress issues such as safeguarding welfare entitlements, providing rent assistance for lower-income families, improving living conditions, delivering more parks and school playgrounds, and enhancing the quality of life.[48] Candidates in commuter constituencies highlight their ability to bring more efficient public services to Ireland's fastest growing areas, whereas candidates in rural areas emphasize government support for farms, roads, tourism, and money for local schools and hospitals.[49] Regional programmatic differences exist, but the need to appeal effectively to local needs remains a constant.

As Sacks described in his classic study of Donegal, politicians actively foster citizen dependencies to stabilize their organizational environment.[50] Parties—and individual candidates—systematically exaggerate their ability to distribute benefits, and they encourage learned dependencies among their client-voters. Although TDs do not have the authority to grant local benefits directly, they possess access to government officials who do. Politicians vie with each other to be the first to claim credit among their constituents, reinforcing the perception among constituents that their TDs influence decisions affecting their material interests.

The all-important "contacts" are vital here. A TD needs to know when the official letter will be issued, so that the TD can issue a letter or make a personal phone call a few days earlier, saying that he or she is "making representations." After the official letter arrives, the TD dispatches a letter expressing delight at the fruit borne by his or her strenuous efforts and asking the grateful recipient to "remember" him or her at the next election. It is vital that locals perceive a candidate as having "pull" (influential contacts that deliver positive results). Sacks described this behavior as "imaginary patronage": the TD creates the appearance of patronage even if the TD's actual influence in securing the goods or services is limited. Voters then reward TDs for delivering fast-track solutions by reaching the remote bureaucrats who make decisions.[51] These tangible benefits—real or perceived—are much more potent in securing votes than ideological claims or even benefits that may be more generally distributed; credit for these latter benefits can be claimed by all the parties and candidates.

This behavior happens at the highest levels of Irish politics. There were tense moments in late October 2010 when the twenty-seven European Union prime ministers met behind closed doors in Brussels to discuss the urgency of adopting significant austerity measures across Europe, with particularly acute consequences for the Irish. The Greeks had already accepted a €110 billion EU/IMF loan, and riots had spread throughout Greece. With Ireland, Portugal, and Spain seen as the next likely victims, one can appreciate the skepticism and finger-pointing faced by Irish Prime Minister (Taoiseach) Brian Cowen as he worked tirelessly to convince his fellow leaders—and the global bond markets—that Ireland's economy was still viable. Yet in the middle of the proceedings, as Ireland's future hung in the balance, Cowen interrupted his meetings and placed a call from his personal mobile phone to a top government official back in Dublin to confirm that three of his constituents from County Offaly had received the greyhound licenses for which they had recently applied. Cowen was assured that the licenses would be granted.[52] The foregoing anecdote, not at all uncommon in the daily life of Irish politicians, suggests that party leaders in Ireland operate in a context that places a high premium on service to the local constituency.

Perhaps not surprisingly, the preeminence of constituency service leaps to the foreground in a 2010 survey of Irish parliamentarians conducted by the parliament. A majority of TDs reported that most of their workload is serving their constituency and representing local interests. The Joint Committee on the Constitution reported of TDs, "They spend (on average) 53 percent of their working time on constituency-based work, 38 percent on legislative work, and 9 percent on 'other' work. The largest single category of constituency-based work was 'working on individual constituents' cases,' which alone accounts for just over 20 percent of the average TD's overall workload."[53] When asked to rank which people a TD should be representing on a scale of 1–6, with 1 signifying the most important, respondents prioritized representing "all voters in the constituency" by a large margin, followed by all voters in the constituency who supported a particular TD or party. They placed little emphasis on representing the country as a whole or national social groups.[54] Irish TDs favor the needs of their constituents over and above those of party supporters and far more than voters from any particular social group. Local politics matter even more during elections. An amazingly high 70 percent of respondents in the 2002 INES reported that they voted for the candidate with whom they had personal contact during the campaign.[55] Irish elections possess a remarkably personalistic character.[56]

Irish TDs perform higher levels of constituency service to boost their personal appeal when they are confronted with greater intraparty competition. The Committee of Public Accounts reported,

> On average, a TD who faced no opponents from the same party in their constituency in 2007 spends 41 percent of their time on constituency-related work. This figure jumps to 62 percent for TDs who faced two or more candidates from the same party in their constituency. Those TDs who, at some point in their career, lost their seat to a fellow party member reported an average of 66 percent of their time spent on constituency work—well above the average figure of 53 percent.[57]

These high levels of constituency service, especially for TDs confronted with intraparty competition, is consistent with the claim that Ireland's PR-STV reinforces the prevalence of localism and the advantages of the major parties. Outdoing copartisans by "bringing home the bacon" helps candidates bolster their electoral appeal against programmatically similar candidates from the same party.

In my parliamentary survey covering the 2007 elections, TDs were asked to rate the importance of various factors that helped them attract votes (see table 3.4). TDs ranked "party policies" second to last among all the factors. The top four factors (the campaign, local organization, constituency service, and individual personality) were ranked highly by TDs from all parties, who agreed that their partisan background had little impact on their ability to attract votes. TDs mostly rated the national party leader, party policies, and national organization as relevant in attracting votes, but there were modest differences between parties, and Fianna Fáil TDs generally did not view these national-level factors as important. Even when TDs deem party policies important, they recognize that other factors also drive electoral competition—especially individual constituent service, personality, and local and national organizational advantages.

Voters share a belief that constituency service is a vital function of TDs. In the 2002 INES, respondents were asked to rank, on a 1–10 scale, the importance of three functions that TDs perform: working for the area, contributing to national debate, and aligning closely with the respondents' political views. A majority of the respondents (59.4 percent) ranked the importance of constituency service as a 10, only 26.9 percent ranked proximity to their own political views as a 10, and 38.2 percent ranked contributing to the national debate as a 10. The 2007 survey, which asked a slightly different set of questions, suggests that citizens see local brokerage as an honest, publicly interested function. When voters were asked whether they saw several traits as important to TDs, 71.4 percent said it was important for TDs to "speak up for their own area," although only about half that many (36.8 percent) said it was important that TDs help individual constituents, and few voters placed a premium on loyalty to parties. Furthermore, the differences between parties were relatively small. Supporters of the Progressive Democrats and of Sinn Féin were less likely to value local community representation than other voters, but only supporters of the Progressive Democrats were less likely to value assistance to individual

TABLE 3.4. OLS Estimates of TDs' Assessments of Factors Important to Voters in the 2007 Election

	Mean (standard deviation) dependent variable	Parameter estimates (standard errors) on party dummy variables			p-value (party effects are zero)[a]	R^2
		Fianna Fáil	Fine Gael	Labour		
Campaign	8.18 (1.74)	0.091 (0.578)	0.255 (0.614)	0.930 (0.687)	0.486	0.222
Party's local organization	7.81 (1.95)	−0.489 (0.640)	−0.288 (0.679)	−0.661 (0.760)	0.809	0.129
Ability to deliver for constituency	7.50 (1.92)	0.044 (0.668)	−0.356 (0.708)	−0.849 (0.793)	0.571	0.151
Personality	7.40 (1.73)	−0.023 (0.544)	0.531 (0.582)	1.192 (0.657)	0.128	0.303
National party leader	6.40 (2.47)	3.003 (0.774)	2.592 (0.821)	2.500 (0.912)	0.003***	0.304
Party's policies	5.93 (2.04)	2.744 (0.657)	1.412 (0.678)	2.296 (0.781)	0.000***	0.270
Traditions and loyalty	5.69 (2.73)	0.398 (0.939)	0.066 (0.997)	0.746 (1.116)	0.858	0.168
Party's national organization	4.73 (2.23)	1.589 (0.755)	2.244 (0.802)	1.006 (0.897)	0.044**	0.192

Note: The TDs were asked how important the factors were for explaining why people voted for them in the 2007 election. The scale was from 1 to 10, with 1 denoting "not important at all" and 10 denoting "very important."

[a]The following represent statistical significance for the p-value at various levels: * < 0.10, ** < 0.05, and *** < 0.01.

voters (in fact, Sinn Féin supporters were the most likely to value this, which speaks to the party's success in building up local organizations). At least by 2007, supporters of the Green Party were as likely as major party supporters to value more localistic services. Although voters' interest in candidates who spoke their mind surged from 43 percent in 2007 to 62 percent in 2011, they still believed that the most important characteristic in a TD was speaking up for the constituency (72.5 percent).

This emphasis on strong personal ties at the local level can have both positive and negative consequences for minor party candidates and independents.[58] Such candidates can initially succeed because they target emerging local issues and promise enhanced delivery of services. Well-known local candidates who have lower levels of party identification and party sentiment in general to capitalize on take advantage of name recognition and personal networks to garner votes.[59] Over the longer term, this electoral success is difficult to sustain, because the larger parties effectively adopt and absorb the very issues that initially offered an electoral foothold to smaller parties and independents. An additional challenge is that, once elected, these independent and minor party TDs' political longevity depends on developing a successful organization that actually delivers on its promises.

A trade-off emerges between addressing local needs effectively and developing or maintaining programmatic distinctiveness. To deliver services effectively to the local constituency and provide access to government officials—the secret to parliamentary success in Ireland—TDs prefer to join government rather than remain in opposition. Historically, smaller parties have joined governing coalitions with parties of different ideological backgrounds—at first almost invariably to remove Fianna Fáil from office, but also because they concluded that they could best promote their policy concerns and attend to local interests by joining government. Once in government, however, these smaller parties and independent TDs face a different problem: how to differentiate themselves programmatically from the larger, dominant party with whom they have joined forces and that is working relentlessly to undermine minor parties' support by exposing trade-offs minor parties made by joining government. Government participation can blunt policy distinctiveness because the need for compromise and collective decision making makes it difficult to criticize policies. In addition, the time and energy spent on governance leaves minor party TDs with less time to maintain strong local organizations.[60] Thus, there is a price to pay for entering government: government parties generally fare worse than opposition parties in general elections, with minor parties that participate in government losing an average of 19 percent of their seats from one election to the next, compared to a drop of only a 5 percent for the major parties.[61] Maintaining links with the electorate requires that parties and candidates find the right mix of ideological appeals and personalistic ties—an especially difficult challenge for minor parties and independents.

Conclusion

Scholarship exploring ideological positions at a given point in time has generally failed to appreciate the evolving character of ideological appeals and the resulting centripetal character of ideological competition among Irish parties. This chapter has redressed this failure. In addition, this chapter has highlighted the challenges facing minor parties, especially given the adaptive capacity of Ireland's major parties to shift their ideological appeals in response to changes in society and to address minor party concerns.

By drawing on multiple sources of data, this analysis has demonstrated that patterns of ideological competition in Ireland are more fully explained by observing shifting ideological and programmatic stands longitudinally. The parliamentary surveys I have undertaken, combined with the INES, demonstrate that while ideological differences exist between TDs from all parties, these differences are not always perceived by voters during elections. Expert surveys confirmed the convergence of party positions across virtually all of the most salient policy areas since the 1990s. This convergence further undermines attempts by minor parties to establish distinctive appeals among the electorate and has continually left voters reverting to voting for major parties as the parties best positioned to serve local constituency needs once in government. Manifesto data captured the fluid nature of major parties' appeals, as these parties regularly shift the emphasis and position of their programmatic offerings to outmaneuver minor parties with a more consistent focus on a narrower set of policies. The interaction of the appeals of major and minor parties over several election cycles illustrates precisely how the centripetal character of ideological competition rewards the larger parties' electoral advantage.

The centripetal character of ideological appeals in the Irish electoral arena has ultimately constrained the political arena further, dampening policy differences among parties competing for office. When this dynamic is combined with the strategies of institutional displacement described in chapter 4 and the organizational advantages enjoyed by Ireland's major parties, set forth in chapter 5, the implications for political representation and the prospects of political accountability come ever more clearly into focus.

FOUR

Shaping the Institutional Domain

Fianna Fáil decided that if they could not have "all the power most of the time," then they might as well have "most of the power all the time."

R. K. Carty

Ireland's historic parties have preserved their electoral predominance by artfully deploying strategies within three overarching domains: ideological, institutional, and organizational. The combined effect of these strategies has been threefold: (1) to prevent programmatic differences from rising to the political surface, thereby disrupting long-term patterns in electoral outcomes; (2) to sidestep contentious issues confronting the electorate; and (3) to preserve the importance of strong personalistic ties between candidates and voters at the local level. In this chapter, my analysis turns to the institutional dimension, to underscore how parties effectively "shrink" the electoral arena by displacing potentially divisive issues from the electoral and parliamentary arenas to nonelectoral institutional domains. As a result, the multitude of emergent issues facing Irish society discussed in chapter 2, including welfare, inequality, abortion, corruption, and immigration, generally are not translated or are incompletely translated into the electoral or parliamentary arenas. The displacement of these issues has mitigated the impact of Ireland's dramatic social change on electoral politics and has served to consolidate the electoral fortunes of Ireland's three historic parties, while making it more difficult for minor parties to enhance their electoral appeal over the longer term.

In stressing how parties deploy strategies to structure electoral patterns, I emphasize the importance of viewing parties as agents. However, in adopting this agency perspective, I am not employing a "rational organizational approach," where parties are assumed to function in a universe of nearly perfect knowledge to achieve purposively a set of preestablished goals. Rather, my analysis treats parties as "natural organizations" operating in a context of uncertainty and imperfect knowledge. Parties act with imperfect knowledge, adopting positions and strategies that can appear at cross-purposes, often resulting in unintended consequences. As mentioned in chapter 1, although parties in Ireland may not have set out to create a set of state institutions purposefully to remove difficult issues from the electoral realm, these institutions, once created for other purposes, have provided the parties with convenient institutional vehicles that elicited this effect. Parties and party leaders utilize state institutions to preserve internal party unity and their broad cross-class electoral appeal, while also inhibiting new parties and issues from reconfiguring long-standing competitive dynamics within the party system.

To help us understand more fully how parties interact within the institutional domain to boost their electoral outcomes, my analysis differs from existing scholarship in two important ways. First, the focus offered here differs from purely institutional explanations that describe institutions as the pivotal explanatory variable in shaping electoral outcomes based on the strong electoral incentives that these institutions provide. Chapters 1 and 2 have already underlined the insufficiency of formal institutional arguments to explain the predominance of Ireland's major parties. Ireland's PR-STV electoral system shapes the electoral behavior of individual candidates and political parties in critical ways, but it cannot fully explain the variation in electoral results over time. This chapter underscores the crucial ways in which Ireland's major parties have interacted with a set of extraparliamentary institutions as a means of preserving their electoral predominance. These institutions have influenced the number and types of strategies available to political parties; however, party leaders have taken advantage of these various institutional mechanisms in different ways depending on how their parties' strategies would affect their overall electoral success. For example, political parties have employed these institutions in one way when they believed they could take credit for enhancing economic policy making and overall governance—which generally occurred when there was clear-cut support for their policies within the electorate. Yet, these same parties have behaved another way when policy issues have divided public opinion and when party elites themselves were internally divided. In these cases, party leaders have taken cover within these various institutions to build consensus, include other actors in the policy-making process, and avoid blame. The ability of party leaders to take the pulse of the public and to respond successfully is a key factor in explaining why and how parties have adapted, strategically employing institutions to maintain their electoral predominance.

During the period of radical social and economic change beginning in Ireland in the 1980s, newer institutions have emerged, and older ones have been used more frequently and in new ways. This period is also marked by heightened competitiveness in Irish elections, with minor parties increasingly challenging the electoral superiority of the historic parties. The success experienced by major party leaders in strategically employing extraparliamentary institutions under a variety of social, economic, and political contexts reinforces the importance of viewing parties and their leaders as agents. These extraparliamentary institutional vehicles are essential, but their full impact can only be appreciated when we factor in the strategic choices of party leaders to utilize them to serve their own evolving electoral interests. My analysis of this period underscores the importance of institutions, but primarily insofar as they provide party leaders with a powerful set of tools to advance their own agendas.

A second way my focus on the institutional dimension differs from that of other scholars is in its attention to how parties interact with the state to maintain their edge in uncertain electoral environments. Consistent with the view of parties as "natural organizations," Irish parties exhibit some characteristics of "cartel" parties as they become increasingly dependent on the state apparatus. Katz and Mair's cartel thesis examines the evolving relationships among civil society, political parties, and the state, revealing a dialectical process whereby parties adapt organizationally and programmatically to changing social contexts. A central feature of their argument is that established parties seek both to set barriers of entry for new parties (via electoral rules and media access) and to provide themselves with state subsidies enabling them to maintain their organizational and electoral advantage.

Irish parties have certainly relied more on state support for their parliamentary and organizational efforts in recent years. Although state financing of parties in Ireland (discussed in more detail in chapter 5) remains comparatively modest, rising levels of state support have permitted parties (with weaker ties to civil society and declining party membership) to more effectively engage electoral politics by professionalizing their organizations. Understanding how political parties are employing state institutions to preserve their electoral predominance requires rethinking. Instead of focusing exclusively or even primarily on how parties increasingly depend on the state for funding and to regulate campaigns, this analysis focuses on the ways established parties manage how issues are addressed via an array of extraparliamentary state institutions that help preserve their electoral success.

New layers of governance networks associated with EU membership, Social Partnership, and quasi-autonomous state agencies (quangos) designed principally to enhance Ireland's competitiveness within the global market have generated additional institutional vehicles by which parties have engaged salient issues confronting Irish society. As a result of the ways party leaders have interacted with these extraparliamentary institutions, many issues have been sidelined—issues that otherwise, if parties had to compete over them openly in the electoral arena, would almost certainly generate unwanted contention, disrupt the electoral advantage of the historic parties, and risk allowing smaller parties to advance electorally. Given the increased levels of competitiveness in Irish elections due to the swelling number of unattached voters, such strategies are especially attractive to established parties. Sidelining potentially contentious issues narrows the programmatic electoral space and prevents new cleavages from altering the overall structure of competition. As a consequence, the growing number of unattached voters is left to base their vote increasingly on perceptions of "competence" and the ability to deliver goods and services locally. Emphasizing "competence" and the delivery of goods and services is a more congenial way for the leading parties to maintain links with voters than relying on deep-seated political divides. The leading parties strategically depoliticize issues with the potential to fracture the electorate—and constituencies internal to the parties themselves—by sidelining them from the electoral arena.

How, why, and what issues become displaced or even depoliticized depends, once again, on the broader electoral strategies that party leaders have employed to help them shape political and electoral competition to advance their interests. In general terms, political parties in advanced democracies select issues in which they perceive that they possess some electoral advantage, while dampening the salience of others. The emergence of contentious issues that either threaten internal party unity or create the potential for the emergence of unwanted issues can thwart the ability of major parties to frame electoral competition to suit their interests. Parties resort to a variety of mechanisms when threatened by unwieldy contention. For example, they can seek to morph contentious value-related issues into resource-related ones: the debate then becomes less about the merits of particular policies and more about their costs and implementation. However, they can also subsume or even remove issues from the realm of electoral and parliamentary politics.

Consider the ways in which parties remove or subsume issues. First, parties can simply avoid an unwanted issue during party competition. Second, if an unwanted issue becomes salient, the main parties can adopt similar positions and generate cross-party consensus, while offering the illusion of choice by advocating slightly different policy approaches. Third, parties can relegate the issue to party competition at subnational levels. Fourth, issues can be displaced to alternative state or extraparliamentary institutions and processes that remove contentious issues altogether from the electoral arena. Leaders of Ireland's major parties have engaged all of these strategies at one time or another, effectively "shrinking" the political arena. As mentioned in chapter 2, even Fine Gael and, to some extent, Labour have pursued these strategies as a way of preserving their broad, catchall appeal during a period of rapid social, economic, and political change.

The following discussion on the primary extraparliamentary institutions employed by parties to displace issues in Ireland focuses on referenda, Social Partnership, tribunals, quangos, and courts. These institutions have been the ones most engaged with policy areas related to Ireland's dramatically changing social and economic landscape. Not surprisingly, these institutions are also most closely related to the cleavages and issues with the greatest potential to alter the dynamics of party competition. The subsequent analysis of how parties address potentially contentious issues outside of the parliamentary arena offers a more complete picture of how parties and the state interact in the contemporary era than does the more limited vision provided by the cartel thesis.

Recurring to Referenda

Referenda have been one of the most important institutional means that parties have employed to frame how pressing cultural, social, and political issues are addressed in a rapidly changing context. Ireland (along with Australia) is a rare case in which every constitutional amendment requires a popular vote. Article 46 of the Irish Constitution declares that a proposal to amend the Constitution must first be passed by both houses of the Oireachtas (the Irish parliament) and then be put to a vote in a referendum. The use of referenda has accelerated in the most recent period of Irish politics, with all but four of thirty-five referenda having taken place since 1972 (table 4.1). In this latter period, nineteen referenda were undertaken at the government's initiative, thirteen were held by governments in response to demands emanating from judicial intervention, and three were initiated as a result of international imperatives.

TABLE 4.1. Irish Referenda, 1937–2013

Referendum	Date	Initiated	Yes (%)	Turnout
Northern Ireland				
Belfast Agreement (Good Friday)	1998	International	94.4	56.3
Religious and moral issues				
Special position of the Catholic Church	1972	Government	84.4	50.7
Adoption boards	1979	Government	99.0	28.6
"Pro-life" (antiabortion) amendment	1983	Government	66.9	53.7
Legalization of divorce	1986	Government	36.5	60.8
Restrict availability of abortion	1992	Courts	34.7	68.2
Freedom to travel for abortion	1992	Courts	62.4	68.2
Freedom of information for abortion	1992	Courts	59.9	68.1
Legalization of divorce	1995	Government	50.3	62.2
Abolish death penalty	2001	Government	62.1	34.8
Protection of human life in pregnancy	2002	Courts	49.6	42.9
Children's rights	2012	Government	58.0	33.5
European integration				
Membership of EC	1972	Government	83.1	70.9
Single European Act	1987	Courts	69.9	44.1
Maastricht Treaty	1992	Courts	69.1	57.3
Treaty of Amsterdam	1998	Courts	61.7	56.2
Nice Treaty (I)	2001	Courts	46.1	34.8
Nice Treaty (II)	2002	Courts	62.9	49.5
Lisbon Treaty (I)	2008	Courts	46.4	53.1
Lisbon Treaty (II)	2009	Courts	67.1	59.0
Fiscal Treaty	2012	Courts	60.3	50.6
Institutional and procedural issues				
Ratify the Constitution	1937	Government	56.5	75.8
Change in voting system	1959	Government	48.2	58.4
Change in voting system	1968	Government	39.2	65.8
Constituency boundaries	1968	Government	39.2	65.8
Voting age (reduced to 18)	1972	Government	84.6	50.7
University representation in Seanad	1979	Government	92.4	28.6
Extension of voting right (Dáil elections)	1984	International	75.4	47.5
Legalize denial of bail by courts	1996	Government	74.8	29.2
Cabinet confidentiality	1997	Courts	52.7	47.2
Recognition of local government	1999	Government	77.8	51.1
International Criminal Court	2001	International	64.2	34.8
Irish citizenship	2004	Government	79.2	59.9
Abolish the Seanad	2013	Government	48.3	39.2
Establish Court of Appeal	2013	Government	65.2	39.2

Note: On left-right, *n* = 256 for Fianna Fáil, 167 for Fine Gael, 75 for Labour, 31 for Greens, 20 for Progressive Democrats, and 28 for Sinn Féin. Sample sizes vary slightly for other issues.

The referendum is perceived by some scholars as a "conservative device," an institution designed to prevent radical changes in Irish society from dramatically altering the landscape of politics in Ireland. Nearly three-quarters of referenda since 1972 have addressed fundamental issues concerning Northern Ireland, Ireland's growing secularization, and Ireland's membership in the EU. These deeply divisive issues struck at the core of what it means to be Irish, and although short-term political polarization occurred as a result of these referenda, polarization subsided over time. The recurrence to referenda to deal with deeply contentious issues has provided legitimacy to the political process without fomenting further interparty and intraparty conflict and division. As a result, referenda have been embraced by both parties and voters as "the way" to deal with certain categories of issues, irrespective of whether the Constitution mandates it or not.

Not all referenda are geared toward deflecting divisive issues. In fact, many of the government-initiated referenda were held to address procedural and institutional issues. Fourteen of nineteen government-initiated referenda passed. Of the five government-initiated referenda that were rejected, four involved governing parties seeking to change the system in ways that voters perceived might increase governing parties' power. For example, Fianna Fáil's two failed attempts to switch the PR-STV electoral system to a single-member district plurality system (in 1959 and 1968) were partisan changes that elicited strong opposition mobilization from Fine Gael, Labour, and the media. In addition, the narrowly defeated 2013 referendum to abolish the Seanad (Ireland's upper parliamentary house) was an attempt by Fine Gael and Labour to capitalize on public opinion in favor of political reform after Ireland's economic and financial meltdown in 2008. Although there was widespread appetite for reform, many voters and opposition groups feared that a unicameral parliament would further solidify the ability of governing parties to pass legislation without scrutiny and would thereby exacerbate Ireland's existing problems. Therefore, Ireland's major parties have not been able to use referenda to bolster their authority in explicit ways. Instead, Ireland's major parties appear to have experienced greater success in referenda when they adopt positions that are more nuanced.

The tendency to recur to referenda has mitigated the impact of significant changes in society on patterns of party competition. Despite dramatic changes in contemporary Ireland, new cleavages with the potential to reshape electoral competition—such as religious versus secular, pro- and anti-EU, and more-trenchant left-right divides—have not materialized. The argument here is that this result has occurred at least partly because these issues have been addressed via referenda and not in general elections. Although it is tempting to conclude that the institution of referenda alone explains the resultant depoliticization, we must not ignore the role of political agency, as party elites have made strategic decisions associated with referendum campaigns, which have resulted in significant, long-term electoral effects. Major party leaders consistently managed this institutional mechanism to handle issues in ways that avoid disrupting long-standing patterns of electoral competition and, for that matter, introducing new ones.

A fuller understanding of how parties use referenda is critical. Referenda in Ireland provide powerful incentives as to how parties, civil society groups, and voters behave. For example, the extraparliamentary character of referenda has provided Ireland's major parties with an institutional vehicle for turning contentious issues over to voters without exposing themselves to the realignment risks of a general election. Although minor parties have used referenda as a bully pulpit to challenge major parties, the nature of referenda as second-order campaigns focused on single issues has limited the longer-term electoral consequences of minor parties. The overall effect has been to keep electoral and referenda competition distinct from one another. The insulation referenda provides has prevented the major parties from having to alter their winning formula of sustaining strong partisan attachments, instead allowing them to offer broad, catch-all ideological appeals during general elections. These institutional factors contribute to an explanation of why and how Ireland's major parties have been able to preserve their electoral predominance during a time of sharp social change and heightened electoral competition.

Party strategies matter as well. The strategic choices of Ireland's party leaders have exploited referenda to maximize their own electoral interests. The various choices party leaders have made *before*, *during*, and *after* referenda campaigns have affected how salient issues in Irish society are translated into the political arena, one of their most critical functions. However, as in the case of the legendary "dog that did not bark" in the Sherlock Holmes story, it is equally important to analyze the contentious issues that are successfully muted or even silenced. Curiously, some hot-button issues simply never appear on the electoral landscape. I argue that, in the Irish context, the silence of many salient issues during elections can be explained partly by the strategies party leaders have employed during referenda, thereby reinforcing the distinction voters perceive between referenda and election campaigns.

Consider a few examples of the types of choices party leaders have made. Governments must decide whether to hold a referendum, and if they choose to hold a referendum, they must make choices about the specific wording of the proposed change to the Constitution and the timing of a referendum. These decisions shape the overall framing of the question and provide inducements to the actors who will either support or oppose it. For example, to influence the framing of EU referenda, the government fought hard to protect certain policies within EU treaty negotiations because the policies were perceived to be important to key elements of the electorate. The "abortion protocol" in the 1992 Maastricht Treaty, the preservation of neutrality in the 1998 Amsterdam Treaty, and the maintenance of the corporate tax rate in the 2012 Fiscal Stability Treaty constitute such policies. By protecting these positions in treaty negotiations, the major parties greatly enhanced the probability that their voters would support a yes vote when an EU referendum was eventually held. On other occasions, a government has chosen to offer a referendum to fulfill a campaign promise made with highly active civil society groups in return for their support during a general election—as was the case in the first abortion referendum in 1983. Still other referenda were only held when the courts forced governments to respond. In each of these scenarios, the decisions of party leaders over whether and when to hold a referendum were greatly influenced by broader electoral interests.

Once a referendum is called, parties must decide how to frame the key issues at stake, what position to take, and how vigorously to campaign. Parties behave opportunistically as they calculate the costs and benefits of engagement in specific referenda campaigns. The choices party leaders make can affect voter turnout because voters are more likely to participate when they are well informed and when ideological alignments are clear. Voter turnout has been highest on the few occasions when the main parties took opposite sides on an issue and lowest when they expressed basic agreement. It is telling that no matter how contentious the issue or how sharp the polarization within the Irish electorate, the two major Irish parties, Fianna Fáil and Fine Gael, have only taken opposing positions four times since 1972. This collusive pattern can be explained by the catchall support base of the main parties and the predilection of party leaders to avoid unwanted splits among their own rank and file and among the broader electorate, at all costs. Although deep historical legacies underscore the catchall nature of the major parties' support, the parties continually adapt strategically to sustain these catchall appeals.

When major party leaders decide whether to take sides on an issue, they must consider how their decision will affect the views of their parliamentary party and rank and file. Meguid's comparative research on niche parties is illustrative for how taking sides can affect broader electoral outcomes. Meguid argues that the survival of niche—or minor—parties depends in large part on the choices exercised by the larger parties. Whereas electorally successful parties will generally seek to dampen or avoid issues where possible, they are sometimes induced—given the growing salience of an issue—to adopt a position on a particular issue. If a challenger party brings an issue before the electorate and then the issue catches fire, an established party has two options. It can mimic the position of the challenger, which undermines the minor party's ability to "own" the issue, eroding their perceived distinctiveness and credibility. As a result, the niche party then generally loses electoral support, because the relevance of their challenge has been reduced. The second option is that established parties can assume an adversarial position directly confronting the challenger party. Meguid argues that niche parties generally increase their vote when this occurs.[1]

The logic of these findings is useful for understanding how parties have behaved during Irish referenda campaigns, as the mandatory nature of a number of constitutional referenda and the growing salience of issues among the electorate has made outright issue avoidance nearly impossible. Increasingly, Ireland's major party leaders cannot altogether avoid dealing with fundamental issues confronting Irish society. As Meguid's comparative work suggests, the decision by a major party leader to take a side on an issue tends to affect the overall salience of that issue as well as the electoral fortunes of both minor and major parties within the electorate. The choice to accommodate or oppose the positions of minor parties is complicated for the leaders of Ireland's major parties. First, the major parties' catchall support base necessarily implies that taking either side might alienate significant constituencies within the electorate, thereby potentially undermining their overall electoral appeal. Similarly, major parties risk weakening party unity or even the possibility of fatally splitting their party if they take a decisive position on an issue. Second, the choice to take an adversarial position could, as the comparative evidence suggests, increase the vote share of minor parties and help them take ownership of a winning issue. An increased vote share for the minor parties may eventually cement their support among a changing electorate or, more dangerously for the established parties, shift the nature of electoral competition away from long-standing Civil War identities.

The very existence of referenda provides major parties, if handled properly, with a powerful tool when forced into the predicament of taking sides.

First, referenda allow a high degree of issue avoidance. That key issues confronting Irish society are being addressed within the political system, although outside the electoral arena, means that parties cannot be accused of being nonresponsive to voter concerns. As long as these key issues can be resolved within this extraparliamentary arena, parties can avoid open competition over them in elections. Second, in deciding whether to adopt a decisive position in a referendum, party leaders must weigh the risks of splitting their constituencies or elevating the importance of an issue that might then become unmanageable in open electoral competition. Taking a back seat could dampen the importance of the contended issue at hand, thereby potentially depriving minor parties of an effective wedge within the electorate. However, taking backseats and simply ceding the outcomes of referendum campaigns to minor parties or civil society groups also risks providing challengers with opportunities to galvanize the electorate and establish a lasting presence within the political landscape. Therefore, when faced with the prospect of a referendum, the leaders of Ireland's major parties must weigh their options carefully.

The strategic choices party leaders make about how to campaign during referenda shapes the array of choices available to voters in subsequent general elections. Not surprisingly, over 80 percent of TDs in my 2010 and 2012 parliamentary surveys admitted that they campaigned less during referenda than in general elections. Ireland's major parties in particular have increasingly—and deliberately—ceded the referenda domain to single-issue groups, who, in turn, mobilize the majority of unattached voters. These single-issue groups are less likely to take their cues from political parties. Winning or losing referenda appears to be less crucial to the major parties than ensuring that the issues—once in referendum—do not spill over into the electoral arena. Major parties often choose not to adopt decisive positions, sometimes even declining to actively campaign during referenda. This gives organizations within civil society an opportunity to win votes not available to them during general elections.

As a consequence of these dynamics, potentially explosive issues addressed in referenda have been kept at arm's length from the domain of electoral politics over the longer term. By relegating the most fractious issues to this mechanism, parties display a high degree of responsiveness and accountability, while avoiding exposure to these issues during all-important general elections. Parties manage this key institution in such a manner that referenda have essentially become a parallel electoral mechanism that leaves the major parties' parliamentary electoral fortunes benignly undisturbed. When election time arrives, more explosive issues, such as abortion, divorce, or European integration, are effectively side-stepped. Abortion has been dealt with in three hotly contended referenda (in 1983, 1992 [three amendments], and 2002), divorce in two (in 1986 and 1995), and EU integration in eight, allowing the established parties to adroitly avoid these issues in general elections. Even though voters identified these issues as important, these issues have remained conspicuously absent during elections, and voters have consistently had difficulty in pinpointing party positions. In 2007, for example, a high percentage of respondents stated that they "did not know" where the parties stood on abortion: for Fianna Fáil, 33 percent; for Fine Gael, 36 percent; for Labour, 39 percent; for the PDs, 41 percent; for the Greens, 45 percent; and for Sinn Féin, 49 percent. As discussed in chapter 2, more voters were unable to place parties on abortion than on any other policy.

Finally, political parties in government must also decide when and how to implement the necessary changes to the Constitution following a referendum. Although the constitutional mandate to legislate for approved referenda issues appears quite straightforward, governments have sometimes simply chosen not to legislate—which has consistently been the case, for example, with abortion. As we shall see later in this chapter, the failure to act on abortion, despite court orders and several referenda, has been driven by the major party leaders' unwillingness to alienate voters. The art of avoidance, often associated with leaders in institutional contexts where there exist voluntary referenda, is operative in the Irish case as well.

Quantitatively speaking, the issues most frequently engaged within referenda reveal distinctive intraparty and interparty divides. Recall table 3.1 in chapter 3, which shows that divisions between the three established parties' TDs in 2007 were far sharper on abortion than on any other issues. In particular, Labour TDs supported notably more progressive abortion laws than the other two major parties, making abortion a potential wedge issue. Labour might be able to mobilize supporters around liberalizing abortion laws, while Fianna Fáil and Fine Gael might be able to mobilize supporters around opposition to this policy. However, there is also a considerable degree of dissent *within* each of the major parties on attitudes toward abortion. Table 4.2, which measures the average distance between a TD and his or her party on a 10-point scale, is indicative. Fine Gael and Labour TDs were, on average, farther from the center of their party on abortion than on any other issue. For Fianna Fáil, only fiscal issues dividing an increasingly laissez-faire wing from moderates were more polarizing.

At its worst, the politicization of abortion could prompt instability and defections among the major parties, opening competition up to new parties. Strategies for defusing conflict over abortion policy are difficult: logrolling and patronage can be insufficient because abortion is a "moral issue" where compromises may be morally unacceptable to many people. Recall the discussion from chapter 2 on figure 2.2, which showed that more Irish voters hold extreme attitudes on abortion than on any other subject examined. As a result, abortion policy has historically led to significant partisan realignment in many democracies, such as the United States.[2] The abortion issue is quintessentially dangerous for parties to address head-on; therefore, Irish leaders have recurred consistently to referenda instead.

Whereas abortion is characterized by a unique and potentially unstable degree of polarization, attitudes toward the European Union are characterized by a potentially unstable degree of elite consensus. Recall from figure 3.2 that although there is some intraparty disagreement among TDs representing the three main parties, the distance between Fine Gael and Fianna Fáil TDs and the center of their party was smaller on European integration than on any other issue. In other words, TDs from these parties shared a remarkable degree of consensus that European integration was a good thing. Among the established parties, only Labour TDs showed much division over the EU. At the same time, almost no visible differences exist between the three parties, and the divisions between the three parties are statistically weaker on this issue than on any other. Referring to table 4.2, note that parties appear to take very ambiguous positions on the European Union: after abortion, voters are less able to place parties' positions on this issue than on any of the other issues surveyed.

The significant minority of the Irish population that has consistently opposed further unification with Europe (see figs. 4.1–2, as well as fig. 2.2 in chapter 2) is not represented by any major party. This, too, indicates a potential source of instability. Given the low levels of intraparty diver-

TABLE 4.2. Average Distance between TDs and Parties by Issue (2007)

	Spending	European Union	Environment	Abortion
Fianna Fáil (*n* = 44)	1.27	.30	.66	.79
Fine Gael (*n* = 31)	1.10	.45	.90	1.24
Labour (*n* = 16)	.63	1.13	.69	1.81
Total (*n* = 101)	1.04	.55	.76	1.14

sity on the European Union, it would be difficult for one or more of the established parties to quickly and credibly change their policy stances on European integration to capture previously unrepresented segments of the electorate. Were voters to base their political decisions on the issue of EU integration, the established parties could likely lose substantial support. The major parties have worked strategically to contain public attitudes on these issues and to preserve a fragile majority in favor of greater integration by displacing conflicts on the issue via referenda.

In general, the major parties' use of referenda on abortion and European integration has succeeded. Table 4.3 shows that at the time of the 2007 election, minor party supporters had not coalesced around strong positions on these issues; instead, minor parties' electoral supporters often held positions that diverged somewhat from the parties' own positions, as shown by the high average distance between voters and parties. Minor party supporters were as internally divided and ambiguous as other citizens. Progressive Democrat, Green, and Sinn Féin supporters were, on average, fairly distant from their parties on abortion—as were Fianna Fáil, Fine Gael, and Labour voters; distances between parties and voters on abortion were higher than on any other issue, across parties. While opposition to further European integration is a potential rallying issue for minor parties, these parties' supporters were divided in 2007. Of all the parties, Green and Sinn Féin supporters were furthest from their party on integration-related issues. For them, integration was second among their most divisive issues, although it was only fourth for the other parties. The continuing divisions within minor parties may be one reason why they have failed to mobilize around emergent issues in Irish politics, and this situation testifies to the strategic successes of major parties.

TABLE 4.3. Average Distance between Voters and Parties by Issue (2007)

	Left-right	Northern Ireland	Spending	European Union	Environment	Abortion
Fianna Fáil	1.11	2.08	1.25	1.60	2.08	2.47
Fine Gael	1.37	2.50	1.58	1.99	2.50	2.21
Labour	1.05	1.66	1.42	1.43	1.66	1.99
Greens	1.48	1.67	1.82	2.03	1.67	2.21
Progressive Democrats	1.55	2.14	1.25	1.32	2.14	2.30
Sinn Féin	1.86	1.64	1.35	2.27	1.64	2.72
Total	1.25	2.10	1.40	1.73	2.10	2.33

Note: On left-right, *n* = 256 for Fianna Fáil, 167 for Fine Gael, 75 for Labour, 31 for Greens, 20 for Progressive Democrats, and 28 for Sinn Féin. Sample sizes vary slightly for other issues.

A careful analysis of the strategic decisions made by political party leaders reveals that regardless of how powerful referenda are in structuring party competition, political parties still have plenty of room to maneuver. The strategic choices made by party leaders matter, and they matter decisively for explaining why major parties have been able to preserve their electoral predominance during this period of dramatic social and economic change. An analysis of the concrete ways that parties have behaved during specific referendum campaigns over social and moral issues and the EU will illustrate the previously described dynamics.

Referenda on Social Issues: Abortion and Divorce

The strategic decisions major party leaders have made with respect to abortion and divorce in the 1980s and 1990s reveal how they successfully avoided fractious internal divisions and prevented the cleavage between religious/conservative and secular/liberal attitudes from becoming a wedge in electoral politics. This was no easy feat. As chapter 2 highlighted, attitudes toward abortion and divorce were undergoing monumental changes beginning in the 1980s, and divisive public clashes between progressives and conservatives were escalating. The major parties sought to balance their historic catchall appeal among voters with the fact that most religiously conservative voters supported them. In contrast, the Labour Party and the other minor parties were generally more progressive on social issues and stood to benefit from the growing proportion of the electorate who were adopting more progressive positions with respect to these issues. Battles between conservative and progressive social forces were waged outright during abortion and divorce referenda. A closer look at these campaigns underscores that while political parties are constantly seeking to reflect changing interests, they are simultaneously trying to frame how these interests are addressed within the political system to preserve their electoral predominance.

In 1982, the antiabortion lobby sought to ensure that no law or court decisions could make abortion legal. These lobbies placed considerable pressure on both Fianna Fáil and Fine Gael to agree to hold a referendum on the issue during the November general election campaign. Both parties agreed because they were scrambling to secure every available vote in this competitive and uncertain electoral environment. When in government with Labour in 1983, Fine Gael fulfilled its promise to hold a referendum that would ensure that neither legislation nor the courts could legalize abortion, despite the risks that this referendum action posed to its own constituencies. Conflicting positions on the referendum existed among and within the parties, with Fianna Fáil in favor, Fine Gael split, and Labour and other minor parties against it. Tellingly, the major parties did not campaign vigorously for or against the referendum, irrespective of their position. Two-thirds of voters supported including a pro-life statement within the Constitution; the referendum passed. The debate, however, was far from over.

Abortion resurfaced in 1992 as a result of the controversial court case *Attorney General v. X*, known as the "X case," and the decision of the governing coalition, led by Fianna Fáil, to prevent Ireland's pro-life laws from being overturned by EC law. In March 1992, the Irish Supreme Court determined that a suicidal pregnant teenager had the right to an abortion: because her life was endangered, the Court found that she was entitled to travel overseas for the procedure. Public and political debate flared in anger over the Court's decision. Legal confusion ensued as to what the Court's decision meant for the availability of abortion in Ireland. Abortion was already being contested as a result of the Maastricht Treaty negotiations, with Ireland requesting an exemption from EC law. This court case added fuel to the fire. Special interest groups on both sides saw an opening to advance their views. Pro-choice lobbies sought a reversal of the 1983 pro-life amendment altogether, and pro-life advocates argued for overturning the ruling of the X case. The government sought not to resolve the abortion debate but only to clarify that the Maastricht Treaty would not eliminate the right of a woman to acquire information about abortions or to travel to another country under EC law for an abortion. The EU referendum was overwhelmingly passed three months later, in June 1992, partly because of the broad consensus among the major parties and the PDs to support the treaty based largely on economic concerns.

The public debate over abortion continued to flare, leading the government to hold three referenda later in the fall. These hotly contested referenda sought to uphold the right to access information regarding abortion and the right to travel to another country to procure an abortion, but they also sought to prohibit abortions from being performed in Ireland. Fianna Fáil's strategic choices about the wording and timing of this referendum powerfully shaped the campaign, the outcome, and the longer-term legacy of the abortion debate for partisan politics in Ireland. The government, led by Fianna Fáil, remained quiet about its plans to hold a referendum over the summer, and when it revealed the wording that it had chosen for the amendment, members of the other parties, including PDs who were also in government, erupted in anger. Decrying that the wording of the referendum did not clarify whether the threat of suicide provided adequate basis for obtaining an abortion, they proposed delaying the referendum altogether. Even the Catholic Church, a consistent supporter of antiabortion positions, adopted an ambiguous stance on the issue because of the decidedly inchoate wording. Nevertheless, the Fianna Fáil Taoiseach, Albert Reynolds, remained steadfast in defending the wording of the measure and argued that the matter was up to the voters to resolve.

The choice to hold the three referenda on the same day as the general election was also crucial. Fiery speeches by a few of its own senators revealed divisions within Fianna Fáil. Although a number of PDs also disagreed with the wording of the referendum, they chose not to speak out, because they were unwilling to risk elevating the salience of abortion further during a general election. A far safer bet was to elevate the importance of economic policies. Calling for a speedy resolution of the matter, special interest groups were given little time to mobilize their campaigns. These factors, together with an internally fractious pro-life coalition, combined to help keep the focus during the general election campaign on the economic issues that Fianna Fáil and PD leaders sought to underscore. Although the eight months previous to the election had been consumed by hotly contested public debate regarding abortion, none of the major parties chose to take decisive positions on the subject, preferring to toss the hot potato to special interest groups contending in the referendum.

Thus, different patterns of competition prevail within these two institutional arenas. That no voters identified abortion as "most important" when asked about issues that mattered to them when casting their vote in the November general election (held on the same day as the referenda) supports this conclusion. Since the Court's ruling and the referendum's outcome contradicted each other, the governing parties could opt to sit on their hands. Despite intense media pressure, mainstream parties in the Dáil simply refused, year after year, to legislate on abortion; they were unwilling to risk alienating elements of the electorate on this hot-button issue. Yet another referendum followed in 2002, concerning the removal of the threat of suicide as grounds for legal abortion in Ireland. This change was rejected by a narrow margin of 50.4 percent to 49.6 percent, signaling continued deep divisions within Irish society. Throughout the fight, the parties in the Dáil remained relatively quiet.

In late 2012, twenty years after the X case, the governing coalition of Fine Gael and Labour finally submitted a proposal to enact regulations to clarify when terminating a pregnancy would be allowable. After an all-night debate, the Protection of Life during Pregnancy Act was signed into law in July 2013. The government was responding to the public outcry over the death of thirty-one-year-old Savita Halappanavar, an Indian citizen who had been living in Ireland for four years. She had died in an Irish hospital after complications from a miscarriage. Public protests across Ireland, Northern Ireland, India, the United States, and parts of Europe reignited the decades-old debate about what to do in the case of the real and substantial risk to the life of the mother. Although the perennial arguments reemerged, the social and political context had shifted decidedly. Pro-choice supporters broadcasted the tragedy of women dying because of doctors refusing to act to save a mother's life, while pro-life advocates argued that concessions, even in the case of the risk of suicide, would pave the way to abortion on demand in Ireland. As they had done previously, governing parties proposed opposing strategies. Labour placed legislating for the X case in their 2011 election manifesto, and all of their parliamentarians signed on in support. In contrast, somewhere between a quarter and a half of Fine Gael TDs were split. Opposition parties and independents were also splintered.

What was critically different this time around was that public opinion had decisively shifted. Sixty-four percent of Irish respondents in 2006 believed that abortion was acceptable in some circumstances, a decisive change from the 1980s, when over 80 percent believed abortion was always wrong. Parties once again sought to balance the need to be responsive to salient concerns within the electorate while sustaining broader catchall appeals. An issue that cleaves deeply, like abortion, holds the potential to alter the overall dynamics of party politics by realigning electoral support and thereby exposing the major parties' electoral predominance to risk.

Data from opinion polls reflect similar liberalizing trends regarding other social attitudes, notably on divorce. Those who considered divorce as "always wrong" declined from 45 percent in 1981 to 27 percent in 1999. The pitched battles surrounding divorce referenda in 1986 and 1995 attest to its salience as a social issue, but as we saw in the abortion debate, divorce curiously evanesced in elections during this same period. A closer look at these campaigns suggests that the outcomes of referenda depended on nonparty special interest groups that focused on sizable portions of undecided and pragmatic voters clustered at the center. The dramatic reversal of opinion during the 1986 campaign on the divorce referendum occurred because a sizable proportion of undecided and pragmatic voters favored the status quo, whereas these swing voters were equally divided in the 1995 divorce referendum (as in the 2002 abortion referenda), which led to evenly split outcomes. These issues are both salient and volatile. Turnout was 61 and 62 percent in the two referenda, with the vote in favor of divorce under certain circumstances surging from 36.5 percent in 1986 to 50.3 percent in 1995. Even though incentives clearly existed for political actors to employ these emotional issues to mobilize support, the main parties ceded this electoral opportunity to interest groups, as predicted.

In the 1980s, several analysts foresaw a clear-cut division emerging within the electorate between religious conservatives and liberals, with Fianna Fáil supporters generally more conservative and Fine Gael and Labour more liberal. These same analysts also inferred from referenda results that a divide between urban and rural would emerge within Irish politics. However, over the longer term, these divisions did not crystallize politically, nor did they reshape longer-term electoral patterns, despite rather dramatic attitudinal changes and key demographic shifts. Religious attitudes appear to divide Irish society into three relatively evenly proportioned groups: conservatives, pragmatic voters and centrists, and liberals. How Irish mainstream parties managed the electoral consequences of these potentially disruptive divisions is once again telling.

From the perspective of this analysis, a crucial result of the referenda on moral issues is that the activist groups who proved most influential in dealing with these issues have not crystallized as viable parties, because of the strategic choices made by major party leaders. For example, two of the most visible leaders of the antidivorce campaign in 1995 (which secured nearly half the vote) ran as independent or minor party candidates in the 1997 general election in Dublin South and Dún Laoghaire and received a derisory 3 percent of first-preference votes. As explained shortly, relevant groups in referenda have proved to be transient single-issue groups that failed to pose any real threat to the parliamentary dominance of the established Irish parties.

In the case of abortion and divorce, Fianna Fáil and Fine Gael artfully balanced the more conservative religious views of party loyalists with outreach to more moderate floating voters, thereby accommodating as many voters as possible—a tactic made easier by quarantining electoral contests from referenda campaigns. Furthermore, the parties that could gain the most from liberalization of these policies (Labour, the Greens, Sinn Féin, and the Progressive Democrats) were deprived of opportunities to capture additional votes, because their issues were successfully relegated to this extraparliamentary arena. As a consequence, the major parties have systematically channeled growing pluralism and liberalism within Irish society without disrupting the overall dynamics of party competition.

It is not the case that these issues lack purchase with the electorate.

According to the INES, 73 percent of respondents in 2002 and 63 percent in 2007 reported that abortion was "very important" or "fairly important" to them. Because the issue is addressed in referenda and courts, voters appear mollified. As we saw in the previous chapter on parties' ideological strategies, party leaders have continually sought to remain as vague as possible on these more divisive issues, in order to attract the broadest possible support. Again, it is perhaps not surprising, therefore, to find that few voters actually know where parties position themselves on the issue (see table 2.1 in chapter 2). The strategy of taking advantage of the institutional cover of referenda as well as shifting their parties' ideological positions on these key issues has proven a powerful combination for party leaders. By preventing voters from differentiating between parties on certain issues such as abortion, party leaders can frame competition around other factors that better advance their electoral interests.

The desire to avoid conflict on moral issues weighs heavily in the larger parties' electoral calculus. Self-identified practicing Catholic voters are more likely to vote for Fianna Fáil and Fine Gael in general elections. The 2007 INES reports that of those respondents who identified themselves as Catholic and attended Mass regularly, 52 percent voted for Fianna Fáil and 33 percent for Fine Gael, with the other parties gaining no more than 6 percent of the vote from this category of voters. By contrast, Fianna Fáil and Fine Gael received respectively only 35 and 33 percent of the vote from those who reported that they were non-Catholics or irregularly attended Mass. The difference in support for minor parties is particularly stark: 23 percent of voters who were not active Catholics supported other parties, while only 6 percent of voters who regularly attended Mass supported minor parties. Nevertheless, despite these rather marked differences in their respective rank and file, the larger parties are remarkably content to avoid any overtly religious or moral issues during elections, because avoiding these issues softens internal conflicts, preserves their broad social appeal, and ultimately diminishes the salience of issues that could generate support for the smaller parties. Their strategy has proven exceptionally effective.

Referenda on the European Union

The state institutions associated with Ireland's economic governance, including requirements related to EU membership, have facilitated consensus among political parties in service of "the national interest," or what many have coined "Ireland Inc." As an institutional mechanism, the referenda process has contributed to building this broad cross-party support. In addition to the referendum concerning Ireland's entry into the European Economic Community in 1973, a constitutionally mandated referendum is held whenever a new EU Treaty is proposed.

Before considering the effects of EU referenda and the strategic choices of party leaders within them, it is critical to recall the overall importance of the EU for Ireland's economic and political evolution. Ireland is regarded as one of the greatest economic beneficiaries of EU membership. Since joining the European Economic Community in 1973, the balance in Ireland's favor between what Ireland paid in and what the EU paid out amounted to €42 billion by 2011 ($58.4 billion in 2011 exchange rates). In essence, every Irish citizen has received nearly $16,769 from the EU over the thirty-eight-year period. The benefits flowing from the EU's Common Agricultural Policy, Single European Market (which provides Ireland with free access to a market of five hundred million people), European Monetary Union, and access to the Structural Funds and the Cohesion Fund boosted Ireland's economic growth by an estimated additional 3 to 4 percent of annual GDP throughout much of the 1990s. Ireland also profited from the significant flow of immigrants from the EU accession states, whose presence bolstered the construction industry when it was the critical engine powering Ireland's economic growth between 2002 and 2007. Since 2009, the EU has become a much more contentious topic because Ireland's banking and debt crisis necessitated an EU/IMF/ECB bailout to the Irish government and resulted in a demoralizing loss of political sovereignty. It remains to be seen whether the Irish electorate will regard the EU as a savior or an Achilles' heel.

From an institutional perspective, without question, the EU powerfully shapes political behavior in Irish politics. Without Ireland's membership in the EU, there may have been no Celtic Tiger, peace in the North, or prospect of economic recovery. Ireland's rapid ascent from the poorest country to the wealthiest and then back to one of the poor and struggling peripheral countries is so intertwined with the EU that conceiving of life outside the EU has become almost impossible for many in Ireland. One might argue that the need to pass EU referenda trumps all other reasons for explaining why the major parties have acted as they have in recent years. The mere weight of necessity structures the choices that party leaders have made with respect to their positions.

Once again, however, an institutional argument alone is insufficient, because it ignores the different ways major and minor party leaders have strategically acted, within this context, both to reflect changing public opinion and to shape how EU issues are translated into the political arena. Not only must we consider the precise ways in which party leaders have behaved within the institutional context that EU referenda have created, but we should also factor in how public opinion on EU issues has influenced the strategies that party leaders have employed. Patterns have emerged depending on the support an issue has among voters. When voter support in favor of policies is unambiguous, party leaders have worked hard to protect these concerns prior to holding a referendum, as we saw with abortion, neutrality, and Ireland's low corporate tax rate. In contrast, when public opinion has been split or uncertain, major party leaders in particular have taken advantage of the institutional cover of the EU to displace these issues—thereby minimizing the blame connected with complex and controversial policies. These strategic decisions highlight that party leaders still have critical decisions to make, with potentially lasting impacts, irrespective of the powerful ways that the EU referenda structure and incentivize political behavior. The choices party leaders make regarding the timing and overall intensity of the campaigning during EU referenda have once again helped them insulate general elections from European issues.

Given the critical role the EU played in facilitating Ireland's spectacular growth in the Celtic Tiger era, Irish public opinion has generally and unsurprisingly favored Ireland's membership in the EU. Data from the European Commission's Eurobarometer imply that a significant majority of Irish citizens think Ireland's membership in the EU is a "good thing," consistently above 70 percent since Ireland joined the Single European Market in the mid-1980s. Irish voters were generally more supportive of economic and monetary union than political union, and they became increasingly skeptical of European integration projects that extended beyond the strictly economic. For example, whereas three-quarters of survey respondents throughout the 1990s favored economic and monetary union, only 53 percent reported that Ireland should work toward political union within the EU. More recent evidence reflects a nosedive in support among Irish voters for full union with the EU, thus revealing a potential political fault line between Europhiles and Euroskeptics, similar to what has occurred in other member states, notably the United Kingdom.

A primary reason the sharpening differences over European policy have not entered into the discourse of Irish electoral competition is that debates over EU policy were largely relegated to referendum campaigns. As mentioned previously, when voters assume that issues, such as European integration, will be addressed in referenda, the need to engage these issues outside this accepted forum is diminished, yet the overall legitimacy

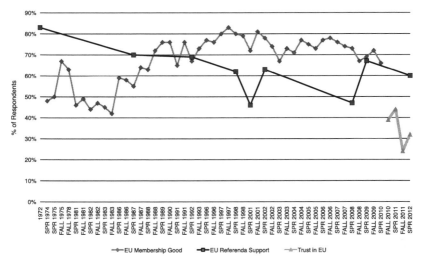

Fig. 4.1. Support for the EU in Referenda and Public Opinion Polls, 1972–2012. (Data from European Commission, "Standard Eurobarometer: Public Opinion," [December 20, 2013 update], http://ec.europa.eu/public_opinion/archives/eb_arch_en.htm.)

of the political process is maintained. Irish referenda results demonstrate that support for European integration has consistently declined, with more rapid falls in pro-European support beginning with the Amsterdam Treaty in 1998 (see fig. 4.1). Even though a majority of Irish citizens in 2002 (77 percent) believed that EU membership was "good" for Ireland and "fairly important" or "very important" to them personally (73 percent), only a bare majority (50 percent) believed European unification should be pushed further. Both the Treaty of Nice and the Treaty of Lisbon (which further reformed the institutions of the EU, first to prepare for enlargement [Nice] and then to make decisions more effectively within an enlarged union [Lisbon]) generated considerable opposition from Irish citizens. Fifty-four percent of Irish voters rejected the proposal of the Nice I referendum in 2001, and 53 percent opposed that of the Lisbon I referendum in 2008—further underscoring Irish citizens' concerns about enhanced integration. The subsequent reversal of both these initial referenda reflects that continued divisions over European issues exist among Irish voters.

European issues are clearly critical to Ireland's overall economic well-being, especially since the humiliating bailout. After the initial EU referenda in 1972, where Labour opposed Ireland's entry into the European

Economic Community but then quickly reversed its decision when it entered into a governing coalition with Fine Gael in 1973 (and remained supportive of further integration in every referendum), a broad and deepening consensus was forged among the main political parties and party leaders in favor of greater European integration. Only Sinn Féin consistently voted no in every EU referendum. The Green Party, the only other anti-EU proponent, shifted from its original opposition to EU integration once it entered government in 2008, offering a supportive or neutral stance in the three subsequent referenda. This broad party consensus in favor of European integration among the major parties exists despite opposition to European integration among substantial sectors of the Irish population, a hostile sector that has expanded dramatically since the banking crisis of 2008 and the EU/IMF bailout in 2010.

European integration has simply not emerged as a contended issue during general elections. Party positions toward integration and strategic action (and inaction) by parties during referenda campaigns highlight the distinctive competitive dynamics in both electoral and referendum arenas. A remarkable disconnect exists between votes in general elections and votes on EU referenda. For example, voters consistently support parties that maintain pro-European positions when they vote in general elections, whereas the percentage of voters who actually voted in favor of integration in EU referenda has varied greatly. Parties promoting European integration have consistently secured more than 80 percent of the overall vote throughout general elections between 1972 and 2011; yet support for further European integration itself has steadily declined since the original EU vote in 1972 (see fig. 4.2). How can broad, pro-European consensus among the parties be so widely confirmed in general elections while support for European integration has declined among the electorate in referenda?

One might argue that European issues simply do not resonate with Irish voters. The average turnout for the nine EU referenda since 1972 has been 51 percent, peaking at 70 percent with the decision to enter the European Economic Community in 1972 and bottoming out at 35 percent in 2001. The exceptionally low turnouts for the defeated Nice I referendum (2001) and the 2012 referendum on the Fiscal Stability Treaty (40 percent) are especially striking. Comparative evidence suggests that the negative bias pervading EU treaty referenda can be attributed to a number of factors, including the second-order nature of referenda, the prevalence of antiestablishment rhetoric, low levels of information and voter turnout, and the overall complexity of the issues being addressed. In addition, the swing to the no vote during campaigns across a broad set of European cases

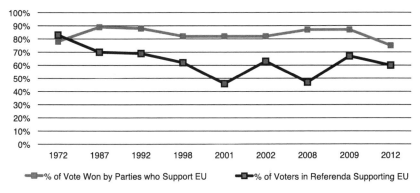

Fig. 4.2. Party Support and Referenda Results for European Integration, 1972–2012. (See ElectionsIreland.org for election and referenda results.)

indicates that when voters have little partisan or ideological basis on which to form their opinion, they are more likely to change their vote during the campaign or not to vote at all. This could help explain the reversals of attitudes that have occurred during Ireland's EU referenda and the lack of support. That Ireland's major parties have maintained a consensus in favor of further EU integration and not always vigorously campaigned to pass these referenda may also have contributed to the swings from no to yes votes in subsequent EU referenda results. Notice the slightly higher turnout in the Nice II referendum (an increase of fourteen percentage points in 2002) and Lisbon II (an increase of six points in 2009). The success of the pro-European positions in these second referenda campaigns is generally attributed to greater clarity on how these issues would affect Ireland, a renewed concern for what might happen if Ireland were left out of European integration altogether, and a more concerted effort on behalf of political parties and civil society groups to mobilize a disengaged electorate.

By limiting programmatic contention over Europe, the major parties have contained disputing views to referenda and limited the possibility that voters would link their concerns over Europe to issues being contested in general elections. Parties have limited supplies of political and social capital and must therefore choose wisely how to spend their resources. Because issues and outcomes associated with EU referenda appear to exert little impact on general election results, the major political parties can keep their powder dry and use these resources in general elections, whereas the minor parties, who tend to use referenda to raise their profile and expend capital, end up strapped for resources when it counts during general elections.

That the Nice I referendum occurred just months before a required general election is noteworthy for several reasons. First, the timing affected levels of financial resources spent during the referendum campaign. Although Irish law no longer permits the government to spend money to mobilize support for its own position in a referendum, individual parties can still deploy their own resources during referendum campaigns. Much less money was spent by the main parties during the Nice I referendum, whereas the yes side outspent the no side by an overwhelming ratio of ten to one on the Nice II referendum. Given both the consensus surrounding European integration among the main parties and the prospect of competition in a coming general election, the major parties had little incentive, in the case of the Nice I referendum, to waste their own valuable resources supporting an initiative that virtually all parties supported and that seemed destined to pass. It was better for them to save these resources for their upcoming general election campaign.

Second, the broad consensus in support of the Nice and Lisbon treaties among the main political parties actually depressed the normal partisan competitive incentives that motivate parties to get out the vote. Because Irish party competition in elections is dominated by personalistic and localized dynamics, voters are much more exercised about ensuring that "their own" get elected in order to deliver local goods and services than they are about more remote ideological issues at the national or international levels. Given party consensus in favor of these EU treaties, incentives for candidates and parties to cooperate during the referenda campaigns have largely been absent; this was especially true for the Nice I referendum, which occurred in the months before a general election. After the general election, during the Nice II referendum campaign, recently elected candidates enjoyed greater freedom to cooperate with candidates from other parties to mobilize the pro-European vote. The PR-STV electoral system's emphasis on developing candidate appeal at the local level serves as a disincentive for campaigning vigorously on behalf of an issue that candidates from other parties also support during referenda. A case in point is the election of the 2002 Fianna Fáil and PD coalition, the first government of any stripe reelected since 1969. These parties were not penalized by voters in the general election for positions they had adopted in the referenda arena—further reinforcing the conclusion that these two competitive arenas are successfully construed as distinct domains for the electorate by the parties' strategic choices, with minimal translation of effects from one to the other.

Third, the increased intensity of the second Nice and Lisbon refer-

endum campaigns, led collectively by political parties and groups in civil
society to educate the public about protecting Ireland's national interests,
focused voters more on European issues than on their evaluation of the
current government. A danger in any second-order election (e.g., local
elections or referenda) is that voters will simply punish or reward incumbents for other issues, which is more likely to occur during hard economic
times—such as existed in both 2001 and 2008. It is all the more telling,
therefore, that opposition parties in favor of the Treaty of Nice worked
hard to decouple evaluations of the government and attitudes toward the
EU: they campaigned for the Nice II referendum with the slogan "Hold
Your Fire. Fianna Fáil Can Wait. Europe Can't!" The central appeal was
not to jeopardize the "national interest" for the sake of partisan politics.

Fourth, Labour and the other major parties would benefit from keeping EU issues contained within referenda campaigns. If voters continued
to keep general elections and referenda distinct, this would reduce the
risk that the growing opposition to EU integration might result in voter
antipathy during elections. Even worse from the perspective of the major
parties, European integration might become a divisive and mobilizing issue
during elections, forcing the parties to take a stand and develop a programmatic linkage with voters. As a divisive issue, European integration risks
advancing the electoral interests of minor parties like the Greens and Sinn
Féin by sustaining their increased appeal within the electorate, instead of
keeping elections focused on party loyalty or constituency service at the
local level. As the only established party on the left, Labour was especially
made vulnerable by the rise of Sinn Féin and the Greens. Any opportunity
to limit these competitors' appeal would bolster Labour's electoral opportunities. Finally, Labour positioned itself as a party committed to what was
in Ireland's best interests, signaling to voters its willingness to act respon-
sibly and effectively as a future leader in government.

Fifth, EU referenda have provided challenger parties with a platform to
elevate their visibility in a party system otherwise dominated by the established parties. Referenda rules require equal media attention to both sides
of an issue, which has given minor parties on the no side a disproportion-
ate amount of airtime compared to the major parties, which all agreed and
were forced to share the media spotlight. For example, Sinn Féin and the
Greens, both of whom opposed integration referenda in 2001 and 2002,
seized the opportunity of EU referenda to underscore their opposition to
the established parties, with the ultimate goal of enhancing their prospects
in upcoming local elections and the all-important general elections. Capitalizing on the free publicity of the no campaign helped these minor parties

in the short run, as both the Greens and Sinn Féin took advantage of their well-organized anti-Nice positions to muster support for their candidates in the 2002 general election, with the Greens trebling their TDs to six and Sinn Féin also gaining a seat. Interestingly, the anti-EU referendum posters and literature for these challenger parties were dominated by individual pictures of local candidates as opposed to slogans articulating the substantive arguments against integration. The minor parties thereby leveraged referenda campaigns to maximize their electoral appeal in upcoming general elections, which would revolve more around personalistic appeals at the local level than around any given ideological ties to voters.

Despite the short-term success experienced by these challenger parties as a result of their anti-European campaigning, electoral momentum has proven difficult to sustain. Pro-European parties, the major parties, have continued to dominate general elections. Perhaps more important, minor parties face continued pressure to alter their positions in favor of the EU, among other things, if they are to be considered worthy of entering into a coalition government. As we saw in the previous chapter, minor parties appear damned either way over the long run, especially because major parties have continually been able to frame electoral competition in ways that mitigate potentially new sources of support for minor parties. The different strategies that party leaders employed within EU referenda have reinforced the separate nature of referenda and general election campaigns. As we have repeatedly seen, the major parties are the long-term beneficiaries.

Recurring to the National System of Wage Bargaining (Social Partnership)

A second key institutional mechanism that major parties regularly utilized from 1987 to 2010 to preserve their electoral predominance was Ireland's national system of wage bargaining, known as Social Partnership (SP). Although SP, Ireland's version of a social pact, fostered consensus among the parties, Ireland's major parties took advantage of these social pacts strategically to attract voters and implement effective economic policies. SP was initiated in 1987 and was widely recognized as one of the principal drivers of Ireland's dramatic economic growth, which experienced an increase in real GDP of 132 percent from 1987 through 2005. The SP model in Ireland entailed a process of consultation, negotiation, and deliberation, with agreements among the leaders of Irish government, trade unions (the Irish Congress of Trade Unions), business leaders (the Irish Business and

Employers' Confederation), farmers, and, eventually, members of the community and voluntary sectors. Introduced during the economic crisis of the mid-1980s (which featured 17 to 20 percent unemployment, 12 to 16 percent inflation, a 125 percent debt-to-GDP ratio, and high levels of emigration), these three-year, renewable national agreements were expanded to encompass broad swathes of economic policy: moderating wage increases, cutting taxes, and improving the effectiveness of public spending.

SP contributed powerfully to Ireland's economic revival and facilitated a consensus that persisted across periods of economic austerity and prosperity. Precisely when the potential existed to shift electoral appeals away from long-standing Civil War loyalties and toward programmatic differences on economic policy, SP fostered consensus among political parties. This shift, in turn, deprived challenger parties of openings into the electoral contests. Furthermore, as the Irish economy rebounded in the 1990s, the number of groups represented within the SP process increased. Its policy domain was extended to include potentially divisive issues such as social exclusion, inequality, and poverty, as well as issues that affected the tangible delivery of material benefits, such as job training, ongoing professional development, and costs of child care. A new model of economic policy making resulted, a model characterized by consultative and participatory relationships between government agencies and organized interests.

Notwithstanding the positive effect that SP had on economic policy in Ireland, the real story for the purposes of this analysis is the impact SP had on electoral competition in the period after 1987, when elections in Ireland became more competitive and fragmented. Recent comparative scholarship suggests that electoral considerations help explain whether governing parties use legislation or engage social pacts to address thorny policies such as wages, the labor market, and welfare reform. Previous explanations have suggested that this choice between pacts and legislation was driven by economic crises and institutional arrangements. Yet these arguments cannot explain variation within or across countries in terms of how political parties deal with these key economic decisions. For example, both Ireland and the United Kingdom faced deep economic crises in the 1980s and possessed similar institutions within the liberal market economy. Despite the similarity in institutions between these two cases, Ireland pursued social pacts to address their economic crisis, and the United Kingdom turned to legislation aimed at weakening the role of unions to deal with their economic challenges. Hamann and Kelly argue that the nature of electoral competition— not economic or institutional factors—shaped the differing decisions to turn to social pacts in Ireland and to legislation in the United Kingdom.[3]

More broadly, Hamann and Kelly highlight several factors that influence electoral and parliamentary competition, including the type of party and party family (e.g., conservative or social democratic) in government, the level of electoral competition measured by vote and seat gains or losses and the closeness of the vote share between the top two parties, the type of governing coalition (minority versus majority or "unconnected" ideologically), and the number of effective legislative parties and the degree of fragmentation this represents. Their overall findings based on sixteen Western European cases support the argument being made in this analysis: namely, that politics matters. Specifically, the strategic choices made by major parties when faced with contentious economic policies are closely related to electoral factors. Moreover, the choices they make can lead to the consolidation of their electoral predominance over the long term, despite constantly changing electoral contexts.

Hamann and Kelly's comparative model holds important implications for the Irish case. From their work, we can see how the increased uncertainty and competitiveness of Irish elections beginning in the early 1980s set the stage for the reemergence and persistence of social pacts in Ireland from 1987 to 2010. Three elections in eighteen months during the 1981 and 1982 period led to significant vote and seat losses for Fianna Fáil, Ireland's predominant party at the time, and revealed the party's growing electoral vulnerability. To regain vote share, Fianna Fáil's influential leader Charles Haughey advocated taking a strong position on the issues of a united Ireland and a conservative stance on abortion and divorce. Other leading party members disagreed, arguing for an emphasis on new economic policies to address unemployment.[4] The fissure between these contending party leaders within Fianna Fáil eventually led Haughey's opponents to break away from Fianna Fáil and form the Progressive Democrats in December 1985. The growing public interest in the PDs' message and fears of further electoral losses led Haughey to reconsider party policies. Haughey concluded that if Fianna Fáil were to offset these new electoral appeals and recapture its electoral predominance as the 1987 election approached, it needed to renew its catchall character via its economic policies rather than by promoting divisive nationalist and social policies.

The possibility of implementing a social pact provided a potential solution to many of the electoral challenges Fianna Fáil faced in 1987. By turning to a social pact, Fianna Fáil sought to strengthen its ties to union members and working-class voters who supported the national wage agreements as a means of representing and guarding their interests. Lest their efforts go unnoticed, Fianna Fáil adopted the proposed title of the first agreement—

Programme for National Recovery—as the slogan for its 1987 election manifesto. This move offset the electoral appeal of the most significant left-leaning parties, Labour and the Workers' Party, both of which had been gaining traction among working-class and union voters due to their advocacy of policies of social protection. Social Partnership also provided Fianna Fáil with the vehicle (and cover) they needed to implement cuts in taxes and public spending advocated previously by Fine Gael but denounced by Fianna Fáil just six months earlier. These economic policies garnered favor from conservative supporters of the right-leaning Fine Gael and PDs.[5] In addition to allowing Fianna Fáil to appeal to voters simultaneously on the left and right, employing social pacts also presented Fianna Fáil with an institutional cover to mitigate the political costs of enacting these controversial policies while serving as a minority government.

The nature of electoral competition and parliamentary activity also helps explain why widespread consensus materialized over time among nearly all of Ireland's political parties in favor of SP, despite initial misgivings by each of the opposition parties in 1987. Every party once in government consistently employed SP to advance their electoral interests, albeit in differing ways as economic and social conditions changed. Increased fragmentation within the legislature, the closeness of elections, the fluctuation in vote gains and losses among the major parties, and a series of "unconnected coalitions" all combined to encourage the political parties initially opposed to SP to embrace SP to enhance their electoral appeal among an increasingly unattached electorate. In 1989, for example, the PDs saw their vote share cut in half. There existed a growing sense among the electorate that SP was working, which incentivized the PDs to shift their position. By the mid-1990s, Fine Gael's full conversion to SP was complete. On the one hand, the Fine Gael Taoiseach, John Bruton, felt "bound" to honor the terms that the previous government, led by Fianna Fáil and Labour, had negotiated with unions and business leaders; on the other hand, he was intent on preventing the consolidation of a new, more robust, left-leaning governing coalition between Labour and Fianna Fáil. Fine Gael's Rainbow Coalition of the mid-1990s not only supported SP but implemented the crucial changes that extended the overall framework to include an even broader array of issues and new social policies. Through use of SP, Fine Gael also sought to broaden its catchall appeal among the electorate.[6]

In practical terms, SP offered parties and individual candidates an institutional vehicle that could provide cover when faced with difficult policy choices that risked triggering adverse electoral ramifications. The 2007 nurses' strike illustrates how parties and candidates relegated important issues strategically to the domain of SP. The nurses' strike had been going on and dominating the headlines for several weeks before the 2007 election was called. The main parties insisted on "respecting the negotiations" that the overall framework of SP mandated occur through the Labour Relations Commission. Meanwhile, the major parties offered sympathy and vague palliatives but copiously avoided assuming a specific stance on this contentious issue. There was no electoral benefit to disrupting a widely supported institutional process by "speaking out," potentially risking the alienation of voters and making the party vulnerable to blame if the policy failed.

Individual candidates also took advantage of recurring to SP opportunistically. For example, in 2007, first-time Fianna Fáil candidate Michael Fitzpatrick in Kildare North maintained the party line in defending the SP process with respect to the nurses' strike, because few votes were to be won by speaking out for nurses. SP provided him with an effective institutional cover while leaving voters with the perception that the issue was adequately addressed through the extraparliamentary means of SP. However, Fitzpatrick was willing to publicly disagree with his own party to suit his own electoral calculus. Fitzpatrick publicly excoriated his party's decision to locate the national children's hospital in Dublin. Fitzpatrick was driven by the calculus that the government's decision would negatively impact local interests—and thus votes. It is one thing to adhere to party positions when less tangible benefits are at stake or when extraparliamentary institutions exist to address contentious issues, but when policies are perceived to conflict with material interests at the local level, candidates jettison national party positions to attract votes locally. Thus, SP provided parties and individual candidates with a valuable tool to bolster their electoral support.

The persistence of governing coalitions consisting of parties with different ideological backgrounds constitutes yet another feature of Ireland's competitive electoral environment that contributed to the growing acceptance of SP. The internal ideological differences that existed within the governing coalitions led by Fianna Fáil and the Progressive Democrats in 1989–92 and 1997–2007 and by Fine Gael and Labour (and the Democratic Left) in 1994–97 consistently made it more difficult for them to reach agreement on more complex and controversial economic and social policies. As comparative evidence suggests, social pacts can be more effective than legislation in securing meaningful reform in such contexts. They provide a vehicle to override internal coalition disagreements by shoring up support outside the legislative arena. This appears to have been the case in Ireland, as divisive and divergent coalition partners relied on SP to achieve consensus and to enact policy and avoid risking erosion of electoral support in the process.

The broad party consensus on SP partly derived from the reluctance of any of the major parties to distance itself too far ideologically from its opponents, particularly because the need may arise to eventually engage one or more of these parties as a coalition partner. The deepening support for SP is consistent with comparative findings by Adams and Somer-Topcu and others that political parties frequently respond to rival parties' policy shifts by shifting their own policies in the same direction in subsequent elections. As SP was increasingly perceived by the electorate to have contributed to Ireland's economic turnaround, it became easier for the parties to accept SP as an integral part of the policy-making process in Ireland. Although SP is commonly discussed in the context of effective economic policy making, it was also a political and electoral strategy. SP was eventually broadened to include a broader array of social policies and issues, which allowed Ireland's major parties to take institutional cover when dealing with complex and potentially divisive issues.

An enduring consequence of SP was to widen the gap between the policy-making process and electoral politics. As a result of this new, multilayered framework of actors and networks, voters had greater difficulty identifying specific policies with specific parties, and assessing credit or blame is more challenging because of the diffused role that parties play in the SP process. Ultimately, the institutionalization of SP has resulted in an obfuscation of the policy-making process, highlighting its technocratic, specialized, and managerial dimensions. TDs also recognize the impact that SP has on the legislative process. According to one former Fine Gael Taoiseach, the reality of the Irish system is that although SP issues were rarely debated explicitly in parliament, the parties in government were ultimately responsible for them, whether they engaged the issues legislatively or not. Stating that "the government makes the policy and the Dáil approves it, or disapproves of it, and if it disapproves of it, there is a general election," he added that although the Dáil is less engaged in policy making and has been even less so with the inception of SP, it still has the final word.[7] In large part because of SP, a broadly consensual approach to economic issues pervades the Irish political process, reducing the competitive space between the political parties on the very issues that define electoral competition and parliamentary contention in many advanced industrial democracies.

Survey data confirms that TDs perceive the SP process as having constrained them, while opening up new, extraparliamentary channels for participation by citizens and social groups. Seventy-nine percent of TDs in my

parliamentary surveys reported that SP had constrained their ability to legislate on economic policy, compared with only 14 percent who stated that
SP enhanced their legislative capacity. Attitudes about the 2011 Croke Park
Agreement, discussed in more detail shortly, were similar. Although the
majority agreed that SP constrained economic policy making, data from an
earlier survey conducted after the 2007 elections shows that overall assessments of the process were still generally positive, at least before the financial
crisis. In terms of the perception of how SP affected levels of participation of citizens with Irish politics, a narrow majority of TDs (43 percent)
reported that they viewed the process as a way of opening up participation
to citizens and social groups, rather than restricting it (39 percent). As discussed shortly, there are substantial reasons to believe this is true, although
the kind of structured participation engendered by SP also has limits.

The major parties' behavior within the SP framework has bolstered
the perception among voters that these parties are best equipped to manage economic policy making. Although explicit evidence of SP's effect on
voter attitudes is difficult to obtain, indirect evidence suggests that SP has
played an important role in shaping the issues that voters identify as most
important to them during elections (see table 2.2 in chapter 2). First, since
the inception of SP, a shift has occurred in the economic issues that have
become salient during election campaigns. Whereas inflation and unemployment had ranked as the most critical issues in every Irish election
between 1969 and 1997, these two concerns did not even appear among the
top ten issues identified by voters in 2002, 2007, and 2011, partly because
of the success of SP's role and changing priorities. Instead, the broader and
more diffuse category of "managing the economy" emerged as the top concern for voters. That label signals a markedly different public perception of
both the process of economic policy making and the role of the state within
that process. The issue of taxation, so integral to the SP framework, also
became less salient. Taxation peaked as an issue in elections in 1997, when
29 percent of respondents indicated that it was the most important. It did
not appear among the top ten issues in 2002 or 2007 and was mentioned
by only 2 percent in the 2011 election (table 2.2). The declining salience of
taxation stems from several potential causes. Certainly a consensus in favor
of a lower tax regime as an essential tool to enhance national competitiveness had grown among all the parties by the early 2000s. In fact, Labour
was the first party to call for tax cuts during the 2007 general election
campaign, despite its left-leaning ideological position. The functioning of
the institutional framework of SP played a role in generating this broad
agreement, trading lower taxes for wage constraints. The consensual and

technocratic nature of the process blurred differences between the parties, further limiting the degree to which voters could distinguish among parties on crucial economic issues.

Finally, longitudinal survey data since the 1980s reveal that two-thirds of respondents report that no competing party would be more effective when evaluating the progress of government policies on a wide array of issues. The 2011 election was the exception, when 80 percent of voters were angered at the governing parties and believed that virtually *any* set of alternative parties would be better. Over the longer term, however, the public perceptions of party platforms appear virtually indistinguishable, as the analysis in chapters 2–3 shows. This holds true even in cases where respondents report negative assessments of progress in a given policy area. The perceptions of narrow programmatic differences among competing parties, coupled with the highly consensual and inclusive framework of SP policy making, bolstered the perception that the major parties were best equipped to manage economic policy making and that interests were being incorporated and appropriately addressed.

The global financial crisis of 2008 created an impetus for renegotiation of the SP framework through an agreement called "Towards 2016." A protracted negotiation among the government, unions, employers, and other social partners ensued. In fact, the overall framework of Social Partnership ended abruptly in 2009, when the government unilaterally imposed austerity measures. However, the Croke Park Agreement (2010) between government and public-sector unions initiated a new form of concession bargaining aimed at fiscal stabilization.

During the 2010 Croke Park negotiations, unions called on the Labour Party to intercede on their behalf, and the party responded by arguing that the government, not political parties, should negotiate wage levels. As a result, the government's austerity measures were unilaterally imposed, leaving key aspects of economic policy making to government bureaucrats, with minimal recourse to the parliamentary arena. Irish party leaders had voluntarily relinquished an opportunity to mobilize potential voters on what was arguably the most important set of economic policy decisions in a generation— issues on which many voters had a strong opinion. To engage these explosive issues publicly might weaken major party leaders' capacity to continue to attract catchall support among the electorate. Moreover, major party leaders once again benefited from avoiding a potential realignment of electoral competition away from traditional, localist politics to more ideologically driven appeals—appeals that could greatly benefit minor parties and independents, who have been angling for such an opportunity since the 1980s.

Regardless of the various combinations of parties that have formed government coalitions since SP began in 1987, there has been little variance in policy outcomes. This underscores the ability of established parties to use the institution of SP to maintain a remarkable policy consensus, which has further reduced head-on competition in both elections and subsequent parliamentary discussions over potentially divisive economic issues. The existence of the SP framework allowed parties to include broader segments of society within the policy-making process, while insulating parties from the wrath of the electorate when unpopular decisions needed to be made. Furthermore, once value issues became translated into resource issues, which occurred regularly within the structure of SP, the debate centered on competence and experience, giving the advantage to established parties.

Although the SP framework did not in itself generate these outcomes, party leaders employed the institutional mechanism that SP made available to them to enhance their electoral appeals and create consensus on difficult decisions. The various ways in which Irish political parties took advantage of state institutions via the SP process is critical for understanding which issues emerged as salient and how they were addressed. This dynamic helps explain the longer-term success that the major parties have been able to sustain during a period of dramatic social change and increasingly competitive elections.

Recurring to Tribunals

A third institutional mechanism that Ireland's major parties, especially Fianna Fáil, have relied on to help preserve their electoral predominance is tribunals. Although tribunals have grown in frequency as a means of addressing concerns about rising levels of corruption, they also serve to insulate parties from corruption charges by removing the charges from the electoral arena to the quasi-judicial arena. Public awareness concerning corruption between politicians and key sectors of the business community, especially the construction industry, increased markedly from the late 1980s. Responding to burgeoning scandals, political parties have sought to walk a fine line between continuing to rely on personalistic relationships that Ireland's electoral system and political culture encourage and transitioning to a more modern, bureaucratic and impersonal mode of politics that downplays these types of relationships. By increasing the use of formal tribunals to adjudicate wrongdoing, elected officials have attempted to balance these two approaches—addressing corruption in a bureaucratic framework, while not undermining a system that relies on strong personalistic ties between voters and individual politicians. Ireland's major parties have actively sustained long-standing formulas of winning elections—that is, delivering strong constituency service and brokering access to the state—by adapting to a rapidly changing electorate that perceives these relationships differently.

Instead of making political corruption a campaign issue to be addressed within the electoral arena, major parties enacted a series of legislative acts and have increasingly relied on independent tribunals to address corruption. Most important among these have been the extraparliamentary tribunals deployed prolifically in the mid-1990s, called bodies of "public inquiry." These bodies, designed to overcome political constraints that can hinder parliamentary mechanisms of scrutiny, were initiated to investigate political corruption. Tribunals, first established under the Tribunals of Inquiry (Evidence) Act of 1921, are mandated by parliament to implement inquiries into "matters of urgent public importance." Tribunals are invested with the powers, privileges, and rights of the Irish High Court, but unlike the courts, which administer justice, the function of the tribunals is to investigate. In contrast to earlier experiences, contemporary tribunals have focused on the internal workings of government agencies, as well as probing the personal finances of politicians and political parties. These tribunals have exerted growing pressure on the government to increase accountability throughout the administration and have resulted in the creation of new regulatory bodies and oversight legislation to monitor the activities of politicians more stringently. Nonetheless, tribunal authorities face great difficulties in prosecuting anyone found to have been corrupt by a tribunal of inquiry, because evidence heard by tribunals cannot be presented in criminal proceedings against the person giving that evidence.

Tribunals, unlike other mechanisms of institutional displacement, have created some costs to major parties and their leaders. Since the mid-1990s, the broadsheet newspapers have added a regular section that includes an average of three articles per day that focus on the tribunals and related issues concerning corruption. Revelations of corruption, despite focusing on select individuals, have generated increasing levels of distrust among the Irish public toward politicians and have undermined public confidence in the political system. The more stringent regulatory environment pervading contemporary Irish politics limits opportunities for patronage and makes it highly unlikely that tougher standards of accountability for public office will ever be undone.

However, the anger expressed by the media and broader public opinion toward politicians has been largely contained within the extraparliamentary realm of tribunals, thereby dampening the electoral consequences of misbehavior. Although previous actions were questionable by contemporary standards, they were not technically "illegal" at the time that they occurred. Furthermore, the relegation of corruption to tribunals has persuaded the voting public that the verdict on any given allegation of misdoing should be in the hands of the legal system, not the electorate. The resulting distancing of corruption from the parliamentary arena—and, consequently, from the realm of electoral politics—suggests that the reliance on tribunals provided a convenient vehicle for party leaders to handle corruption in a way that largely muzzled parliamentary debate, while allowing party leaders to claim that something was being done to address malfeasance. Therefore, governing parties have had it both ways, standing up to corruption while preserving a cozy system that has allowed favor-mongering and other patrimonial practices to thrive.

Fianna Fáil, in particular, yet again proved its mastery at preempting a damaging issue and remaining in power, managing to be perceived as responsive to the need for reform by supporting the establishment of tribunals at the exact time when the party was the most significant object of scrutiny. Parties perceived as "less corrupt" were unable to exploit the failings of Fianna Fáil, partly because no party was completely free of corruption scandals among its own ranks. Furthermore, parties of all stripes had grown accustomed to maximizing close personal relationships within their constituencies to win votes.

Curiously, although political corruption has increasingly taken center stage in Ireland since the mid-1980s and 1990s, the parties and individual candidates most closely associated with allegations of improper behavior have not been punished at the polls for their behavior. Fully 18 percent of INES respondents in 2002 and 11 percent in 2007 reported "honesty and integrity" as the most important issue to them in those respective elections, yet politicians and parties associated with corruption did not suffer at the polls. During this period of intense public concern about corruption, a primary target of anticorruption investigations, Fianna Fáil, remained in government for all but three years from 1987 to 2008. Levels of party support from public opinion data show that Fianna Fáil has been declining steadily since the revelations of corruption in 1989, with the exception of a brief spike in support in 1998 (see fig. 4.3). Despite these longer-term trends, however, Fianna Fáil has been the majority party of a governing coalition after every election between 1989 and 2011. While recognizing the multitude of factors that influence both public opinion results and elec-

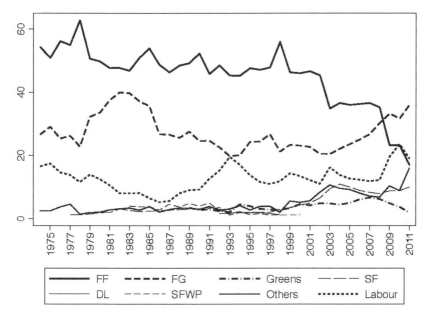

Fig. 4.3. Evolution of Party Support in Irish Public Opinion Polls, 1975–2011. (Data from public opinion polls was supplied by Michael Marsh, Trinity College Dublin. In years when there were several polls conducted, he averaged the results for the parties in order to come up with the figures for this graph. In addition to the parties identified previously, SFWP is Sinn Féin the Workers Party and DL is the Democratic Left Party.)

tions, the fact that Fianna Fáil fared so well in elections during this period of heightened concern about corruption among its party leaders further reinforces the perception that Irish politicians and parties have successfully insulated themselves from the fallout of corruption. Fianna Fáil's ability to continually form governments in an era when two of its longer-serving party leaders came under unrelenting pressure because of corruption charges underscores this claim.

The startling case of former Fianna Fáil Taoiseach Bertie Ahern is particularly telling. Sixty-four percent of respondents in a 2006 Ipsos MRBI poll believed that the Taoiseach was wrong to have accepted €50,000 in personal payments from his friends while he was Minister for Finance in 1993. Another 66 percent felt that Ahern was wrong to accept £8,000 from his personal backers in Manchester in 1994. Nevertheless, despite these damaging and much-publicized allegations, the perennially popular Ahern-led Fianna Fáil romped in 2007 to its third straight victory in a general election. When an RTÉ exit poll asked voters whether the discussion over Ahern's personal finances had influenced their vote, 75 percent reported no, 16 percent stated that it led them to vote against Fianna Fáil, 6 percent said that it led them to vote for Fianna Fáil, and 3 percent were undecided. The scandal-tainted Ahern remained Taoiseach for an additional year before resigning.

Individual candidates often suffer no adverse electoral consequences from corruption scandals. Indeed, several TDs with the highest totals in first-preference voting in 2007 were precisely those who had corruption cases pending, including Ahern, Beverly Cooper-Flynn, and the disgraced former Fine Gael front-bencher Michael Lowry. Despite these charges, these candidates were compensated with voter support at the local level, a result reinforced by the effects of the PR-STV electoral system, which richly rewards responsive constituency service with voter loyalty. The greater the public media buzz enjoyed by local personalities is, even if resoundingly negative, the greater the support from the base will be.

While allegations of corruption may not have resulted in altered voter preferences, it raised concerns about each of the parties among the broader public. For example, when asked in the 2002 INES how widespread corruption such as bribe taking was among politicians in Ireland, 69 percent of respondents reported that corruption was "very" or "quite" widespread. When the same survey asked respondents to rate the honesty of the six main parties, 60 percent of respondents considered Fianna Fáil dishonest, compared with 59 percent for Sinn Féin (tainted by its connections to the Provisional IRA), 51 percent for Fine Gael, 45 percent for Labour, 44 percent for the Progressive Democrats, and 37 percent for the Green Party. Thus, none of the parties were considered by the public to be very honest. The minor parties have had fewer explicit scandals, so these results may indicate that they have been lumped in with the major parties in the eyes of many voters.

In the end, growing awareness of widespread and persistent corruption has not resulted in greater changes in party support, because parties have found ways to balance reforming the system with perpetuating strong personal ties between individual politicians and voters—the lifeline of Irish electoral success. The introduction of tribunals and legislation demonstrated a degree of responsiveness by Ireland's major parties to growing concerns among the electorate over corruption, helping parties preserve the baseline legitimacy of the Irish system and their role within it. The very collapse of party systems in places such as Italy and Venezuela, due partly to their party leaders' failure to increase levels of accountability and to overcome political corruption, reinforces the importance of how Ireland's major parties responded and adapted to their own problems.

Nevertheless, Irish party leaders have been reluctant to undermine clientelistic and brokerage relationships altogether, even when questionable, precisely because doing so would undermine a long-standing arrangement that has proven to be mutually beneficial for parties and voters alike. Virtually all parties have offered some innocuous reforms aimed at fighting corruption, but as representatives elected within this system, they depend on strong linkages with voters at the local level to get elected. Therefore, real parliamentary-sponsored efforts to introduce effective anticorruption measures, beyond elementary legislation and the creation of independent tribunals, have been largely absent. These patterns of party behavior help explain why the major parties have survived a challenge to their longer-term electoral predominance. The precise ways in which party leaders have maximized these cultural and institutional realities to their advantage underlines the critical role of agency in the broader narrative of the present study.

Recurring to Quasi-Autonomous State Agencies

A fourth institutional vehicle that the major parties have used to shrink the electoral and parliamentary arenas has been the proliferation of quasi-autonomous state agencies. These state agencies, called "quangos," are "organizations operating at a national level established and funded by the Government to perform a public function, under governing bodies with a plural membership of wholly or largely appointed persons."[8] Depending on the criteria adopted, the number of agencies identified as quangos varies considerably from a couple hundred to as many as a thousand. The variation arises from classification decisions, such as whether to include government ministries, regulators, tribunals, local government organizations, universities, and subdivisions of health and social service agencies. Although agencies have existed from the foundation of the state, they have mushroomed in the last two decades, further reinforcing a general trend toward a more professional and managerial style of Irish governance (see fig. 4.4).[9] The recent explosion in the number of agencies is attributed to several factors, including requirements of Ireland's EU membership, public-sector reforms, and commitments in Social Partnership. Political responsiveness also played a role, as governments sought to demonstrate their commitment to addressing emerging policy issues and public tasks and still deliver

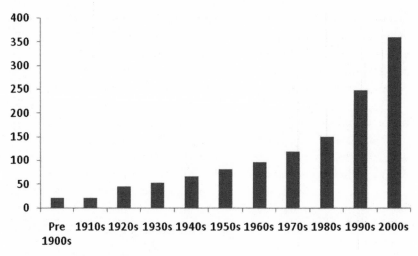

Fig. 4.4. Number of Total Irish State Agencies by Decade

services effectively in an increasingly complex modern world. This goal has been achieved through the creation of state agencies.

State agencies have assumed an ever larger range of public functions and control of an increased share of public expenditure, and there have been vast increases in the numbers of public-sector employees carrying out their work. Quangos were initially formed to address a variety of needs, including providing advice (23 percent), implementing policy (15 percent), regulating policy (13 percent), providing information (13 percent), registering public information (6 percent), undertaking promotional activities (6 percent), providing policy coordination (4 percent), assisting commercial development (3 percent), and various other purposes (18 percent). The biggest growth in agencies has been in delivery, regulatory, adjudicatory, and advisory or advocacy functions. By the middle of the first decade of the twenty-first century, several departments were allocating large percentages of their total budget to quangos, including Enterprise, Trade, and Employment (90 percent); Health and Children (87 percent); Communications; Marine and Natural Resources (55 percent); and Arts, Sports, and Tourism (47 percent).[10] Although considerable variation exists across departments, the clear trend is toward increased reliance on quangos across vast tranches of Irish governance, especially among those focusing on economic issues.

In principle, these public bodies enhance the effectiveness of Irish public policy making in an era of complex relations between state, market, and society. However, their proliferation poses challenges for political accountability and for policy coherence. First, the creation of agencies in Ireland has been ad hoc in nature, rather than a structured program of delegation and decentralization. As comparative evidence confirms, these agencies were not created because of technical imperatives; instead, their creation was an instance of policy diffusion or policy transfer. This instance highlights the deliberate choices of party and government leaders to use these institutional mechanisms not only to address issues but also to serve their own interests. Second, despite considerable legislation to enhance parliamentary accountability, implementation of the legislation has been inconsistent and ad hoc as well. Departmental and parliamentary oversight of public bodies has been "less than effective . . . and is rife with problems of inconsistency, exclusions and lack of clarity."[11] According to a 2005 study that identified the existence of 482 public bodies, only 225 were established by an act or order of parliament; fully 257 of them remain undefined. In addition, few mechanisms exist to oversee the selection and appointment process for five thousand government appointments to these public bodies. As a result, accusations of political favoritism and patronage politics have proliferated.

However, increased complexity of the policy-making process, reinforced by the heightened role of public bodies, has rendered it more difficult to hold elected officials accountable for the conduct of governance. Even highly publicized financial scandals associated with the chief executive of Ireland's former national job training authority (FÁS) or the banking crisis of 2008 have focused attention on who serves on the boards of public bodies, rather than addressing a more systematic concern over the proliferation of these boards or the inability to monitor their efforts once established.

Major parties have been reluctant to abolish these boards for several reasons. First, these agencies can, in some cases, improve the efficiency of government services. Second, they provide an additional source of patronage in an era when extending such benefits is increasingly difficult. Despite Fine Gael and Labour's promises to reform the process of appointments to these boards and bring an end to political cronyism in 2011, the practice continues. At least twenty past or present party members, strategists, or donors have been named to key boards, and five out of six judges nominated by the government have links to Fine Gael or Labour, along with two of the three members of the Judicial Appointments Advisory Board appointed by Minister for Justice Alan Shatter. Finally, most crucially for the purposes of the argument in the present study, the further bureaucratization of government services is the latest means by which the policy process can be obfuscated. In a highly complex and technical policy-making arena, one of the few areas left for parties to compete over—namely, competence—has also become nearly impossible for voters to assess. In sum, an important consequence of the greater proliferation of these state bodies is that policy making has been relegated to this technocratic realm, providing another mechanism by which issues are siphoned off from electoral competition or parliamentary accountability.

Recurring to the Courts

Another closely related strategy that parties have successfully utilized to mute potentially contentious issues has been to defer to the judiciary. For example, in recent years, challenges have been made to the conservative religious nature of the Irish constitution and early subsequent legislation that banned contraception (the Criminal Law Amendment Act of 1935) and abortion (the Offences against the Person Act of 1861 and the Eighth Amendment of the Constitution, made in 1983) and that made homosexuality a criminal offence (the Offences against the Person Act of 1861). However, Irish political parties have been reluctant to tackle these issues directly via legislation. Instead, these potentially explosive cultural issues are carefully delayed or avoided. Consequently, interest groups, seeking to challenge these laws, have sought relief from both Irish and European courts. In 1973, for instance, the Irish Supreme Court ruled in the *McGee* case that the Irish Constitution did not provide the state with the right to forbid the use of contraception to married couples. It took Irish parties five years to enact legislation in the Dáil to allow the use of contraception for married couples.

Irish public opinion on homosexuality—first on decriminalizing it and then on extending rights such as gay marriage and adoption for gay parents—has undergone relatively brisk change but has been matched by glacial treatment in the legislative arena. Irish attitudes toward homosexuality have dramatically shifted, as the percentage of respondents who considered homosexuality "always wrong" collapsed from 59 percent in 1981 to just 23 percent in 2006. Those who reported that homosexuality was never wrong went from 3 percent in 1981 to 53 percent by 2006. Despite rapid changes in attitudes, shifts in the law were secured only after the courts dictated such action. Minor parties have been quick to stake out their positions on these issues, whereas the established parties have been reluctant to take a stand. For example, homosexuality was finally decriminalized in 1993 by an act of the Dáil, marking the end of a fifteen-year campaign spearheaded by Senator David Norris to reverse the law. But the law was overturned only when the European Court of Human Rights ruled that Irish law was in violation of Article 8 of the European Convention on Human Rights, a provision that decriminalized homosexuality. Just as in the case of contraception, a long delay occurred between the court decision and subsequent legislation to bring the judicial ruling into effect. Parliament acted only after a legal obligation forced its hand.

By the late 2000s, public opinion toward homosexuality had shifted even more dramatically, as the debate concerning marriage equality and civil unions intensified in the press. The percentage of Irish citizens who felt that same-sex couples should receive legal recognition jumped from 51 percent in 2006 to a whopping 84 percent in 2008; those opposed declined from 16 percent to 10 percent. Of the 84 percent that supported legal recognition of same-sex unions in 2008, 51 percent agreed that it should be called "marriage," while 33 percent preferred the term "civil partnership." The growing sentiment among the electorate is that the religious and legal dimensions of marriage should be separated as fewer Irish citizens view marriage as inherently a religious act. A further division revealed itself among the Irish electorate when asked in the same 2008 survey about adoption by same-sex couples: 39 percent were in favor of allowing same-sex couples to adopt children, whereas 37 percent rejected it. Sixty-four percent of all respondents also stated that no difference to their voting would occur if a political candidate in their constituency supported same-sex marriage. In addition to delaying legislation, the strategy by the established parties has been to focus on the separation of legal and religious aspects of the issue to preserve internal party unity and avoid fractious conflicts among large blocks within their electoral base, especially until consensus exists within the electorate. After years of debate and political controversy, this broader consensus emerged, and the Civil Partnership Act was passed in 2012. It extended to same-sex couples tax and inheritance rights similar but not equal to those extended to partners in civil marriages. This example reinforces that delaying legislation while issues remain divisive and removing them to the judicial arena can deprive minor parties from taking advantage of an issue to mobilize new voters, thereby limiting the extent to which unsettling changes in society can alter the nature of Ireland's electoral competition.

Immigration constitutes another area where Ireland underwent considerable changes with little impact on electoral politics. Consider the challenges surrounding the growing numbers of immigrants who were coming to Ireland starting in the late 1990s. Historically, Ireland had been among the most homogeneous countries in Europe, but it was transformed from a country of emigration to one of immigration. Ireland's immigrants doubled from 5 to 10 percent of its overall population between 2002 and 2006 alone. The number of immigrants arriving in Ireland during the 2000s would be equivalent to the United States receiving 6.75 million immigrants per year, as opposed to the one million annually that actually arrived during that same period. The surge in immigration was in response to Ireland's rapid economic growth since the 1990s and its liberal immigration policies. The absence of quotas on work permits and the decision to grant the ten EU accession states free access to Irish labor markets upon their entry into the EU in 2004 prompted a significant spike in immigrants seeking to live in Ireland.

As immigration issues heated up in the early 2000s, it was not political parties that mobilized and led the debate for how best to address immigration-related policies. Instead, a 2003 Supreme Court ruling and subsequent citizenship referendum in 2004 led to the removal of the right to permanent residence for "nonnational" parents of children born in Ireland. This was a marked shift toward a more stringent immigration policy, albeit still relatively liberal by European standards. By and large, parties remained on the sideline as other actors within civil society motivated public debate. However, party leaders did frame the debate during the referenda in economic, rather than ethnic, terms. Whereas ethnic appeals would have divided the electorate, economic appeals attracted cross-sector support. As a result of these strategies, party leaders garnered overwhelming support for the amendment to the Constitution. Opportunistic party leaders once again demonstrated that they can act decisively if needed but that they will not do so unless they can act to resolve issues in ways that will not undermine their electoral fortunes.

For this reason, political parties chose not to directly address immigration in the 2007 election, even though it had become increasingly salient within the electorate. Parties managed the controversy strategically by consciously avoiding this contested issue during the election, preferring to handle it quietly by offering to create a new government bureaucracy concerned with immigrant issues. Party leaders deliberately chose not to play the immigration card, even though the potential existed for electoral mobilization around these issues, as indicated by the public opinion highlighted in chapter 2. The Irish are not immune to prejudice, and latent racist and xenophobic attitudes certainly exist.[12] Nevertheless, party leaders decided not to politicize this divisive issue. As Michael McDowell, then leader of the PDs, made clear, one could mobilize votes on immigration, but such a strategy would ultimately be divisive and not serve the interests of the parties or the state. The unwillingness of minor parties to carve out a niche around a specific issue like immigration in fear that it might undermine their chances of attracting broader support among the electorate plays directly into the hands of the major parties, which excel at this catchall approach.

Party Strategies and the Reshuffled Institutional Dimension, 2008–12

The 2011 election results and the events surrounding it provide an interesting counterfactual to the results we have observed thus far in this chapter. In particular, Fianna Fáil's severe electoral losses illustrate the profound results that can occur when a major party is unable to displace issues or take institutional cover to shield themselves from blame when policies fail. The most obvious outcome of the 2011 election was that the governing coalition of Fianna Fáil and the Green Party was severely chastised by an angry electorate for presiding over the financial meltdown triggered in 2008 and for the government response to it. Fianna Fáil's twenty seats represented a historic low; the Green Party fared even worse, losing all six of its seats. A complacent and perhaps hubristic Fianna Fáil had been in government for a decade and a half, rewarded by a grateful electorate who perceived it to be the most competent party when it came to managing the extraordinarily successful Celtic Tiger economy. The scope of the sudden financial meltdown (which affected every sector of Irish society) and the frenzied national and international media attention on the crisis exposed Fianna Fáil to unprecedented criticism from which it could not escape. The 2011 INES confirms that 80 percent of respondents held Fianna Fáil accountable for the financial crisis and the disastrous economic consequences that ensued.

Analysis of economic indicators and public opinion polls between 2005 and 2011, as well as the 2011 INES and the 2011 RTÉ exit poll, emphasizes the degree to which the government parties were specifically blamed for their role in the financial collapse. Consumer confidence and industrial production had begun declining in mid-2007, but the Irish economy took a nosedive in September 2008, with the sudden announcement of the government's blanket bank guarantee for all deposits and liabilities of the nation's banks. In the succeeding two years, unemployment spiked from 4 to 15 percent, and per capita income declined by 20 percent. Nevertheless, a study of key economic indicators concluded that, with the exception of unemployment, economic variables had no statistical effect on levels of support for Fianna Fáil in public opinion polls. Instead of a gradual decrease in support for Fianna Fáil in conjunction with slumping economic indicators and heightened awareness of the party's role in this decline, Fianna Fáil's support collapsed in relation to two critical events: the September 2008 government bank guarantee and the October 2010 decision to withdraw from the international bond market—the final step on the path to the EU/IMF/ECB bailout. In the Red C public opinion poll, there was a decline of 11 percentage points in Fianna Fáil support immediately after the bank guarantee in September 2008 and an additional drop of 5 percentage points after the decision on the bond market was announced in October 2010, but support for the party leveled off after both decisions. The final margin (an overall drop of 24 percentage points in Fianna Fáil's support between the two elections) was closely related to the EU/IMF/ECB loan announcement in November 2010 and to the abysmal final days of the Cowen administration, which were dominated by the shell-shocked Taoiseach barely surviving an internal contest over party leadership, his bungled cabinet reshuffle, and his delaying tactics in relation to calling an early election.

That most voters blamed Fianna Fáil for Ireland's economic woes is especially important, given that economic issues were identified by voters as those that most influenced their vote. According to the RTÉ exit poll, 49 percent of respondents ranked economic concerns as most important in determining their vote, while an additional 36 percent claimed that their anger toward the government and incumbents determined their vote. The most salient issues from the previous several elections (health, education, and crime) barely registered among voters in the exit poll, receiving only 2 percent, 1 percent, and 0.5 percent, respectively. The perception of Fianna Fáil as the most competent party to deal with economic issues had crumbled, and with it collapsed its historic levels of electoral support. The party that had proven so adept at managing complicated issues by embedding themselves deep within Ireland's set of extraparliamentary institutions—and thriving electorally as a result—was left bereft of the cover provided by these institutions and was harshly punished.

Some argue that this electoral backlash could visit serious adverse longer-term effects on Fianna Fáil and even lead eventually to the party's demise. After the 2011 election, one noted scholar of Fianna Fáil's history argued that the core elements of the party's historical success have all been compromised. Noel Whelan stated, "Devoid of its original driving mission, stripped of its reputation for economic competence and economic probity, lacking critical mass in the Oireachtas and depleted in personnel at the local government and local cumann [branch] level, Fianna Fáil may now be in terminal decline."[13] First, the infighting of the 1970s and 1980s and the subsequent revelations of sordid corruption have eroded party unity and undermined Fianna Fáil's moral authority. When coupled with the emergence of a stable peace in the North, the party's core identity has been undermined. Second, a subtle shift has occurred in terms of local political organizations. Inspired by the example of former Taoiseach Bertie Ahern, local machines have encouraged followers and financial resources to be loyal to individual candidates more than to the party. Over time, this has rendered parties less relevant and made it more difficult to find new candidates to pick up and lead the party "franchise," especially in urban areas where Fianna Fáil's support has declined most precipitately. Whelan predicted that generations will be required for Fianna Fáil to overcome their current predicament.

In contrast to Fianna Fáil, the other established parties were able to take advantage of institutional mechanisms to strengthen their electoral standing. Although the financial crisis of 2008 and the conditions of the 2010 EU/IMF/ECB loan reshuffled and greatly limited the array of policy choices available to the leaders of Ireland's major parties, party leaders were able to parlay those constraints to their advantage. The EU/IMF/ECB framework greatly inhibited the scope of economic policy making and resulted in minimal programmatic differences among competing parties on economic issues. Approximately 88 percent of TDs in my parliamentary survey believed that the EU/IMF loan agreement constrained TDs' abilities to make economic policy. Similarly, large majorities agreed that the loan agreement constrained social policy making as well. At the same time, the scale of Ireland's economic woes and concomitant feelings of despair and rage among the electorate regarding the political system's ineffectiveness provided incentives to parties to respond boldly to the crisis with a wide array of political reforms. Indeed, the reform of political institutions was second of the most prevalent themes among party platforms during the 2011 campaign, signaling the willingness of political parties to advance their positions by advocating institutional reform—even toward institutions that they had largely supported and benefited from in the past.

However, since the adoption of the EU/IMF/ECB framework effectively minimized the range of alternative policies to address the economic crisis, the imperative of institutional reform became the clarion call for all.

As we would predict, the major parties joined the parade, successfully co-opting this newly emergent salient issue, preventing opponents from taking full advantage of the rage within the electorate. Rather than accepting the argument that parties had no other option than to resign themselves to the EU/IMF/ECB framework, my argument is that party leaders actively contributed to establishing a more limited policy framework because it allowed them to contain the catastrophe to a predetermined extraparliamentary arena.

The period between 2008 and 2011 in Ireland was marked by a devastating financial crisis and zigzagging government responses that failed to regain the confidence of the international markets needed to stabilize the national economy. Although Fianna Fáil shouldered the blame for this catastrophe, the great majority of Ireland's party leaders supported the austerity measures ultimately adopted by the Fianna Fáil government under the guise of the "national interest." In 2008, Labour was the only party that voted against the bank guarantee. They adopted what some considered a populist position, claiming that the people who would suffer most from this measure were Ireland's defenseless pensioners, not the cosseted and inept bankers who were actually to blame. Mainstream commentators criticized Labour, suggesting that it was ironic that Labour "ended up voting against a piece of legislation which gives the Government of the day enormous powers over the banking sector, even to the point of nationalisation, given that it was a long-held aspiration of Labour to nationalise the banks."[14]

By 2010, the Fianna Fáil and Green government announced a four-year austerity plan that would cut government spending by €10 billion and raise taxes by €5 billion between 2011 and 2014—a 5 percent downward adjustment in the overall budget—to win approval from its EU partners and the IMF and secure the emergency rescue package. Although parties disagreed over how best to tackle the economic crisis during the parliamentary debate on this budget (Fine Gael proposed cuts over five years instead of four; Labour wanted to commit to only a one-year budget plan because it thought the cuts were too harsh), only Sinn Féin voted against the Finance Bill in November 2010, paving the way for the EU/IMF/ECB loan.

The terms of how the EU/IMF/ECB deal would be implemented permitted party leaders to pin the blame for unpopular economic policies on international institutional actors, thereby allowing parties to coalesce around a common defense. In some ways, the conditions inspired by the international lending community and the EU replaced the institutional framework previously provided by Social Partnership, which had disintegrated in the wake of the crisis. The pervasive consensus that emerged across the political spectrum argued that Ireland could recover only by adopting orthodox economic measures such as increasing taxes and slashing the budget. This approach, they argued, would signal the government's commitment to macroeconomic stability to global markets, thereby restoring growth by improving conditions favorable to investment. As long as the parties continued to maintain a consensus around these policies, the focus of political discourse remained centered around issues of competence and delivery, not alternative visions of Ireland's future. This familiar pattern enhanced the position of Ireland's major parties, which are perceived to be best positioned to lead any governing coalition because of their size, perceived competence, and ability to deliver.

Even when public opinion polls indicated great public ambivalence and opposition toward the EU/IMF/ECB deals and after the 2011 elections produced a cohort of TDs who were skeptical of these policies, the government did not seriously debate or revisit these policies. As table 4.4 notes, solid majorities or pluralities of respondents in the 2011 INES supported providing taxpayer-funded relief to people behind on their mortgages and "burning the bondholders" who held stakes in collapsing banks (rather than taking out public debt to repay the bondholders). The public was evenly divided on whether the government was right to accept the bailout. Winning candidates responding to the Comparative Candidates Survey after the 2011 election exhibited an almost identical pattern, the public being evenly divided on the bailout. Yet, once the new parliament was seated, there was little serious debate over reversing the bailout deal or making adjustments to the course of fiscal and social policy. Although the sample sizes from individual parties are small, they suggest that all of the major parties were torn by conflicting attitudes toward these issues and that such conflict may have prevented them from developing unambiguous stances.

TABLE 4.4. Percentage of Respondents to the 2011 INES and Comparative Candidates Survey Who Supported Selected Policies

	Government wrong to accept bailout		Government should burn bondholders		Taxpayers should fund mortgage relief	
	Voters	TDs	Voters	TDs	Voters	TDs
Total disagree	41	48	17	29	20	22
Total agree	39	43	58	55	52	57
Disagree strongly	16	33	6	19	7	7
Disagree slightly	26	15	10	10	13	15
Neither	19	9	26	16	29	22
Agree slightly	20	25	26	36	33	46
Agree strongly	20	19	32	19	19	10

The institutional cover provided by the EU/IMF/ECB deal explains why parties from across the political spectrum were so willing to openly seek institutional reform during the 2011 election campaign, even of those institutions that had contributed to their overall electoral predominance over previous decades. The very institutions that had previously sustained Ireland's economic growth, including Social Partnership and the proliferation of state agencies, were perceived by analysts to have contributed to the excesses of the Celtic Tiger. They were also regarded as fundamentally weakening the quality of representative democracy and accountability in Irish politics. The pattern of Ireland's major party leaders behaving opportunistically—adopting policy positions directly contradictory to earlier stands in order to mirror Irish public opinion—was taken to new levels during the 2011 campaign.

When the 2011 election arrived, 36 percent of respondents in the RTÉ exit poll indicated that they were angry or felt let down by the government and politicians in general—a response that was not even an option in the previous election poll. In keeping with their opportunistic and highly flexible programmatic approach, Irish parties offered campaign policy documents setting forth virtually identical plans for political reform. This patterned response reinforces the behaviors described in the previous chapter whereby party positions converge on popular issues to prevent any one party from "owning" that particular issue and from gaining an electoral advantage. Fine Gael and Labour, even though they had relied on many of the very institutions they now critiqued when they were in government, successfully pinned the blame for the recent failings of these institutions on Fianna Fáil. The election revolved around competency, not alternate policies.

Instead, a policy bidding war unfolded as parties tried to outpromise each other in terms of what they were willing to do to fix Ireland's broken political system. True to form, despite all the heated calls for electoral reform in the run-up to the election, this issue became muted during and after the campaign. This is hardly surprising, as those elected by a particular system are least likely to alter it; they are the beneficiaries of the status quo. Consistent with long-standing practice, Taoiseach Enda Kenny promised during the campaign that his ministers would avoid constituency service for the first one hundred days in office, in order to more effectively address their national responsibilities. Nevertheless, seventy days into his term as Taoiseach, Kenny himself had "added up an impressive level of local involvement. . . . The Taoiseach had raised a flag at the Galway-Mayo Institute of Technology, sounded the starting horn at the West of Ireland Women's Mini-Marathon, opened the Mayo Ploughing Championship, turned the first sod at May Abbey National School. . . . And his Spartan, outcomes-focused cabinet members were doing the same around the country."[15]

Despite the disappearance of electoral reform as an issue, parties across the spectrum offered a multitude of other reforms during the campaign, many focused on increasing accountability and enhancing meaningful access for civil society's interests within the political process. Because all Irish parties hopped on the reform bandwagon of the day, minor parties were once again deprived of the chance of either shaping the reform legislation or taking credit for it. Ireland's major parties were therefore able to avoid the blame for practices they supported over the years, while claiming credit for proposing reform.

The increased focus on political reform produced several websites that sought to facilitate debate about how to improve the accountability and efficiency of Irish political institutions. According to one of the leading sites that rated party platforms on their reform agenda, Reformcard.com, Fine Gael rated highest in the strength of its overall reform package. Fine Gael proposed four pillars within its "New Politics" proposals: a new, single-house legislature (i.e., the abolishment of the Seanad, Ireland's upper house); an improved Dáil; a more open government; and a more empowered civil society. The key features of Fine Gael's reform agenda included significant modifications both in how interests are represented within Social Partnership and in the leadership of state agencies. These measures, it was argued, would enhance transparency and increase parliamentary oversight across economic and social policy. Labour focused its reform proposals on public-sector pay and enhancing the transparency and accountability of state boards, making this layer of "political cronyism" subject to enhanced Dáil scrutiny. Even Fianna Fáil, which had had plenty of opportunities to reform the political system during its fifteen years in government, proposed its own set of reforms. Among them was the proposal that ministers would cease to be TDs for the duration of their ministerial terms, so that they could become more effective managers in their respective areas of responsibility. They also proposed a greater role for a citizens' assembly, limited constitutional reform, public-sector reform, and adjustments to how state boards were administered.

Although it was still too early at the time of this writing to evaluate which reforms the government would enact, it is already clear that, as we would predict, the appetite for reform among party leaders has diminished rapidly in the aftermath of the election. According to my 2012 parliamentary survey, when asked to rate the importance, in terms of improving the quality of democracy in Ireland, of reforming various aspects of Ireland's political system, only four of ten areas received ratings above 5.0 on a scale of 1 (not important at all) to 10 (very important): these areas were public service (7.7), quangos (7.7), the number of women TDs (6.6), and the Constitution (6.5). There was less support for previously visible reforms such as changing or abolishing the Seanad (4.9), reducing the number of TDs (4.5), and altering the PR-STV electoral system (3.6). TDs generally share similar (although not identical) priorities for reform, regardless of the party to which they belong. In addition to waning support at the elite level, the once-busy websites now languish unvisited or have shut down due to lack of funding. It also unclear whether the heralded Convention on the Constitution, consisting of randomly selected citizens and political representatives, will lead to any significant reforms. The preservation of narrow programmatic differences, especially among the major parties, reduces the choices available to the electorate. Ultimately, strategies that major party leaders have employed within the institutional domain during the 2011 election to insulate themselves from the fiscal tumult of the previous years further reinforced the likelihood that the major parties will continue to predominate electorally in the future.

Conclusion

The leaders of Ireland's major parties have artfully deployed a broad array of institutional mechanisms to contend with dramatic changes in Irish society and politics, to sideline conflicts, and, ultimately, to maintain their electoral predominance. Rather than confronting contentious issues directly in the electoral arena, parties have consistently preferred to consign them to extra-electoral and extraparliamentary institutions. These practices have effectively shrunk the electoral arena, while preserving and even strengthening the electoral position of Ireland's established parties. Why would party leaders risk direct confrontation and expose their parties to the vagaries of the electorate, when issues can be handled with less exposure to electoral risk? Parties have not intentionally created these institutions to insulate themselves from the uncertainties of the electoral market. Rather, party leaders have employed a variety of strategies within these extraparliamentary institutions in order to advance their own electoral agendas during a period of social and electoral uncertainty. As a net result, contention has been removed from the electoral arena, and new cleavages have been inhibited from destabilizing persistent patterns of party competition.

My treatment of the institutional dimension makes two important contributions toward better understanding party leaders and parties as agents, as well as the strategies they employ to maintain their predominance. First, I highlight the critical interaction between party leaders and the array of extraparliamentary institutions they have at their disposal. Although Ireland's set of institutions powerfully structures the choices that parties and voters have available to them, a strict institutional argument is insufficient. The analysis in this chapter has demonstrated how major party leaders have taken advantage of these institutions to protect their longer-term electoral interests. These leaders have engaged Ireland's institutional framework effectively to address emerging issues within a modernizing Ireland, but they have also sought to insulate themselves from contentious issues when the electorate was divided. How party leaders have managed change reinforces the importance of political agency arguments.

Second, the analysis in this chapter has extended our understanding of the precise means by which parties rely more fully on the state for their survival. An analysis that concentrates solely on how established parties increasingly depend on the state for funding, campaign regulation, and media access is insufficient. I have extended such analysis by including the ways in which Ireland's major parties have actively employed evolving state institutions to manage how issues within society are addressed. In particular, we have seen how parties have utilized various institutions to help frame whether, how, and where societal conflicts get translated into the political system. This approach both broadens our view of the multifaceted relationships between political parties and the state and reminds us that parties do not simply reflect society's interests but also actively shape them. The strategic use of institutional mechanisms to relegate contentious issues to the extraparliamentary arena is reinforced by other adaptive mechanisms: namely, opportunistic ideological flexibility and organizational repositioning.

FIVE

Shaping the
Organizational Domain

The ongoing electoral predominance of Ireland's major parties is intricately linked with their ability to adapt their organizational structures and outreach to keep pace with rapidly changing social and electoral environments. As we have seen, the centripetal character of ideological competition and the institutional displacement of issues have contributed powerfully to prevent changes in society from altering the nature of electoral competition. With little separating Ireland's parties programmatically during elections, personal appeals and organizational capacity are the primary mechanisms by which candidates and parties establish and maintain linkages with voters and distinguish themselves from one another among the electorate. Although it is has been fifty years since Basil Chubb famously suggested that the role of the TD is to "go about persecuting civil servants," the demand for unusually robust constituency service and the expectation that TDs will serve as brokers between voters and the state continue to dominate Irish politics.[1] On average, 40 percent of voters choose their TDs primarily based on the candidate's ability to look after the constituency's needs. Additionally, people from all sectors of Irish society, including educated and upper-income citizens, continue to use their elected representatives in a brokerage capacity to access goods and services from the state.[2] Major parties possess an advantage when it comes to carrying out this vital brokerage role.

Ireland's parties now face a more demanding electoral environment than they faced in elections prior to the 1980s. It is characterized by lower turnout, lower party attachment, and increased numbers of floating voters. Taken together with the complex and technocratic character of the issues facing modernizing Ireland, parties have had to respond energetically to these challenges or suffer the consequences. As a result, major party organizations have become more centralized, professionalized, and bureaucratized. These modernizing trends, in turn, have had important consequences, enhancing the parties' overall ability to coordinate efforts at the national level. In addition, these trends have improved how parties select candidates and leaders, raise money, and communicate policy priorities. At the same time, the imperative of efficient local delivery of goods and services and the personalized nature of electoral appeals incentivize parties to field candidates who can simultaneously sustain multiple linkages to government offices at every level. Successful candidates must cultivate linkages at the national party level and navigate Ireland's complicated civil service protocols to deliver goods, services, and information locally. Minor parties and independents, with their weaker national party organizations, are less able to navigate such protocols. The parties' ability to work effectively at both the national and local levels has been crucial for their longer-term electoral success.

Consistent with the literature on party organizations that emphasizes the importance of studying parties as political systems in their own right, this chapter analyzes the interplay among and between parties' various components, most notably the rank and file, activists, parliamentary representatives and leaders, and party headquarters.[3] How parties are organized shapes their electoral and ideological strategies and, subsequently, their electoral fortunes. We have already seen how Ireland's ideological spectrum has narrowed despite widespread changes in society. The analysis in this chapter focuses on the concrete organizational strategies that leaders of Ireland's major parties have employed to mobilize voters in a sharply altered social and political context.

An increasingly professional party organization, combined with the constraining effects of ideological dampening and institutional displacement discussed in chapters 3 and 4, has heightened the parties' reliance on brokerage politics at the local level. Contrary to what we might intuitively expect, therefore, party modernization in the Irish case actually places a heavier stress on personalistic, nonideological appeals at the local level, as candidates emphasize "performance" and delivering local goods and services. Modernization has also weakened the influence of ideologically motivated activists within parties. Somewhat paradoxically, the very modernization of party organization has strengthened, rather than weakened, the emphasis on more traditional, local politics.

Because of declining levels of party attachment and voter turnout, as well as growing voter apathy, candidates and parties must work harder and more creatively to continuously mobilize their core supporters, while gaining the support of those ever-swelling ranks of the fickle "floating voters," those who lack a close connection with any party. Simultaneously, candidates must appeal to a broader electorate to win sufficient lower-preference votes away from competing candidates to ensure their election. These multiple and sometimes contradictory demands impel parties to perform a balancing act: getting out one's core party vote while not being so partisan as to alienate other parties' supporters. This act requires ever greater professional and personnel resources to sustain visibility in the media and new social networks (the air campaign) while providing constituency service to local communities (the ground campaign). Accomplishing all of this requires more money. Similar to the advantages major parties have enjoyed on the ideological dimension, the major parties have also proven more adept at attracting resources to maintain their organizational edge over the medium and longer term.

As we have seen throughout the analysis in this book, Ireland's major parties have enjoyed certain long-standing advantages. For example, the founding of Ireland's party system and its historical legacies, the dynamics of its PR-STV electoral system, and a political culture that values personal relationships at the local level have all combined to give the major parties an electoral edge. The parties that established mass organizations and occupied the political playing field at the onset of the initial mobilization of the electorate captured an enduring loyalty of voters early in the country's political history. As a result, Ireland's major parties enjoyed numerical and geographic superiority, flexible administrative structures, and strong national and local organizations from the very beginning. These advantages have made it difficult for newcomers to overcome the organizational edge of the major parties. Nevertheless, these legacies cannot explain why the major parties have survived electorally over the longer term as society changed and as more competitive elections emerged.

This chapter examines the precise ways in which Ireland's major parties have altered their organizational strategies to preserve their advantage. It explores multiple features of Irish parties that underscore the relatively high organizational autonomy of national party leaders as well as TDs at the local level and the consequences of this relative autonomy for party behavior.[4] We will see that contemporary Irish parties embody a somewhat contradictory reality, one that is increasingly modern but tenaciously traditional and local.

This chapter also advances our understanding of political parties in several significant ways. First, it addresses an empirically and theoretically compelling question: what factors account for party ability to adapt organizationally? Levitsky's work on the Peronists in Argentina found that lower levels of institutionalization—often a source of inefficiency, disorder, and ineffective representation—tend to enhance parties' flexibility during times of crisis.[5] He identifies several internal organizational features that facilitate this flexibility, including leadership autonomy, leadership renovation, and pliable rules and procedures within the party.[6] Ireland's major parties have also exhibited remarkable flexibility in adapting to changes in the electoral environment, but they operate somewhat differently. Major party leaders in Ireland have enjoyed considerable autonomy, but one only becomes a party leader by proving one's commitment and loyalty and by rising through the ranks. Leadership renovation has not always been as fluid in Ireland as Levitsky found for the Peronists; set rules and procedures hold real importance within the Irish parties. Despite this fact, party leaders in Ireland have proven adept at changing the rules and restructuring their organizations in response to electoral defeats.

Second, the various organizational responses employed by Irish parties and described in this chapter challenge the utility of existing party typologies. Irish parties manifest the qualities of several different party types, including electoralist and catchall parties, cartel parties, and parties modeled after business firms or franchises.[7] Irish parties exemplify electoral professional parties in that all aspects of party internal organization and external relations function to maximize electoral opportunities. These aspects include programmatic flexibility, limited discretion of party members in policy making, increased polling as a guide to crafting a winning message, and leadership autonomy.[8] Similar to electoral professional parties, Irish parties also display characteristics of catchall parties. Increased marginalization of the rank and file, a concentration of power and resources in the parliamentary party, and the further professionalization and high capitalization of campaigns are characteristic of Irish party development.[9] At the same time, Irish parties exhibit the tendencies of cartel parties: an increased reliance on state resources and institutions has allowed them to assert the power of the parliamentary party and to develop the permanent professional organization so vital to electoral success in the modern era.[10] Irish parties also behave like business firms: a high level of autonomy holds sway in Ireland for individual political entrepreneurs to promote themselves and their local "franchises" within the party.[11] In this chapter, we will see the heterodox nature of major Irish parties not only as a key factor in explaining their long-term electoral predominance but also as a challenge to the existing consensus on how political science conceptualizes party types more generally.

Finally, this chapter reinforces the need for a longitudinal and multidimensional analysis. The origins of the Irish party system are crucial for understanding the broad, catchall appeal and highly flexible and autonomous nature of the established parties. However, Ireland's dramatic social, economic, and political changes have placed a strain on long-standing party attachments. As we would expect, the major parties have worked hard to sustain their electoral advantages and to maintain a particular way of doing politics. Only by analyzing party strategies longitudinally and along multiple dimensions—institutional, ideological, and organizational—can we truly appreciate the ways in which Ireland's major parties have preserved their electoral predominance over the longer term. A dialectical process is at work here: the impact of organizational changes is reinforced by the actions of parties on these other dimensions. Therefore, we must keep in mind the effects (discussed previously) of the centripetal character of ideological competition and institutional displacement of issues; they greatly enhance the ability of parties to adapt organizationally to bolster their support.

Major Parties Sustain Their Historical Size Advantage

The electoral success of Ireland's major parties has been enhanced by the unusual degree of organizational autonomy and flexibility enjoyed by their leadership.[12] Despite some similarities across parties, the internal structures of Irish parties vary in important ways and have evolved in response to electoral challenges. Since a prolific literature exists describing the origins of Irish parties, only an abbreviated narrative will be offered here, with an eye toward explaining how parties have modified their internal structures over time to maintain and strengthen their effective links with voters.

Party Origins

From the outset, Fianna Fáil fashioned itself organizationally as a great national movement rather than as a mere political party, seeking to extend its reach to every family and community in the country.[13] Local organizational development was crucial from the beginning. The movement depended on tightly knit, activist communities throughout the country, united in their willingness to support the party leader at all costs in order to win and wield power.[14] Fianna Fáil, the argument goes, was essentially a secular echo of the organizational space occupied by the Catholic Church in Irish society.[15] Despite significant recent erosion of its once formidable base, Fianna Fáil successfully maintained its overall hegemony within the party system between 1932 and 2011. Fianna Fáil became the hinge on which party competition swung: its continued viability in an era of coalition politics has forced the other parties to act in response to its moves. Indeed, Fianna Fáil's envied success fostered imitation among the other parties in their quest for votes.

In contrast to Fianna Fáil, Fine Gael was historically a more poorly organized party that revolved around key notables and individuals at the local level—a cadre type of party. They placed less emphasis on mass involvement and tolerated a lax and sometimes nonexistent network of local branches.[16] Garret FitzGerald and another former Fine Gael Taoiseach, John Costello, laughed about the fact that neither of them had ever formally become a member of the party, despite the century-long involvement of their iconic Fine Gael families.[17] Nevertheless, Fine Gael also maintained local (even if small or moribund) branches in virtually every corner of Ireland.

The third-largest party, Labour, had the weakest of the major party organizations and was for some time largely considered less a modern mass-based political party and more a loose coalition of like-minded independent TDs.[18] Of the remaining smaller parties that have been competitive since the late 1980s, only the Green Party was formed independently, as both Sinn Féin and the Progressive Democrats emerged as disgruntled splinter groups from the two Civil War parties. These smaller parties have enjoyed limited success in extending their reach outside Dublin, although Sinn Féin (recently freed of the taint of terrorism) has shown some capacity for maturing into an effective national party, with considerable strength in the border region.

Organizational and Geographic Superiority

Fianna Fáil and Fine Gael owe much of their long-term electoral success to their extensive organizational reach, especially the local branches that they have developed in nearly every small town and rural parish throughout the country. At the local level, branches (*cumainn* in the case of Fianna Fáil and Sinn Féin) are the key organizational building block for parties.[19] These branches generally consist of at least three to five members in rural areas and closer to ten in more urban areas. Branches are required to meet at least once annually and elect various officers.

Minor parties, independents, and, to some extent, Labour lack these vital local capillaries.[20] Despite the much-lamented decline in active party participation in the most recent period, independent TD Catherine Murphy claims that the advantage of the main parties over independents and smaller parties lies in their ability to sustain member involvement and, consequently, activate member turnout when it really counts.

> [Local party organizations] are the eyes and ears of the community without doing a whole lot, they would be passive on a committee, but they will go back and report what is happening. They do not function as *cumainn* [local branches] anymore; they function as election machines now. . . . They still turn out for elections.[21]

In the contemporary era of accelerating electoral competitiveness and increasing floating voters, the major parties' ability to deliver efficient local electoral machines has continued to be critical to their success. However, changes have been implemented to take full advantage of the geographic and numerical superiority of the major parties as society has changed.

In recent decades, national party headquarters have intervened in local party bodies, sometimes to wrest power away from ineffective local leaders (more focused on the personal than on the party) and sometimes to reinvigorate their organizational networks around the country and preserve their mobilizational edge over the smaller parties. One example of this intervention lies in the reform of "paper branches." These phantom branches existed in name only, usually with three or four active members and an additional roster of dozens of inactive individuals. Using these fictive "wards," influential local party leaders manipulated local party organization and candidate selection.[22] Incumbent TDs used this ruse to stack the deck in their favor, employing paper branches to ensure their own nomination for office time after time. Paper branches have also ensured that local party leaders maintain their primacy, insulating themselves (and the party) from incumbency challenges. As a result, this fictive but effective organizational vehicle eliminated new blood at the source, as well as stifling the "circulation of local elites," slowly atrophying party organization at the local level. As Carty describes it,

> Irish deputies . . . do not hesitate to use their considerable influence within the local party to keep able and aggressive young men and women out of any positions which might allow them to short-circuit the TD's brokerage relationships and build an independent

base of support. . . . Too often talent-suppression practices of this kind result in the promotion of decidedly mediocre individuals, handicapping the parties' ability to provide the system with effective political leadership.[23]

The use of paper branches and the fact that socially mobile citizens are increasingly uninterested in becoming involved in politics begin to explain the declining party identification among the Irish. The reform of paper branches was initiated by Fine Gael (under Garret FitzGerald) when that party was in opposition in the late 1970s and by Fianna Fáil when it was in opposition in 1982–87.[24] In both cases, these reforms halted the effects of declining membership and vote share and helped the major parties enhance their electoral outcomes in subsequent elections.

Nevertheless, party membership still matters at the local level. The sheer numerical superiority and geographical reach of the major parties is telling—even when factoring in the varying levels of real engagement by members within these local branches. Between 1970 and 1986, Fianna Fáil grew its branches from twenty-two hundred to nearly three thousand, Fine Gael averaged sixteen hundred branches, and Labour had nearly five hundred.[25] Although the political parties guard updated membership statistics, anecdotal evidence suggests that membership levels are falling. A 2005 internal Fianna Fáil study reported three thousand existing branches.[26] While some of these branches may no longer be active in holding regular meetings and serving as the locus of community relations, others persist as the backbone of the party locally and provide candidates in general elections with the geographical and community-based means to reach the party faithful. That local organizations still provide some limited financial resources to their national party headquarters is another reason parties are reluctant to eliminate them.[27] Only a minority of individual TDs report receiving any financial support from their local branches. Of TDs interviewed in my 2010 parliamentary survey, 19 percent admitted to accepting money from these sources, and half of these were from Fine Gael; 50 percent of those TDs who relied on local funds received, on average, 35 percent or less of their overall resources for the campaign from the local organization.[28] Ultimately, the most successful candidates combine reliance on rank-and-file party members and local volunteers with an inner circle of family and friends to cultivate a vibrant and loyal electoral base.[29] Evidence from the Comparative Candidates Survey suggests that the size of the campaign team still has some impact on a candidate's chance of victory. Among nonincumbent candidates from major parties, those that won their races had a mean of 117 party volunteers and 53 personal volunteers, while those that lost had a mean of 81 party volunteers and 48 personal volunteers. In terms of minor party candidates, incumbents had nearly three to four times more party and personal volunteers than nonincumbent candidates. This confirms the critical organizational advantage that officeholders maintain over their rival candidates.

The next level upward from the branches consists of a "constituency council," which includes representatives from each branch within every Dáil constituency; this body also elects officers and has regular meetings. This level coordinates candidate nomination and selection at local, national (i.e., general), and European elections. Above the constituency level is the national conference (called the "*ard fheis*" for Fianna Fáil, Sinn Féin, and the PDs). Party conferences are held annually and typically are better attended in election years. Historically, these conferences have allowed members to have their voices heard and to engage parliamentary members and the party leadership in debate. The highest organizational level of Irish parties is the national executive, which consists of the party leader (and deputy leader), nationally elected officers, and other elected members, including parliamentary leaders and membership representatives. Irish political parties have relied heavily on the party leader both to instill a vision for the party and to rally the grassroots to action.

In recent years, major parties have found additional organizational vehicles outside the micro level to energize party faithful, attract unattached voters, and balance local and national interests. Fianna Fáil initiated a regional structure in the mid-2000s, whereby four paid officers are assigned to bolster the party. They are charged with increasing responsiveness to emergent local issues. These regional representatives are, in the words of Dorgan, "expected to go to meetings, to be talking to TDs, candidates, councillors, and interested people, and they are expected to make sure that the general secretary is briefed on what is going on. If I am briefed, the party leaders are briefed."[30] Fine Gael implemented a similar structure at the regional level. Five full-time organizers cover different regions: two are active in Dublin, where the party experienced significant electoral erosion between 1987 and 2007.[31] The shift toward paid regional officers is evidence of the diminished reliance on local branches, as well as the intrusive role for the national party in controlling every level of the organization.

The organizational life of Irish parties also supports ancillary and affiliate organizations, the most important of which are youth and women's organizations, but they can also include farmers, unions, and local county and town councillors. These groups were founded in the 1970s as the parties regenerated themselves after crushing electoral defeats (Fianna Fáil between 1973 and 1977, Fine Gael between 1977 and 1981).[32] Fianna Fáil and Fine Gael have well-established youth wings (Ógra Fianna Fáil and Young Fine Gael), which are active during election campaigns as roving groups of canvassers are brought in to "hit" certain constituencies. Involving young people (the bulk of them recruited from families who traditionally supported the party) has been an important element in sustaining the continued electoral vitality of the larger parties. In fact, one of the main organizational responses to Fianna Fáil's massive electoral defeat in 2011 has been an attempt to regenerate the party by attracting young supporters. Within two years of this devastating loss, Ógra Fianna Fáil resurfaced as the largest party organization on many of Ireland's largest college campuses, including Trinity College Dublin and University College in Dublin, Cork, and Galway.[33]

One final development within party organizations has been the growing professionalization and centralization of party headquarters. In addition to overseeing the various levels of the organization, the party has increased its focus on policy development and public and media relations. As Irish elections have shifted since 1977 from short-term, local, and volunteer-driven campaigns dependent principally on parochial party machines to campaigns characterized by long-term strategies designed by national campaign committees, the reliance on the media has grown. Greater need exists for a more coordinated approach by parties to ensure a consistent message. These media blitzes focus more on national party leaders and rely heavily on consultants and new technologies, combined with sophisticated market research to target specific constituencies within the electorate.[34]

The modern era of media-dominated campaigns began in Ireland in the 1977 general election, when Séamus Brennan, then the young general secretary of Fianna Fáil, imported the media-savvy campaign techniques he had observed while attending the 1976 U.S. Democratic National Convention. On his return to Ireland, he helped Fianna Fáil to score a landslide victory.[35] Campaigns since then have increasingly focused on how the "message" is communicated through mass media, and in this process, party headquarters have held the reins. This need to develop and communicate a coordinated media campaign has added financial and personnel pressure on political parties already strapped for resources. The advantage once again goes to the major parties, which have greater numbers to staff these campaigns and to raise the necessary financial resources to fund them and which also draw the most media attention.

For example, half of the electorate watched the television debate between the leaders of Fianna Fáil (Taoiseach Bertie Ahern) and Fine Gael (Enda Kenny, leader of the opposition) in the 2007 election.[36] According to RTÉ exit polls, 53 percent believed that Ahern won, compared with only 18 percent who plumped for Kenny.[37] Expanded television coverage in the 2007 election reinforced the trend in Irish politics to focus on the leaders of the two main parties: the debate influenced the late surge of support for Fianna Fáil and Bertie Ahern in the final weeks of the campaign, as 55 percent of voters who made up their mind in the final week voted for Fianna Fáil.[38] Independents and smaller parties complained that the media's focus on the two primary parties' candidates made it practically impossible for them to keep their policies and candidacies in the public eye.

The television debates, combined with the three main parties' daily press conferences during the election and live TV coverage of party conferences, seriously hindered the independents' ability to attract media attention.[39] Press conferences, although perhaps less effective than door-to-door canvassing, shaped voter preferences in several ways. First, 12 percent of respondents in the RTÉ exit poll suggested that choosing the set of ministers that will form the government was the most important determinant of their vote. This factor benefits incumbents on the grounds of experience.[40] Daily press conferences provided governing parties with an opportunity to demonstrate experience as they responded to questions about their policies, and these conferences also revealed the depth of the front-bench teams (made up of ministers or policy spokespersons). Understandably, the major parties generally had more elected TDs and, as a result, deeper benches.

In addition, whereas the three major parties enjoyed regular media coverage of their press conferences, the smaller parties struggled to attract attention, resulting in anorexic coverage of their respective leadership teams and policies.[41] The media spotlight remained unwaveringly on the three major parties, considered the most likely to form a governing coalition. Although some minor parties (and independents) have possessed the potential to broker a successful coalition, the leadership of any government has historically emanated from Fianna Fáil or Fine Gael, further strengthening their role within the party system.

Given the ever-growing relevance of media encounters, the role of party headquarters and party press officers (who script nearly all press conferences, speeches, and press releases) has increased during elections. The party's message is carefully framed for the media as well as for the voters, their ultimate audience. In this sense, the media have become a vital link between Irish parties and voters. More important, the personnel and financial resources required to engage the media are great; the major parties consistently outspend and outperform their minor party challengers.

The Importance of Geographic and Numerical Superiority

As we have seen, Irish voters favor those who look after the needs of the constituency and who reach out to them personally, especially during election campaigns. Although most candidates and their teams try to knock on every single door in their constituency during the campaign, they often rely on local knowledge and contacts to concentrate their ground campaign in areas where they are more likely to attract support. To achieve this level of knowledge and geographic coverage, candidates and parties build and sustain active local machines to go door-to-door on their behalf on a regular basis. INES data (2002, 2007, and 2011) indicate that a large percentage of voters reported voting for a candidate from a party by whom they were directly contacted during the election campaign (fig. 5.1). These data reinforce the importance of making and maintaining these local connections.

According to the 2002 INES, 52 percent of voters who were contacted by Fianna Fáil voted for that party, nearly double the rate achieved by any other party. Fine Gael's numbers increased in 2007 and even more dramatically in 2011, a reflection of the improved efficiency of party organization. All the opposition parties in 2011 had significant gains in making personal contact with voters.[42] Fianna Fáil, absolutely devastated at the polls, was still quite efficient in its organizational outreach, as 43 percent of INES respondents who were contacted by the party cast their vote for them. If it were not for this tenacious organizational reach, Fianna Fáil may have been eliminated altogether, given the mood for "revenge" in the electorate.

This broad organizational reach is important to bear in mind: even though smaller parties have become better at cultivating relationships with potential voters, the major parties maintain advantages in the number—and often quality—of candidates that they can field in elections. In numerical terms, major parties ran more than twice as many candidates as did all of the minor parties together in elections from 1989 to 2011. In the 2011 election, for example, the major parties fielded a total of 248 candidates (for 166 seats), and the minor parties ran just 108. Independents, not included in the comparison between major and minor parties, have seen an increase in candidates as well; there were more than twice as many independent candidates as there were candidates from the minor parties in 2011. The numerical superiority of major parties extends further back than just the

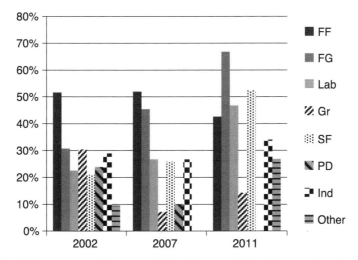

Fig. 5.1. Percentages of Respondents Who Reported Being Contacted by a Party for Which They Voted (INES 2002–11)

late 1980s. In all elections since 1948, major parties have fielded 69 percent of all candidates, while minor parties have only put forward 15 percent.

The major parties also appear to have accumulated larger numbers of quality candidates. The ability to nurture a local organization capable of attracting and mobilizing voters in greater numbers depends on having a strong candidate. The major parties have proven adept at this crucial first step. As we shall see later in the chapter, over 80 percent of all TDs since 1973 were local councillors before being elected to the national parliament. Given that the major parties have the edge on local councils too, they rely on these already proven local organizers to run for national office and to take advantage of their local networks to staff their campaigns and raise sufficient financial resources.

In addition, a deeper pool of supporters working on behalf of candidates allows for broader and more effective opportunities to cultivate their relationships with loyal voters and influence potential ones. Ultimately, the foundation for all other organizational capacity is having active, visible candidates who make personal connections in local contexts, and the major parties continue to thrive in this respect across much of the country. Dublin poses the greatest challenge for the two Civil War parties, because they have experienced serious declines in their electoral support there. They have had greater difficulty maintaining ties with that urban electorate because it is more anonymous, more fractured, and less connected.

The Resource Advantage for Major Parties

It is not surprising that greater reliance on financial resources impacts party competition in Ireland. As in other advanced democracies, a study based on the 2002 election found that "all things considered, the candidates that outspend the others are much more likely to be winners."[43] In a highly competitive and uncertain electoral market, pressure has mounted for candidates to spend their way to victory. Although limits on television advertising level the playing field somewhat, there is inexorable pressure to spend more.[44] Nevertheless, as reported by the Standards in Public Office Commission, any attempts to relax the limits on campaign expenditures would inevitably lead to additional advertising that "will grow in line with that increase, as will the gap between those, both individuals and parties, who are in a position to incur higher levels of expenditure and those who are not."[45]

Although deeper financial resources are increasingly necessary to be successful in Irish politics, tracking the actual trends is very difficult. Annual reports from the Standards in Public Office Commission are self-admittedly not capturing the resources used to fund the electoral activities of parties. There have been slight spikes in political donations for the years in which there was a general election (1997, 2002, 2007), but these levels still do not accurately reflect what political insiders suggest is actually being raised and spent.[46] For example, these figures indicate that Sinn Féin received more donations than even Fianna Fáil in 2001 and 2007, which is highly unlikely given the size of the two parties. However, besides this anomalous finding, Fianna Fáil enjoyed a substantial edge over the other parties during this period, with very small differences separating the remainder of the parties, including Fine Gael—the second-largest party at the time.

A more telling indicator of the financial advantage of the larger parties can be found in the report on the 2007 election from the Standards in Public Office Commission. Total spending was largely consonant with the relative electoral outcomes for the respective political parties. The parties that received the most votes nationally also spent more money during the campaign, in approximately the same proportions. Fianna Fáil's total expenditures were the highest, at €3.7 million, followed by Fine Gael at €2.8 million, the Labour Party at €1.5 million, the Progressive Democrats at just over €1 million, Sinn Féin at less than €700,000, and the Green Party at €550,000.[47]

The major parties have maintained their financial advantage by relying on a greater diversity of funding sources as well as by increasing the amount of state subsidies provided to winning candidates and parties. Major parties and their candidates have therefore been able to reinforce their organizational advantage by maintaining this financial one, which, in turn, has helped consolidate the strong incumbency effect in Irish elections. The two most common sources of financial support for Irish political parties during the period between 1997 and 2006 were business interests and private individuals.[48] Fianna Fáil and the PDs, the two parties in government at that time, received the highest proportion of their donations from business, industry, and the private sector: 85 percent and 70 percent, respectively, compared with only 55 percent for Fine Gael, 6 percent for Labour, and zero for Sinn Féin.[49] Furthermore, within this category, construction and property developers accounted for 32 percent (FF) and 34 percent (PDs) of donations during this boom period—a finding that came under considerable scrutiny in the tribunals investigating inappropriate relationships between politicians and developers in the 1980s and 1990s.[50] Fine Gael relied most on individual donations (45 percent), followed by the PDs (30 percent), Fianna Fáil (15 percent), and Labour (4 percent), with Sinn Féin once again reporting no donations in this category. Trade unions (64 percent) and elected representatives' salaries (26 percent) were the primary sources for Labour's donations during this period. Sinn Féin was unique in that 77 percent of its donations in this period came from international supporters.[51]

Unwillingness or inability to attract donations from corporations and business interests has greatly limited party financing across the board. For example, Fine Gael experienced a short-lived, if highly principled, episode of not accepting corporate donations under the leadership of Michael Noonan, a strategic choice that was jettisoned after Fine Gael's collapse in 2002—an electoral disaster attributed subsequently to the weak organizational and financial status of the party under Noonan's leadership.[52] Pat Rabbitte, former leader of the Labour Party, stated in 2007 that his party members genuinely wanted to compete with Fianna Fáil and Fine Gael for more seats but were reluctant to admit that this required more money and even less willing to acknowledge the need to solicit private donations more aggressively. The Labour Party grudgingly tolerated Rabbitte raising external financial support to offset the costs of a sophisticated media and public relations campaign.[53] Yet Labour's reluctance to go wholeheartedly down the path of private solicitation ensured that it still lagged considerably behind Fianna Fáil and Fine Gael in terms of corporate donations; only 6 percent of its donations came from businesses during this period. The smaller parties and independents have been less willing to accept donations from corporations and business interests altogether (with the exception of the PDs), which has inhibited their ability to grow organizationally.[54] That the governing parties received more resources from businesses implies that businesses are quick to back the parties that have proven proficient at advancing the interests of the private sector. The smaller parties once again miss out, and Labour's ties to unions make it more difficult for them to attract support from business interests. This has left the two major parties as the primary beneficiaries of corporate support and has further challenged the other parties' ability to compete organizationally with them.

Labour still received a majority of its declared financial donations (64 percent) from trade unions between 1997 and 2005, yet it consistently won a smaller proportion of the union vote in elections than Fianna Fáil. Labour's reluctance to raise funds among the private sector added a further limiting financial constraint on the organizational capacity of the party. Between 2006 and 2011, Labour slightly altered the sources of its financial support, disclosing that 58 percent of the party's donations were from business, industry, and the private sector; 21 percent from individuals; and 20 percent from trade unions.[55]

Because minor parties and independents have had little access to corporate donations, they have had to compensate by finding alternative funding sources such as TD salaries, international donations, and even personal wealth. These limited sources retard the ability of these parties to expand organizationally. For example, because a vast majority of its donations come from Sinn Féin organizations abroad, Sinn Féin has gained a majority of its financial donations from those who do not or, in this case, cannot vote for the party in elections. A unique feature of that party is that all its elected officials accept the equivalent salary of the average industrial wage and turn the remainder over to the party to help maintain the organization. Sinn Féin now resembles the Fianna Fáil of the 1930s and 1940s in its ambition to create a national movement rather than to present itself as a mere conventional political party, and it relies more heavily than the other parties do on committed party militants from both sides of the border. This profile has allowed Sinn Féin to compete with the other parties despite having fewer financial resources at its disposal. The Green Party also reported that 95 percent of its national party donations between 2006 and 2011 were from the party's elected officials. This practice not only limited the resources the party brought in but also illustrates the challenge the party faced in getting voters to "put their money where their mouth is" in terms of their support for environmental issues in politics.

The other primary means by which Ireland's major parties consolidated their resource advantage was by increasing state subsidies for winning candidates and parties, both during campaigns and while in office. Unlike many countries in Western Europe, Ireland's political parties receive comparatively low levels of public financing. A 2002 commission found that TDs were significantly underresourced when compared with other parliaments internationally. Parliament began to address this issue in the late 1990s in response to the criticism that parties had become far too dependent on the business community for financial resources.[56] Increases in state support for parties included higher salaries for TDs, senators, and committee chairs; better budgets for staff support; and greater numbers of state-funded personnel for the parties in parliament.[57] Parties represented in the Dáil were awarded additional staff and infrastructure resources based on their number of seats.[58] Many of these resources contributed directly or indirectly to political campaigns, whether by helping staff donate larger sums to parties or by allowing TDs to pursue a higher volume of casework and credit claiming. These increases have strengthened the major parties, marking a dramatic shift from the late 1980s, when many TDs lacked sufficient funds to run an office.[59] The increase in state funding has made party organizations even more dependent on national party leaders for many aspects of party activity, because resources are now funneled through the leaders' offices.[60]

These additional resources have also been helpful for smaller parties, but they have not been enough to push newer parties over the entry barrier within electoral politics. Facing a perpetual uphill battle in raising money to fund their operations, state resources have permitted the smaller parties an opportunity—in some cases for the first time—to professionalize their operations. However, because the major parties are awarded the lion's share of state funding, their already considerable financial and organizational advantage has been strengthened even further.[61]

The major parties receive more financial support each year, in terms of both funding of party leaders and qualified party funding, because these benefits are allocated on the basis of a pro rata share of the vote. In 2007, state resources accounted for 16 percent of Fianna Fáil spending, 7 percent of Fine Gael spending, and 10 percent of Labour spending. In contrast, the percentage of overall spending for the smaller parties supplied by the state was 4 percent for the PDs, 5 percent for Sinn Féin, and 1 percent for the Greens.[62] In the 2002 election, the percentage of publicly allocated funding unused by the major parties was considerably smaller (FF, 13 percent; FG, 21 percent; Labour, 33 percent) than that of smaller parties (PDs, 13 percent; SF, 57 percent; Greens, 78 percent).[63] The major parties receive more than the minor parties, and because of the professional and technical resources at their disposal, they have also been more efficient at deploying these resources once allocated.

Financial Resources for Incumbent TDs

In addition to the overall funding for the various parties, it is useful to examine the resources available to individual candidates. Like their parties, candidates from the major parties enjoy a financial advantage over candidates from the smaller parties and independents. Whereas the major parties report between half and two-thirds of their donations as supporting the national party and the remainder flowing to local candidates, nearly all of the donations received by the smaller parties went directly to the national party, leaving individual candidates strapped for cash. As a result, fewer candidates want to run for office under minor party labels, because they are even more likely to accumulate debt when doing so, not to mention the uphill battle they will face on other fronts. Despite a growing proportion of major party money going to candidates in general, the national party headquarters of all parties generally offer scant financial support to individual candidates, forcing candidates to rely on either constituency-based fund-raising or their own personal campaign contributions.

According to evidence from my parliamentary surveys, a vast majority of TDs from across all the parties report receiving little or no financial support from their parties during general election campaigns. Although the major parties have resources to fund their national campaigns, individual candidates and incumbent TDs from all parties must generate a substantial share of their own money. This dynamic further reinforces highly personalized campaigns at the constituency level. My 2010 parliamentary survey revealed that, on average, TDs received less than 10 percent of their funding from their national parties during the 2007 election. Forty-one percent of respondents indicated that they received no funds from national headquarters. Table 5.1 reveals the percentages of sources that the average TD relied on to finance the 2007 campaign: 53 percent from their own resources, 10 percent from the national party, 17 percent from individual donations, 6 percent from corporate donors, and 13 percent from "other" sources. The only statistically significant result from the analysis undertaken using the data from my survey pertained to how much major party TDs relied on individual donations; otherwise, one's party identification did not significantly influence how individual campaigns were funded in

2007. There were only slight changes in the 2011 campaign, where the average TD relied on the following sources: 49 percent from personal funds, 21 percent from the national party, 13 percent from individual donations, only 1 percent from corporate donors, and 14 percent from "other" sources. TDs reported an increase, from the 2007 election, of 11 percentage points in their reliance on the national party, as well as a drop by 5 percentage points in corporate donations and a decline by 4 percentage points in individual donations. Both parliamentary surveys support the view that the financial challenges of individual TDs are very different from those facing national parties.

Not surprisingly, incumbents experience a significant advantage given the growing costs of elections and the advantages that major parties and their candidates enjoy. Between 1918 and 2007, 71 percent of incumbents who have run for reelection have been returned to the Dáil. (In the 2011 election, 65 percent of TDs seeking reelection won, but given that this election experienced the highest number ever of TDs choosing not to run again (39), incumbents made up only 49 percent of the new Dáil—well below the norm.[64]) By comparison, the reelection rates of incumbents in the U.S. House and Senate between 1964 and 2006 were 93 percent and 82 percent, respectively.[65] In an earlier comparative study of twenty-five countries, Ireland had the fourth-highest incumbency return rate, at 76 percent, behind the United States, Australia, and Germany (85, 80, and 79 percent, respectively). Ireland was comparable to the United Kingdom (76 percent) and slightly ahead of Japan, Sweden, New Zealand, and Malta. The overall average of countries in the study was 68 percent.[66]

Candidates from smaller parties often possess less political experience

TABLE 5.1. TDs' Sources of Campaign Funding for the 2007 General Election (%)

Party	Personal/ salary	National party	Individual donations	Corporate donations	Other sources
Fianna Fáil	53.4	8.9	20.9	7.5	8.5
Fine Gael	53.7	12.7	11.1	4.2	16.4
Labour	50.2	8.8	23.9	4.3	10.4
Greens	70.0	8.8	13.8	0.0	7.5
Sinn Féin	11.7	10.0	11.7	3.3	60.0
Independents	56.2	0.0	6.3	12.5	25.0
Total	52.5	9.7	17.3	5.8	13.3

Note: Similar to the analysis in the previous chapter, the null hypothesis is that partisan differences do not influence the source of a TD's funding. The party dummies are all zero, and the question is whether the equation reveals enough information to reject the null. The reference category is the breakdown of funding for minor party TDs, which means that the coefficients for the three major parties indicate how many percentage points more or less the major party TDs rely on the different sources to finance their campaigns.

and notoriety to attract support from voters and also lack the organizational acumen to know how best to raise adequate funds. First-time candidates from smaller parties face an even more daunting uphill battle. New candidates have to spend additional money simply to gain name recognition to be successful. Evidence from the Comparative Candidates Survey reveals that minor party challengers spend approximately €14,700 on their campaigns, major party incumbents spend nearly twice this amount (averaging €27,800), and major party challenger candidates spend almost thrice this amount (an average of €38,000). Challenger candidates from major party organizations clearly enjoy an advantage because they can rely on larger pools of support, but they also need to raise additional funds to gain selection in their party. As a new candidate, Lucinda Creighton, a Fine Gael TD elected for the first time in 2007 to a seat in the Dublin South-East constituency, needed to spend more on publicity than her more experienced opponents in the eighteen months preceding the formal election campaign. An aggressive fund-raiser, Creighton recruited a cadre of volunteers to stage fund-raising events. Unlike candidates from smaller parties, however, 15 percent of Creighton's campaign expenses were covered by her national party that year, as Fine Gael focused efforts to win seats in Dublin.[67]

First-time candidates from the smaller parties generally did not attract a similar level of support from their party's headquarters. For example, Green Party and Sinn Féin candidates in Kerry South entered the 2007 campaign with only three weeks remaining, largely because their parties were unable to find candidates willing to assume the financial burden required to run a viable campaign.[68] These candidates ran at the last minute on a shoestring and on only a part-time basis, mostly as "testimonial" candidates to raise the profile of their party. In other instances, challenger parties enjoyed popular support but were unable to secure candidates because of financial and organizational obstacles. A recent noteworthy example was the case of Democracy Now, led by several media and sports celebrities who were riding the wave of popular discontent due to Ireland's economic and political crises in 2011. Ultimately, they chose not to field candidates, due to financial and other organizational constraints.[69]

Like first-time candidates and candidates from smaller parties, independents are more vulnerable organizationally and financially than major party candidates. Initial success inevitably catalyzes a reaction against them by their more institutionalized and organizationally robust competitors, who relentlessly target their seats in subsequent elections. Since the foundation of the Irish Free State in 1922, 60 percent of independent TDs failed to win reelection; of those who were reelected, only 20 percent won reelection between 1973 and 2011.[70] Fourteen independents were elected in 2002, but only five gained election in 2007; this figure rose to fourteen again in 2011. It is easier to target an independent candidate than a party, as the former does not enjoy reliance on core electoral support. Major parties can also employ their resources to bolster support outside the formal election period. Ultimately, this link between organizational and financial strength has allowed candidates from the larger parties to enjoy an electoral advantage. The fifteen independent candidates elected in the watershed 2011 election must overcome these organizational handicaps to survive beyond one term.

Ireland's major parties enjoy geographical, numerical, and financial superiority over their minor party rivals. The major parties have benefited from certain advantages from the outset of the party system and have relied on their organizational strengths to maintain these advantages. The remainder of this chapter provides further evidence for why Ireland's major parties have proven to be so flexible organizationally and how they have adapted their organizational strategies at both the national and local levels to electorally outperform minor parties over the longer term.

Organizational Autonomy and Flexibility

In addition to the major parties' geographic and numerical superiority, they have developed flexible internal structures and procedures that have allowed them to adapt more readily to Ireland's constantly changing social and electoral environments. Consistent with Levitsky's findings in the case of Argentina, higher levels of leadership autonomy in Ireland's major parties have enhanced the degree of flexibility enjoyed by party leaders. This organizational flexibility has further advanced major parties' longer-term electoral predominance, especially when contrasted with the experience of minor party leaders who enjoy lower levels of organizational autonomy. Once again, a longitudinal and multidimensional approach is important to highlight why this is the case.

From the founding of the state, Ireland's major parties enjoyed strong partisan attachments with broad, cross-class programmatic appeal. As we saw in chapter 3, they have been relatively free to engage ideological competition more pragmatically and to mobilize voters by relying heavily on strong personalistic ties in local communities. The resulting, relatively fluid nature of ideological appeals has lent major party leaders an unusual degree of autonomy and flexibility to structure internal party organization, including granting individual candidates and constituencies the freedom to run their campaigns as they see fit. Although major party leaders established sets of rules and procedures for how leadership would be exercised within their parties, they have consistently modified these organizational structures as society and elections have changed. In sum, the populist origins, strong mass links, and fluid ideological appeals of Ireland's major parties combined to give their leaders the organizational flexibility they regularly employ.

By contrast, the leaders of Ireland's minor parties have not enjoyed a similar degree of organizational autonomy and flexibility. As discussed in chapter 3, Ireland's minor parties have adopted a more ideological profile, often presenting themselves as more internally "democratic" than their opponents. The more a party relies on any one programmatic position or one specific social group for its electoral success, the harder it is for party leaders to adapt their positions when conditions change. Likewise, the more a party employs internally democratic practices to determine, for example, how it selects its policies or chooses leaders, the more difficult it is for party leaders to change strategies quickly. As a result, Ireland's minor party leaders have enjoyed much less autonomy and flexibility than their major party counterparts.

The flexibility and autonomy of Ireland's major parties have proven critical to their success. As elections in the recent period have included candidates from more parties and as the length of campaigns has swollen to the point where cycles of general and local elections follow one another in rapid succession, all parties have been forced to renew their membership continuously at local and national levels. This necessity has enhanced the authority of national party leaders, the parliamentary party, and party headquarters, with an attendant decrease in the influence exercised by members and local branches. Growing reliance on professionalization has increased the cadre of full-time employees serving party leaders and the parliamentarians.[71] Party headquarters have become decisively involved in determining every aspect of elections, from policy to candidate selection.[72] Although national party leaders still ostensibly include local members and branches in the process of candidate selection, their role is diminished. By contrast, the smaller parties provide rank-and-file members with a genuine voice in determining policy formation and coalition strategies. They do this partly to differentiate themselves from their competitors and to compensate for the organizational handicap that prevents them from employing the resources that major parties take for granted, such as media and campaign consultants. Short on professional staffs, smaller parties depend on volunteers. In sum, major party leaders enjoy greater autonomy and flexibility vis-à-vis their rank-and-file membership, which has allowed them to adapt more readily to competitive dynamics that emerge within each election.

There are several noteworthy trends when one considers the various ways in which parties select candidates and party leaders and decide on policy. In terms of candidate selection, the main difference between major and minor parties is that major parties have a much larger pool of interested and potentially viable candidates from which to choose, while minor parties may only have one or two candidates interested in running. Therefore, the major parties' selection process entails candidates demonstrating their organizational prowess. Successful major party candidates must gain sufficient support from within the local organization to be nominated, but national party leaders play a pivotal role in this process and can, in most cases, name additional candidates or even disregard local recommendations. As later sections will illustrate, part of major party leaders' strategy to more effectively mobilize the vote and manage transfers of lower-preference votes within each constituency is to retain a higher level of control over candidate selection. Party headquarters have managed candidate selection ever since the 1997 general election.[73] Fianna Fáil, Fine Gael, and Sinn Féin have the highest level of involvement from party headquarters in candidate selection.[74] In response to competition from all parties, Fianna Fáil removed the guaranteed reselection of incumbent TDs in 2002, to ensure that candidates maintain party loyalty and to incentivize the continuous cultivating of strong local party machines.[75] This shift is consistent with Levitsky's observation in the Argentinian case that more flexible parties facilitate renovation in party leadership. Although a tried-and-true path to higher levels of leadership within Ireland's major parties remains in place, this change in the rules for candidate selection strengthens the hand of central leadership. Candidates are thereby encouraged to work continually, between elections and not just in the periods leading up to election campaigns, to strengthen and sustain their personal networks within the constituency. Again, the smaller parties, notably the Greens (and previously the PDs), have experienced considerable difficulty in attracting viable local candidates, leaving them more reliant on those simply willing to put their names forward.[76] The financial, organizational, and personal resources required to run an effective campaign often take years to establish. Furthermore, developing such an organization is even more difficult if one lacks connections on local councils or in the Dáil to help them provide access to state goods and services for their constituents. Without significant numbers of party members serving on local councils, minor parties also lack the best route to identify, test, and train new candidates.

Yet another organizational strategy that national party leaders employ to outflank recalcitrant local party leaders and candidates while energizing the rank and file has been to allow party members to vote directly for a particular candidate. The introduction of the "one person, one vote" principle into the internal party processes was intended to weaken the hold of long-standing party cadres. In the past, that local notables stacked the local branch with a handful of supportive delegates was sufficient to ensure their candidacy. The introduction of procedures that are more democratic has forced major party candidates to develop broader networks of supporters, because there are greater numbers of members voting during the nomination stage. Thus, internal voting procedures that are more democratic were rationalized in terms of mobilizing the base. For major parties, the stage of candidate selection helps national party leaders observe which candidates can develop the organizational wherewithal to compete successfully during elections. Although introducing voting procedures that are more democratic was intended to mobilize more supporters, rather than surrendering candidate selection to the rank and file altogether, major party leaders have identified highly visible and "electable" candidates and placed them on local selection ballots, thereby powerfully shaping the available choice. Voting for these handpicked candidates differs from what generally occurs in smaller parties, where the participatory process is seen as essential to the nature of the party. While the smaller parties have generally employed approaches to candidate selection that are more democratic, the larger parties have moved in the direction of shaping the choices available to the voters. For example, Fianna Fáil's party headquarters shifted toward internal party elections in urban areas after its disastrous local and European elections in 2009, where their numbers slipped behind Labour and Fine Gael on the Dublin City Council. Considering the absolute electoral wipeout they suffered in the capital in 2011, this shift accentuates the unusual degree of organizational flexibility enjoyed by the major party leaders, which makes possible these evolving organizational strategies.

The methods by which Irish parties select leaders at the national level have varied widely. At one extreme, Fianna Fáil's party leader is elected exclusively by sitting TDs, ensuring that the leader enjoys the loyalty of parliamentary colleagues. This selection process is crucial for maintaining party unity and discipline, as TDs depend on the party leader for their own promotion to cabinet and other positions in future governments.[77] Once elected, the Fianna Fáil leader enjoys a high degree of relative autonomy to chart the party's course with respect to personnel, ideology, and overall party organization. Fine Gael employs different combinations of TDs, local representatives, and party members in the election of their national leaders. Labour and the Greens occupy the opposite end of the spectrum, employing a "one person, one vote" method within the party rank and file. These latter two parties have successfully catalyzed the participation and identity of rank-and-file members through these internal party elections. Finally, Sinn Féin nominally "elects" its party president each year at the party conference (*ard fheis*). However, Gerry Adams has run unopposed since 1983. In general, the shift toward a mode of electing leaders that is more democratic has been one of the primary ways that smaller parties have sought to animate current members and attract new ones. At a time when central offices of all parties are assuming greater control over nearly every dimension of party organization, involving the rank and file in leadership elections enhances their sense of belonging. The drawback for party leaders, of course, is that a more mobilized rank and file often demands a greater voice in policy, thereby imposing a limiting factor on the ability of the leaders of smaller parties to adopt opportunistic electoral strategies.

Policy formation is the realm in which major party parliamentarians and party leaders wield the most autonomy and authority and where the rank and file is least involved. Fianna Fáil, Fine Gael, and Labour each allow members to raise concerns at their respective annual party conferences, but specific policy formulation remains exclusively with the parliamentary party's policy committee and the front-benchers. Whereas party conferences historically were platforms for debating policy among members and parliamentary leaders, this organizational arena has evanesced in an era dominated by television and the mass media. The media presence at party conferences has altered the character of the debates: the attention has shifted toward projecting a polished image to the broader electorate rather than airing potentially acrimonious differences in public. Conor Lenihan, former Fianna Fáil TD and minister as well as the son of a celebrated Fianna Fáil front-bencher, describes the evolving functions of the party conference: "The 1980s saw the end of activist power over policy, and since then, power in the policy sense is a function of the parliamentary elite and the party's advisors. Its current importance lies in its ability to generate publicity, send messages to activists and the public, and, more than anything else, boost morale."[78] Therefore, from an organizational standpoint, members exert little influence over policy, in stark contrast to the influence they previously held.[79]

The Green Party once again represents the opposite end of the spectrum in terms of membership involvement in determining policy. Although the impetus for programmatic appeals remains centrally driven, the Greens have a more formal consultative process involving the rank and file. Specifically, the Greens have held party conventions to determine party strategy on such momentous decisions as whether to enter into a governing coalition in 2007 (and to stay in the coalition in 2009) and whether to support the Lisbon Treaty in 2008 and 2009. In these cases, party members and the leaders of the parliamentary party conducted a lively public debate and then put them to a vote of all party members. The party ignored advice by its party leader to leave government in September 2010, because a majority of the members were committed to securing legislation on climate change, although doing so meant that they would likely lose favor with the electorate on a broader set of issues.[80] The Greens, therefore, represent a more policy-driven and democratically focused "aggregator" type of party; they will not endorse certain measures without the declared support of the party membership.[81] The Greens have held party votes on key aspects of electoral strategy in referenda and general election campaigns. This inclusion of the rank and file has limited the autonomy and organizational flexibility enjoyed by Green Party leaders.

In contrast to the Greens, Fianna Fáil has been the least internally democratic in its election of leaders, in its formation of policy, and even, more recently, in the realm of candidate selection. Evidence from my parliamentary survey reinforces the differences between major and minor parties in terms of how they select their policies. Table 5.2 indicates the average distance between a TD's position and the perceived official party position on specific policies. We generally assume that grassroots activists and members tend to be more policy driven and extreme in their ideological positions, whereas top leaders tend to be more centrist and electorally motivated. Therefore, when TDs are more centrist than the party, policy is likely influenced by the grassroots, and when TDs are less centrist than the party, policy is likely driven by central leaders. The findings confirm the claim that when making choices about policy, Ireland's major parties are more top-down than minor parties. Major party TDs in the parliamentary survey reported a greater gap between their position and their party's position, which implies that the party platform is most likely set by party leaders rather than TDs' sincere preferences. In contrast, minor party TDs hold policy views more closely in line with their party's official platform. Although minor party TDs were less extreme on social issues, they seem to

TABLE 5.2. Average Reported Difference between TDs' Position and Their Party's Position (2007)

	Left-right (positive is right)	Northern Ireland (positive is abandon)	Spending (positive is more social spending)	European Union (positive is pro-Europe)	Environment (positive is antiprotection)	Abortion (positive is ban abortion)
Fianna Fáil	−.77	−.38	.68	−.11	−.07	.23
Fine Gael	−.68	.13	.10	−.13	−.19	.11
Labour	−.81	.19	.13	.50	−.44	.44
Greens	.00	.00	−.25	1.50	1.00	2.33
Sinn Féin	.00	.00	−.33	1.00	1.00	−.33
Total	−.70	−.10	.34	.08	−.10	.28

perceive a great deal of ideological convergence between themselves and their parties, as indicated on the left-right placement.

Consistent with expectations of vote-seeking, "hunter" parties that have broad, catchall appeal, of which Fianna Fáil is the prime example within the Irish context, the unusually high degree of autonomy and flexibility that major party leaders enjoy in virtually every aspect has been used to their advantage. Historically, Fianna Fáil relied on a die-hard support base willing to grant its leaders considerable leeway. Although Fianna Fáil's core support has declined in recent years, it still enjoys the support of 30 percent of those voters who claim to be close to any particular party.[82] Both its ability to navigate and balance the competing demands of rank-and-file loyalty and the organizational flexibility enjoyed by its party leaders are keys to understanding the electoral success of major parties over the longer term.

Organizational Strength at National and Local Levels

Ireland's major parties also enjoy stronger organizational links at the local and national levels. Possessing more elected officials consistently at both levels has served to advance the electoral interests of the major parties. Balancing the sometimes contradictory demands for greater centralization at the level of party headquarters with an appropriate degree of flexibility and autonomy at the level of individual candidates and their local organizations has also been important for ongoing major party success.

Greater centralization helps national party organizations coordinate their candidate selection and vote management to maximize their vote during competitive elections. A few votes in either direction can dramatically alter outcomes. This organizational centralization can reinforce the major parties' advantages once they are elected, due to their ability to channel state resources in targeted ways. Meanwhile, strong local "franchises" help parties establish ties with an increasingly unattached electorate. That nearly 40 percent of Irish voters prefer a candidate who looks after the needs of the constituency reinforces the significance of TDs prepared to serve as community and social workers at the local level. A review of how major party leaders deal with this delicate balance between robust organizations at the national and local levels will illustrate precisely how major parties have been able to sustain their longer-term electoral predominance.

Establishing a Local Machine

Successful candidates in Irish elections have effective local machines that consist of loyal personal and party supporters who help TDs stay connected on the ground throughout the constituency. Gaining the nomination is more about having the right personal qualities and the ability to cultivate a network around one's self than it is about policy differences. Much depends, therefore, on how effective candidates are at generating a personal network at the local level. Unlike party competition in many advanced industrial democracies, where political parties generally mobilize specific constituencies within civil society largely by deepening affiliations with leading social groups, Irish parties seek support from voters across all social demographic groups. Successful candidates must identify and foster relationships with leading individuals in every local community across the constituency, and the candidates depend on these influential community members to get their message out. Successful Irish candidates also generally cultivate a smaller and more active inner circle of supporters who sustain and deepen these relationships.

One of the most effective ways in which Irish parliamentarians have established their credibility is by inheriting a local machine from a family member. The inherited local machine gives them an advantage during their initial campaign and a foundation they can consolidate, through sustained effort, in subsequent campaigns. Since 1922, family members of previous TDs have occupied 10 percent of all Dáil seats. On average, this number has increased to 18 percent since 1965, when a majority of the politicians from the Civil War era reached the end of their careers. Prior to 1965, Fine Gael had the most family legacies in parliament, but Fianna Fáil overtook

Fine Gael and dominated in this respect until Fianna Fáil's electoral collapse in 2011. The three historic parties have been far more successful than their minor party competitors in securing family seats. In fact, 92 percent of all TDs who have held family seats are from these established parties, with Fianna Fáil (46 percent) and Fine Gael (35 percent) far outperforming the other parties in this method of maintaining strong local ties. To understand how the historic parties have maintained local ties better than their competitors—and therefore to understand their predominance—we must explore the additional methods that parties and candidates employ to consolidate their local machines.

Methods of Outreach

Results from my 2010 parliamentary survey underscore the critical role that personal and local relationships play. When asked what methods of reaching out to voters were most essential to the success of their 2007 campaigns, 63 percent of TDs surveyed responded that door-to-door canvassing was the single most effective means of connecting with voters.[83] In a similar study of the 2011 election, that figure rose to 68 percent. When asked to rate various means of interfacing with voters (measured on a 10-point scale, with 1 denoting "not important at all" and 10 signaling "very important"), the more personal and intimate the means of reaching out to voters in the 2007 election were, the higher the ratings were among the TDs. As table 5.3 shows, door-to-door canvassing (8.6), local constituency newsletters (6.4), and personal letters (5.8) were rated higher than less-personal contact, such as national party literature (4.3), the Internet (3.6), or even larger-scale rallies (3.6).

Using a basic multivariate regression model, I examined whether TDs' party membership affected their assessments of various techniques in a statistically significant way. The results indicate that the TDs' party affili-

TABLE 5.3. Ordinary Least Squares Estimates of TDs' Assessments of the Importance of Methods Used to Inform Voters (2007 Election)

	Mean	Fianna Fáil	Fine Gael	Labour
Methods of contacting voters				
Door-to-door canvassing	8.62	8.9	9.2	9.6
Rallies	3.56	3.0	3.7	4.0
Methods of informing voters				
Personal letters*	5.83	5.6	7.8	8.4
Newsletters	6.37	5.7	7.4	6.8
Internet	3.64	3.6	3.7	4.3
National party literature*	4.33	4.8	6.0	6.2

ations did not affect the ratings of these different campaign methods.[84] The only statistically significant estimate was in the case of the utility of personal letters, where Fine Gael and Labour TDs were far more likely to consider them important than were TDs from minor parties. Thus, the tried-and-true means of successful electioneering for candidates regardless of party is establishing and maintaining personal connections with voters. Candidates capable of effectively developing personal linkages with voters have been rewarded for their efforts. Successful canvassing requires time, numbers, the willingness of candidates to campaign year-round, and an ability to listen to the needs of constituents. This finding would seem to help minor parties, because canvassing is a low-cost method of reaching voters. However, the reception candidates receive on the doorstep is influenced by what candidates can offer in return, such as access to public goods and services. Because the major parties have already limited the extent to which ideological differences shape voter preferences, the ability to deliver for the constituency is what remains to distinguish candidates among voters. Therefore, major parties possess an inherent organizational advantage even when canvassing, because of what they can promise to the people they meet.

Successful TDs clearly perceive the importance of these local connections. When asked to rate the factors that influenced why voters supported them in the 2007 and 2011 elections, TDs consistently rated local factors highest (see tables 5.4–5). If one considers the factors rated in the top three for both elections, local and personal factors score higher than party factors such as policy, party leader, and national party organization. TDs of all parties rated their campaign as among the top three reasons why constituents voted for them in both elections. Other top reasons why TDs perceived that voters supported them include local organization (FF, FG, and SF), the TD's personality (FG, Labour, and SF), experience in office (Labour and SF) and constituency service (FF). Party policy only appeared as highly significant for Fine Gael TDs in 2011, but it was much less important for the other parties. Perhaps not surprisingly, Fianna Fáil TDs downplayed their party policies, party leader, and national organization in 2011. Overall, in the eyes of TDs, local factors and establishing strong local connections greatly outweighed other factors in explaining why their constituents voted for them.

One of the most common means by which successful candidates develop their organizational advantage is by establishing a local machine. Successful candidates build a tight local organization around supporters who are dedicated to them personally. Celebrated vote getter Frank Fahey (former

TABLE 5.4. Top Three Answers of TDs in 2007 Election to "How important was each of the following in determining why people voted for you in the last election?" (1–10 Scale)

	First answer	Second answer	Third answer
Fianna Fáil	Campaign (8.2)	Constituency service / local organization (7.9)	Constituency service / local organization (7.9)
Fine Gael	Campaign (8.2)	Local organization / personality (7.6)	Local organization / personality (7.6)
Labour	Campaign (8.4)	Experience in office / personality (7.9)	Experience in office / personality (7.9)
Sinn Féin	Party leader (8.3)	Campaign (8.0)	Personality / local organization / constituency service (7.3)
Greens	Constituency service (7.5)	Experience in office (7.3)	Campaign (7.0)
Independents	Local organization (10.0)	Campaign (9.0)	Constituency service (8.0)
Total	Campaign (8.2)	Local organization (7.8)	Constituency service (7.5)

TABLE 5.5. Top Three Answers of TDs in 2011 Election to "How important was each of the following in determining why people voted for you in the last election?" (1–10 Scale)

	First answer	Second answer	Third answer
Fianna Fáil	Campaign (7.9)	Constituency service (7.5)	Local organization (7.4)
Fine Gael	Campaign (7.7)	Personality (7.6)	Policies (7.3)
Labour	Campaign (8.2)	Local organization (7.5)	Experience in office / personality (7.2)
Sinn Féin	Campaign (7.8)	Local organization (7.7)	Experience in office (8.5)
People Before Profit Alliance	Local organization / campaign (10.0)	Local organization / campaign (10.0)	Experience in office (8.5)
Socialists	Experience in office (9.0)	Campaign (8.3)	Policies (7.5)
Independents	Campaign (7.8)	Policies (7.5)	Constituency service / experience in office / personality (7.1)
Total	Campaign (7.9)	Local organization / Personality (7.2)	Local organization / personality (7.2)

FF TD for Galway West) suggested that successful candidates must target the most high-profile and community-engaged individuals—doctors, lawyers, teachers, sports coaches, postal carriers, union representatives, housewives, shop owners, publicans, electricians—and that these individuals, in turn, get out the existing vote and identify potential additional supporters.[85] Because of the importance attached to personal relationships, introductions by these local community notables are ultimately more productive than a volunteer army knocking on every door in the constituency. Even canvassing, however, has become more sophisticated for the more successful candidates. Party organizations study the returns from the previous election and determine—with a high degree of accuracy, almost to the level of each individual house—who received first-preference votes and from whom.[86] Such precise information leads candidates to target specific neighborhoods and families in the lead-up for the next election. Voter loyalty is then rewarded with special treatment subsequent to the election, via increased attention from the TD and access to state resources for those areas with growing or already significant levels of support.

Cultivating relationships with local community leaders is even more crucial in recent times, given that the long-standing practice of weekly "clinics," or advice centers, across the constituency are commonly viewed by candidates as less effective than previously. Though holding clinics was more critical in an earlier era, when it was more difficult for individuals to travel to meet with a TD, they are still conducted today.[87] Candidates in the contemporary era hold regular clinics each week in designated pubs, schools, and town halls, especially in the more rural areas.[88] According to a 2010 study of brokerage politics in Ireland, 89 percent of rural TDs and 76 percent of urban TDs engage in clinics.[89] On average, TDs report spending between eight and twelve hours per week in these clinics, with rural TDs spending nearly twice as many hours than their urban counterparts.[90] In an electoral context in which constituency service plays a critical role, advertising these clinics throughout the constituency strengthens the ties with local candidates, benefiting incumbents in particular. Of TDs who do not hold clinics, 60 percent believe there is no longer a need for them, but 20 percent offer "office hours" in their parliamentary offices in place of meeting throughout the constituency.[91] The personnel and financial resources needed to sustain clinics, attend local meetings, and respond to the hundreds of individual requests for favors that come across a TD's desk each week place considerable pressure on a local politician's organization.

A well-trod Irish phenomenon is the expectation that TDs attend funerals or wakes within their constituency. This practice, vibrantly alive in more rural areas even today, used to be a common practice even in urban areas. One Dublin politician tells the story of trying to win support by appearing at funerals that Fianna Fáil TD Ray Burke, a prolific campaigner, had over-looked. After many attempts failed because Burke showed up to funerals, the challenger finally found a funeral that was about to begin with the government minister nowhere in the congregation. At the very last moment, Burke materialized, swinging the incense and striding in with the priest and the coffin to serve Mass. Not just a legacy of a more traditional period, such is politics as practiced in Ireland today, although attending funerals is more common in rural than urban constituencies. Sixty percent of rural TDs still agree that attending funerals is important, compared to only 10 percent of urban TDs. Attending funerals remains heavily valued by the historic Civil War parties. For example, in a 2010 study of brokerage politics in Ireland, 73 percent of Fianna Fáil TDs and 68 percent of Fine Gael TDs reported that attending funerals was an important part of their job, whereas only 42 percent of Sinn Féin TDs and 12 percent of Labour TDs reported the same. That younger and more inexperienced politicians are just as likely as their older and more seasoned veteran colleagues to consider this practice as important highlights its ongoing relevance.[92] One young rural Fine Gael TD reported that it is not unusual to attend ten funerals and wakes in one week. This ongoing practice may also help explain why the established parties continue to outperform their minor party challengers in rural constituencies, because the members of the established parties have proven willing and able to perform this tried-and-true local practice.

The People Who Make Up the Local Organization

Given demands on TDs' and candidates' time, personnel, and financial resources, candidates with greater numbers of volunteers and staff have the advantage. Evidence from my two parliamentary surveys reinforces the organizational challenges these practices pose. First, successful candidates must recruit volunteers to mobilize voters during the campaign and to maintain personal links even outside of elections (see table 5.6). Of the major parties, Fianna Fáil and Fine Gael TDs report larger volunteer forces than their Labour colleagues, an accounting that corresponds with the fact that Labour possesses a smaller number of local branches and members. Sinn Féin and People Before Profit TDs indicate fairly significant and regular volunteer support compared with quite small numbers for the Green Party and Socialist TDs. Independents also rely on large numbers of volunteers, compensating for a lack of other resources. The daunting task of mobilizing and coordinating these volunteers can deter some candidates from running in the first place. Once successful, TDs must then maintain these high numbers to remain successful over the medium and longer term.

Greater numbers of volunteers are perhaps even more crucial for smaller party TDs and independents, who cannot rely on a national party for personnel or financial resources. According to my 2010 parliamentary survey, when asked which group of supporters were most essential for the success of their campaigns, over 50 percent of all TDs recognized family as most important; 33 percent, party volunteers; 9 percent, paid staff; and 7 percent, friends (table 5.7). Interestingly, only TDs from the three established parties reported paid staff as important in their 2007 campaigns (FF, 7 percent; FG, 10 percent; Labour, 19 percent). By the 2011 election, Sinn Féin TDs also recognized the importance of paid professionals. Candi-

TABLE 5.6. Number of Volunteers per TD Local Organization (2007 and 2011 Elections)

	During campaign		Since campaign	
	2007	2011	2007	2011
Fianna Fáil	111.4	152.9	32.4	92.6
Fine Gael	114.8	102.0	28.3	33.3
Labour	70.0	56.4	36.8	23.4
Greens	27.5	—	10.0	—
Sinn Féin	180.0	177.5	56.7	69.6
People Before Profit Alliance	—	275.0	—	100.0
Socialists	—	47.5	—	27.5
Independents	214.3	138.0	43.8	70.7
Total	108.7	110.2	32.1	46.9

TABLE 5.7. Groups Most Important for TDs' Campaigns (2010 and 2012 Parliamentary Surveys)

	Family		Friends		Party volunteers		Paid staff	
Party	2007	2011	2007	2011	2007	2011	2007	2011
Fianna Fáil	55	53	7	13	32	47	7	13
Fine Gael	61	46	7	15	26	39	10	7
Labour	47	44	0	7	38	44	19	7
Greens	75	—	0	—	25	—	0	—
Sinn Féin	0	25	0	0	100	75	0	0
People Before Profit Alliance	—	0	—	0	—	100	—	0
Socialists	—	0	—	50	—	100	—	0
Independents	0	75	50	17	50	11	0	0

dates that can maintain a full-time staff to develop campaign strategy and follow up on casework enjoy a major organizational advantage, whereas independent or minor party candidates are unlikely to amass the financial resources needed to hire full-time staff. Sinn Féin also stood out in its use of volunteers: whereas TDs from all parties recognize the importance of party volunteers for effective campaigns, 100 percent of Sinn Féin TDs in 2007 and 75 percent in 2011 indicated that party volunteers were critical to the success of their local organizations. In the end, the ability to rely on personal supporters and party loyalists is critical for candidates of all parties. However, those candidates that can rely on resources from their party and support from personal resources have the overall organizational edge.

Tom Sheahan, former Fine Gael TD from Kerry South, provides an instructive example of how an individual candidate builds up an effective local machine. His 2007 campaign revealed the dual imperative of attracting core party support and building a personal network loyal to the candidate. Vote share for Fine Gael had declined precipitously in Kerry South over the preceding years and paralleled the personal trajectory of TD Michael Begley. In 1963, Michael Begley was easily elected. He had lost his parliamentary seat by 1989 and then lost his Kerry County Council seat in 1991. Both Sheahan and longtime Kerry South Fianna Fáil TD John O'Leary attribute Begley's collapse to his reluctance to maintain the requisite local relationships and to do the grinding "hard slog" of local constituency work. Sheahan recalled the day that Begley stopped holding monthly clinics in his home, because he was getting tired of them. At that time, Sheahan's father prophesied, "That is the end of Begley's career."[93] The thirty-three local FG branches withered as a result of Begley's political demise.

Sheahan recounts how he revitalized his local organization by a combination of hard slog and initiating his own personal network that encompassed the Fine Gael faithful. He claimed that the secret to his success consisted of an intense cultivation of personal networks. Before running in the 2004 local elections, Sheahan had fought to secure water grants for his local community. Subsequently, he won a local council seat in 2004 and began establishing relationships with other councillors to more effectively deliver social services. His alliance with longtime councillor Michael O'Connor-Scarteen, a member of a family whose involvement in Fine Gael politics dated back to the Civil War, cemented his popularity among the core Fine Gael voters, who had supported other local candidates in the absence of a candidate of their own over the past fifteen years.[94] Sheahan capitalized on his extended family's considerable geographical dispersion throughout the constituency (he had three brothers in Killarney, one in Killorglin, and one in Glenbeigh) and on the support of local notables in the towns, to cultivate personal relationships. Sheahan worked hard to foster youth support, canvassing in nightclubs and creating events for young people so that they felt they were being heard.[95] In sum, Sheahan solidified his support base and reached out to unattached voters by developing a vast web of interpersonal relationships. The Sheahan candidacy underscores the importance of having strong organizational links to individuals and the local community and similarly broad-reaching personal relationships within the party and the local community.

Sheahan was defeated in the 2011 election despite the upsurge in support for Fine Gael nationally and locally, losing his seat to a younger member of his own party, Brendan Griffin. Local insiders suggest that Sheahan lost precisely because he was unable to balance maintaining constituency relationships and delivering the goods with his commitments in Dublin. Griffin, it is argued, was a highly visible local councillor whose tireless work on behalf of party supporters and likely voters built on his already impressive work within the party, first as a member of Young Fine Gael, then as a parliamentary assistant for a Fine Gael TD in the neighboring constituency, and finally as a member of the Kerry County Council.

Griffin's defeat of Sheahan underscores two critical factors that affect one's ability to successfully establish and then maintain a local machine. First, candidates—especially those from the major parties—must simultaneously develop key relationships within the party organization and among the party faithful and establish a personal machine. A careful mix of presenting oneself as loyal to the party and as an individual candidate who "owns" the "franchise" provides the winning electoral combination over the longer term. In the 2011 election, Griffin generated a better blend of the requisite party and personal support. Second, geography matters. Whereas two of three successful candidates in the Kerry South constituency in the 2011 election were from the same geographic area within this large rural constituency, Griffin benefited from being the sole strong contender in his part of the constituency. This strengthened his claim to be the candidate best positioned to serve the interests within the constituency.

Managing the Vote within Constituencies

Responding to the challenges presented by a more intensely competitive electoral arena, the major parties have been determined to add increased

sophistication to how the vote is "managed." The first element of this strategy is an increased reliance on polls to target successful candidates and the
identification of marginal constituencies where highly focused campaign
efforts could tilt the outcome. Few candidates can afford to conduct their
own public opinion polls and research, so major party candidates have the
advantage because their national party can pick up the bill. Second, parties
also craft their ideological and organizational appeals to induce voters who
are loyal to competing parties to transfer their lower-preference votes to
their candidates. Again, major party candidates have the edge because they
can rely on intraparty and interparty transfers to stay in the election long
enough to secure a seat. Consider the following evidence showing how
these practices benefit major party candidates as they seek to balance local
and national interests during election campaigns.

Polling and Research

The major parties have become adept at employing research to identify
slates of candidates within and across constituencies, a process necessitat-
ing increased technical skill.[96] Frank Flannery, Director of Elections for
Fine Gael in 2007, argued that Fine Gael decided on specific candidate
selection and numbers of candidates per constituency based not only on
the party's own prospects but also on the outlook and strategies of its likely
coalition partners and opposition within each constituency. According to
him, Fianna Fáil and Fine Gael alone have the organizational capacity and
professional and technical competency to target certain seats to defeat
opponents.[97]

As noted previously, candidate selection has become an art. First, marginal constituencies must be identified where incumbent TDs won by a
slim margin in the previous election. Extensive research is then required to
analyze the specific geographic areas within the constituency and the characteristics and policies that would appeal to those voters. Based on these
findings, party leaders seek to either influence the selection of a candidate
or handpick one with those strengths. They then deploy party financial and
personnel resources to promote the candidate. Flannery credits Fine Gael's
use of these tactics aimed at the Progressive Democrats as the reason why
the PDs lost six of their eight seats in 2007. He correctly predicted that
Fine Gael would implement a similar targeting of Green candidates in the
2011 election.[98] Although this ability to defeat smaller parties' candidates
may be overstated, major parties indisputably have superior organizational
resources at their disposal, making it difficult for the smaller parties to
compete successfully over the medium and longer term. This organiza-

tional advantage becomes evident when these enhanced professional and technical resources are combined with the major parties' ability to manage vote transfers by having party candidates compete actively only in limited and agreed on geographical areas of the constituency.

The episodic success of independent candidates—a hallmark of the Irish electoral system—reflects the ability of individual candidates to target perceived shortcomings in the major parties' policies or the individual candidates' appeals at the local level. However, as previously discussed, independents have had a remarkably difficult time in winning consecutive elections. Given that the long-term electoral success of independents depends on the same ingredients as successful candidates from the major parties, independents must also strike the proper balance among personal charisma, delivery of local services, and programmatic offerings. Independents must accomplish this balance without sophisticated and professionally staffed national party organizations, and they must build a competitive local organization, sometimes from scratch—something that has proven immensely difficult to sustain over the longer term.

The reliance on increasingly sophisticated polling to select candidates and to target potentially vulnerable constituencies raises the cost of electioneering, once again benefiting the leading parties, which have superior organizational and financial resources. Given their organizational advantage in terms of fund-raising, the major parties can spend more to acquire the expensive professional and technical expertise required to conduct sophisticated market research and to design effective campaign strategies. The two main opposition parties actually reported spending more than Fianna Fáil on market research in 2007 (Fine Gael spent €140,000; Labour, €70,000; Fianna Fáil, €58,000).[99] However, these figures may not reflect reality, because Fianna Fáil reported spending eight times as much as Fine Gael on research in 2002, which suggests that Fine Gael completed its research well in advance of the election being called, therefore avoiding the legal requirement to report its spending levels. By contrast, the Greens and PDs did not report any expenditure on research.[100] The organizational advantage for the major parties is evident.

Somewhat paradoxically, TDs from all parties report that campaign consultants, focus groups, and surveys were not critical in enhancing their individual 2007 campaigns.[101] Fifty-eight percent of TDs in my parliamentary survey declared that campaign consultants were not important at all, 50 percent felt this way about focus groups, and 42 percent stated that surveys had no importance. If one includes the responses from those who rated these electoral tools as unimportant to some degree, the percentages increase to 79 percent for electoral consultants, 73 percent for focus groups, and 63 percent for surveys. TDs from the major parties, with the exception of Fine Gael, reported a slightly lower rating of importance for these electoral tools—especially for those who rated the tools as not important at all.[102] These findings indicate that greater professionalization and sophistication at the national level is not necessarily experienced equally at the constituency or candidate level. Expensive technical tools are primarily employed by the party at the national level. That the national parties spend their resources on consultants, focus groups, and surveys in campaign lead-ups gives candidates from the larger parties a head start. This boost frees up individual TDs to focus their personal resources in a more targeted way in their local campaign.

Vote Transfers

Major parties also enjoy an organizational advantage in their ability to employ their organizational depth to maximize their share of transfers from both intraparty and interparty lower-preference votes in the PR-STV electoral system. As table 5.8 demonstrates, the overall pattern in the percentage of transfers that parties receive in each election confirms the advantage maintained by the major parties. Parties normally receive a percentage of transfers similar to their percentage of first-preference votes.[103] This advantage is not automatic; rather, major party leaders preserve their edge by engaging in elaborate strategies to capture the transfer of lower-preference votes.[104] In an electoral arena where a handful of votes can alter elections and where voting along strict party lines is less prevalent, parties must optimize the most efficient transfer of votes among their own partisan supporters. Carefully calculating the number and provenance of candidates in each constituency is vital to success. To avoid spreading their lower-preference votes too thinly, the historic parties, especially Fianna Fáil, have reduced the number of candidates they run in each constituency.[105] Since the 1990s, Fianna Fáil has typically entered only the number of candidates in each constituency that are likely to get elected, thereby reducing wasted vote transfers and maximizing the number elected in an overall context of a declining vote share. If, for example, Fianna Fáil had run even fewer candidates in 2011 in some constituencies, such as Dublin South, they may not have split the vote and been thereby deprived of a seat that their first-preference vote warranted. In this case, the party did not make the difficult decision to intervene and prevent incumbents from running for reelection, although their running jeopardized the party's overall results; in other words, the lack of an imposed centralized strategy proved damaging to the party. Such cases underscore the critical impact that sophisticated vote management can have on outcomes and the pressure that this places on national party leaders to advance such strategies, sometimes even over and often against the will of individual candidates.

Candidate provenance is the other critical factor that parties consider when determining which candidates to put forward. This is especially true for the major parties, which generally run multiple candidates in each constituency to harvest as many votes as possible from the various regions of the constituency. Voters exhibit at least as much loyalty to their locale as toward a particular party, and many voters are very willing to vote for a locally known candidate of a party different from their own.[106] Fianna Fáil and Fine Gael generally choose candidates from geographically diverse areas within constituencies to maximize second-preference votes, so as to keep at least one candidate in the hunt for a seat and potentially get others elected.

The management of internal party competition, together with the ability to attract transfer votes, requires a high degree of coordination between the national and local levels. Intense intraparty competition can bolster overall party support and broaden organizational reach within a constituency; organizations at the local level are heavily dependent on the presence of an energetic or charismatic councillor or TD to galvanize efforts. Internal party rivalries incentivize candidates to develop their organization at an early stage and to maintain them, lest they succumb to other candidates within the party. The more solid the support for a given party candidate is, the more likely these partisan colleagues are to support each other and encourage transfer of lower-preference votes among their own loyalists.

However, internal rivalries can also bring negative consequences. Internal party competition can foment intraparty divisions, resulting in organizational fragmentation.[107] In addition, intraparty competition splits up the party vote, risking an outcome whereby the party can fail to elect any of its

TABLE 5.8. Share (%) of Transfers in Irish General Elections, 1992–2011

Election	Fianna Fáil	Fine Gael	Labor	Sinn Féin	Greens	Progressive Democrats	Workers' Party	People Before Profit Alliance	Other	Non-transferable
1992	29.8	29.5	5.8		2.8	5.6	5.8	—	5.5	14.6
1997	31.9	25.2	13.1	0.4	2.8	4.0	0.3	—	9.0	12.1
2002	26.2	27.6	13.3	0.4	5.0	3.4	0.1	—	8.7	11.9
2007	25.8	31.3	14.2	0.6	5.9	2.2	0.1	—	5.8	10.8
2011	17.1	29.0	17.7	0.9	0.9	—	0.0	1.0	11.5	15.3

candidates, as described shortly. Finally, in cases where a single candidate enjoys overwhelming popularity, the party label can become too closely identified with a single personality, thereby undermining overall party appeal over the long term because voters become so closely linked to a candidate and not the party.[108]

In 2007, Fine Gael's decision at the national level to run two candidates in the Kerry South constituency was successful because the party's increased vote share allowed first-time candidate Tom Sheahan to benefit from his fellow party member's transfers and win a seat. Within the Fine Gael vote, Sheahan enjoyed a decisive geographical advantage in that he was born in the western part of the constituency, lived in the eastern part, and had ten brothers and sisters conveniently spread throughout the constituency and all working feverishly on his behalf. Séamus Cosái Fitzgerald, the losing Fine Gael candidate, could be easily pigeonholed as an exclusively Dingle candidate, from a fishing and tourist town on a remote peninsula, even though he worked hard to overcome this disadvantage by campaigning throughout the constituency for eighteen months.[109]

The decision by the Fianna Fáil national party to geographically split the Kerry South constituency in 2007 ultimately cost them the election of their second candidate because of how campaigning worked on the ground locally. Independent TD Jackie Healy-Rae strategically exploited Fianna Fáil's decision to split the constituency, emphasizing John O'Donoghue's absence in Healy-Rae's strongholds and repeatedly seeking to convince voters that O'Donoghue had "abandoned them" and was "unconcerned about their interests." O'Donoghue ended up winning more votes in Killarney, the largest city, which affected the vote sufficiently to alter how lower-preference votes were transferred. In the end, only O'Donoghue, the incumbent Minister for Arts, Sports and Tourism, won a seat for Fianna Fáil; the party's candidate Tom Fleming lost by just over fifty votes. Given that candidates who enjoy more popularity are expected by party leaders to intentionally lower their vote sufficiently to get another party candidate elected, some considered Fleming's near losses in the 2002 and 2007 elections to be as much O'Donoghue's fault as Fleming's.[110]

Managing vote transfers astutely both in terms of national strategy and local implementation has become especially crucial in the contemporary era of multiparty competition. A comparison of the 1973 and 2007 elections provides a telling contrast between party competition in these two periods. In the 1973 election, an electoral pact between Fine Gael and Labour was formed with the express purpose of producing more efficient transfers of lower-preference votes to candidates from these two parties.

As a result of this strategic electoral alliance, Fianna Fáil won fewer seats (47.6 percent in 1973 compared to 51.7 percent in 1969), even though it enlarged its vote share by 1 percent since the last election. The inverse was true for Fine Gael and Labour, the two parties forming the National Coalition in 1973. Their vote share declined from 51.1 percent to 48.8 percent, but they increased the percentage of seats they won from 47.6 percent in 1969 to 50.7 percent in 1973.[111]

In the more recent era of multiparty competition (as exemplified in 2007), voting pacts and transfer patterns have continued to play an important, though diminished, role. One of the characteristics of this latter period has been a decline in straight party voting, combined with a growing complexity of transfer patterns, given the wider range of candidates and parties competing for office. Straight party voting declined for all the major parties between 1973 and 2007, including a decline of 13 percentage points for Fianna Fáil, 10 percentage points for Fine Gael, and 27 percentage points for Labour.

Transfer patterns have also been more complex in the recent era, even though there was the option of the same electoral coalition between Fine Gael and Labour in both 1973 and 2007. Recall that if a second-preference or lower-preference vote is designated for a candidate who has either been elected or eliminated, that vote is transferred to the next preference on the voter's ballot. In 2007, a slightly higher percentage of Labour transfers went to Green candidates (37 percent) than to Fine Gael candidates (34 percent) when candidates from both parties were still available. However, when only a Fine Gael candidate remained, the Labour transfer rate increased to 46 percent. The intention of Fine Gael and Labour to create a winning electoral coalition and avoid uncertainty from the impact of transfers did not result in the anticipated outcome in 2007, partly because the proliferation of parties and candidates across each of the forty-three constituencies made transfers more complex and unpredictable than they had been in the earlier election period. Despite some losses, Fianna Fáil and Fine Gael maintained high levels of party voting in 2007 (67 and 64 percent, respectively), whereas Labour has experienced a much steeper decline. Furthermore, while transfer votes from Fine Gael to Labour have remained stable, Labour transfers to Fine Gael declined. The sheer complexity of optimally managing transfer patterns in contemporary elections represents yet one more source of organizational advantage for the major parties. They command greater technical and professional resources to manage this uncertainty better than the competition, endowing the major parties with a medium- and longer-term electoral advantage.[112]

Leveraging Access to State Resources

The third primary organizational advantage major parties have over minor parties and independents is their capacity to elect candidates to secure local council seats as well as ministerial positions in government. This allows the major parties to provide their constituents with access to information and/ or goods and services from the state. Given that Irish citizens place such high expectations on their elected officials to meet their local needs, the major parties' track record in delivering for their constituents plays to their strength. To win elections is one thing, but then being able to use the spoils of victory to maintain voter support is another skill altogether. The major parties have proven effective at linking these two political imperatives by establishing and maintaining strong links between representatives on local councils and the national parliament and by taking advantage of ministerial positions to serve their constituents.

Linking Local and National Elected Representatives

The TDs who have succeeded over the longer term have maintained their personal relationships at the local level by fostering close relationships with the members of the local county and city councils. These bodies are largely in control of the delivery of local services. Since TDs can no longer hold other elected positions, these linkages have taken on even greater significance in recent years. Indeed, the parties that succeed over the longer term have elected officials on local councils and in the national parliament. As a result, major parties enjoy an organizational advantage because of their ability to identify, attract, and cultivate sufficient numbers of quality candidates to compete and succeed locally and nationally. Independents and minor parties have routinely struggled to maintain enough links to voters in both types of elections.

The significance of maintaining strong ties to local councils is evident when comparing the correlation between outcomes in local and general elections. Parties experience roughly the same results in both types of elections. By and large, successful local elections enhance the local organizations of parties, which, in turn, fuels success in subsequent general elections. The corresponding trends in local and national elections are striking: when a party wins in local elections, there is a parallel surge in support in general elections. For example, the Greens and Sinn Féin enjoyed a much stronger presence on local councils beginning in 1999, which certainly contributed to the electoral success of these parties in the subsequent 2002 general election, when both parties elected an additional four TDs. That

Fine Gael overtook Fianna Fáil as the largest party after the 2009 local elections certainly contributed to the former party's crushing success at the national level in 2011.

Likewise, poor local results signal subsequent electoral erosion at the national level. The dismal performance of Fianna Fáil in the 2004 and 2009 local elections, where they experienced a 10 percent decline in their shares of votes and seats in each election, signaled a weakening acceptance of the party at the local level and foreshadowed their cataclysmic result in the 2011 general election. Similarly, that the Greens did not win a single local seat in 2009 demonstrated weakness at the local level in key constituencies and presaged their loss of all six of their Dáil seats in 2011. These examples illustrate that a sine qua non of Irish political success is sustaining strong organizational roots both locally and nationally. This task has proven much more difficult for minor parties to perform over the longer term.

Political entrepreneurs establish and sustain these essential local relationships in a variety of ways. Historically, elected TDs have had a family member who was previously a TD, who served as a local councillor, or who was a local personality in business, sports, or entertainment-related activities. One-quarter of Irish TDs since 1973 had family members previously in the Dáil, and fully 80 percent were local councillors before becoming TDs. In 1973, 28 percent of TDs had family members who were past or current members of the Dáil; this figure had risen to 37 percent three decades later.[113] Serving as a local councillor remains the tried-and-tested route to the Dáil, with three-quarters of all TDs elected since 1989 having first been a member of a local council.[114] Simple significance tests on whether winning and losing candidates possess different background experiences, from the 2007 Comparative Candidates Survey, also confirmed that local councillors are substantially more likely to win elections (see table 5.9). Parties use local political office to identify and "test-drive" new candidates. Once elected to county councils, candidates gain valuable experience about how to work the system. In addition to building a web of local contacts and administrative procedures, these candidates rejuvenate the membership of the local party as fresh adherents are gained. Without access to this step in the ladder of professional development, candidates must find alternative ways of building their base, which have not proven nearly as effective. Evidence from the 2007 Comparative Candidates Survey suggests that losing candidates actually spent greater time participating within and belonging to civil society groups than their winning counterparts. The path to national office clearly runs through local councils.

A significant legal change affecting the relationship between local political office and national parties occurred in 2003, when the dual mandate was terminated by legislation: TDs, senators, and members of the European Parliament (MEPs) could no longer be members of local councils while also serving in the Irish or European parliaments.[115] Before 2003, TDs found it convenient to hold both the TD post and a local council office, because more than half of all government spending, though funded by central government transfers, is allocated locally. Furthermore, since local councils control many local services, they offer a rich source of patronage. In addition, councillors are dispositive on issues pertaining to planning permission/zoning, roads, medical cards, waste management, and so on. TDs are responsible for issues perceived to be more removed from the local scene. Given that electoral success is indisputably shaped by a given candidate's ability to deliver goods to the local level, the elimination of the dual mandate deprived TDs of an important resource, rendering it more difficult for TDs to confer favors and deliver the goods to local constituents. TDs have compensated by developing close links with copartisans in local government—something that independent and minor party candidates have been poorly positioned to do.

Because the elimination of the dual mandate was intended to create a more efficient division of labor and to provide additional leadership positions previously monopolized by powerful local bosses, it was welcomed by many. In fact, as a result of this reform, one-third of the newly elected TDs in 2007 had only recently become councillors in 2004, a stepping-stone that had been made available by the resignation of TDs from local councillorships in 2003.[116] However, some felt that the end of the dual mandate weakened the office of local councillor, because real power is still perceived to lie with TDs. Once TDs were no longer present on the council to ensure that agreements reached would be funded at the national level,

TABLE 5.9. Candidates' Experience in Politics (2007 Comparative Candidates Survey)

	Mayor ($p = .17$)	Local Council ($p < .01$)	Oireachtas ($p < .01$)	Government ($p < .01$)
Losing candidates	.174	.522	.174	.022
Winning candidates	.266	.800	.855	.429
Total	.212	.637	.448	.187

local councillors were regarded as having lost their ability to influence outcomes.[117] Indeed, the real winners in the reform were nonelected, technical, professional staff, the county managers and planners who make many of the specific decisions within the local area.[118]

Predictably, candidates responded to the elimination of the dual mandate by naming family members and close associates to take their place on local councils. Though serving on the local council remains a useful apprenticeship for aspiring TDs, the prohibition has resulted in TDs articulating strong personal relationships with councillors to meet the "service" needs of their constituents. Because experience as a local councillor continues to be the preferred path toward candidacy for parliament, incumbent TDs colonize local councils with friends, allies, and family members to propagate their influence and eliminate potential challenges to their parliamentary seats. For example, one TD who had two sons serving on the county council was notorious for claiming that a vote for him delivered "three for the price of one."[119] In addition, since local councillors have a decisive say over favors essential to servicing the constituency, the presence of allies and family members on local councils makes it possible to channel the flow of goods to the targeted parts of the constituency.

Given that major parties possess a deeper pool of candidates to fill seats at both the local and national levels and then to orchestrate delivery of services to satisfy constituents' needs, they have been better at maintaining this vital symbiotic linkage between politics at both levels. As we have seen, success at the local level generates the experience and the networks that pave the way to win Dáil elections.[120] The sheer size of their candidate pools ensures, however, that the major parties are better positioned to field viable candidates at both levels. Preserving this vital link to county and city governments has proven essential for electoral success during general elections.

Channeling State Resources to Serve Local Constituencies and Strengthen the Party

The other primary means by which major parties have strengthened their brokerage capacity has been by assuming ministerial positions within the government. The perks of office benefit individual ministers as well as the major parties themselves. One of the most effective tools for proving one's capacity to serve local interests is being a member of a governing party or, even better, a government minister. The appeal of having a cabinet minister in your constituency has been an enduring feature of Irish politics. When Michael Begley was chosen as Parliamentary Secretary to the Minister for Local Government in 1973, County Kerry's first minister in over thirty years, the *Kerryman*'s front page stated "Bonfires Blaze for Begley: The Hills of Dingle Peninsula blazed in jubilation last Sunday night as Deputy Michael Begley rode in triumph in his native town."[121] Irish politicians energetically employ their role as government ministers to cultivate their status among their local constituencies.

At the most basic level, parties in government can leverage the resources of the civil service associated with their government responsibilities. Ministers enjoy an advantage because additional benefits accompany ministerial office, including salaries, staffing, extra office resources, and the support of civil servants, all of which reinforces incumbents' daunting resource edge over challengers, especially those from smaller parties. Government ministers possess more resources to conduct both their ministerial and constituency workloads, and they can rely more heavily on the civil service to assist them. In fact, the cabinet and ministers of state have over a hundred civil servants and privately recruited staff working solely on constituency queries, costing the exchequer at least €4 million annually.[122] These personnel and financial resources facilitated governing parties' responsiveness to their constituencies, which further enhances the advantage they enjoy when the incumbent candidates compete with challengers. They also strengthen individual TDs—more than the TDs' respective parties—because resources are allocated to support the specific operations of the minister.

Ministers who have control over discretionary accounts—such as the Minister for Finance; the Minister for Arts, Sports, and Tourism; the Minister for Social and Family Affairs; and the Minister for Community and Gaeltacht Affairs (Irish speaking regions)—possess an even greater capacity to deliver for their constituents.[123] A study of the distribution of grants per constituency from the Departments of Health, Education, and Transportation highlights this power of the purse strings. The largest number of grants was awarded to the constituencies of the ministers for the relevant departments and the constituency of the Minister for Finance.[124] It is also revealing that the finance ministry is the traditional stepping-stone to becoming Taoiseach. However, access to state resources is not all that matters in this ministry; how these funds are allocated locally to maximize party advantage also matters. Canny ministers will use these allocations to bolster their own support bases among the TDs of their own parties.

Another weapon at the disposal of party leaders is the power to select cabinet ministers and ministers of state (junior ministers). Parties historically have dispersed ministries among TDs from different regions, which is

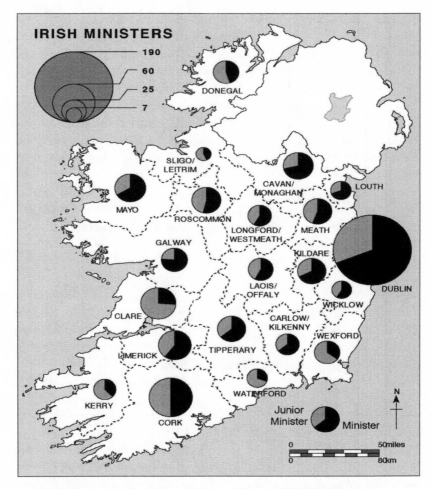

Fig. 5.2. Geographic Distribution of Ministerial Posts, 1937–2011. (Data represented here was compiled by the author from multiple sources, including "Members Database," House of the Oireachtas, http://www.oireachtas.ie/members-hist/; and ElectionsIreland.org.)

another way parties can both reward loyal and strong TDs and enhance the popularity of their TDs in local areas by giving them additional resources to better serve and deliver to those areas. Although the number of cabinet ministers has remained stable at fifteen due to a constitutional mandate, the number of ministers of state (formerly known as parliamentary secretaries) mushroomed from seven to twenty between 1977 and 2007.[125] The power to appoint senior government ministers provides party leaders with a formidable tool to discipline or reward parliamentarians, in a system where supine backbenchers wield little authority. This vehicle also allows party leaders to extend the geographical reach of the party, carefully choosing ministers from as many different constituencies as possible. Candidates are chosen by party leaders as much for their geographic provenance as for merit. The geographic distribution of the ministerial posts is shown in figure 5.2. Since 1937, governments led by Fianna Fáil have occupied 74 percent of the cabinet ministries and 72 percent of the junior ministries, whereas governments led by Fine Gael have occupied only 26 percent of the former and 28 percent of the latter. The overall electoral success of the major parties, especially Fianna Fáil, was enhanced by both their remarkable ability to adapt organizationally and their exceptional capacity to efficiently employ state resources to advance their agendas. Because government ministries are such powerful tools for delivering goods and services to constituents, minor parties have consistently been willing to trade their policy distinctiveness in exchange for a ministerial post. As we have seen throughout this analysis, this may benefit minor parties in the short term but may not necessarily do so in the longer term.

In the end, the ability of Ireland's major parties to reward loyal TDs who, in turn, take advantage of state resources to enhance their service to their local constituencies reinforces the role of constituency service and corresponding electoral loyalty to a party as a primary means of garnering electoral support. Fianna Fáil, a classic vote-seeking and office-seeking party, is a master at this game. It perfected local constituency service for generations, which, in turn, reinforced its electoral success and its ability to maintain its capillaries at the local level in a rapidly changing environment in which parties have been stretched financially.

Conclusion

Party organization in Ireland has undergone a broad process of modernization, concomitant with the experience of the country as a whole. This process has led to growth, albeit uneven, in professionalization and centralization among Irish parties. The parties that have modernized most robustly—namely, the major ones—have adapted organizationally in a myriad of ways that further enhance their organizational and electoral advantage.

The professionalization and centralization of Fianna Fáil, Fine Gael, and Labour provide their party leaders with a level of insulation from the demands of their rank and file. This insulation, in turn, endows them with a level of organizational autonomy and flexibility not available to the leaders of smaller parties. This enhanced autonomy provides these leaders with an ability to adapt and respond to electoral challenges with greater alacrity than can opponents who lack such flexibility and resources. This, in turn, reinforces the electoral advantage we have identified in chapters 3 and 4.

Additionally, the major parties have enjoyed organizational advantages provided by growing centralization, professionalization, and increasing technical competence. The taxing resource demands of modern campaigns and the complexity of conducting sophisticated market analysis and fine-tuning campaigns in a media-driven environment require finer-tuned national party organizations. A whole range of activities and practices, ranging from elaborate calculations of candidate selection to optimizing vote transfers to engendering a powerful local network, all depend on enhanced party organizational capacity. Paradoxically, this increased modernization ultimately reinforces the importance of traditional, local politics, for such politics is what remains to distinguish candidates and parties once the institutional displacement of issues and centripetal character of ideological competition have effectively blurred, in the eyes of voters, many of the most salient differences among the various parties.

SIX

Shaping Democracy's Choices

> The outcome of the game of politics depends on which of a multi-
> tude of possible conflicts gains the dominant position.
>
> E. E. Schattschneider

How major parties maintain their electoral predominance in a competitive system, especially in the context of a rapidly changing and modernizing society, is the central puzzle that this book has sought to analyze. Given that in a study of forty-seven democracies, only half of all major parties persistently retained their electoral predominance over long periods, it is surprising how little is actually known about the precise mechanisms by which major parties survive electorally. How major parties and their leaders actively reconstitute themselves and their linkages with the electorate during periods of rapidly evolving social conditions has been undertheorized and understudied.

Entrepreneurial party leaders are perpetually on the prowl for winning ideological, institutional, and organizational strategies to ensure their long-term electoral advantage. The narrative of this book describes how, by employing these strategies, the leaders of Ireland's major parties have maintained their electoral predominance over long periods in the face of potentially destabilizing forces in the social, economic, and political environment. Despite the rising involvement of competing interest groups, social movements, and the media in performing key interest-formulation functions often associated with parties, party leaders have succeeded in structuring electoral competition to their advantage by engaging in these strategies.

The perspective adopted by this analysis argues that political parties are best viewed as agents that actively shape the array of choices available to voters during elections, rather than as primarily responding to the electorate's evolving set of demands. Instead of viewing parties as resulting primarily from historical legacies and partisan identities, larger sociological conditions, and/or electoral rules, I have identified a number of mechanisms that party leaders utilize to translate electorally salient issues into the political arena—or sometimes to deliberately ignore them. Although approaches that focus on historical legacy, partisan identity, sociology, and electoral systems contribute in critical ways to our understanding of the conditions and incentives that influence how parties compete, they fail to explain how parties survive and even thrive when these factors that are more "fixed" undergo dramatic change. The analysis in this in-depth case study offers a fresh perspective on how major party leaders simultaneously employ a set of strategies within multiple domains to structure electoral competition in ways that advance their own long-term electoral interests.

In the Irish case, we have seen how major party leaders adopt strategies that seek to enhance their considerable electoral advantage in each of these domains—ideological, institutional, and organizational. In the ideological domain, major party leaders work to preserve the centripetal nature of programmatic competition. Dampening programmatic contention serves these parties' longer-term electoral interests. Within the institutional domain, party leaders often displace potentially controversial and divisive issues to extraparliamentary institutions such as referenda and national systems of wage bargaining, thereby further muting the salience of highly contentious issues during elections. Additionally, within the organizational domain, major parties combine centralized national party organizations with strong local machines revolving around individual candidates, to mobilize the electorate around local issues. The cumulative effect of these strategies within these distinctive domains has been a constrained political arena. As a result of the choices of major party leaders, Ireland's minor parties and independents have experienced difficulty surviving electorally over the longer term.

In this chapter, following a brief summary of the key findings put forward in this book, I will set those findings in a broader comparative context. The party strategies discussed in this book are not unique to Ireland. In some country cases, major party leaders have successfully tamed politically explosive issues by employing strategies similar to those described in the foregoing analysis, thereby maintaining their party's electoral predominance. In other cases, the choices major party leaders have made have led to fragmentation, party decline, and even democratic collapse. Within the comparative context of this chapter, I will discuss how the set of behaviors and strategies attributed to major party leaders in this analysis affect the overall quality of democracy. A key question is whether major party leaders can continue to manage how social interests are translated—or, perhaps even more important, not translated—into the political arena, without risking voter alienation and potentially undermining the representative process altogether. The choices political entrepreneurs make affect the choices available to the electorate, thereby also affecting the overall quality of democratic representation.

Party Choices on Multiple Dimensions over Time: Findings from the Irish Case

The longitudinal and multidimensional approach employed in this analysis helps explain how major parties have, over time, shaped the choices available to the electorate, in an effort to limit the effects of social change on patterns of electoral competition. The Irish case is telling for these purposes. Ireland's three historic parties have won the support of more than three-quarters of the electorate since the 1930s, despite dramatic social, economic, and political changes. The demand side of Irish politics has been dramatically altered by the rapid modernization of Irish society. Peace in Northern Ireland, the decline of the Catholic Church as an institutional and moral force in Irish politics and society, the transformation of Ireland's economy, and an influx of immigrants combined to turn Irish society on its head in less than a generation. Accompanying these changes was a growing diversity of attitudes on contentious moral issues (abortion, divorce, and homosexuality), on the role of the state in the economy, and on Ireland's place in a globalized world. In addition, the number of unattached voters has grown significantly, such that floating voters now represent a majority of the electorate. Few other established democracies have weathered social changes as dramatic as those that have taken place in Ireland, which makes Ireland a useful case for gaining a fuller appreciation of how parties adapt to changing contexts.

A striking feature of Irish electoral competition during this period of unprecedented change has been the puzzling disconnect between increasingly salient issues confronting the Irish public and those issues over which parties compete during general elections. Curiously, the greater heterogeneity on the demand side has not resulted in altered patterns of electoral competition. In the context of general elections, rather than casting their ballots based on intense programmatic battles over increasingly salient moral issues, the economy, or Ireland's place within the EU, Irish voters generally vote for the candidate who will best serve the local constituency and who they know personally.

The persistence of localist politics in a modernizing Ireland has largely been a result of the success of major party leaders' strategies to mute and constrain competition within the electoral arena. During the very period when dramatic change within Irish society could have reshuffled the political landscape, the party landscape became somewhat ossified instead. As long as ideological differences among the parties remained narrow and major parties exercised control over access to state resources, an emphasis on local politics further bolstered the electoral advantage enjoyed by major parties. Although Ireland's ideological spectrum has always been perceived as relatively narrow in comparison with those in other European party systems, it has remained narrow largely due to the choices Ireland's major party leaders have made on the ideological and institutional dimensions to constrain the electoral arena.

This book has discussed the set of strategies Irish party leaders have employed within three critical domains—ideological, institutional, and organizational—to preserve their electoral predominance. Within the first, ideological domain, Ireland's major parties have employed a number of mutually reinforcing strategies similar to those adopted by major parties in other advanced democracies. These include shifting ideological positions in response to changes on the demand side; managing the salience and ownership of issues by adopting accommodating versus adversarial positions; and claiming, as their own, electorally successful policy positions borrowed from competitors. This last strategic adaptation, co-opting popular issues promoted by minor parties, especially those that do not threaten to divide their parties internally or polarize the electorate, has proven exceptionally successful.

Evidence from two parliamentary surveys undertaken by this author, combined with the INES, demonstrates that while ideological differences exist between parliamentarians from all parties, these differences are often unperceived by voters during elections. Expert surveys confirm this same convergence of party positions across virtually all of the most salient policy areas since the 1990s. Ideological convergence among the major parties further undermines attempts by minor parties to establish distinctive programmatic appeals among the electorate, because once the most distinctive policies of minor parties are shared with most other parties, voters are more likely to cast their vote on the basis of other factors. Since major parties have consistently offered a broader array of policies and enjoy a privileged position to deliver local goods and services once in government, their electoral advantage is reinforced. Manifesto data further capture this more fluid nature of the programmatic appeals of minor parties, as major party leaders regularly shift the emphasis and position of their programmatic offerings to outmaneuver the narrower policy focus generally adopted by minor parties. The interaction of major and minor party appeals over several election cycles illustrates precisely how the centripetal character of ideological competition consistently reinforces the larger parties' electoral advantage.

Through mechanisms within the second domain, major parties have sought to shape the choices available to voters by displacing controversial and potentially divisive issues to a set of extraparliamentary institutions such as referenda, national systems of wage bargaining, tribunals, quangos, and courts. Newly emergent issues that are relevant to voters but do not align with the major parties' Civil War legacies have been disproportionately displaced to these alternative extraparliamentary arenas. Referenda campaigns have addressed key moral and political issues, as well as critical economic and social policies associated with Ireland's membership in the EU. Essential policies on taxes, wages, and social welfare have been addressed and decided on as part of Social Partnership, Ireland's national system of wage bargaining. Growing concerns over corruption, especially about the improper relationships between politicians and the business and financial sectors, have been dealt with in tribunals of inquiry. A proliferation of quangos have assumed an ever-larger range of public functions, accounted for an increased share of public expenditure, and generated a considerable increase in the numbers of public-sector employees carrying out their work. Finally, major parties increasingly rely on courts to deal with controversial issues and often only recur to legislation when courts require them to or when public opinion has shifted sufficiently that policy debate will not undermine party unity. The decision to legislate over abortion in 2013, twenty-one years after a controversial Supreme Court case, is a recent example of this dynamic.

Using extraparliamentary mechanisms to address highly contentious issues has had a mixed overall impact on democratic representation in Ireland. On the one hand, recurring to these mechanisms provides party leaders with a useful vehicle to address changes on the demand side of Irish politics and to deal proactively with important issues confronting Irish society. Furthermore, since citizens can vote directly on issues in referenda, participate in groups that negotiate with the government on taxes and wages, take up issues that directly affect their lives via the courts, and rely on the state to hold politicians accountable via tribunals, party leaders can legitimately claim that pressing politically salient issues are being addressed. On the other hand, by removing contentious issues from the electoral arena, Ireland's major parties effectively constrain the array of choices available to Irish voters in general elections. Since the principal arena wherein voters can hold parties accountable consists of the electoral arena, the use of extraparliamentary mechanisms to address contentious issues obfuscates the accountability function of elections.

The strategies of party leaders seeking to preserve their electoral advantage via the third, organizational domain build on and interact dynamically with strategies employed in the ideological and institutional domains. The internal autonomy and flexibility that scholars identify as enjoyed by party leaders in other contexts vis-à-vis rank-and-file members is certainly evident in the case of Ireland's major parties.[1] As we have seen, growing professionalization and centralization at the national level has provided Ireland's major party leaders with greater control over candidate selection, geographic vote management, and policy emphasis during campaigns. The major parties have also fostered greater candidate autonomy at the local level by allowing strong local "franchises" centered on attractive candidates who mobilize their own personal networks. The ability of local candidates to establish their own personal machines, to influence lower-preference vote transfers, and to generate access to state resources for their constituents is enhanced by their mutually beneficial connections with the national party organization. Ultimately, the interplay between robust local and national organizations has bolstered the capacity of Ireland's major parties to deliver to their constituents goods, services, and access to state entitlements.

The multidimensional approach offered by the analysis in this book is crucial for understanding how Ireland's major parties have survived and thrived electorally over long periods. Since party strategies on one dimension influence what is possible and strategically advantageous on other dimensions, studies that isolate a single dimension of party strategy often ignore or underappreciate the multidimensional character of party competition. This book's analysis of the Irish case demonstrates how leaders can enhance their longer-term electoral effectiveness by dynamically and interactively employing strategies across these three dimensions. Strategies within the ideological and institutional dimensions combine to frame if, when, where, and how salient issues in Irish society are translated into the political arena; in turn, they shape what choices have been available to voters during elections. Additionally, organizational strategies interact with these ideological and institutional strategies, allowing party leaders to focus their attention on tactics that allow them to deliver goods and services to their constituents more effectively.

Comparative Applications: Institutional Displacement and the Persistence of Localism

As noted in chapter 1, no obvious or clear-cut patterns distinguish types of major parties that fail from those that have survived and preserved their electoral predominance over long periods. The foregoing analysis of the Irish case suggests that the strategic choices party leaders make shape diverse outcomes. Although explanations that emphasize historical legacies, ideological background, organizational structures, and institutional frameworks are useful, they do not, in and of themselves, explain the variation in electoral outcomes among major parties. To better appreciate the broader analytic usefulness of this study's description of the adaptive mechanisms employed by major parties in Ireland, this section provides an initial explanation of how these strategies are at work in other party systems. The comparative analysis offered here is suggestive of a further and more exhaustive future comparative research agenda.

Two particularly relevant findings from the Irish case that provide analytical leverage for comparison are the ability of major Irish parties to displace salient and often highly contentious issues to extraparliamentary institutions and their capacity to maintain the primary locus of electoral competition on localist, brokerage politics, even during a period of rapid modernization. Given that the contemporary political science literature has focused much of its attention on how parties behave within the ideological domain, there appears to be particular comparative and analytic value in examining party strategies within the two other domains I have identified. For example, I have shown repeatedly in the foregoing analysis that ideological strategies are often greatly influenced by party choices within the institutional and organizational domains. Applying a similar multidimensional approach to other cases is suggestive of how major parties behave in other comparative contexts.

Institutional Displacement of Issues

The desire for political parties to insulate themselves from thorny and potentially divisive issues is by no means a phenomenon unique to Ireland. As the epigraph from Schattschneider at the outset of this chapter attests, parties generally try to focus electoral competition on the issues and programmatic appeals where they can gain advantage. Likewise, they seek to dampen the salience of issues where other parties have the edge or where they are less certain about their own and/or voter positions. We often think of parties seeking to affect the salience and ownership of issues via the ideological positions they stake out during campaigns. However, this study has underscored the ways in which parties also shape electoral competition by muting those very issues through displacement to extraparliamentary institutions. Strategies to remove issues from the realm of electoral and parliamentary politics include avoiding and co-opting issues ideologically, relegating issues to subnational levels of governance, and displacing issues to alternative state or extraparliamentary institutions and processes. The most frequently used extraparliamentary institutions employed in the Irish case include referenda, national bargaining agreements (social pacts), quangos, and courts. Again, whereas previous studies have highlighted how parties have adapted ideologically to shape party competition, this analysis has underscored how party leaders have employed strategies within the institutional domain to complement their strategies within other domains for preserving their electoral success.

Comparative studies of how these extraparliamentary institutions operate in a variety of country contexts have identified key points of differentiation: their prevalence, the types of issues they address, and their impact on the political system. However, this literature rarely emphasizes the ways in which party leaders employ these institutions as vehicles to displace contentious issues from the electoral arena. Moreover, the extent to which these other institutions influence the programmatic appeals that parties employ during election campaigns is typically neglected. As a result, how these institutional arrangements shape the choices voters have available to them during elections is often ignored: if voters and parties know that certain issues will be addressed outside parliament, parties and voters may not select candidates who share their positions on those issues. Future comparative studies would benefit from an additional focus on how parties in a number of different country contexts employ these institutions to frame the demand side of politics.

Referenda

Referenda and systems of wage bargaining (the latter of which will be discussed shortly) provide illustrative examples of institutions that play a role in the displacement of issues in a broad set of countries. Referenda are commonly employed in a wide range of comparative cases. There are three basic types: mandatory, government-initiated, and citizen-initiated. Switzerland, perhaps the most widely known case, employs all three types of referenda. However, countries as diverse as Uruguay, Venezuela, Italy, Denmark, Lithuania, and Latvia also employ multiple types of referenda. New Zealand and Slovenia employ only citizen initiatives, whereas Australia and Ireland require mandatory referenda on government-initiated constitutional changes. Increasing attention has been given to the types and frequency of referenda in these cases. However, less attention has been paid to how political parties use these institutions strategically to manage how social interests are engaged within the electoral arena.

The array of types of referenda available within a country affects the electoral strategies and incentives on which party leaders can call. Mandatory referenda generally address changes to the constitution or deal with major treaties, and they therefore require broad levels of support to pass. Nevertheless, as we have seen in the Irish case, party leaders still have considerable influence even in the case of mandatory referenda, because of the choices they make before, during, and after referenda campaigns. Government-initiated referenda generally deal with intensely controversial conflicts. In these contexts, party leaders employ referenda for different strategic reasons. When party leaders are in a weak position, they often use referenda as a means of enlisting public support for difficult decisions. In other cases, leaders seeking to uphold the unity of a party or coalition use referenda to avoid internal conflict. In still other contexts, party leaders may seek to electorally neutralize an issue by resolving it to voter satisfaction.[2] If these types of referenda occur only infrequently, they tend to have only short-term effects on electoral competition, levels of polarization, and policy outcomes. By contrast, the practice of holding more numerous or regular referenda can have a longer-term, cumulative impact on the political system, as different actors and issues assume a central role in shaping policy outcomes depending on the different arenas. As in the case of Ireland, regularly and frequently deciding on EU integration and moral issues via referenda has created an alternative realm for policy resolution that has insulated major parties from potentially harmful divisions and, at the same time, prevented minor parties from appealing to voters on these issues during elections.

Citizen-initiated referenda, in contrast to constitutionally required and government-initiated ones, tend to mobilize the electorate around issues that parliaments are not addressing or that cut across existing cleavages within a system. These instruments of direct democracy allow new actors, such as social interest groups and minor parties, to take the lead in framing the debate over salient single issues confronting society. They sometimes introduce new veto players into the legislative process, with a decisive impact on the political decision-making process in places like Switzerland, Italy, and the state of California. For example, vibrant referenda campaigns that have resulted in outcomes preserving the status quo may not represent the last word, especially when activist social interest groups and large portions of the electorate remain mobilized around an issue. Persistent mobilization of this kind often induces long-term, gradual policy reform.[3] Notwithstanding their policy relevance, these activist social interest groups, which initially crystallize around referenda campaigns, rarely become long-term politically viable forces in national elections, which suggests that parties have managed to isolate the impact of such groups on electoral competition.

In most cases, initiatives serving direct democracy have facilitated broad consensus. The presence of the abrogative referendum, which allows voters to initiate the partial or total repeal of laws, has opened up the political system and facilitated social reform in Italy. For instance, in situations where politicians have been unable to resolve certain salient issues such as abortion, divorce, and electoral reform, allowing voters to decide through referendum has overcome political impasses.[4] The referenda process in Switzerland has increased the level of consultation and negotiation over a wide variety of issues. Ironically, the use of referenda in Switzerland has contributed to a perceived reduction in the transparency of political procedures, as social conflicts and other divisive issues have been removed from the public realm of parliament and transferred to the semipublic arena of preparliamentary processes. According to Marxer and Pallinger, this development has favored the creation of elite policy cartels in Switzerland that steer politics in certain directions—a process over which the public has little or no control.

Similar to the case of Ireland, the use of referenda in Switzerland has contributed to relative electoral continuity among major parties and some measure of representation, but with potential consequences for the quality of democracy. On the one hand, citizens are given a voice on key policies confronting society. From 1980 to 2007, there were, on average, nine referenda per year in Switzerland, a considerably higher rate than in the Irish experience. Compared with the mandatory referenda used in Ireland, a wider range of types of referenda exists in Switzerland: 37 percent were popular initiatives, 30 percent were abrogative referenda, and another 20 percent were mandatory referenda.[5] Swiss citizens therefore have regular opportunities to vote in referenda over a wide range of issues. On the other hand, elites in both contexts still frame the overall referendum process in ways that influence where, when, and how social interests are translated into the political arena. That only 7 percent of Swiss legislative decisions eligible to be tested via referenda were actually challenged suggests that Swiss parties have largely satisfied voters' overall policy concerns. That, again like the Irish case, differences exist between Swiss voters' preferences in elections and their preferences as expressed during referenda suggests that elites have been able to successfully frame competition in ways that have insulated the dynamics of the electoral arena from that of referenda and, in turn, shielded major parliamentary parties from the intensity and focus of contentious referendum battles.

A potentially rich vein of future research on the relationship between referenda and the dynamics of party politics should focus on precisely how and why parties frame issues the way they do during referendum campaigns. For example, to what extent do the growing numbers of referenda in Switzerland affect the types of issues that are competed over during national parliamentary elections? Of particular comparative interest from the perspective of this analysis would be to identify the types of issues that are salient in the general elections of country cases that employ referenda and to what extent their use affects the electoral strategies that parties in different country contexts employ within the ideological and organizational domains to preserve their electoral predominance.

Social Pacts

National wage agreements—that is, social pacts—provide parties with another institutional mechanism with which to displace salient and potentially divisive issues from the parliamentary and electoral arenas. The Irish experience at once confirms and challenges recent comparative scholarship on social pacts. Ireland conforms to Hamann and Kelly's argument that endeavors to explain the choice to form social pacts. They contend that under certain conditions, governing parties prefer creating social pacts instead of legislating directly to address thorny policies such as wages, the labor market, and welfare reform. Hamann and Kelly argue that the calculus used by governing parties to recur to the use of social pacts is driven by a number of factors: the type of party and party family in government, the level of electoral competition, minority versus majority governing coalitions, the level of ideological "connectedness" versus "unconnectedness" among coalition partners, and the number of effective legislative parties and the degree of fragmentation this number represents.[6] In turn, the choice to continue social pacts depends largely on the degree to which the system of wage bargaining leads to successful policy outcomes in the eyes of voters. For example, electorally successful governments in both Italy and Spain relied less on social pacts in the 1980s but rediscovered pacts in the mid-1990s, when electoral competition combined with economic decline to threaten the popularity of incumbent parties.

In Ireland, disastrous economic conditions during the 1980s, combined with the highly competitive nature of Irish elections during this period, encouraged Fianna Fáil to reach out to unions in an attempt to bolster its diminishing electoral appeal. Fianna Fáil deepened its support of Social Partnership (SP) in the period it was serving as a minority government in 1987 and during its participation in an "unconnected" governing coalition in 1989.[7] As SP was increasingly perceived by the electorate to have contributed to Ireland's economic turnaround, it became easier for parties originally opposed to SP to accept it as an integral part of the policy-making process. As Adams and Somer-Topcu and others have shown, political parties frequently respond to rival parties' policy shifts by shifting their own policies in the same direction in subsequent elections. SP eventually expanded to include a broader array of social policies and issues, which allowed Ireland's major parties to employ SP to take institutional cover when dealing with complex and potentially divisive issues.

Electoral factors can also incentivize party leaders to legislate instead of initiating social pacts. A declining vote share, for instance, does not necessarily lead to the creation of social pacts. In Sweden, for example, the historically successful Social Democrats increased their willingness to legislate even in the face of union antagonism because the center and rightist opposition was gaining traction among the electorate. Social Democratic party leaders sought to diminish the electoral appeal of their opponents by taking a tougher stand on unions.[8] In the United Kingdom, governing parties also chose legislation over social pacts. The strategy of enacting stringent economic legislation proved so successful electorally for the Conservatives in the 1980s that the Labour Party under Tony Blair radically altered its traditional relationship with unions to offset the Conservatives' electoral appeal. This shift toward legislating and minimizing the direct role of unions in policy making was vital in Labour's revival in the mid-1990s.

These cases suggest that the choice to displace issues via social pacts depends on whether major parties rely on those issues to help mobilize their core electorate and sufficient numbers of floating voters to win elections. If parties depend on mobilizing voters and differentiating themselves from other parties based on their programmatic positions on wages, the labor market, and welfare reform, they appear to be less likely to initiate social pacts. In Ireland, many issues related to taxation and social welfare had been important to voters during elections throughout the 1980s and 1990s. However, after peaking in 1997, these issues were increasingly addressed by the terms of Social Partnership, and broad consensus emerged, making the issues less relevant during elections. The very process of SP contributed to altering the electoral relevance of class-related appeals and deprived minor parties of an opportunity to establish a more left-right basis for party competition at the very time when changes in Irish society were pointing in that direction.

Future research should also examine how prominently the issues addressed within social pacts influence voters during election campaigns. Are the issues that citizens identify as most important the same ones that shape party competition in general elections? If significant numbers and types of issues are addressed in extraparliamentary realms, parties can focus attention on a less risky set of issues during elections. The availability of extraparliamentary vehicles influences, in turn, the range and types of strategies parties can then employ within the ideological and organizational dimensions. Additional comparative research on these questions will advance our understanding of how, when, and why the displacement of issues to extraparliamentary institutions is likely to occur.

A Comparative Case Study: Germany

A rich comparative research agenda consists of further study of cases where major parties have survived despite dramatic changes in society and where a number of these extraparliamentary institutions exist. The case of Germany presents us with one such example. German patterns of major party competition and adaptation resemble those in Ireland in that major parties have survived in several markedly different electoral contexts, but the patterns differ in that Germany's major parties have distinctive ideological foundations. Germany has experienced dramatic social, economic, and political change—and even increased electoral competition, with the emergence of new parties–and yet has been characterized by remarkable continuity within the electoral landscape, with its two largest parties dominating governing coalitions. Along with the Social Democrats, the Christian Democratic Union and its Bavarian counterpart, the Christian Social Union, have maintained their overall electoral predominance throughout the period of postwar reconstruction, rapid economic growth, and social modernization since the 1960s, through unification in 1991, and into the contemporary period. These parties have responded nimbly to changes in the electoral environment by adapting their ideological, institutional, and organizational strategies. As a result of deftly employing strategic adaptations within multiple domains, Germany's major parties may actually enjoy greater relevance than ever in brokering any potential governing coalition, despite slightly lower levels of vote shares in recent elections. Like their Irish counterparts, the unusual ability of these major parties to continually shift their coalitional strategies has enhanced their capacity to sustain their electoral predominance.

Of particular interest is the way German parties have exploited state institutions to preserve their predominance. For example, Germany's major political parties have taken advantage of the division between federal and state powers, the preponderance of semistate or "parapublic" bodies, and plebiscitary practices at the state and local level to encourage a more consensual approach to policy making. Parapublic bodies address issues relating to economic management, industrial relations, social welfare, immigration, and university reform and serve as political shock absorbers by depoliticizing the policy process and ensuring that more consensual, gradualist polices will prevail.[9] This layer of decision making outside the parliamentary arena includes citizens in the political process via their participation in highly centralized associations such as employers groups, unions, churches, and private welfare associations.[10] The declining numbers of German citizens participating in politics through elections is partially offset by the fact that representation of their interests takes place in these alternative arenas. In addition, the increased reliance on plebiscitary vehicles since the late 1980s (ballot initiatives and referenda at the state and local levels, candidate preference ballots in local elections, the direct election of mayors) provide further examples of alternative ways of including citizens in politics. The displacement of issues to various extraparliamentary arenas, similar to the Irish strategies discussed in chapter 4, has effectively defused salient policy concerns among the electorate while including new social groups and actors in the German political process.

Much like Ireland's major parties, Germany's major parties have consistently responded to challenges in the electoral environment by adopting ideological and organizational strategies. Equally important, however, is that Germany's parties have also employed strategies on the institutional dimension to structure the policy-making process in ways that favor consensus and incremental policy making. As in Ireland, the cumulative effect of these party strategies has constrained the electoral arena and served to preserve the major parties' electoral predominance. Ultimately, the German case exhibits remarkable continuity that cannot solely be understood by sociological factors, electoral rules, or cultural legacies.

The Persistence of Local, Brokerage Politics in a Modernizing Context

The evidence of persistent localism and brokerage politics in the rapidly modernizing Irish society presents a second potentially rich opportunity for further comparative analysis. Although an extensive literature exists on clientelistic politics in traditional societies with lower levels of economic development, only more recently have studies highlighted the persistence of clientelism in economically advanced countries such as Austria, Italy, Belgium, and Japan.[11] Earlier studies of clientelism argued that lower levels of economic development encouraged clientelistic behavior, since voters at such levels tended to be poorer, less well-educated, ethnically homogenous, and more dependent on family and friends for their economic, social, and political survival—all conditions that made them more susceptible to accept offers of particularistic benefits and patronage from political elites.[12] More recent scholarship by Kitschelt and Wilkinson argues that intense party competition, socioeconomic heterogeneity, and inequality in societies at intermediate levels of economic development create incentives for clientelistic strategies, especially in countries undergoing rapid social, economic, and political change.[13] The evolving social and political context alters the degree to which different kinds of linkages with voters will be effective, leaving parties with difficult decisions about whether to adopt more clientelistic or more programmatic appeals.

Kitschelt and Wilkinson's framework makes an important contribution to our understanding of the persistence of local, brokerage politics in Ireland's modernizing context. It also helps provide a rationale for why Irish party leaders seek to combine programmatic and clientelistic appeals to attract support. Ireland has experienced rapid social change, which has altered the homogeneous character of Irish society. As socioeconomic changes have taken root, some voters are increasingly interested in programmatic appeals, others remain eager to take advantage of brokerage politics, and still others prefer a mixture of these options. Ireland has also experienced increased levels of electoral competitiveness, given the high percentage of floating, uncommitted voters within the electorate that express interest in candidates from a number of parties. This open electoral market provides parties with strong incentives to seek support at the margins of other partisan camps. The competitiveness of elections incentivizes candidates to offer both programmatic and clientelistic appeals to potential voters; relying on clientelistic appeals can become too costly as a country develops economically, because the average voter in these contexts requires more goods and services to satisfy their needs in return for electoral support. In addition, Ireland's strong executive control over the allocation of state resources encourages parties to emphasize their ability to deliver goods and services locally, which further reinforces the importance of brokerage appeals.[14]

Although the framework developed by Kitschelt and Wilkinson proves very helpful, it perhaps underappreciates how contending parties frame ideological competition within an economically developing country to affect whether clientelistic appeals are attractive to voters. For example, Ireland's major parties have simultaneously employed a wide array of strategies on multiple dimensions, all of which have combined to reinforce localism as the driving force in electoral politics. By employing the strategies discussed at length in the foregoing analysis within the ideological, institutional, and organizational domains, Ireland's major parties have constrained the ideological choices available to voters. As a result, Irish party leaders retain an enhanced role as "brokers." Elected representatives serve as intermediaries between constituents and the state, often channeling entitlements and access to the state in the local community. In an era of increasingly competitive elections where ideological differences have been minimized and where voters place a very high value on constituency service, the party remains a critical resource for local candidates in Ireland, who are otherwise relatively autonomous. A more comprehensive understanding of how party strategies on multiple dimensions affect the combination of clientelistic and programmatic appeals allows for a fuller and more complete explanation of the persistence of localism in the Irish context.

As mentioned previously, a number of other countries have sought to maintain local, clientelistic relationships in the face of modernization. Parties that have employed similar strategies in other cases have experienced a wide array of electoral outcomes, ranging from decline and even eventual collapse to survival and success, as in the Irish case. What appears to differentiate these outcomes is the extent to which major parties captured and controlled the distribution of state resources for their own benefit, as opposed to facilitating the distribution of state resources for the benefit of local constituents more generally. Considering cases of major party predominance in Venezuela, Italy, and Japan reveals how electoral politics that is similarly locally oriented but has different intended uses of patronage can lead to different outcomes.

Country Case Studies

Venezuela

From the inception of competitive party politics in the contemporary era in 1945 until the political crisis beginning in 1993 and deepening in 1998, the Venezuelan party system witnessed moderate levels of competition between the two largest parties with democratic inclinations, the Social Democratic AD (Acción Democrática) and the Christian Democratic COPEI (Comité de Organización Política Electoral Independiente). These parties won more than 85 percent of the vote in presidential elections between 1973 and 1993. However, their vote share collapsed by 1998, when (rather remarkably) neither of the two main parties fielded a candidate in the presidential election won by Hugo Chavez. A fatal combination of leaders from the two historic parties adopting similar ideological positions, an unusual degree of organizational rigidity among the major parties, and a predatory approach to state oil revenues undermined the ability of party leaders both to adapt to changes in society and to represent interests within society.

The cases of the electoral collapse of Venezuela's AD and COPEI stand in stark contrast to the experience of major Irish parties. Unlike the Irish case, where major parties consistently employed state institutions to include broader interest groups and address salient issues among the electorate within the political process, party elites in Venezuela employed their privileged access to state institutions and its resources principally to advance their own narrow, personalistic interests. Party politics in Venezuela from 1945 to 1993 increasingly revolved around an intra-elite system for distributing the wealth of a state-led oil-rich "booty" economy.[15] Again, in contrast to the Irish case, the state-funded clientelism that existed was generally distributed through state institutions like the welfare system, rather than a party "brand." The visible linkages that Irish parties and local candidates have developed to claim credit for favors and constituency service had not been sufficiently developed by Venezuelan parties. As a consequence, goods and services that Venezuelan parties distributed primarily to their supporters through state institutions were viewed by voters as examples of corruption.[16] As long as the money flowed from state oil resources, party elites had little incentive to interrupt this revolving door of privilege. Cash was flowing generously into the pockets of party elites and their supporters.

While Venezuelan party elites enjoyed this cozy situation, poverty was both widespread and growing. Shockingly, despite its vast oil wealth, Venezuela's per capita GDP declined between 1978 and 2003 by a greater percentage than in all but five countries in the world, and these other five cases all experienced protracted civil wars.[17] Not surprisingly, the Venezuelan populace blamed corrupt party leaders for siphoning off the country's oil wealth.[18] By 1998, only 19 percent of Venezuelans identified with one of the major parties.[19] Kleptocratic parties experienced a nearly complete loss of legitimacy among voters, and voters turned to a nonparty populist actor, Hugo Chavez, to address a growing social deficit long ignored by the major parties.[20] The way party elites employed their privileged access to state institutions for their own personalistic benefits sowed the seeds for their own demise and ultimately led to the collapse of competitive party politics in Venezuela.

In sum, through inability or disinterest, Venezuelan party leaders did not develop new linkages with emerging sectors. Drawing on lessons from the analysis provided in this book, we can see that Venezuela's major parties failed to rearticulate their ideological positions to reflect the growing (and legitimate) demands of the popular sectors, to enhance the coherence and responsiveness of the party organization, and to transform their predatory relationship with state institutions. The failure resulted in a collapse of the party system, though such an outcome was not inevitable. In the end, the virtual disappearance of Venezuela's major parties was a consequence not only of economic crisis and growing poverty and inequality but also of a failure of party leadership to adapt successfully to changing conditions. Very critically for the purposes of the analytic approach adopted by this book, the sources of the demise of Venezuelan parties rest principally not in structural factors but in the very actions and inaction of Venezuelan party elites.

Italy

Italy in the 1990s provides a case whereby long-standing patterns of party competition and long-dominant parties virtually disappear in the context of sustained economic growth and secularization, combined with episodic economic distress, corruption, calls for electoral reform, and the rise of new opposition parties. The Christian Democrats (DC) had held the position of prime minister continuously from 1946 until 1982 and had formed part of every government for nearly five decades until 1994. The main opposition party, the Italian Communist Party (PCI), consistently performed well in elections over the course of five decades but was never able to expand beyond its base and make a serious bid for executive power—partly because of Western Europe's ideological landscape shaped by the Cold War. But in 1994, the relatively stable pattern of party competition disappeared almost overnight. The Christian Democrats' vote share collapsed, while the Communists dissolved and began a tortuous decade-long process of institutional reinvention into a vastly different leftist party.

These two major parties in Italy found themselves unable to adapt successfully within the ideological and organizational domains, but a factor that proved ever more important in their demise was their overdependence on increasingly corrupt and ineffective clientelistic governance practices. A severe economic downturn and escalating corruption undermined the state-run system of patronage (e.g., jobs, contracts, and money) that constituted the principal organizational and institutional advantage that governing parties enjoyed over opposition parties. Desperate efforts on the part of DC party elites to plunder diminishing state coffers and outright buy votes backfired, alienating a substantial share of the electorate. Without expensive state-financed patronage to offer, the DC lost its ability to maintain key political linkages with key allies in civil society. The failure of DC party leaders to articulate meaningful ideological or personalistic/ material linkages with voters finally caught up with them in the cataclysmic 1994 elections.

Localism in Italy, which entailed large-scale reliance on state institutions and resources that blurred the relationship between state and party, made the DC and allied parties overly dependent on patronage, which is always a finite resource. The party did little to innovate ideologically or organizationally and was mostly a bystander in debates over new electoral rules and federalism in the early 1990s. This stands in great contrast to the almost frenetic interest that major party leaders display in shaping how issues such as political reform are addressed in Ireland, where a different form of localism has allowed party leaders to enjoy greater degrees of freedom. Although it is natural for party leaders to look after their own interests and to fall to the temptation to become dependent on the state for survival, a party cannot ultimately survive if it does not maintain some form of effective linkages with voters. The combination of the lack of ideological and organizational flexibility displayed by the leaders of the DC and an overreliance on state resources to benefit personal gain over and above society's interests resulted, ultimately, in the party's demise.

Japan

The contemporary Japanese party system represents a case of major party survival in the face of increased electoral pressures, shifts in the underlying cleavages, and a significant change in the electoral system, but only after a major crisis threatened the long-term dominance of the Liberal Democratic Party (LDP) and greatly enhanced the competitiveness of the opposition. Japan has experienced intense modernization, the end of foreign policy divisions from the Cold War, and subsequent (until very recently) economic stagnation. At the same time, Japan underwent a transition from an electoral system based on single nontransferable voting to a mixed-member electoral system. Although the LDP experienced some decline in its vote share during this period of change and faced a more united opposition after a period of crisis in the 1990s, it remains a formidable electoral force in Japan, even regaining control of the government in 2012.

Two dimensions of clientelism help explain the LDP's longer-term electoral dominance in Japan. First, LDP party leaders took advantage of Japan's political institutions, such as fiscal centralization and legislative malapportionment, to buttress personal, clientelistic relationships and to outmaneuver opposition candidates. The combination of patronage and fiscal centralization meant that voters in state-dependent areas of the country were reluctant to support opposition candidates who would be unable to provide public works, agricultural and industrial subsidies, and state employment. Like in Ireland, the candidate-centered electoral system (based on single nontransferable voting, which fostered intraparty competition for seats) and a salient urban-rural cultural divide allowed pockets of modern, programmatically oriented politics to coexist with pervasive localism. Legislative malapportionment ensured that patronage-dependent rural areas were massively overrepresented, which, in turn, led to a serious deficit of experienced local opposition leaders (especially in the rural sector) who could mobilize voters and stand as viable candidates for national office.

Second, party organization in Japan was also greatly influenced by the prevalence of local brokerage politics and the institutional features that facilitated them. Localism in Japan, like its counterpart in Ireland, is simultaneously reinforced by way of party strategies within the organizational, institutional, and ideological domains alike. The LDP's internal party organization was designed to maximize its capacity to manage government resources by keeping conflict inside the party and ensuring that losing factions retained some access to patronage. The LDP relied on several complementary institutions to reinforce each other and facilitate clientelistic relationships.[21] They include the *koenkai*—personal support organizations that exist outside the party apparatus—and institutionalized factions within the party caucus that fought for the spoils of office. LDP policies have traditionally been set through the party's powerful Policy Affairs Research

Council and its tightly hierarchical leadership and decision-making structure, which allows for closed-door deal making and political horse trading rather than open, acrimonious debate. Japan's previous electoral system of single nontransferable voting, like PR-STV in Ireland, encouraged intraparty competition and interacted with these party organizations in complex ways that encouraged politicians' responsiveness to constituents. In turn, these elements of party strategy within the organizational and institutional domains have affected the ideological strategies of Japanese politics in a way that fuels localism. The net effect of these strategies is to make interparty ideological differentiation difficult while maintaining intraparty ideological differences even at the expense of internal party ideological cohesion.

The LDP, again like Irish parties and unlike their Italian and Venezuelan counterparts, has adjusted its programmatic appeals and strategies in response to a changing electoral context. The institutional-level changes in the electoral system in the 1990s, combined with depleted government coffers due to its flagging economy, curbed parties' abilities to deliver highly particularistic local benefits. Ideological differences among the parties narrowed, but parties have been forced to offer distinctive and far-reaching policies with fewer resources available to fund them. The emergence of two electorally viable catchall centrist parties has transformed the electoral landscape. Unlike the cases of party collapse in Venezuela and Italy, where parties apprised themselves wholesale of state resources to benefit themselves, Japanese major parties employed their privileged access to state institutions more strategically and targeted policies to benefit constituents and bolster their longer-term electoral dominance. Unlike the major parties in Venezuela and Italy, the Japanese parties accomplished this without undermining their legitimacy or becoming too dependent on any single strategy to adapt to the changing political context.

Democracy's Choices

This study has highlighted the various ways in which the leaders of Ireland's major parties have preserved their parties' electoral predominance over the longer term by constraining the electoral arena while also employing successful mechanisms to channel salient issues. The brief comparative overview of major party predominance, both failed and successful, suggests the wider relevance of the three adaptive mechanisms employed by major party leaders in Ireland to successfully maintain their electoral predominance. Understanding more adequately how major parties in other contexts address the challenge posed by changing electoral environments and rapidly modernizing contexts requires further research in line with the approach adopted in this analysis. In pursuing these questions, scholars may gain analytic leverage by being more attentive to the cumulative role that the strategies adopted by major party leaders within the ideological, institutional, and organizational domains have on long-term party failure or success.

The examination of the supply side of politics offered in this analysis draws our attention to two key phenomena important for our appreciation of the quality of democratic representation. First, we have observed how major parties act strategically within multiple dimensions on the supply side to powerfully shape the choices available to voters on the demand side during elections. Second, we have also observed that mainstream parties regularly converge toward some consensus on salient issues addressed within the electoral arena. These empirical observations raise important, corresponding normative questions. The degree to which parties successfully frame what is offered to the voters in elections calls into question the extent to which democratic governments are responsive to demands within civil society. Meanwhile, the frequent convergence of programmatic positions potentially limits the choices that voters are offered during elections.

The question in this final section is whether these strategic choices of the parties undercut the quality of democracy and the degree to which citizens' interests are adequately addressed within the political system. For some scholars, the tendency for parties to act powerfully to ensure self-preservation ultimately risks a growing disconnect between parties and their constituents. For others, the tactics displayed in the Irish context are indicative of responsive party adaptation in the context of rapid modernization. As society changes, so must the manner in which interests are mediated between parties and voters, which implies that the democratic process takes on a different look than in previous eras. To adjudicate between these competing perspectives, it is helpful to think about the key functions that we expect parties to perform within democracies.

The quality of democracy is affected, powerfully but often subtly, by how parties perform their representative and institutional functions.[22] The representative function of parties includes aggregating interests and values within society, providing symbolic identities and a stable set of political goals, and structuring electoral competition. At the broadest level, the institutional function of parties involves gaining office and filling various roles within legislative and executive offices that determine how policy is actually approved and implemented within a political system.[23] Parties are critical actors for ensuring the state's ability to provide the elements of effective democratic governance, which include high-quality democratic practice, the protection of citizen rights, economic growth, and effective remedy of serious social problems.[24]

One important school of thought on parties in advanced industrial democracies has advanced the argument that the rift between the representative and institutional (or governing) functions of parties is widening, with serious negative consequences for the quality of democracy.[25] These scholars—including Katz and Mair, who advanced the well-known "cartel party" thesis—assert that parties have become less effective in their representative role and have come to rely increasingly on the state for their survival. Parties, they submit, are less well connected within civil society and receive and respond to less feedback from citizens outside of government.[26] Increasing reliance on institutional, rather than representative, functions can, over the long term, erode accountability and responsiveness.[27]

Some have argued that such erosion has occurred in Ireland. For example, some popular accounts of the Irish banking crisis describe erosion in the quality of representation and accountability within Irish political life. Critics claim that a lack of accountability existed among party leaders (especially in Fianna Fáil) who enjoyed an all-too-cozy relationship with prominent banking and construction executives during the twilight years of the Celtic Tiger economy, in the first decade of the twenty-first century. Others point to Ireland's growing dependence on the EU for economic policy making, suggesting that the locus of accountability has shifted from the Irish voter to bureaucrats at the supranational level.[28] The argument is that with voters perceiving only minor ideological differences between the parties, the representative character of competitive party politics in Ireland is constrained even further, leaving voters with little to choose from among the competing parties in elections. Seen in this light, some scholars and analysts think that party politics is more about preserving electoral success and bolstering parties' institutional roles and less about how the interests of civil society are aggregated and translated into the political arena.

In somewhat the same vein, Mair has argued that in such contexts, where national debts have skyrocketed, where the legacies of past policies dominate the policy agenda, and where pressure from external lenders, bondholders, and supranational authorities has increased, relations between politicians and civil society worsens. Once a widespread perception exists that voters can more easily change governments than they can alter actual policies, Mair contends, a failure of representation occurs, and a "democracy without choices" results.[29] He argues that when viable public policies have been enacted by external political actors and not by political parties elected by voters, representative democracy as a whole can suffer.

In extreme situations, the alienation of voters can lead to dramatic party decline or even a collapse of the party system. In countries like Italy and Venezuela during the early 1990s, major parties had become ideologically and organizationally inflexible. When party inflexibility combined with overdependence on the state to provide material benefits to party insiders, it is no surprise that they were unable to navigate the punishing dynamics of economic downturn and social change. In Venezuela, the party system collapsed altogether and was replaced by a semi-authoritarian regime. These cases confirm that it is one thing for parties to actively shape the choices available to voters on the demand side and quite another for them to basically ignore changing social interests. Clearly, party leaders must maintain at least some responsiveness to evolving voter concerns or risk disappearing altogether.

In Japan, a greater degree of party adaptation has occurred. For years, the LDP shaped the demands of the electorate by structuring their internal organizations and policy choices to maximize the distribution of key benefits. Rather than capturing the state for their own benefit, the LDP leaders became masters at funneling state resources to benefit key constituencies. As ideological concerns shifted and as state resources became scarcer due to two decades of economic decline in Japan, the LDP and opposition parties adapted their strategies to compete within a media-intensive electoral environment that was still highly personalistic. The ability of the LDP to adapt ideologically, institutionally, and organizationally has helped the party return from the brink and regain power, albeit with different strategies and constraints. Ultimately, these adaptive strategies have not undermined voter participation or the overall quality of representative democracy in Japan.

Together with the case of Japan, Ireland's major parties are at the other end of a continuum from the major parties of Venezuela and Italy. These former cases comprise parties that powerfully and constantly shape political demand while responding effectively (and creatively) to evolving voter preferences. Like the case of Japan, Ireland's major parties have repeatedly constrained the choices available to voters during elections by deploying strategies on multiple dimensions. Despite criticisms that voters enjoy sharply limited choices during elections, Ireland's major parties have thus far avoided the degree of voter alienation that has occurred elsewhere. In fact, the set of strategies that Ireland's major parties have employed to

shape voter demands has not seriously undermined the representative process at the heart of democracy. Instead, these strategies have resulted in an
effective formula for democratic representation.

Ireland's major parties have weathered dramatic social, economic, and
political changes without capsizing by allowing for interest representation to occur in a variety of ways. Citizens are hyperrepresented at the
local level due to the prominence of constituency service by elected TDs
in Ireland, such that virtually every citizen has access to the political system through their elected representatives. Irish citizens have also had their
voices directly heard through referenda on a wide array of issues, including contentious moral issues, Northern Ireland, European integration,
the electoral system, citizenship, and the relationship of the state with the
Catholic Church. That the major parties have remained on the sidelines for
many of the referenda campaigns (sometimes resulting in a perceived failure to aggregate interests) has paved the way for social interest groups to
perform a key mobilizing role. Finally, citizen concerns were represented
through the participation of civil society (and quasi-corporatist interest
groups such as business and labor) in the national system of wage bargaining (Social Partnership) for over two decades.[30] These practices may have
arguably resulted in less transparency in parliament as government parties negotiated behind closed doors, but the inclusion of additional actors
within the policy arena facilitated enhanced participation.[31] Although SP
collapsed in late 2009, the bias toward consultative and partnership-based
processes remains.

Increased reliance on extraparliamentary institutions has not closed
off public debate in ways that the cartel thesis might predict but, rather,
has redirected contention into extraparliamentary arenas. Furthermore,
strong networks at the local level have ensured that the linkages between
politicians and voters continue to be vibrant and that the representation
function of parties at the local level remains robust. Thus, Ireland's major
parties have demonstrated a remarkable ability to both constrain choice at
the national level and yet give the voters what they appear to value most—
accessible and often intimate local representation.

The Irish case challenges normative arguments about how effective and
meaningful representation occurs within a system. Essential for the quality
of democratic governance is the degree to which citizens have their voices
heard and meaningfully included in the governing process.[32] Parties need
not be the sole actors aggregating interests, conducting debate, and social-
izing citizens within the system. The long-term success of Ireland's established parties may actually be closely linked with their ability to mitigate

divisions and thereby foster consensus. This inclusiveness has provided an effective means through which voters can express themselves and a vehicle through which parties can fortify their role as the principal arbiters of Irish politics.

A numbing consensus among parties may have confounded voters at times, but it also appears to have helped depolarize the electorate in ways that contributed both to the emergence of peace in Northern Ireland and to Ireland's economic growth from the late 1980s. For example, party leaders across the political spectrum realized that peace in Northern Ireland, let alone unification, was never going to be possible without the consent of citizens in the North and cooperation between the governments of the United Kingdom and the Republic of Ireland. Even Fianna Fáil, who originally opposed the Anglo-Irish Agreement in 1985 that outlined these key principles, and Sinn Féin, who had traditionally supported a united Ireland at all costs, ultimately supported the peace process. Broad partisan consensus around a peace agreement made the Republic of Ireland a more credible and attractive negotiating partner (because it was unlikely the agreement would be undermined later) and reduced potential support for violence and radicalism. Muted partisan polarization allowed democracy to deliver in a way that it otherwise might not have done, illustrating that creative, ambitious policy making is still possible amid multiparty consensus.

The depolarized, consensus-oriented environment has also been crucial for Ireland's economic progress in recent decades. Political parties in both government and the opposition supported the transformative institutional developments I have outlined in this analysis (i.e., the EU, SP, quasi-autonomous state bodies, and the legal context). Initially, much of this support was part of a broad consensus to solve Ireland's national economic crisis, beginning with Fine Gael's willingness to support Fianna Fáil's austerity measures as part of the 1987 Tallaght Strategy. Once the Celtic Tiger ushered in over a decade of economic and social transformations, Irish political parties deepened their commitment to and use of these institutions to maintain Ireland's economic growth. What began as crisis management became a new form of consensus governance that included additional social actors in official decision making but that also added layers to the political system and potentially distanced voters from decisions. The persistence of widespread consensus among Ireland's political parties since Ireland's economic collapse in 2008 and the lack of debilitating protests like those in Greece, Spain, and Italy have combined to help Ireland on the road to economic recovery.

Critics have argued that citizen inclusion in multiple forums for policy debate and decision making has lowered the degree to which political parties are held accountable for overall policy outcomes in elections. These multiplying loci of accountability, it is argued, have allowed major parties to evade blame for voters' frustration with the political system. The multiple opportunities for policy input have often incentivized party leaders to focus on structuring the political arena to facilitate their own electoral success, rather than on representing citizens. Yet, as we have seen repeatedly, Ireland's major parties have consistently found ways to give Irish voters what they want: attentive constituency service and access to state resources. Even if voters are not entirely satisfied with the programmatic options available to them, they have a voice in policy making and in selecting the representatives who look after their needs—key elements of an effective democracy. The lack of significant public outcry toward parties—other than the important exception of the crushing electoral defeat dealt to governing parties following the economic crisis of 2008—may indicate that voters perceive few, if any, formulas for effective representation other than the current set of institutional arrangements.

As we have seen, the strategies employed by Ireland's major parties have consistently weakened minor parties' capacity to challenge long-standing patterns of party competition. Voters often complain that there are no meaningful differences among the parties anymore and that they live in a democracy "without choices," so voters in Ireland instead focus on candidates that can deliver goods and services, which sustains localist politics. They appear willing to accept parties with little meaningful difference because they know that important issues will be addressed via extraparliamentary institutions. In quite a fundamental sense, these are "democracy's choices." In the end, Ireland's major parties have been able to structure party competition in ways that constrain broader, national-level political choices while responding to the needs of their constituents. The parties have accomplished this, at least in part, by consistently removing, sidelining, and finessing contentious issues.

Therefore, rather than viewing these choices in entirely negative terms—as party leaders preserving their parties at the expense of voters' choices—we might consider that parties are facilitating the complex and changing interests that characterize contemporary democratic governance in a globalizing context. Major, electorally successful parties continually seek to constrain the political arena to ensure their electoral fortunes by employing strategies on the ideological, institutional, and organizational dimensions. However, no political party or set of parties in a developed democratic system—no matter how adept they might be in shaping the supply side of the political arena—can ultimately survive over the medium or longer term without giving or being perceived to give effective response to the demands of the electorate. The survival of any political party depends on its ability to maintain the balance between, on one hand, representing citizens' interests and demands and, on the other, shaping those interests and demands in ways that allow for effective democratic governance. Failure by party leaders to strike this balance goes well beyond the electoral success or failure of parties; it affects the very quality of representative democracy as a whole.

Appendix

List of Major Political Parties from Table 1.1

Europe

The following are identified as the twenty-two "always major" parties in Europe: Social Democratic Party of Austria (SPO), Austrian People's Party (OVP), Danish Social Democrats (SD), Finnish Social Democratic Party (SDP), Agrarian Labour Union / Centre Party (KESK), German Christian Democratic Union (CDU), German Social Democrats (SPD), Greek New Democracy (ND), Irish Fianna Fáil (FF), Irish Fine Gael (FG), Italian Communist Party / Left Democrats (DS) /The Olive Tree / Democratic Party (PD), Dutch Labour Party (PvdA), Norwegian Labour Party (DNA/A, also appears as A/Ap), Portuguese Social Democratic Party (PSD-PP) / Democratic Alliance (AD), Portuguese Socialist Party (PS), Spanish Socialist Workers' Party (PSOE), Spanish People's Alliance / People's Party (PP), Swedish Social Democratic Party (SAP), Swiss Radical Democratic Party (FDP), Swiss Social Democratic Party (SPS), British Conservative Party (C), British Labour Party (LAB).

The following are identified as the five "major-minor (now major)" parties in Europe: Danish Liberals (V), Finnish National Coalition Party (KOK), French Socialist Party (PS), French Union for a Popular Movement (UMP), Norwegian Conservative Party (H).

The following are identified as the eleven "major-minor (now minor)" parties in Europe: Belgian Christian Democratic Party (CVP-PSC/CD&V), Belgian Socialist Party (PSB-LSP/SP), Belgian Liberal Party (PL-LP/PVV/VLD), Danish Conservatives (KF), Finnish Democratic Alternative (SKDL), French Communist Party (PCF), Greek Pan-Hellenic Socialist Movement (PASOK), Dutch Catholic People's Party (KVP) / Christian Democratic Appeal (CDA), Portuguese Communist Party (PCP), Swedish Liberal People's Party (FP), Christian Democratic People's Party (formerly Swiss Catholic Conservatives) (CVP/PDC).

The following are identified as the two "dissolved" parties in Europe: Italian Christian Democracy (DC), Spanish Central Democratic Union (UCD).

Latin America

The following are identified as the six "always major" parties in Latin America: Liberal Party of Colombia (PL), Costa Rican National Liberation Party (PLN), Mexican Party of the Democratic Revolution (PRD), Jamaican Labour Party (JLP), People's National Party (PNP), Trinidadian People's National Movement (PNM).

The following are identified as the two "major-minor (now major)" parties in Latin America: Bolivian National Democratic Action Party (ADN), Colombian Conservative Party (PCC/PSC).

The following are identified as the three "major-minor (now minor)" parties in Latin America: Bolivian Nationalist Revolutionary Movement (MNR/ADRN/AMNR/MNRA), Dominican Social Christian Reformist Party (PRSC/PR), Ecuadorian Democratic Left (ID).

The following is identified as the one "dissolved" party in Latin America: Democratic and Popular Union (UDP/MIR).

Asia-Pacific

The following are identified as the six "always major" parties in the Asia-Pacific: Australian Labor Party (ALP), Australian Conservative

Party (ACP), Indian National Congress (INC), Japanese Liberal Democratic Party (LDP), New Zealand Labour Party (LAB), New Zealand National Party (NAT).

The following is identified as the one "major-minor (now major)" party in the Asia-Pacific: Israeli Worker's Party of the Land of Israel (Maipah/ILP/OI).

The following are identified as the two "dissolved" parties in the Asia-Pacific: Japanese Liberal Party (LP), Japanese Left Wing Socialists (LWSP) / Japan's Socialist Party (JSP).

North America

The following are identified as the three "always major" parties in North America: Liberal Party of Canada (LPC), U.S. Democratic Party (D), U.S. Republican Party (R).

The following is identified as the one "major-minor (now major)" party in North America: Cooperative Commonwealth Federation (CCF) / New Democratic Party (NDP).

The following is identified as the one "dissolved" party in North America: Progressive Conservative Party of Canada (PC).

Notes

1. Table 1.1 is based on the analysis of Scott Mainwaring and Edurne Zoco, in "Political Sequences and the Stabilization of Interparty Competition: Electoral Volatility in Old and New Democracies," *Party Politics* 13, no. 2 (2007): 155–78. They included all countries with at least one million inhabitants that had, as of 2006, experienced at least four consecutive lower-chamber elections during which the country's Polity score was consistently 2 or higher (including not only the years of the elections but all years in between). A Polity score of 2 or higher is designed to eliminate authoritarian regimes because these type of regimes control elections, which favors the governing party and tends to limit electoral volatility. I updated the electoral data of the forty-seven countries Mainwaring and Zoco used in their analysis, to include elections up until 2012 where possible, and I isolated the results for major parties.

2. All countries included in table 1.1 held their first democratic election prior to 1980. The table includes only "original parties," defined as parties that came into existence prior to a country's third election, and "major parties," defined as parties having attained a 15 percent vote share in any single election during their history. A number of major parties have disappeared in other Latin American countries. Because these countries did not meet the selection criteria employed within this data set, their major parties are not counted, but the overall number of disappearing major parties is still quite small.

3. Jana Morgan, *Bankrupt Representation and Party System Collapse* (University Park: Pennsylvania State University Press, 2011); Jason Seawright, *Party-System Collapse: The Roots of Crisis in Peru and Venezuela* (Stanford: Stanford University Press, 2012).

4. The following are identified as the original sixteen left-leaning or Social Democratic parties in Europe: Swiss Social Democratic Party (SPS), Finnish Social Democratic Party (SDP), Social Democratic Party of Austria (SPO), Danish Social

Democrats (SD), French Socialist Party (PS), German Social Democrats (SPD), Irish Labour Party (Lab), Italian Communist Party / Left Democrats / The Olive Tree / Democratic Party (PD), Dutch Labour Party (PvdA), Norwegian Labour Party (DNA/A; also appears as A/Ap), Portuguese Socialist Party (PS), Spanish Socialist Workers' Party (PSOE), Swedish Social Democratic Party (SAP), UK Labour Party (Lab), Belgian Socialist Party (PSB-LSP/SP), Greek Pan-Hellenic Socialist Movement (PASOK). These parties are so defined by their membership in the Party of European Socialists, the members of which are listed at http://www.pes.eu/. The lone exception is the Italian Communist Party, which moderated its ideology in the wake of the Soviet Union's collapse and whose ideology can be found at http://www.partitodemocratico.it/. The following are identified as the original sixteen center-right parties in Europe: Italian Christian Democracy (DC), German Christian Democratic Union (CDU), Irish Fine Gael (FG), Austrian People's Party (OVP), Norwegian Conservative Party (H), Spanish People's Alliance (AP) / People's Party (PP), French Union for a Popular Movement (UMP), Greek New Democracy (ND), Portuguese Social Democratic Party (PSD-PP) / Democratic Alliance (AD), Finnish National Coalition Party (KOK), Swedish Moderate Coalition Party (MSP), Belgian Christian Democratic Party (CVP-PSC/CD&V), Christian Democratic People's Party (CVP/PDC), Dutch Catholic People's Party (KVP) / Christian Democratic Appeal (CDA), Danish Conservatives (KF), Portuguese Social Democratic Center Party (CDS). These parties are so defined by their membership in the European People's Party, the members of which are listed at http://www.epp.eu/member-parties. The lone exception is the United Kingdom's Conservative Party, which is a member of the Alliance of European Conservatives. Their center-right ideology can be found at their website (http://www.conservatives.com/). The following are identified as the original eleven centrist parties in Europe: Finnish Agrarian Labour Union / Centre Party (KESK), Danish Liberals (V), Dutch Liberal Party (PvdV) / People's Party for Freedom and Democracy (VVD), Swiss Radical Democratic Party (FDP), Irish Fianna Fáil (FF), UK Liberal Party / Liberal Democratic Party (LDP), Belgian Liberal Party (PL-LP/PVV/VLD), Swedish Centre Party (CP), Swedish Liberal People's Party (FP), Norwegian Center Party (SP), French Radical Party (RAD/UDF). These parties are so defined by their membership in the Alliance of Liberals and Democrats for Europe Party, the members of which are listed at http://www.alde.eu/. The exceptions are the Norwegian Center Party, whose centrist ideology is spelled out on its website (http://www.senterpartiet.no/category11868.html), and the French Radicals, whose ideology is outlined at http://www.partiradical.net/.

5. In addition to the United Kingdom, the other countries included here are Australia, Canada, India, Ireland, Jamaica, New Zealand, and the United States.

6. Mainwaring and Zoco, "Political Sequences."

7. Russell J. Dalton and Martin P. Wattenberg, *Parties without Partisans: Political Change in Advanced Industrial Democracies* (Oxford: Oxford University Press, 2000); Philippe C. Schmitter, "Parties Are Not What They Once Were," in *Political Parties and Democracy*, ed. Larry Jay Diamond and Richard Gunther (Baltimore: Johns Hopkins University Press, 2001), 67–89; Richard Gunther, Jose Ramon Montero, and Juan J. Linz, eds., *Political Parties: Old Concepts and New Challenges* (Oxford:

Oxford University Press, 2002); Peter Mair, Wolfgang C. Muller, and Fritz Plasser, eds., *Political Parties and Electoral Change: Party Responses to Electoral Markets* (London: Sage, 2004).

8. Arturo Valenzuela and J. Samuel Valenzuela, "Party Oppositions under the Chilean Authoritarian Regime" (Working Paper 125, Woodrow Wilson International Center for Scholars, Washington, DC, 1983), 15, http://www.wilsoncen ter.org/sites/default/files/125.Party%20Opposition.Valenzuela%20%2526%20 Valenzuela.pdf.

9. Anthony Downs, *An Economic Theory of Democracy* (New York: Harper, 1957), 96–97.

10. Downs, *Economic Theory*, 131.

11. Herbert Kitschelt and Steven I. Wilkinson, "Citizen-Politician Linkages: An Introduction," in *Patrons, Clients, and Policies: Patterns of Democratic Accountability and Political Competition*, ed. Herbert Kitschelt and Steven I. Wilkinson (Cambridge: Cambridge University Press, 2007), 1–49.

12. Bonnie Meguid, *Party Competition Between Unequals: Strategies and Electoral Fortunes in Western Europe* (Cambridge: Cambridge University Press, 2008).

13. Michael Laver and Ernest Sergenti, *Party Competition: An Agent-Based Model* (Princeton: Princeton University Press, 2011), 10.

14. Important organizational studies are represented by Angelo Panebianco's *Political Parties: Organization and Power* (Cambridge: Cambridge University Press, 1988), Herbert Kitschelt's *The Logics of Party Formation* (Ithaca: Cornell University Press, 1989), and Steven Levitsky's *Transforming Labor-Based Parties in Latin America: Argentine Peronism in Comparative Perspective* (Cambridge: Cambridge University Press, 2003).

15. Levitsky, *Transforming Labor-Based Parties*.

16. Seawright, *Party System Collapse*.

17. Russell J. Dalton, David M. Farrell, and Ian McAllister, *Political Parties and Democratic Linkage: How Parties Organize Democracy* (Oxford: Oxford University Press, 2011).

18. Timothy J. McKeown, "Case Studies and the Limits of the Quantitative Worldview," in *Re-thinking Social Inquiry: Diverse Tools, Shared Standards*, ed. Henry E. Brady and David Collier (Oxford: Rowman and Littlefield, 2004), 153.

19. Alexander L. George and Andrew Bennett, *Case Studies and Theory Development in Social Sciences*, BCSIA Studies in International Security (Cambridge, MA: MIT Press, 2005), 205–32.

20. Herbert Kitschelt, "The Demise of Clientelism," in Kitschelt and Wilkinson, *Patrons, Clients, and Policies*, 323.

CHAPTER 2

1. Giacomo Sani and Giovanni Sartori, "Polarization, Fragmentation, and Competition in Western Democracies" in *Western European Party Systems: Continuity and Change*, ed. Hans Daalder and Peter Mair (Beverly Hills, CA: Sage, 1983), 307–40.

2. Michael Marsh et al., *The Irish Voter: The Nature of Electoral Competition in Ireland* (Manchester: Manchester University Press, 2008), 32.

3. Richard Sinnott, *Irish Voters Decide: Voting Behaviour in Elections and Referendums since 1918* (Manchester: Manchester University Press, 1995), 177–78.

4. Data from the 1982, 1989, and 1991 Ipsos MRBI Polls and the 2002 Irish National Election Study (INES). A considerable percentage of respondents reported that Northern Ireland was "not very important" or "not at all important": 32 percent in 1982, 29 percent in 1989, 15 percent in 1991, and 32 percent in 2002. In 1982 and 1989, the responses stated "unimportant" rather than "not at all important." The numbers do not add up to 100 percent because the figures for those who responded "don't know" were not included.

5. In the February 1982 general election, several of the imprisoned hunger strikers ran for the Dáil, and one even won a seat.

6. *Chief Constable's Annual Reports* for 1970–96, http://cain.ulst.ac.uk/issues/vio lence/death95w.htm. These figures do not include deaths that occurred outside Northern Ireland.

7. Marsh et al., *Irish Voter*, 66–67, 70–71.

8. Data for 1978–2002 from Peter Mair and Michael Marsh, "Political Parties in Electoral Markets in Postwar Ireland," in Mair, Muller, and Plasser, *Political Parties and Electoral Change*, 234–63; data for 2007 and 2011 from the INES. (http://www.rte.ie/news/2007/0525/RTEExitPoll2007details.ppt, no longer available, but see http://www.rte.ie/news/2007/0525/89361-election1/, which contains some, but not all, of the information in the poll). In this context, "close" includes those who feel close to or sympathize with a particular party, whereas the graph separates the sympathizers from those feeling close. The 2007 and 2011 INES asked whether voters were close to a party or not, thereby eliminating the "sympathizer" category, which explains the higher levels of attachment in this election compared with the previous surveys. In addition, for 2007 and 2011, the percentage of respondents who answered "not attached" was calculated from questions vo680_07 and vo690_07 (2007) and qe1 and qe6 (2011). Due to different question format across the surveys, the total amount of respondents does not equal 100 percent for these two years.

9. For a thorough discussion of party attachment in Ireland, see Marsh et al., *Irish Voter*, 59–79.

10. Mair and Marsh, "Political Parties in Electoral Markets," 234–63.

11. Michael Marsh, "Voting Behavior," in *Politics in the Republic of Ireland*, ed. John Coakley and Michael Gallagher, 5th ed. (London: Routledge in association with PSAI Press, 2009), 172.

12. R. K. Carty, *Party and Parish Pump: Electoral Politics in Ireland* (Ontario: Wilfred Laurier University Press, 1981).

13. *Constitution of Ireland*, http://www.taoiseach.gov.ie/eng/Historical_Informa tion/The_Constitution/. For the quote from Mary McAleese's speech to the General Synod 2008 of the Church of Ireland in Galway, see the transcript at http://ireland.anglican.org/cmsfiles/pdf/Synod/2008/journal2008.pdf, page cxxxvii.

14. "Many Faiths in a Changing Ireland," *Irish Times*, May 15, 2008; "Muslims Have Integrated Well Despite Recent Arrival," *Irish Times*, May 14, 2008.

15. Data for 1974 and 2005 from the Communications Office of the Irish Bishops' Conference; data for 1981 and 1999 from the World Values Survey (which has had three waves, in 1981, 1990, and 1999); data for 2012 from Patsy McGarry, "Catholics' Beliefs Not Always by the Book," *Irish Times*, November 30, 2012.

16. According to World Values Survey data from Ireland since 1981, belief in God has remained at 97 percent, belief in a life after death at 82 percent, and belief in sin at 87 percent.

17. These figures represent the percentage of respondents in the World Values Survey who reported having "a great deal" of confidence in the church.

18. Andrew M. Greeley, *Religion in Europe at the End of the Second Millennium: A Sociological Profile* (New Brunswick, NJ: Transaction, 2003), 158–60.

19. Data for 1981, 1990, and 1999 from the World Values Survey (WVS); data for 2006 from Richard Layte et al., *The Irish Study of Sexual Health and Relationships* (Dublin: Crisis Pregnancy Agency and Department of Health and Children, 2006), 104–7 (http://www.ucd.ie/issda/static/documentation/esri/isshr-report.pdf). The WVS used a 1–10 scale in which 1 denotes "never justifiable" and 10 denotes "always justifiable." In order to compare the rest of the results with the 2006 data, I converted the WVS responses into the 2006 categories. I combined the WVS 2–4 responses and labeled them "abortion is nearly never justified," and the WVS 6–9 responses were combined to create the category "abortion is sometimes justifiable." The categories for abortion in the 2006 ISSHR survey were "always wrong," "mostly wrong," "sometimes wrong," and "never wrong."

20. Results from the 2007 INES suggest that public opinion continues to be evenly split on abortion attitudes.

21. Layte et al., *Irish Study of Sexual Health and Relationships*, 105.

22. Stephen Collins, "Over 70% Support X-Case Legislation on Abortion," *Irish Times*, February 11, 2013.

23. Between 2002 and 2007, Ireland has been ranked in the top five most globalized countries in the world based on the A. T. Kearney / Foreign Policy Globalization Index. The index includes scores on four dimensions: economic, personal, technological connectivity, and political engagement. See http://www.foreignpolicy.com/articles/2007/10/11/the_globalization_index_2007.

24. Data from the Central Statistics Office, Dublin, http://www.cso.ie.

25. Central Statistics Office; Brian Nolan and Bertrand Maitre, "A Comparative Perspective on Trends in Income Inequality in Ireland," *Economic and Social Review* 31, no. 4 (October 2000), 329–50.

26. Central Statistics Office.

27. Michael Marsh, "Irish Voting Behavior" (unpublished manuscript, 2009). Marsh provides a useful summary of how the economic voting literature has been received in the Irish context.

28. Peter Mair, *The Changing Irish Party System: Organisation, Ideology, and Electoral Competition*, (London: Frances Pinter Publishers, 1987), 76–77.

29. James Adams, Andrea B. Haupt, and Heather Stoll, "What Moves Parties? The Role of Public Opinion and Global Economic Conditions in Western Europe," *Comparative Political Studies* 42, no. 5 (May 2009): 611–39.

30. The 2007 results are used because, of the three national election studies that have been conducted thus far, they offer the most complete set of questions.

31. Stephen Collins, "Vast Majority Happy Ireland Is in EU," *Irish Times*, November 27, 2012.

32. Bryan Fanning, Jo Shaw, Jane-Ann O'Connell, and Marie Williams, *Irish Political Parties, Immigration, and Integration in 2007* (Dublin: University College Dublin, 2007); this source, available at http://www.ucd.ie/mcri/Political%20Par

ties,%20Immigration%20and%20Integration.pdf, presents research conducted on behalf of the Migration and Citizenship Initiative, University College Dublin.

33. Pat Lyons, *Public Opinion, Politics, and Society in Contemporary Ireland* (Dublin: Irish Academic Press, 2008), 160–61.

34. Corrie Potter, "Left-Right Self-Placement in Western Europe: What Responses and Non-Responses Indicate" (Political Behavior Group, University of Wisconsin Madison, 2001), 3.

35. Marsh et al., *Irish Voter*, 31–58. For more on left-right placement, see Peter Mair, "Left-Right Orientations," in *The Oxford Handbook of Political Behavior*, ed. Russell J. Dalton and Hans Dieter Klingemann, (Oxford: Oxford University Press, 2007), 206–22.

36. The 2002 INES reported that 34 percent of respondents placed the Greens on the left in 2002.

37. Richard Sinnott, "Appendix 4: The Electoral System," in *How Ireland Voted 2002*, ed. Michael Gallagher, Michael Marsh, and Paul Mitchell (Basingstoke, Hampshire: Palgrave MacMillan, 2003), 260.

38. The quota represents the minimum number of votes that absolutely guarantees election. It is calculated by dividing the total valid votes by one more than the number of seats to be filled and then adding one, disregarding any fraction. See Sinnott, "Appendix 4: The Electoral System," 246–77.

39. Basil Chubb, "The Electoral System," in *Ireland at the Polls: The Dáil Elections of 1977*, ed. Howard Rae Penniman (Washington, DC: American Enterprise Institute for Public Policy, 1978), 27; Sinnott, *Irish Voters Decide*, 95; Mair and Marsh, "Political Parties in Electoral Markets," 234–63.

40. David Davin-Power, "The End of the Affair," in *The Week in Politics: Election 2011 and the 31st Dáil*, ed. Deirdre McCarthy (Dublin: RTÉ Publishing, 2011), 10–11.

41. John Coakley, "The Election and the Party System," in Gallagher, Marsh, and Mitchell, *How Ireland Voted 2002*, 240. Fianna Fáil ranks first in percentage of seats and second, behind the Labour Party in the United Kingdom, in percentage of votes won.

42. Peter Mair, "The Election in Context," in Gallagher and Marsh, *How Ireland Voted 2011: The Full Story of Ireland's Earthquake Election*, ed. Michael Gallagher and Michael Marsh (Basingstoke, Hampshire: Palgrave Macmillan, 2011), 285–88.

43. Michael Marsh, "Explanations for Party Choice," in *How Ireland Voted 2007: The Full Story of Ireland's General Election*, ed. Michael Gallagher and Michael Marsh (Basingstoke, Hampshire: Palgrave Macmillan, 2008), 120.

44. Stefano Bartolini and Peter Mair, *Identity, Competition, and Electoral Availability: The Stabilisation of European Electorates, 1885–1985* (Cambridge: Cambridge University Press, 1990), 19.

45. Michael Gallagher, "Ireland: The Discreet Charm of PR-STV," in *The Politics of Electoral Systems*, ed. Michael Gallagher and Paul Mitchell (Oxford: Oxford University Press, 2005), 522; David M. Farrell, *Electoral Systems: A Comparative Introduction* (Basingstoke, Hampshire: Palgrave Macmillan, 2001), 141; Séan Dorgan, interview by Sean McGraw, Dublin, September 2007. See also Sean Donnelly, "Number Cruncher: Sean Donnelly's Result Analysis," in McCarthy, *Week in Politics*, 71.

46. In the 1989 election, 65 percent of voters voted for more than one party. In 2002, most individuals voted for candidates from two (34 percent) or three (28 percent) parties. See David M. Farrell and Shaun Bowler, "Voter Behavior under STV-PR: Solving the Puzzle of the Irish Party System," *Political Behavior* 13, no. 4 (December 1991): 303–20; Marsh et al., *Irish Voter*, 14–30.

47. Stephen Collins, ed., *The Irish Times Nealon's Guide to the 30th Dáil and 23rd Seanad* (Dublin: Gill and Macmillan, 2007). There were only eleven cases in 2011 (and fourteen in 2007) where the seats were changed as a result of transfers. In other words, if a candidate is not in the running after the first count, the chance of winning a seat is only 10 percent. See Donnelly, "Number Cruncher," 69.

48. The two largest parties are generally the only ones that run multiple candidates in the same constituency. Fianna Fáil and Fine Gael candidates accordingly faced their toughest competition from members of their own party: as Michael Gallagher noted, "56 percent of Fianna Fáil TDs, and 37 percent of Fine Gael TDs, who suffer defeat at an election, lose to a running mate rather than to a candidate of another party." Overall patterns for candidates from every party reveal that interparty losses comprise 61 percent of all electoral defeats in Ireland between 1927 and 1997, almost double the 34 percent comprised of intraparty losses (Gallagher, "The (Relatively) Victorious Incumbent under PR-STV: Legislative Turnover in Ireland and Malta," in *Elections in Australia, Ireland, and Malta under the Single Transferable Vote: Reflections on an Embedded Institution*, ed. Shaun Bowler and Bernard Grofman [Ann Arbor: University of Michigan Press, 2000], 97).

49. These incumbency rates were calculated by Sean Donnelly, the Irish author, political analyst, and pollster who founded ElectionsIreland.org.

50. James A. Walsh, ed., *People and Place: A Census Atlas of the Republic of Ireland* (Maynooth, County Kildare: National Institute for Regional and Spatial Analysis, National University of Ireland, Maynooth, 2007), 329.

51. Neal G. Jesse, "A Sophisticated Voter Model of Preferential Electoral Systems," in *Elections in Australia, Ireland, and Malta under the Single Transferable Vote: Reflections on an Embedded Institution*, ed. Shaun Bowler and Bernard Grofman (Ann Arbor: University of Michigan Press, 2000), 69.

52. In my analysis, the urban constituencies include Cork NC, Cork SC, Dublin Central, Dublin MW, Dublin North, Dublin NC, Dublin NE, Dublin NW, Dublin South, Dublin SC, Dublin SE, Dublin SW, Dublin West, Dun Laoghaire, and Limerick East; the rural constituencies include Carlow-Kilkenny, Cavan-Monaghan, Clare, Cork East, Cork NW, Cork SW, Donegal NE, Donegal SW, Galway East, Galway West, Kerry North, Kerry South, Limerick West, Longford-Westmeath, Mayo, Sligo-Leitrim North, Roscommon-Leitrim South, Tipperary North, Tipperary South, and Waterford; and the commuter constituencies include Kildare North, Kildare South, Laois-Offaly, Louth, Meath East, Meath West, Wexford, and Wicklow.

53. For the purposes of my argument, I am simplifying the evolution of the Civil War parties into what eventually became the two "established" parties of Fianna Fáil and Fine Gael. For more on the early development of these parties, see J. J. Lee, *Ireland, 1912–1985: Politics and Society* (Cambridge: Cambridge University Press, 1989); Sinnott, *Irish Voters Decide*.

54. Lee, *Ireland, 1912–1985*, 69.

55. J. H. Whyte, "Ireland: Politics without Social Bases," in *Electoral Behaviour: A Comparative Handbook*, ed. Richard Rose (New York: Free Press, 1974), 619–51.

56. Whyte, "Ireland," 619–51.

57. Sean McGraw, "Managing Change: Party Competition in the New Ireland" (PhD diss., Harvard University, 2009), 140–57.

58. Marsh et al., *Irish Voter*, 31–58.

59. For the purposes of this analysis, I used three categories: upper and middle class (ABC1), working class (C2DE), and farmers (F1/F2).

60. Michael Marsh and Kevin Cunningham, "A Positive Choice, or Anyone but Fianna Fáil," in Marsh and Gallagher, *How Ireland Voted 2011*, 182–83.

61. Mair, *Changing Irish Party System*, 221.

62. Farrell, *Electoral Systems*, 4–7.

63. Farrell, *Electoral Systems*, 140.

64. See Farrell, *Electoral Systems*, 145; Bowler and Grofman, *Elections in Australia, Ireland, and Malta*.

65. Wolfgang Hirczy de Mino and John C. Lane, "Malta: STV in a Two-Party System," in Bowler and Grofman, *Elections in Australia, Ireland, and Malta*, 192–93.

66. Giovanni Sartori, "The Influence of Electoral Systems: Faulty Laws or Faulty Method?" in *Electoral Law and Their Political Consequences*, ed. Bernard Grofman and Arend Lijphart (New York: Agathon, 1986), 43–65.

67. See Farrell, *Electoral Systems*, 124–25.

68. Michael Gallagher, "Constituency Service, the Role of the TD, and the Electoral System" (report to the Oireachtas Joint Committee on the Constitution, November 18, 2009), available at https://www.tcd.ie/Political_Science/staff/michael_gallagher/PresentationToCtteNov09.pdf, 1–4.

69. Gallagher, "Constituency Service," 3.

70. Sinnott, *Irish Voters Decide*, 279–97. See also Min Shu, "Cope with Two-Dimensional Cleavage Structure: Party Politics in Referendums on European Integration" (paper presented at Workshop 19, "Cleavage Development: Causes and Consequences," ECPR Joint Sessions, Edinburgh, March 28—April 2, 2003).

71. Marsh et al., *Irish Voter*, 39–42.

72. The three highest response categories for each election are bolded in table 2.2.

73. The PDs won fourteen seats and 12 percent of the first-preference votes in their initial general election.

74. Richard Sinnott, "The Voters, the Issues, and the Party System," in *Ireland at the Polls, 1981, 1982, and 1987: A Study of Four General Elections*, ed. Howard Rae Penniman and Brian Farrell (Durham, NC: Duke University Press, 1987), 55–98. As Sinnott explains, for an issue to become an electoral one, there must be conflicting goals or objectives by the parties, or at least one party must be seen to have a more effective strategy (62–64).

75. Marsh et al., *Irish Voter*, 286.

76. Marsh et al., *Irish Voter*, 2. The variables used in the empirical tests are generated from the INES (2002–7).

77. Because evaluations of housing, crime, and local economy were not included in the 2011 INES, I developed a model incorporating only economy and health. This model produced even lower pseudo-R^2 values, ranging from .088 to .058.

78. Laver and Sergenti, *Party Competition*, 185–205.

79. James Adams, Michael Clark, et al., "Are Niche Parties Fundamentally Different from Mainstream Parties? The Causes and the Electoral Consequences of Western European Parties' Policy Shifts, 1976–1998," *American Journal of Political Science* 50, no. 3 (July 2006): 513–29.

80. In the 2007 election, Fianna Fáil candidate Cyprian Brady was elected in Dublin Central after having received just over nine hundred first-preference votes from his party colleague Taoiseach Bertie Ahern.

81. Marsh et al., *Irish Voter*, 137.

82. These figures are the average scores calculated from the data in table 2.2.

83. INES 2011, QB14–15.

84. INES 2011, QB16.

85. David Farrell and Jane Suiter, "It's the Policy, Stupid," in McCarthy, *Week in Politics*, 54.

86. Farrell and Suiter, "It's the Policy, Stupid," 56.

87. See "RTÉ Exit Poll 2007," *RTÉ News*, May 25 2007, http://www.rte.ie/news/2007/0525/RTEExitPoll2007. The ten issues included jobs stimulus, the abolition of the Health Services Executive, welfare cuts, whether to renegotiate the interest paid to the EU, whether to renegotiate with some bank bondholders, greater emphasis on taxes in the budget, whether to reverse the minimum wage cut, measures to deal with negative equity, increases in third-level education fees and charges, and the abolition of the Seanad.

CHAPTER 3

1. See Niamh Hardiman and Christopher T. Whelan, eds., *Politics and Democratic Values* (Dublin: Gill and Macmillan, 1994).

2. Michael Gallagher, "Societal Change and Party Adaptation in the Republic, 1960–1981," *European Journal of Political Research* 9 (1981): 269–85.

3. Laver and Sergenti, *Party Competition*, 10.

4. John Coakley, "The Rise and Fall of Minor Parties in Ireland, 1922–2011," in *Radical or Redundant? Minor Parties in Irish Politics*, ed. Liam Weeks and Alistair Clark (Dublin: History Press Ireland, 2012), 46–78.

5. Laver and Sergenti, *Party Competition*, 10.

6. Laver and Sergenti, *Party Competition*, 124–25.

7. Shaun McDaid and Kacper Rekawek, "From Mainstream to Minor and Back: The Irish Labour Party, 1987–1992," *Irish Political Studies* 25, no. 4 (2010): 625–42.

8. Ian Budge and Judith Bara, "Introduction: Content Analysis and Political Texts," in *Mapping Policy Preferences: Estimates for Parties, Electors, and Governments 1945–1998*, ed. Ian Budge et al. (Oxford: Oxford University Press, 2001), 3.

9. Budge and Bara, "Introduction," 6–7.

10. Andrea Volkens, "Quantifying the Election Programmes: Coding Procedures and Controls," in Budge et al., *Mapping Policy Preferences*, 93–109.

11. Ian Budge, "Theory and Measurement of Party Policy Positions," in Budge et al., *Mapping Policy Preferences*, 81–82.

12. The following are the mean ideological distances between TD and party and between voter and party, respectively, on key issues: left/right, 1.57 and 1.95; Northern Ireland, 1.44 and 2.13; tax/spend, 1.59 and 2.08; EU, 1.05 and 2.66; envi-

ronment, 1.30 and 2.90; abortion, 1.80 and 3.27. Standard deviation was calculated as s = $\sqrt{\Sigma((\text{self-placement} - \text{party placement})^2/n)}$. The mean distance recorded here is affected by outliers, so the median voter and the median TD are likely to be closer to their parties than these results indicate.

13. Torbin Iversen, "Political Leadership and Representation in West European Democracies: A Test of Three Models of Voting," *American Journal of Political Science* 38, no. 1 (1994): 45–74.

14. Lawrence Ezrow, Catherine E. De Vries, Marco Steenbergen, and Erica E. Edwards, "Mean Voter Representation and Partisan Constituency Representation: Do Parties Respond to the Mean Voter Position or to Their Supporters?" *Party Politics* 17, no. 3 (2011): 275–301.

15. The sample size of the parliamentary survey was too small to use a reliable multivariate model or to include minor party and independent TDs.

16. The Green Party's first-preference vote share declined from 5 percent in 2007 to 2 percent in 2011, and the party lost all six of its seats in 2011. Sinn Féin increased its first-preference vote from 7 percent in 2007 to 10 percent in 2011 and saw its seats rise from five in 2007 to fourteen in 2011.

17. James Adams, Michael Clark, et al., "Niche Parties"; James Adams and Lawrence Ezrow, "Why Do European Parties Represent? How Western European Parties Represent the Policy Preferences of Opinion Leaders," *Journal of Politics* 71, no. 1 (January 2009): 206–23; James Adams and Zeynep Somer-Topcu, "Policy Adjustment by Parties in Response to Rival Parties' Policy Shifts: Spatial Theory and the Dynamics of Party Competition in Twenty-Five Post-War Democracies," *British Journal of Political Studies* 39 (2009): 825–46; Adams, Haupt, and Stoll, "What Moves Parties?"

18. There were no expert surveys conducted during the 2011 election.

19. Kenneth Benoit and Michael Laver, *Party Policy in Modern Democracies* (London: Routledge, 2006), 229.

20. Perhaps it is not surprising that experts perceived Fianna Fail's largest shift on any policy to be a shift of 4.1 points on the Northern Ireland scale, given that they had worked to secure peace in the North by working closely with the British government.

21. See "RTÉ Exit Poll 2007," *RTÉ News*, May 25, 2007, http://www.rte.ie/news/2007/0525/RTEExitPoll2007.

22. Farrell and Suiter, "It's the Policy, Stupid," 54.

23. Ironically, only after the fear of Greece's default and concerns about Italy's debt crisis did Ireland receive the more favorable terms of a lowered interest rate. See Arthur Beesley and Derek Scally, "Irish Bailout Costs to Fall by €800 Million as EU Deal Agreed," *Irish Times* (Dublin), July 22, 2011, for details of the rate reduction.

24. Suiter and Farrell, "It's the Policy, Stupid," 40.

25. Suiter and Farrell, "It's the Policy, Stupid," 39–43.

26. Data for Ireland from the Manifesto Project Database include manifestos for eighteen parliamentary elections held between 1948 and 2007, with more reliable data for manifestos beginning in 1977 and 1981, when parties published their official manifesto documents. Fifty-six categories from the Comparative Manifestos Project were examined individually and amalgamated into seven broader issue

domains: external relations, freedom and democracy, political system, economy, welfare and quality of life, fabric of society, and social groups.

27. Christoffer Green-Pedersen, "The Growing Importance of Issue Competition: The Changing Nature of Party Competition in Western Europe," *Political Studies* 55, no. 3 (October 2007): 607–28.

28. Averages for the size of Western European and Irish manifestos were obtained from the Manifesto Project Database (v. 2009). Western European averages for this same period were 307 in the 1970s, 512 in the 1980s, 584 in the 1990s, and 909 in the 2000s (data accessed October 2008).

29. Green-Pedersen, "Issue Competition," 615–17; Benoit and Laver, *Party Policy*, 99–104.

30. Stephen Collins, *Breaking the Mould: How the PDs Changed Ireland* (Dublin: Gill and MacMillan, 2005), 124.

31. These top issues ranged from, for both parties, *environmental protection* and *welfare state expansion;* for Fianna Fáil, *farmers, labor groups, technology and infrastructure,* and *noneconomic demographic groups* (e.g., the elderly); and, for Fine Gael, *economic orthodoxy, market regulation,* and *incentives.*

32. The top three issues in 1981 for Fianna Fáil were *technology and infrastructure* (8.2 percent), *productivity* (7.6 percent), and *farmers* (7.6 percent). Fine Gael highlighted *incentives* (9.9 percent), *social justice* (9.1 percent), and *government efficiency.* Based on the results for each election, the top three issues received, on average, 34 percent of the overall manifesto for Fianna Fáil and 37 percent for Fine Gael.

33. Budge et al., *Mapping Policy Preferences,* 227. The *traditional morality positive* category includes favorable mentions of traditional moral values; prohibition, censorship, and suppression of immorality and unseemly behavior; maintenance and stability of family; and religion. The *traditional morality negative* category includes opposition to traditional moral values; support for divorce, abortion, and so on; and negative positions to those mentioned for the *traditional morality positive category.*

34. In 2007, the Greens devoted 0.5 percent to *traditional morality positive* and 0.1 percent to *traditional morality negative.*

35. Coakley, "Minor Parties in Ireland, 1922–2011," 77–78.

36. For more on Clann na Talmhan, which was concerned primarily with protecting the status of farmers neglected by Fianna Fáil's policies, see Lee, *Ireland, 1912–1985,* 295.

37. These policy domains were those mentioned previously in this discussion: *welfare state expansion, non-economic demographic groups* and *social justice.*

38. Michael McDowell, interview by Sean McGraw, Dublin, September 2007.

39. McDowell was referring to the leaders of Labour, Green, and Sinn Féin, respectively.

40. Michael McDowell, interview by Sean McGraw, Dublin, May 2007.

41. An analysis of the vote in the Dublin South-East constituency demonstrates that Creighton delivered a sizable vote in these middle-class areas. In addition, Gormley edged out McDowell by three hundred votes partly because he was able to win the transfer votes of the independents and Sinn Féin (i.e., the primarily "left" vote) and enough transfers from Andrews (FF) and O'Callaghan (FF) to win the last seat. In the final count, 510 of O'Callaghan's votes were nontransferable, and McDowell only lost to Gormley by 304 votes.

42. Peter Cassells, interview by Sean McGraw, Dublin, February 2007.

43. The original top three issues for the Greens were *environmental protection, antigrowth economy*, and *social justice*.

44. Nicole Bolleyer, "The Irish Green Party: From Protest to Mainstream Party?" *Irish Political Studies* 25, no. 4 (2010): 603–23.

45. See Adam Przeworski and John Sprague, *Paper Stones: A History of Electoral Socialism* (Chicago: University of Chicago Press, 1986). See also Herbert Kitschelt, *The Transformation of European Social Democracy* (Cambridge: Cambridge University Press, 1994), for a description of similar tensions within social democratic parties.

46. Lynn Ni Bhaoighealláin, interview by Sean McGraw, County Kerry, Ireland, August 2007.

47. Eimear Noelle O'Leary, "'Political Gatekeepers': An Analysis of the Brokerage Activities of TDs and MLAs" (PhD diss., University College Cork, 2011), 229.

48. Sean McGraw, interviews with the top eight finishers in Dublin South-East in the 2007 election, Dublin, July 2007.

49. McGraw, "Managing Change," 444–47, 456–59.

50. Paul Martin Sacks, *The Donegal Mafia: An Irish Political Machine* (New Haven: Yale University Press, 1976).

51. Sacks, *Donegal Mafia*, 7.

52. Sean McGraw, interview with former government advisor, Dublin, June 2011.

53. Michael Gallagher, *Results of Survey of Members of Both Houses of the Oireachtas: The Electoral System, Representative Role of TDs, and Proposals for Change* (interim report of the Joint Committee on the Constitution, February 2010), 3; see also 37–38, tables 3–5. The three most important activities identified by TDs were all constituency-based activities, not their parliamentary activities.

54. Gallagher, *Results of Survey of Members of Both Houses of the Oireachtas;* Oireachtas Committee of Public Accounts Records, http://www.oireachtas.ie/documents/committees30thdail/j-constitution/report_2008/Article1620100204.pdf. The average ranks of importance for who TDs think they should be representing, on a 1–6 scale, are as follows: all voters in a constituency, 1.56; all those in the constituency who voted for a TD, 2.77; all those in the constituency who voted for the TD's party, 3.37; all voters in the country, 3.38; all those in the country who voted for the TD's party, 4.03; members of a particular social group, 4.9.

55. The 2011 INES indicates that a high percentage of voters selected a candidate on whose behalf they had been contacted during the election. The following are the percentages of INES respondents who reported voting for a party by whom they were contacted during the campaign: Fine Gael, 67 percent; Sinn Féin, 52 percent; Socialists, 50 percent; Labour, 47 percent; Fianna Fáil, 43 percent; Independents, 34 percent; Green Party, 14 percent.

56. Marsh et al., *Irish Voter*, 210.

57. Gallagher, *Results of Survey of Members of Both Houses of the Oireachtas*, 17.

58. See Liam Weeks and Alistair Clark, eds., "Minor Parties in Irish Political Life," special issue, *Irish Political Studies* 25, no. 4 (2010).

59. Liam Weeks, "We Don't Like to Party: Explaining the Significance of Independents in Irish Political Life" (paper presented at the First Annual International Conference on Minor Parties, Independent Politicians, Voter Associations, and

Political Associations in Politics, Institute of Local Government Studies, University of Birmingham, November 29–December 1, 2007).

60. Eoin O'Malley, "Punch Bags for Heavyweights? Minor Parties in Irish Government," *Irish Political Studies* 25, no. 4 (2010): 544.

61. O'Malley, "Punch Bags," 547–48.

CHAPTER 4

1. Bonnie Meguid, *Party Competition Between Unequals: Strategies and Electoral Fortunes in Western Europe* (Cambridge: Cambridge University Press, 2008).

2. Greg D. Adams, "Abortion: Evidence of an Issue Evolution," *American Journal of Political Science* 41, no. 3 (1997): 718–37.

3. Kirsten Hamann and John Kelly, *Parties, Elections, and Policy Reforms in Western Europe: Voting for Social Pacts* (London: Routledge, 2011).

4. Hamann and Kelly, *Parties, Elections, and Policy Reforms*, 62.

5. Hamann and Kelly, *Parties, Elections, and Policy Reforms*, 63–65.

6. Hamann and Kelly, *Parties, Elections, and Policy Reforms*, 66–69.

7. Tim Hastings, Brian Sheehan, and Padraig Yeates, *Saving the Future: How Ireland's Social Partnership Shaped Ireland's Economic Success* (Dublin: Blackhall Publishing, 2007), 205.

8. Paula Clancy and Grainne Murphy, *Outsourcing Government: Public Bodies and Accountability* (Dublin: TASC [A Think Tank for Action on Social Change] and New Island, 2006), 10.

9. Niamh Hardiman and Colin Scott, "Governance as Polity: An Institutional Approach to the Evolution of State Functions in Ireland," *Public Administration* 88, no. 1 (March 2010): 170–89.

10. Clancy and Murphy, *Outsourcing Government*, 22.

11. Clancy and Murphy, *Outsourcing Government*, 15.

12. Steve Garner, *Racism in the Irish Experience* (London: Pluto, 2004), 59–66.

13. Noel Whelan, *Fianna Fáil: A Biography of the Party* (Dublin: Gill and Macmillan, 2011), 8.

14. Stephen Collins, "Handling of Seismic Events Was Good for Irish Politics," *Irish Times (Dublin)*, October 4, 2008, 15.

15. Fiach Kelly, "Kenny Ignores Own Pledge to Avoid Constituency Service," *Irish Independent*, May 17, 2011.

CHAPTER 5

1. Basil Chubb, "Going about Persecuting Civil Servants: The Role of the Irish Parliamentary Representative," *Political Studies* 11, no. 3 (October 1963): 272–86.

2. E. O'Leary, "Political Gatekeepers," 175.

3. Andre Krouwel, "Party Models," in *The Handbook of Party Politics*, ed. Richard S. Katz and William J. Crotty (London: Sage, 2006), 249–69.

4. Kitschelt, *European Social Democracy*, 207–53; Levitsky, *Transforming Labor-Based Parties*; Panebianco, *Political Parties*, 15.

5. Levitsky, *Transforming Labor-Based Parties*, 3–4.

6. Levitsky, *Transforming Labor-Based Parties*, 13.

7. Krouwel, "Party Models," 262–63.

8. Moshe Maor, *Political Parties and Party Systems: Comparative Approaches and the British Experience* (London: Routledge, 1997) 105–7.

9. Maor, *Political Parties*, 108–10; Krouwel, "Party Models," 256–58.

10. Maor, *Political Parties*, 111–13; Krouwel, "Party Models," 258–60.

11. Krouwel, "Party Models," 260–61.

12. For more detailed descriptions of party organization, see Mair, *Changing Irish Party System*, 93–106; Michael Gallagher and Michael Marsh, *Days of Blue Loyalty: The Politics of Membership of the Fine Gael Party* (Dublin: PSAI Press, 2002), 40–47; Michael Marsh, "Parties and Society," in *Politics in the Republic of Ireland*, ed. John Coakley and Michael Gallagher, 4th ed. (London: Routledge in association with PSAI Press, 2005), 160–82; Basil Chubb, *The Government and Politics of Ireland*, 3rd ed. (London: Longman, 1992).

13. David Farrell, "Ireland: Centralization, Professionalization and Competitive Pressures," in *How Parties Organize: Change and Adaptation in Party Organizations in Western Democracies*, ed. Richard S. Katz and Peter Mair (London: Sage, 1994), 219.

14. Dick Walsh, *The Party: Inside Fianna Fáil* (Dublin: Gill and Macmillan, 1986), 4.

15. Carty, *Parish Pump*, 142–43.

16. Mair, *Changing Irish Party System*, 121. See also Gallagher and Marsh, *Days of Blue*.

17. Garret FitzGerald, interview by Sean McGraw, Dublin, February 2007.

18. Mair, *Changing Irish Party System*, 124.

19. Farrell, "Ireland," 219. Farrell suggests that the local branches were outgrowths of the Irish Republican Army battalions and companies that had existed since the time of the War of Independence from Britain. One could also trace these organizational units back to the nineteenth century and Daniel O'Connell's development of parish networks in the Catholic Emancipation movement: see Sean McGraw and Kevin Whelan, "Daniel O'Connell in Comparative Perspective, 1800–1850," *Eire-Ireland: An Interdisciplinary Journal of Irish Studies* 40, nos. 1–2 (2005): 60–89.

20. Pat Rabbitte, interview by Sean McGraw, Dublin, October 2007.

21. Catherine Murphy, interview by Sean McGraw, County Kildare, Ireland, July 2007.

22. In the past, three delegates from each local branch would be dispatched to a constituency's nomination convention to vote on candidates for the upcoming election. Paper branches consisted of exactly the same number of people (three) as a branch could send as delegates to the constituency's convention. In other cases, names on the register may not have even known they were included. This proved an effective way to rig nomination conventions.

23. Carty, *Parish Pump*, 137.

24. Frank Wall (General Secretary of Fianna Fáil, 1981–91), interview by Sean McGraw, Dublin, December 2007.

25. For more on party membership, see Mair, *Changing Irish Party System*, 104; Farrell, "Ireland," 227.

26. Seán Dorgan, interview by Sean McGraw, Dublin, October 2007. According to Seán Dorgan (Fianna Fáil General Secretary), party leaders chose not to eliminate smaller, more rural, and often moribund branches.

27. Dorgan, interview, October 2007; Rabbitte, interview; Frank Flannery, interview by Sean McGraw, Dublin, October 2007.

28. One caveat for these results is that the survey did not specifically ask TDs about local party funding. They were asked about national party funding, private donations, self-funding, and "other" and were asked to specify what was meant by "other."

29. Jim O'Callaghan, interview by Sean McGraw, Dublin, July 2007; Wall, interview.

30. Dorgan, interview, October 2007.

31. Flannery, interview.

32. G. FitzGerald, interview ; Wall, interview.

33. Sean McGraw, interview of Fianna Fáil party official, Dublin, November 2012.

34. Farrell, "Ireland," 221–22.

35. Harry McGee, "Seamus Brennan," *IrishTimes.com*, July 9, 2008, http://www.irishtimes.com/blogs/politics/2008/07/09/seamus-brennan/.

36. "RTÉ Exit Poll 2007," *RTÉ News*, May 25, 2007, http://www.rte.ie/news/2007/0525/RTEExitPoll2007.

37. "RTÉ Exit Poll 2007," *RTÉ News*, May 25, 2007, http://www.rte.ie/news/2007/0525/RTEExitPoll2007. In 2011, there was controversy over the number of debates and which party leaders would be included in them. It was also the first election in which there was a debate in Irish on national television. The RTÉ exit poll reported the following results for which leader "came out the best" among respondents who watched the debate where leaders of the five main parties were present: Martin (Fianna Fáil), 32 percent; Kenny (Fine Gael), 29 percent; Gilmore (Labour), 14 percent; Adams (Sinn Féin), 5 percent; Gormley (Greens), 2 percent. Seventeen percent reported that there was no clear winner.

38. Fifty-five percent of voters who made up their mind on how they would vote in the election supported Fianna Fáil, compared with only 14 percent who voted for Fine Gael, 10 percent for Labour, and 22 percent for others. Although there were many factors that contributed to this increased support for Fianna Fáil, the debate was a key factor. See http://www.rte.ie/news/2007/0525/RTEExitPoll2007.

39. Murphy, interview.

40. "RTÉ Exit Poll 2007."

41. In contrast to the three main parties, which typically had at least thirty to fifty press members at their press conferences, there were only about ten press members present for the many press conferences of the Greens that I attended during the campaign.

42. Note that Fine Gael was by far the most efficient in 2011: two-thirds of INES respondents reported being contacted by Fine Gael during the election and also voting for them. The other opposition parties in this election, including Labour, Sinn Féin, and the Socialists, witnessed 20 percent increases in the numbers of respondents who reported being contacted during the campaign.

43. Kenneth Benoit and Michael Marsh, "Incumbent and Challenger Campaign Spending Effects in Proportional Electoral Systems: The Irish Elections of 2002," *Political Research Quarterly* 63, no. 1 (2010): 159–73.

44. Wall, interview.

45. Standards in Public Office Commission, "Donation Statements furnished by Political Parties for 2006" (Report by the Standards in Public Office Commission to the Chairman of Dáil Éireann Pursuant to Section 4(1) of the Electoral Act 1997), http://www.sipo.gov.ie/en/Reports/Annual-Disclosures/Disclosure-by-Political-Parties/2006-Donation-Statements/.

46. Elaine Byrne, "Irish Political Party Financing" (paper presented at the Annual Conference of the Political Studies Association of Ireland, University College Cork, October 20–22, 2006); Standards in Public Office Commission, *Annual Reports*, http://www.sipo.gov.ie/en/Reports/Annual-Reports/.

47. See "Election 2007: Following the Money," *Sunday Business Post*, December 12, 2007.

48. Byrne, "Party Financing."

49. The breakdown of support for Fianna Fáil by industry is 32 percent from construction and property developers, 26 percent from businesses and the financial sector, 9 percent from the hospitality sector, 7 percent from the motor sector, 5 percent from the drinks industry, 4 percent from auctioneers (real estate agents), and 2 percent from lawyers.

50. "Cowen Abandons Fianna Fáil Tent at Galway Races," *Irish Times*, December 3, 2008.

51. In terms of Sinn Féin's external support, 44 percent of their donations were from the Friends of Sinn Féin organization in America, 21 percent was donated by elected representatives in Northern Ireland, and 12 percent came from the Friends of Sinn Féin organization in Australia.

52. Flannery, interview.

53. Rabbitte, interview.

54. See "Green Ministers' Pay Rises to Go to Party," *Irish Times*, November 20, 2007.

55. Standards in Public Office Commission, "Donation Statements furnished by Political Parties for 2011," April 1, 2013, http://www.sipo.gov.ie/en/reports/annual-disclosures/disclosure-by-political-parties/2011-donation-statements/.

56. Jon Pierre, Lars Svasand, and Anders Widfelt, "State Subsidies to Political Parties: Confronting Rhetoric with Reality," *West European Politics* 23, no. 3 (2000): 1–24.

57. Farrell, "Ireland," 223; Oireachtas (Ministerial and Parliamentary Offices) (Secretarial Facilities) (No. 5) Regulations 2004, S.I. No. 888/ 2004, Irish Statute Book, http://www.irishstatutebook.ie/2004/en/si/0888.html.

58. *Annual Report of the Houses of the Oireachtas Commission, 1 January 2004 to 31 December 2004* (Dublin: Stationery Office, 2005), http://www.oireachtas.ie/parliament/media/about/annualreports/Houses-of-the-Oireachtas-Commission-Annual-Report-2004.pdf.

59. John O'Leary, interview by Sean McGraw, County Kerry, Ireland, August 2007.

60. Farrell, "Ireland."

61. Colm Ó Caomhanaigh (General Secretary of the Green Party), interview by Sean McGraw, Dublin, December 2007. See also Desmond O'Malley, Catherine Murphy, and Dan Boyle, "Life in a Minor Party," in Weeks and Clark, *Radical or Redundant?*, 84

62. Byrne, "Party Financing."

63. Byrne, "Party Financing."

64. Séan Donnelly, e-mail message to Sean McGraw, August 2011. After the 2011 election, the new Dáil consisted of 49 percent incumbents, 24 percent TDs who ran for the first time in that election, 22 percent TDs who had run before but were elected for the first time in that election, and 5 percent former TDs returning to parliament. The incumbency rates for the three constituencies in the case study were 67 percent for Dublin South-East, 76 percent for Kildare, and 80 percent for Kerry South.

65. "Reelection Rates over the Years," OpenSecrets.org, http://www.open secrets.org/bigpicture/reelect.php?cycle=2006 (accessed November 2013).

66. Richard E. Matland and Donley T. Studlar, "Determinants of Legislative Turnover: A Cross-National Analysis," *British Journal of Political Science* 34, no. 1 (2004): 87–108.

67. Lucinda Creighton, interview by Sean McGraw, Dublin, July 2007.

68. John Hickey, interview by Sean McGraw, Dublin, August 2007; Ni Bha-oighealláin, interview.

69. Alan O'Keefe, "Democracy Now Celebs Ditch Their Election Bid," *Herald. ie,* January 31, 2011, http://www.herald.ie/news/democracy-now-celebs-ditch-their-election-bid-27972149.html.

70. Data based on election figures from ElectionsIreland.org.

71. Farrell, "Ireland," 223.

72. Sinnott, *Irish Voters Decide*; Mair and Marsh, "Political Parties in Electoral Markets"; Gallagher and Marsh, *How Ireland Voted 2007*.

73. Wall, interview.

74. Farrell, "Ireland," 227.

75. Ian Hughes et al., *Power to the People? Assessing Democracy in Ireland*, (Dublin: TASC at New Island Press, 2007), 276.

76. Michael McDowell, interview by Sean McGraw, Dublin, July 2007; Ó Caom-hanaigh, interview.

77. This procedure has not always maintained party unity. Fianna Fáil's fractious leadership strife occurred after the retirement of de Valera and Lemass, as competing leaders sought to win support from parliamentary colleagues. The disunity peaked under Charles Haughey, whose controversial and abrasive leadership was challenged unsuccessfully three times in the early 1980s. Disaffected Fianna Fáil members who disliked Haughey eventually formed the PDs in 1985 to oppose him.

78. Conor Lenihan, interview by Sean McGraw, Dublin, March 2007.

79. Brendan Halligan, interview by Sean McGraw, Dublin, May 2007; Wall, interview. According to Frank Wall, Charles Haughey (former Fianna Fáil Taoiseach) explicitly told him that policy development was the parliamentary party's responsibility whereas party organizational matters were the concern of the national executive and party headquarters.

80. John Gormley (former Green Party TD and party leader), interview by Sean McGraw, Dublin, April 2013.

81. For a discussion of vote-seeking, office-seeking, and policy-seeking parties, see Kaare Strøm and Wolfgang C. Müller, "Political Parties and Hard Choices," in *Policy, Office, or Votes? How Political Parties in Western Europe Make Hard Choices*, ed.

Wolfgang C. Müller and Kaare Strøm (Cambridge: Cambridge University Press, 1999), 1–35.

82. Twenty-one percent of respondents in the 2011 INES claimed to be close to a particular party. The breakdown of the parties to which they were closest was as follows: Fine Gael, 42 percent; Fianna Fáil, 31 percent; Labour, 11 percent; Sinn Féin, 15 percent; the Greens, less than 1 percent; and other, 1 percent.

83. A study of the 2004 local elections in Ireland found that virtually 100 percent of candidates personally conducted door-to-door canvassing during that campaign. Second among their popular election activities was erecting posters, undertaken by 85 percent of candidates in 2004 (Liam Weeks and Aodh Quinlivan, *All Politics Is Local* [Cork: Collins, 2009], 124).

84. In this analysis, the null hypothesis is that party identification does not influence a TD's position on these policy issues. The party dummies are all zero, and the question is whether the equation reveals enough information to reject the null. The reference category is the means of minor party candidates; therefore, the coefficients for the three major parties indicate how many points the means of the major party TDs are apart from those of the minor party TDs on the 10-point scale. The discrepancies are small and statistically insignificant ($p < 0.05$) for all the variables except personal letters; therefore, we can conclude that party identification does not explain the variance among the party means for these various methods of reaching out to voters.

85. Frank Fahey, presentation at the Fianna Fáil Ard Fheis (national party conference), Dublin, March 2007.

86. Fahey's presentation to the Fianna Fáil Ard Fheis in 2007 included detailed maps of local neighborhoods where his local constituency office had identified which houses supported him. E-mail Sean McGraw at mcgraw.4@nd.edu for a detailed map of the 2007 election results indicating levels of support that Labour received in each neighborhood (street by street) within the constituency, constructed by Labour TD Ruairí Quinn from Dublin South-East.

87. J. O'Leary, interview; Breeda Moynihan Cronin, interview by Sean McGraw, Killarney, County Kerry, Ireland, August 2007.

88. Bernard Durkan, interview by Sean McGraw, Dublin, July 2007.

89. E. O'Leary, "Political Gatekeepers," 169–70.

90. Evidence from my 2010 and 2012 parliamentary surveys indicates the following results for the average number of hours spent in clinics each week as reported by TDs who were elected to parliament in 2007 and 2011, respectively: Fianna Fáil, 13.1 and 7.8; Fine Gael, 10.9 and 6.4; Labour, 7.4 and 5.7; Sinn Féin, 19.0 and 10.8; independents, 19.0 and 10.0; Greens, 4.3 in 2007. There are also differences in terms of the average number of hours TDs from urban, commuter, and rural constituencies spent in clinics in 2007 respectively: urban, 8.3; commuter, 13.4; and rural, 15.9 hours. These hours declined for 2011 to 5.7 hours, 6.3 hours and 9.5 hours respectively.

91. E. O'Leary, "Political Gatekeepers," 170.

92. E. O'Leary, "Political Gatekeepers," 171–74.

93. J. O'Leary, interview; Tom Sheahan, interview by Sean McGraw, County Kerry, Ireland, August 2007.

94. Michael O'Connor-Scarteen, interview by Sean McGraw, Kenmare, County Kerry, Ireland, August 2007.

95. Sheahan, interview.

96. Dorgan, interview, October 2007; Flannery, interview; Rabbitte, interview.

97. Flannery, interview.

98. Flannery, interview. In each of the six constituencies where the Green Party's incumbent was defeated in 2011, Fine Gael and Labour won additional seats, and Fianna Fáil won fewer seats. In addition, an independent won in Dublin South, a Socialist in Dublin North, and a People Before Profit candidate in Dun Laoghaire.

99. Fianna Fáil only reported €18,000 for market research, but this figure includes €40,000 that the party spent on local opinion polls ("Election 2007: Following the Money").

100. "Election 2007: Following the Money."

101. In my 2010 Irish parliamentary survey, 102 of 166 elected TDs were interviewed face-to-face.

102. Fine Gael TDs reported lower scores for all three electoral tools, especially compared to other electoral tools such as door-to-door canvassing, rallies, and radio exposure. Nevertheless, an OLS estimate of TDs' assessments of the importance of various methods used to inform voters in the 2007 general election campaign indicates a statistically significant result for Fine Gael TDs' perception of the importance of using electoral consultants. Fine Gael TDs may have ranked electoral consultants lower compared to other electoral tools, but when all factors were considered, they perceived using consultants as more important than did TDs from minor parties.

103. Donnelly, e-mail.

104. Adrian Kavanagh, "Geography and Irish Elections: A Case Study of the 2007 General Election," (paper presented at the Annual Conference of the Political Studies Association of Ireland, Dublin, October 19–21, 2007).

105. It is widely considered that Fianna Fáil fielded too many candidates per constituency throughout the country in the 2011 general election.

106. This dimension becomes more relevant in a sprawling constituency like Kerry South, which is spread over a much broader and more remote geographical area, thereby elevating the appeal of local candidates over party candidates.

107. Jackie Foley (longtime Fine Gael party activist in Kerry South from the 1960s to the present), interview by Sean McGraw, County Kerry, Ireland, August 2007.

108. Darren Scully, interview by Sean McGraw, County Kildare, Ireland, July 2007.

109. Sheahan, interview; Séamus Cosái Fitzgerald, interview by Sean McGraw, Dingle, County Kerry, Ireland, August 2007.

110. John O'Donoghue, interview by Sean McGraw, Cahersiveen, County Kerry, Ireland, August 2007; Tom Fleming, interview by Sean McGraw, County Kerry, Ireland, August 2007.

111. Ted Nealon, *Nealon's Guide to the 23rd Dáil and Seanad: Election '73* (Dublin: Gill and MacMillan, 1974); Michael Gallagher, "The (Relatively) Victorious Incumbent under PR-STV: Legislative Turnover in Ireland and Malta," in *Elections in Australia, Ireland, and Malta under the Single Transferable Vote: Reflections on an*

Embedded Institution, ed. Shaun Bowler and Bernard Grofman (Ann Arbor: University of Michigan Press, 2000).

112. The inability to attract lower-preference transfers was disastrous for Fianna Fáil in 2011. Labour received 19 percent of first-preference votes, and Fianna Fáil won 17 percent; yet Labour won thirty-seven seats compared to Fianna Fáil's twenty.

113. Statistics compiled from previous *Nealon Guides to the Irish Parliament* and information collected from the candidates in the Thirtieth Dáil. The typical Dáil during this period averaged thirty-six TDs who were family members of previous or current TDs. In my 2010 parliamentary survey, 19 percent of the 102 TDs interviewed had relatives with previous political experience.

114. Weeks and Quinlivan, *All Politics Is Local*, 159.

115. The Local Government Bill (2003) abolished the dual mandate under which TDs and senators could be members of local authorities while also serving in the Oireachtas. Under the act, a majority of TDs in the Twenty-Ninth Dáil and Seanad had to relinquish their local authority seats. See "Dual Mandate Comes to an End," *RTÉ News*, June 2, 2003, http://www.rte.ie/news/2003/0602/dualmandate.html.

116. Collins, *Nealon's Guide to the 30th Dáil and 23rd Seanad*, 180–82.

117. Michael Healy-Rae, interview by Sean McGraw, County Kerry, Ireland, May 2007.

118. Murphy, interview.

119. Campaign speeches made during the official election campaign, May 2007.

120. This relationship was especially true for the Green Party. However, after several Green councillors became TDs, the local organization was shorn of councillors in the aftermath of the 2002 and 2007 general elections. The loss of all Green candidates in the 2009 local election clearly hurt them in 2011, when they lost all six of their Dáil seats.

121. "Bonfires Blaze for Begley," *Kerryman*, March 17, 1973.

122. "Ministers' Constituency Staff Cost €4m a Year," *Irish Times*, November 8, 2007.

123. Jane Suiter, "Pork Barrel Spending in Ireland—Fact or Fiction?" (PhD diss., Trinity College Dublin, 2009).

124. Jane Suiter, "The Geo-Politics of Irish Education Spending" (paper presented at the Annual Conference of the Political Studies Association of Ireland, National University of Ireland, Galway, October 17–19, 2008).

125. Brendan Tuohy (former General Secretary of the Communications, Energy, and Natural Resources Department), interview by Sean McGraw, Dublin, December 2007. The 1924 Ministers and Secretaries Act (section 7) provided for the appointment of a maximum of seven "parliamentary secretaries" to act as junior ministers. In 1977, this provision was repealed and replaced by a measure allowing for the appointment of "ministers of state" from among members of either House to a maximum figure of, initially, ten and, subsequently, fifteen (since 1980), seventeen (since 1995), and twenty (since 2007).

CHAPTER 6

1. Kitschelt, *Party Formation*; Levitsky, *Transforming Labor-Based Parties*.

2. Theo Schiller, "Conclusions," in *Referendums and Representative Democracy:*

Responsiveness, Accountability, and Deliberation, ed. Maija Setala and Theo Schiller, ECPR Studies in European Political Science (London: Routledge, 2009), 214.

3. Schiller, "Conclusions," 211–12.

4. Wilfred Marxer and Zoltan Tibor Pallinger, "Stabilizing or Destabilizing? Direct-Democratic Instruments in Different Political Systems," in Setala and Schiller, *Referendums and Representative Democracy*, 46.

5. Marxer and Pallinger, "Stabilizing or Destabilizing?," 48–50.

6. Hamann and Kelly, *Parties, Elections, and Policy Reforms*. Hamann and Kelly define "unconnected" coalitions as consisting of parties that are from different ideological backgrounds.

7. Fianna Fáil entered into a coalition government with the Progressive Democrats in 1989, which marked the first time the party had formed a coalition government because it was unable to form the government on its own.

8. Hamann and Kelly, *Parties, Elections, and Policy Reforms*, 165–68.

9. Peter J. Katzenstein, *Policy and Politics in West Germany: The Growth of a Semisovereign State* (Philadelphia: Temple University Press, 1987), 58–80.

10. Katzenstein, *Policy and Politics in West Germany*, 58–80.

11. Kitschelt and Wilkinson, "Citizen-Politician Linkages," 41.

12. Kitschelt and Wilkinson, "Citizen-Politician Linkages."

13. For example, see Beatriz Magaloni, Alberto Diaz-Cayeros, and Federico Estévez, "Clientelism and Portfolio Diversification: A Model of Electoral Investment with Applications to Mexico," in Kitschelt and Wilkinson, *Patrons, Clients, and Policies*, 182–205. See also Kitschelt and Wilkinson, "Citizen-Politician Linkages," 46–47.

14. Kitschelt and Wilkinson, "Citizen-Politician Linkages," 26–41.

15. Anibal Romero, "Rearranging the Deck Chairs on the Titanic: The Agony of Democracy in Venezuela," *Latin American Research Review*, 32 (1997): 7–36; Terry Lynn Karl, *The Paradox of Plenty: Oil Booms and Petro-States* (Berkeley: University of California Press, 1997).

16. Seawright, *Party System Collapse*.

17. Alan Heston, Robert Summers, and Bettina Aten, Penn World Table Version 7.0, Center for International Comparisons of Production, Income, and Prices at the University of Pennsylvania, June 2011.

18. Romero, "Rearranging the Deck Chairs," 23–24.

19. Jana Morgan, "Partisanship during the Collapse of Venezuela's Party System," *Latin American Research Review* 42 (2007): 83.

20. Seawright's *Party System Collapse* offers a two-stage model of the collapse. First, voters grew disillusioned with the traditional parties because they perceived them to be self-serving and corrupt, but they still voted for these parties (albeit apathetically), because they were averse to risk. Second, voters became angry, which political psychology has found to lower the risk of changing one's behavior. This anger, fueled by a sense of being underrepresented, lowered people's risk aversion enough to abandon traditional parties. Even though the Left was fairly small and, as Seawright notes, "clearly incapable of electing a president" (135), it was big enough to make a presidential candidate noticeable to centrist voters disinterested in AD and COPEI.

21. Ellis S. Krauss and Robert Pekkanen, *The Rise and Fall of Japan's LDP: Political*

Party Organizations as Historical Institutions (Ithaca: Cornell University Press, 2011), 270.

22. Peter Mair, "Democracy beyond Parties" (working paper 05/06, Center for the Study of Democracy, University of California, Irvine, 2005), http://repositories. cdlib.org/csd/05–06; Schmitter, "Parties Are Not What They Once Were."

23. Schmitter, "Parties Are Not What They Once Were," 67–89.

24. Scott Mainwaring and Timothy R. Scully, eds., *Democratic Governance in Latin America* (Stanford: Stanford University Press, 2009).

25. Mair, "Democracy beyond Parties"; Mair, "Election in Context."

26. Krouwel, "Party Models," 251–52, 258–61.

27. Mair, "Election in Context."

28. Mair, "Election in Context."

29. Mair, "Election in Context," 15. Mair cites an earlier study by Krastev, who argued that stability in the Balkans in the early 2000s was due to outside pressure, EU and IMF budgetary constraints, and the like.

30. Lucio Baccaro and Simoni Marco, "The Irish Social Partnership and the Celtic Tiger Phenomenon," (discussion paper, International Institute for Labour Studies, Geneva, 2004); Seamus Ó Cinnéide, "Democracy and the Constitution," *Administration* 51, nos. 1–2 (Spring–Summer 2003): 326–40.

31. Alan Dukes (former TD and leader of Fine Gael), interview by Sean McGraw, Dublin, February 2007. See also Rory O'Donnell and Damian Thomas, "Social Partnership and the Policy Process," in *Social Policy in Ireland: Principles, Practice, and Problems*, ed. Séan Healy, Brigid Reynolds, and Micheál Collins, rev. ed. (Dublin: Liffy, 2006).

32. Albert O. Hirschman, *Exit, Voice, and Loyalty: Responses to Decline in Firms, Organizations, and States* (Cambridge, MA: Harvard University Press, 1970).

Bibliography

Adams, Greg D. "Abortion: Evidence of an Issue Evolution." *American Journal of Political Science* 41, no. 3 (1997): 718–37.

Adams, James, Michael Clark, Lawrence Ezrow, and Garrett Glasgow. "Are Niche Parties Fundamentally Different from Mainstream Parties? The Causes and the Electoral Consequences of Western European Parties' Policy Shifts, 1976–1998." *American Journal of Political Science* 50, no. 3 (July 2006): 513–29.

Adams, James, and Lawrence Ezrow. "Why Do European Parties Represent? How Western European Parties Represent the Policy Preferences of Opinion Leaders." *Journal of Politics* 71, no. 1 (January 2009): 206–23.

Adams, James, Andrea B. Haupt, and Heather Stoll. "What Moves Parties? The Role of Public Opinion and Global Economic Conditions in Western Europe." *Comparative Political Studies* 42, no. 5 (May 2009): 611–39.

Adams, James, Samuel Merrill, and Bernard Grofman. *A Unified Theory of Party Competition: A Cross-National Analysis Integrating Spatial and Behavioral Factors.* Cambridge: Cambridge University Press, 2005.

Adams, James, and Zeynep Somer-Topcu. "Policy Adjustment by Parties in Response to Rival Parties' Policy Shifts: Spatial Theory and the Dynamics of Party Competition in Twenty-Five Post-War Democracies." *British Journal of Political Studies* 39 (2009): 825–46.

"Ahern-Kenny Debate Attracts Almost One Million Viewers." *Independent*, 18 May 2007.

Alliance of Liberals and Democrats for Europe Group. Website. http://www.alde.eu/.

Annual Report of the Houses of the Oireachtas Commission, 1 January 2004 to 31 December 2004. Dublin: Stationery Office, 2005. http://www.oireachtas.ie/parliament/media/about/annualreports/Houses-of-the-Oireachtas-Commission-Annual-Report-2004.pdf.

Baccaro, Lucio, and Simoni Marco. "The Irish Social Partnership and the Celtic

Tiger Phenomenon." Discussion paper, International Institute for Labour Studies, Geneva, 2004.

Bartolini, Stefano, and Peter Mair. *Identity, Competition, and Electoral Availability: The Stabilisation of European Electorates, 1885–1985.* Cambridge: Cambridge University Press, 1990.

Beesley, Arthur, and Derek Scally. "Irish Bailout Costs to Fall by €800 Million as EU Deal Agreed." *Irish Times* (Dublin), July 22, 2011.

Benoit, Kenneth, and Michael Laver. *Party Policy in Modern Democracies.* London: Routledge, 2006.

Benoit, Kenneth, and Michael Marsh. "Incumbent and Challenger Campaign Spending Effects in Proportional Electoral Systems: The Irish Elections of 2002." *Political Research Quarterly* 63, no. 1 (2010): 159–73.

Blaney, Niall. Interview by Sean McGraw. Dublin, October 2007.

Bolleyer, Nicole. "The Irish Green Party: From Protest to Mainstream Party?" *Irish Political Studies* 25, no. 4 (2010): 603–23.

"Bonfires Blaze for Begley," *Kerryman,* March 17, 1973.

Bowler, Shaun, and Bernard Grofman, eds. *Elections in Australia, Ireland, and Malta under the Single Transferable Vote: Reflections on an Embedded Institution.* Ann Arbor: University of Michigan Press, 2000.

Budge, Ian. "Theory and Measurement of Party Policy Positions." In *Mapping Policy Preferences: Estimates for Parties, Electors, and Governments, 1945–1998,* edited by Ian Budge, Hans Dieter Klingemann, Andrea Volkens, Judith Bara, and Eric Tanenbaum, 75–90. Oxford: Oxford University Press, 2001.

Budge, Ian, and Judith Bara. "Introduction: Content Analysis and Political Texts." In *Mapping Policy Preferences: Estimates for Parties, Electors, and Governments, 1945–1998,* edited by Ian Budge, Hans Dieter Klingemann, Andrea Volkens, Judith Bara, and Eric Tanenbaum, 1–16. Oxford: Oxford University Press, 2001.

Budge, Ian, Hans Dieter Klingemann, Andrea Volkens, Judith Bara, and Eric Tanenbaum, eds. *Mapping Policy Preferences: Estimates for Parties, Electors, and Governments, 1945–1998.* Oxford: Oxford University Press, 2001.

Byrne, Elaine. "Irish Political Party Financing." Paper presented at the Annual Conference of the Political Studies Association of Ireland, University College Cork, October 20–22, 2006.

Carty, R. K. *Party and Parish Pump: Electoral Politics in Ireland.* Ontario: Wilfred Laurier University Press, 1981.

Cassells, Peter. Interview by Sean McGraw. Dublin, February 2007.

Central Statistics Office. *Census 2011 Reports.* March 29–December 13, 2012. http://www.cso.ie/en/census/census2011reports/.

Central Statistics Office. *Unemployment Rates.* http://cso.ie/indicators/default.aspx?id=2LRM03.

Central Statistics Office. Website. http://www.cso.ie.

Chubb, Basil. "The Electoral System." In *Ireland at the Polls: The Dáil Elections of 1977,* edited by Howard Rae Penniman, 21–34. Washington, DC: American Enterprise Institute for Public Policy Research, 1978.

Chubb, Basil. "Going about Persecuting Civil Servants: The Role of the Irish Parliamentary Representative." *Political Studies* 11, no. 3 (October 1963): 272–86.

Chubb, Basil. *The Government and Politics of Ireland.* 3rd ed. London: Longman, 1992.

Clancy, Paula, and Grainne Murphy. *Outsourcing Government: Public Bodies and Accountability.* Dublin: TASC (A Think Tank for Action on Social Change) and New Island, 2006.

Coakley, John. "The Election and the Party System." In *How Ireland Voted 2002,* edited by Michael Gallagher, Michael Marsh, and Paul Mitchell, 230–46. Basingstoke, Hampshire: Palgrave Macmillan, 2003.

Coakley, John. "The Rise and Fall of Minor Parties in Ireland." *Irish Political Studies* 25, no. 4 (2010): 503–38.

Coakley, John. "The Rise and Fall of Minor Parties in Ireland, 1922–2011." In *Radical or Redundant? Minor Parties in Irish Politics,* edited by Liam Weeks and Alistair Clark, 46–78. Dublin: History Press Ireland, 2012.

Collins, Stephen. *Breaking the Mould: How the PDs Changed Ireland.* Dublin: Gill and MacMillan, 2005.

Collins, Stephen. "Handling of Seismic Events Was Good for Irish Politics." *Irish Times,* October 4, 2008: 15.

Collins, Stephen, ed. *The Irish Times Nealon's Guide to the 30th Dáil and 23rd Seanad.* Dublin: Gill and Macmillan, 2007.

Collins, Stephen. "Over 70% Support X-Case Legislation on Abortion." *Irish Times,* February 11, 2013.

Collins, Stephen. "Vast Majority Happy Ireland Is in EU." *Irish Times,* November 27, 2012.

Constitution of Ireland. http://www.taoiseach.gov.ie/eng/Historical_Information/The_Constitution/.

"Cowen Abandons Fianna Fáil Tent at Galway Races." *Irish Times,* December 3, 2008.

Creighton, Lucinda. Interview by Sean McGraw. Dublin, July 2007.

Cronin, Breda Moynihan. Interview by Sean McGraw. Killarney, County Kerry, Ireland, August 2007.

Currency Converter. http://www.oanda.com/currency/converter/.

Dalton, Russell J., David M. Farrell, and Ian McAllister. *Political Parties and Democratic Linkage: How Parties Organize Democracy.* Oxford: Oxford University Press, 2011.

Dalton, Russell J., and Martin P. Wattenberg. *Parties without Partisans: Political Change in Advanced Industrial Democracies.* Oxford: Oxford University Press, 2000.

Davin-Power, David. "The End of the Affair." In *The Week in Politics: Election 2011 and the 31st Dáil,* edited by Deirdre McCarthy, 10–11. Dublin: RTÉ Publishing, 2011.

Donnelly, Sean. E-mail message to Sean McGraw. August 2011.

Donnelly, Sean. "Number Cruncher: Sean Donnelly's Result Analysis." In *The Week in Politics: Election 2011 and the 31st Dáil,* edited by Deirdre McCarthy, 58–89. Dublin: RTÉ Publishing, 2011.

Donnelly, Sean. Website. ElectionsIreland.org.

Dorgan, Séan. Interview by Sean McGraw. Dublin, September 2007.

Dorgan, Séan. Interview by Sean McGraw. Dublin, October 2007.

Downs, Anthony. *An Economic Theory of Democracy*. New York: Harper, 1957.

"Dual Mandate Comes to an End." *RTÉ News*, June 2, 2003. http://www.rte.ie/news/2003/0602/dualmandate.html.

Dukes, Alan. Interview by Sean McGraw. Dublin, February 2007.

Durkan, Bernard. Interview by Sean McGraw. Dublin, July 2007.

"Election 2007: Following the Money." *Sunday Business Post*, December 12, 2007.

European Commission. Standard Eurobarometer. Last updated December 20, 2013. http://ec.europa.eu/public_opinion/archives/eb_arch_en.htm.

Ezrow, Lawrence, Catherine E. De Vries, Marco Steenbergen, and Erica E. Edwards. "Mean Voter Representation and Partisan Constituency Representation: Do Parties Respond to the Mean Voter Position or to Their Supporters?" *Party Politics* 17, no. 3 (2011): 275–301.

Fahey, Frank. Presentation at the Fianna Fáil Ard Fheis. Dublin, March 2007.

Fanning, Bryan, Jo Shaw, Jane-Ann O'Connell, and Marie Williams. *Irish Political Parties, Immigration, and Integration in 2007*. Dublin: University College Dublin, 2007.

Farrell, David M. *Electoral Systems: A Comparative Introduction*. Basingstoke, Hampshire: Palgrave MacMillan, 2001.

Farrell, David M. "Ireland: Centralization, Professionalization, and Competitive Pressures." In *How Parties Organize: Change and Adaptation in Party Organizations in Western Democracies*, edited by Richard S. Katz and Peter Mair, 216–41. London: Sage, 1994.

Farrell, David M., and Shaun Bowler. "Voter Behavior under STV-PR: Solving the Puzzle of the Irish Party System." *Political Behavior* 13, no. 4 (December 1991): 303–20.

Farrell, David M., and Jane Suiter. "It's the Policy, Stupid." In *The Week in Politics: Election 2011 and the 31st Dáil*, edited by Deirdre McCarthy, 54–57. Dublin: RTÉ Publishing, 2011.

Farrell, David M., and Jane Suiter. "The Parties' Manifestos." In *How Ireland Voted 2011: The Full Story of Ireland's Earthquake Election*, edited by Michael Marsh and Michael Gallagher, 29–46. Basingstoke, Hampshire: Palgrave MacMillan, 2011.

FitzGerald, Garret. Interview by Sean McGraw. Dublin, February 2007.

Fitzgerald, Séamus Cosái. Interview by Sean McGraw. Dingle, County Kerry, Ireland, August 2007.

Flannery, Frank. Interview by Sean McGraw. Dublin, October 2007.

Fleming, Tom. Interview by Sean McGraw. County Kerry, Ireland, August 2007.

Foley, Jackie. Interview by Sean McGraw. County Kerry, Ireland, August 2007.

Gallagher, Michael. "Constituency Service, the Role of the TD, and the Electoral System." Report to the Oireachtas Joint Committee on the Constitution, November 18, 2009. https://www.tcd.ie/Political_Science/staff/michael_gallagher/PresentationToCtteNov09.pdf.

Gallagher, Michael. "Ireland: The Discreet Charm of PR-STV." In *The Politics of Electoral Systems*, edited by Michael Gallagher and Paul Mitchell, 511–34. Oxford: Oxford University Press, 2005.

Gallagher, Michael. "The (Relatively) Victorious Incumbent under PR-STV: Legislative Turnover in Ireland and Malta." In *Elections in Australia, Ireland, and Malta under the Single Transferable Vote: Reflections on an Embedded Institution*, edited by Shaun Bowler and Bernard Grofman, 81–113. Ann Arbor: University of Michigan Press, 2000.

Gallagher, Michael. *Results of Survey of Members of Both Houses of the Oireachtas: The Electoral System, Representative Role of TDs, and Proposals for Change*. Interim report of the Oireachtas Joint Committee on the Constitution, February 2010. Dublin: Stationery Office.

Gallagher, Michael. "Societal Change and Party Adaptation in the Republic, 1960–1981." *European Journal of Political Research* 9 (1981): 269–85.

Gallagher, Michael, and Michael Marsh. *Days of Blue Loyalty: The Politics of Membership of the Fine Gael Party*. Dublin: PSAI Press, 2002.

Gallagher, Michael, and Michael Marsh, eds. *How Ireland Voted 2007*. Basingstoke, Hampshire: Palgrave Macmillan, 2008.

Gallagher, Michael, and Michael Marsh, eds. *How Ireland Voted 2011: The Full Story of Ireland's Earthquake Election*. Basingstoke, Hampshire: Palgrave Macmillan, 2011.

Garner, Steve. *Racism in the Irish Experience*. London: Pluto, 2004.

Garry, John, Fiachra Kennedy, Michael Marsh, and Richard Sinnott. "What Decided the Election?" In *How Ireland Voted 2002*, edited by Michael Gallagher, Michael Marsh, and Paul Mitchell, 119–42. Basingstoke, Hampshire: Palgrave Macmillan, 2003.

George, Alexander L., and Andrew Bennett. *Case Studies and Theory Development in the Social Sciences*. BCSIA Studies in International Security. Cambridge, MA: MIT Press, 2005.

Greeley, Andrew M. *Religion in Europe at the End of the Second Millennium: A Sociological Profile*. New Brunswick, NJ: Transaction, 2003.

"Green Ministers' Pay Rises to Go to Party." *Irish Times*, November 20, 2007.

Green-Pedersen, Christoffer. "The Growing Importance of Issue Competition: The Changing Nature of Party Competition in Western Europe." *Political Studies* 55, no. 3 (October 2007): 607–28.

Gormley, John. Interview by Sean McGraw. Dublin, April 2013.

Gunther, Richard, Jose Ramon Montero, and Juan J. Linz, eds. *Political Parties: Old Concepts and New Challenges*. New York: Oxford University Press, 2002.

Halligan, Brendan. Interview by Sean McGraw. Dublin, May 2007.

Hamann, Kerstin, and John Kelly. *Parties, Elections, and Policy Reforms in Western Europe: Voting for Social Pacts*. London: Routledge, 2011.

Hamann, Kerstin, and John Kelly. "Voters, Parties, and Social Pacts in Western Europe." Paper presented at the Fifteenth International Conference of the Council for European Studies, Chicago, March 29–April 2, 2006.

Hardiman, Niamh, and Colin Scott. "Governance as Polity: An Institutional Approach to the Evolution of State Functions in Ireland." *Public Administration* 88, no. 1 (March 2010): 170–89.

Hardiman, Niamh, and Christopher T. Whelan. *Politics and Democratic Values*. Dublin: Gill and Macmillan, 1994.

Hastings, Tim, Brian Sheehan, and Padraig Yeates. *Saving the Future: How Ireland's Social Partnership Shaped Ireland's Economic Success*. Dublin: Blackhall Publishing, 2007.

Healy-Rae, Michael. Interview by Sean McGraw. County Kerry, Ireland, May 2007.

Heston, Alan, Robert Summers, and Bettina Aten. Penn World Table Version 7.0. Center for International Comparisons of Production, Income, and Prices at the University of Pennsylvania, June 2011.

Hickey, John. Interview by Sean McGraw. Dublin, August 2007.

Hirczy de Mino, Wolfgang, and John C. Lane. "Malta: STV in a Two-Party System." In *Elections in Australia, Ireland, and Malta under the Single Transferable Vote: Reflections on an Embedded Institution*, edited by Shaun Bowler and Bernard Grofman, 178–204. Ann Arbor: University of Michigan Press, 2000.

Hirschman, Albert O. *Exit, Voice, and Loyalty: Responses to Decline in Firms, Organizations, and States*. Cambridge, MA: Harvard University Press, 1970.

Houses of the Oireachtas. Members Database. http://www.oireachtas.ie/membershist/.

Hughes, Ian, Paula Clancy, Clodagh Harris, and David Beetham, eds. *Power to the People? Assessing Democracy in Ireland*. Dublin: TASC at New Island, 2007.

Ipsos MRBI. Website. http://www.ipsosmrbi.com.

Irish Conservative Party. Website. http://www.conservatives.com/.

Irish National Election Study (INES) 2002–7. Trinity College Dublin, 2008. http://www.tcd.ie/ines/files/codebook_27_05_2009.pdf.

Irish National Election Study (INES) 2011. Trinity College Dublin, 2011. http://www.tcd.ie/ines/.

Iversen, Torbin. "Political Leadership and Representation in West European Democracies: A Test of Three Models of Voting." *American Journal of Political Science* 38, no. 1 (1994): 45–74.

Jesse, Neal G. "A Sophisticated Voter Model of Preferential Electoral Systems." In *Elections in Australia, Ireland, and Malta under the Single Transferable Vote: Reflections on an Embedded Institution*, edited by Shaun Bowler and Bernard Grofman. Ann Arbor: University of Michigan Press, 2000.

Karl, Terry Lynn. *The Paradox of Plenty: Oil Booms and Petro-States*. Berkeley: University of California Press, 1997.

Katzenstein, Peter J. *Policy and Politics in West Germany: The Growth of a Semisovereign State*. Philadelphia: Temple University Press, 1987.

Kavanagh, Adrian. "Geography and Irish Elections: A Case Study of the 2007 General Election." Paper presented at the Annual Conference of the Political Studies Association of Ireland, Dublin, October 19–21, 2007.

Kearney, A. T., and Foreign Policy. *The Globalization Index 2007*. http://www.foreignpolicy.com/articles/2007/10/11/the_globalization_index_2007.

Kelly, Fiach. "Kenny Ignores Own Pledge to Avoid Constituency Service." *Irish Independent*, May 17, 2011.

Kitschelt, Herbert. "The Demise of Clientelism." In *Patrons, Clients, and Policies: Patterns of Democratic Accountability and Political Competition*, edited by Herbert Kitschelt and Steven I. Wilkinson, 298–321. Cambridge: Cambridge University Press, 2007.

Kitschelt, Herbert. *The Logics of Party Formation*. Ithaca: Cornell University Press, 1989.

Kitschelt, Herbert. *The Transformation of European Social Democracy*. Cambridge: Cambridge University Press, 1994.

Kitschelt, Herbert, and Steven I. Wilkinson. "Citizen-Politician Linkages: An Introduction." In *Patrons, Clients, and Policies: Patterns of Democratic Accountability and Political Competition*, edited by Herbert Kitschelt and Steven I. Wilkinson, 1–49. Cambridge: Cambridge University Press, 2007.

Kitschelt, Herbert, and Steven I. Wilkinson. *Patrons, Clients, and Policies: Patterns of Democratic Accountability and Political Competition*. Cambridge: Cambridge University Press, 2007.

Krauss, Ellis S., and Robert Pekkanen. *The Rise and Fall of Japan's LPD: Political Party Organizations as Historical Institutions*. Ithaca: Cornell University Press, 2011.

Krouwel, Andre. "Party Models." In *The Handbook of Party Politics*, edited by Richard S. Katz and William J. Crotty, 249–69. London: Sage, 2006.

Laver, Michael, and Ernest Sergenti. *Party Competition: An Agent-Based Model*. Princeton: Princeton University Press, 2011.

Layte, Richard, Hannah McGee, Amanda Quail, Kay Rundle, Grainne Cousins, Claire Donnelly, Fiona Mulcahy, and Ronan Conroy. *The Irish Study of Sexual Health and Relationships*. http://www.ucd.ie/issda/static/documentation/esri/isshr-report.pdf. Dublin: Crisis Pregnancy Agency and Department of Health and Children, 2006.

Lee, J. J. *Ireland, 1912–1985: Politics and Society*. Cambridge: Cambridge University Press, 1989.

Lenihan, Conor. Interview by Sean McGraw. Dublin, March 2007.

Levitsky, Steven. *Transforming Labor-Based Parties in Latin America: Argentine Peronism in Comparative Perspective*. Cambridge: Cambridge University Press, 2003.

Lyons, Pat. *Public Opinion, Politics, and Society in Contemporary Ireland*. Dublin: Irish Academic Press, 2008.

Magaloni, Beatriz, Alberto Diaz-Cayeros, and Federico Estévez. "Clientelism and Portfolio Diversification: A Model of Electoral Investment with Applications to Mexico." In *Patrons, Clients, and Policies: Patterns of Democratic Accountability and Political Competition*, edited by Herbert Kitschelt and Steven I. Wilkinson, 182–205. Cambridge: Cambridge University Press, 2007.

Mainwaring, Scott, and Timothy R. Scully, eds. *Democratic Governance in Latin America*. Stanford: Stanford University Press, 2009.

Mainwaring, Scott, and Edurne Zoco. "Political Sequences and the Stabilization of Interparty Competition: Electoral Volatility in Old and New Democracies." *Party Politics* 13, no. 2 (2007): 155–78.

Mair, Peter. *The Changing Irish Party System: Organization, Ideology, and Electoral Competition*. London: Frances Pinter, 1987.

Mair, Peter. "Democracy beyond Parties." Working paper 05/06, Center for the Study of Democracy, University of California, Irvine, 2005. http://repositories.cdlib.org/csd/05-06.

Mair, Peter. "The Election in Context." In *How Ireland Voted 2011: The Full Story of Ireland's Earthquake Election*, edited by Michael Gallagher and Michael Marsh, 283–97. Basingstoke, Hampshire: Palgrave Macmillan, 2011.

Mair, Peter. "Left-Right Orientations." In *The Oxford Handbook of Political Behavior*, edited by Russell J. Dalton and Hans Dieter Klingemann, 206–22. Oxford: Oxford University Press, 2007.

Mair, Peter, and Michael Marsh. "Political Parties in Electoral Markets in Postwar Ireland." In *Political Parties and Electoral Change: Party Responses to Electoral Markets*, edited by Peter Mair, Wolfgang C. Müller, and Fritz Plasser, 234–63. London: Sage, 2004.

Mair, Peter, Wolfgang C. Müller, and Fritz Plasser, eds. *Political Parties and Electoral Change: Party Responses to Electoral Markets*. London: Sage, 2004.

Manifesto Project Database. CMP data, Version 2007a. https://manifesto-project. wzb.eu.

"Many Faiths in a Changing Ireland." *Irish Times*, May 15, 2008.

Maor, Moshe. *Political Parties and Party Systems: Comparative Approaches and the British Experience*. London: Routledge, 1997.

Marsh, Michael. "Explanations for Party Choice." In *How Ireland Voted 2007: The Full Story of Ireland's General Election*, edited by Michael Gallagher and Michael Marsh, 105–31. Basingstoke, Hampshire: Palgrave Macmillan, 2008.

Marsh, Michael. "Irish Voting Behavior." Unpublished manuscript, 2009.

Marsh, Michael. "Parties and Society." In *Politics in the Republic of Ireland*, edited by John Coakley and Michael Gallagher, 160–82. 4th ed. London: Routledge in association with PSAI Press, 2005.

Marsh, Michael. "Voting Behavior." In *Politics in the Republic of Ireland*, edited by John Coakley and Michael Gallagher, 168–97. 5th ed. London: Routledge in association with PSAI Press, 2010.

Marsh, Michael, and Kevin Cunningham. "A Positive Choice, or Anyone but Fianna Fáil." In *How Ireland Voted 2011: The Full Story of Ireland's Earthquake Election*, edited by Michael Gallagher and Michael Marsh, 172–204. Basingstoke, Hampshire: Palgrave Macmillan, 2011.

Marsh, Michael, Richard Sinnott, John Garry, and Fiachra Kennedy. *The Irish Voter: The Nature of Electoral Competition in the Republic of Ireland*. Manchester: Manchester University Press, 2008.

Matland, Richard E., and Donley T. Studlar. "Determinants of Legislative Turnover: A Cross-National Analysis." *British Journal of Political Science* 34, no. 1 (2004): 87–108.

Marxer, Wilfred, and Zoltan Tibor Pallinger. "Stabilizing or Destabilizing? Direct-Democratic Instruments in Different Political Systems." In *Referendums and Representative Democracy: Responsiveness, Accountability, and Deliberation*, edited by Maija Setala and Theo Schiller, 34–55. ECPR Studies in European Political Science. London: Routledge, 2009.

McCashin, Tony, Niamh Hardiman, and Diane Payne. "Understanding Irish Attitudes to Poverty and Wealth." In *Irish Social and Political Attitudes*, edited by John Garry, Diane Payne, and Niamh Hardiman, 43–59. Liverpool: Liverpool University Press, 2006.

McDaid, Shaun, and Kacper Rekawak. "From Mainstream to Minor and Back: The Irish Labour Party, 1987–1992." *Irish Political Studies* 25, no. 4 (2010): 625–42.

McDowell, Michael. Interview by Sean McGraw. Dublin, May 2007.

McDowell, Michael. Interview by Sean McGraw. Dublin, July 2007.

McDowell, Michael. Interview by Sean McGraw. Dublin, September 2007.

McGarry, Patsy. "Catholics' Beliefs Not Always by the Book." *Irish Times*, November 30, 2012.

McGee, Harry. "Seamus Brennan." *IrishTimes.com*, July 9, 2008. http://www.irish-times.com/blogs/politics/2008/07/09/seamus-brennan/.

McGraw, Sean. Interview with Fianna Fáil party official. Dublin, November 2012.

McGraw, Sean. Interview with former government advisor. Dublin, June 2011.

McGraw, Sean. Interviews with the top eight finishers in Dublin South-East in the 2007 election. Dublin, July 2007.

McGraw, Sean. Irish parliamentary survey with elected TDs. Dublin, 2010.

McGraw, Sean. Irish parliamentary survey with elected TDs. Dublin, 2012.

McGraw, Sean. "Managing Change: Party Competition in New Ireland." PhD diss., Harvard University, 2009.

McGraw, Sean, and Kevin Whelan. "Daniel O'Connell in Comparative Perspective, 1800–1850." *Eire-Ireland: An Interdisciplinary Journal of Irish Studies* 40, nos. 1–2 (2005): 60–89.

McKenna, Fionnula. "Annual Deaths in Northern Ireland, by 'Status' of Person Killed, August 1969 to December 1995." CAIN Web Service. http://cain.ulst.ac.uk/issues/violence/death95w.htm (accessed 2008).

McKeown, Timothy J. "Case Studies and the Limits of the Quantitative Worldview." In *Re-thinking Social Inquiry: Diverse Tools, Shared Standards*, edited by Henry E. Brady and David Collier, 139–67. Oxford: Rowman and Littlefield, 2004.

Meguid, Bonnie M. *Party Competition between Unequals: Strategies and Electoral Fortunes in Western Europe*. Cambridge: Cambridge University Press, 2008.

Ministers and Secretaries Act, 1924. Irish Statute Book. http://www.irishstatutebook.ie/1924/en/act/pub/0016/.

"Ministers' Constituency Staff Cost €4m a Year." *Irish Times*, November 8, 2007.

Morgan, Jana. *Bankrupt Representation and Party System Collapse*. University Park: Pennsylvania State University Press, 2011.

Morgan, Jana. "Partisanship during the Collapse of Venezuela's Party System." *Latin American Research Review* 42 (2007): 78–98.

Müller, Wolfgang C., and Kaare Strøm. *Policy, Office, or Votes? How Political Parties in Western Europe Make Hard Decisions*. Cambridge: Cambridge University Press, 1999.

Murphy, Catherine. Interview by Sean McGraw. County Kildare, Ireland, July 2007.

"Muslims Have Integrated Well Despite Recent Arrival." *Irish Times*, May 14, 2008.

Nealon, Ted. *Nealon's Guide to the 23rd Dáil and Seanad: Election '73*. Dublin: Gill and Macmillan, 1974.

Ni Bhaoighealláin, Lynn. Interview by Sean McGraw. County Kerry, Ireland. August 2007.

Nolan, Brian, and Bertrand Maitre. "A Comparative Perspective on Trends in Income Inequality in Ireland." *Economic and Social Review* 31, no. 4 (October 2000): 329–50.

Norwegian Centre Party. Website. http://www.senterpartiet.no/category11868.html.

O'Callaghan, Jim. Interview by Sean McGraw. Dublin, July 2007.

Ó Caomhanaigh, Colm. Interview by Sean McGraw. Dublin, December 2007.

Ó Cinnéide, Seamus. "Democracy and the Constitution." *Administration* 51, nos. 1–2 (Spring–Summer 2003): 326–40.

O'Connor-Scarteen, Michael. Interview by Sean McGraw. Kenmare, County Kerry, Ireland, August 2007.

O'Donnell, Rory, and Damian Thomas. "Social Partnership and the Policy Process." In *Social Policy in Ireland: Principles, Practice, and Problems*, edited by Séan Healy, Brigid Reynolds, and Micheál L. Collins, 117–46. Rev. ed. Dublin: Liffey, 2006.

O'Donoghue, John. Interview by Sean McGraw. Cahersiveen, County Kerry, Ireland, August 2007.

Oireachtas (Ministerial and Parliamentary Offices) (Secretarial Facilities) (No. 5) Regulations 2004. Irish Statute Book. http://www.irishstatutebook.ie/2004/en/si/0888.html.

O'Keefe, Alan. "Democracy Now Celebs Ditch Their Election Bid." *Herald.ie*, January 31, 2011. http://www.herald.ie/news/democracy-now-celebs-ditch-their-election-bid-27972149.html.

O'Leary, Brendan. "Towards Europeanisation and Realignment? The Irish General Election." *West European Politics* 10, no. 3 (2011): 455–65.

O'Leary, Eimear Noelle. "'Political Gatekeepers': An Analysis of the Brokerage Activities of TDs and MLAs." PhD diss., University College Cork, 2011.

O'Leary, John. Interview by Sean McGraw. County Kerry, Ireland, August 2007.

O'Malley, Desmond, Catherine Murphy, and Dan Boyle. "Life in a Minor Party." In *Radical or Redundant? Minor Parties in Irish Politics*, edited by Liam Weeks and Alistair Clark, 79–93. Dublin: History Press Ireland, 2012.

O'Malley, Eoin. "Punch Bags for Heavyweights? Minor Parties in Irish Government." *Irish Political Studies* 25, no. 4 (2010): 539–61.

Panebianco, Angelo. *Political Parties: Organization and Power*. Cambridge: Cambridge University Press, 1988.

Partido Democratico. Website. http://www.partitodemocratico.it/.

Parti Radical. Website. http://www.partiradical.net/.

Party of European Socialists (PES). Website. http://www.pes.eu/.

Pierre, Jon, Lars Svasand, and Anders Widfelt. "State Subsidies to Political Parties: Confronting Rhetoric with Reality." *West European Politics* 23, no. 3 (2000): 1–24.

Potter, Corrie. "Left-Right Self-Placement in Western Europe: What Responses and Non-Responses Indicate." Political Behavior Group, University of Wisconsin–Madison, 2001.

Przeworski, Adam, and John Sprague. *Paper Stones: A History of Electoral Socialism*. Chicago: University of Chicago Press, 1986.

Rabbitte, Pat. Interview by Sean McGraw. Dublin, October 2007.

"Reelection Rates over the Years." OpenSecrets.org. http://www.opensecrets.org/bigpicture/reelect.php?cycle=2006.

Romero, Anibal. "Rearranging the Deck Chairs on the Titanic: The Agony of Democracy in Venezuela." *Latin American Research Review* 32 (1997): 7–36.

RTÉ. *General Election 2011—Exit Poll*. Dublin: Millward Brown Lansdowne, 2011. http://www.rte.ie/news/election2011/election2011-exit-poll.pdf.

"RTÉ Exit Poll. 2007." *RTÉ News*, May 25, 2007. http://www.rte.ie/news/2007/0525/RTEExitPoll2007.

Sacks, Paul M. *The Donegal Mafia: An Irish Political Machine*. New Haven: Yale University Press, 1976.

Sani, Giacomo, and Giovanni Sartori. "Polarization, Fragmentation, and Competition in Western Democracies." In *Western European Party Systems: Continuity and Change*, edited by Hans Daalder and Peter Mair, 307–40. Beverly Hills, CA: Sage, 1983.

Sartori, Giovanni. "The Influence of Electoral Systems: Faulty Laws or Faulty Method?" In *Electoral Laws and Their Political Consequences*, edited by Bernard Grofman and Arend Lijphart, 43–65. New York: Agathon, 1986.

Schiller, Theo. "Conclusions." In *Referendums and Representative Democracy: Responsiveness, Accountability, and Deliberation*, edited by Maija Setala and Theo Schiller, 207–19. ECPR Studies in European Political Science. London: Routledge, 2009.

Schmitter, Philippe C. "Parties Are Not What They Once Were." In *Political Parties and Democracy*, edited by Larry Jay Diamond and Richard Gunther, 67–89. Baltimore: Johns Hopkins University Press, 2001.

Scully, Darren. Interview by Sean McGraw. County Kildare, Ireland, July 2007.

Seawright, Jason. *Party System Collapse: The Roots of Crisis in Peru and Venezuela*. Stanford: Stanford University Press, 2012.

Sheahan, Tom. Interview by Sean McGraw. County Kerry, Ireland, August 2007.

Shu, Min. "Cope with Two-Dimensional Cleavage Structure: Party Politics in Referendums on European Integration." Paper presented at Workshop 19, "Cleavage Development: Causes and Consequences," ECPR Joint Sessions, Edinburgh, March 28–April 2, 2003.

Sinnott, Richard. "Appendix 4: The Electoral System." In *How Ireland Voted 2002*, edited by Michael Gallagher, Michael Marsh, and Paul Mitchell, 260–61. Basingstoke, Hampshire: Palgrave Macmillan, 2003.

Sinnott, Richard. *Irish Voters Decide: Voting Behaviour in Elections and Referendums since 1918*. Manchester: Manchester University Press, 1995.

Sinnott, Richard. "The Rules of the Electoral Game." In *Politics in the Republic of Ireland*, edited by John Coakley and Michael Gallagher, 105–34. 4th ed. London: Routledge in association with PSAI Press, 2005.

Sinnott, Richard. "The Voters, the Issues, and the Party System." In *Ireland at the Polls, 1981, 1982, and 1987: A Study of Four General Elections*, edited by Howard Rae Penniman and Brian Farrell, 55–98. Durham, NC: Duke University Press, 1987.

Standards in Public Office Commission. *Annual Reports*. http://www.sipo.gov.ie/en/Reports/Annual-Reports/.

Standards in Public Office Commission. "Donations Statements Furnished by Political Parties for 2006." http://www.sipo.gov.ie/en/Reports/Annual-Disclosures/Disclosure-by-Political-Parties/2006-Donation-Statements/.

Suiter, Jane. "The Geo-Politics of Irish Education Spending." Paper presented at the Annual Conference of the Political Studies Association of Ireland, National University of Ireland, Galway, October 17–19, 2008.

Suiter, Jane. "Pork Barrel Spending in Ireland—Fact or Fiction?" PhD diss., Trinity College Dublin, 2009.

Tuohy, Brendan. Interview by Sean McGraw. Dublin, December 2007.

Valenzuela, Arturo, and J. Samuel Valenzuela. "Party Oppositions under the Chilean Authoritarian Regime." Working Paper 125, Woodrow Wilson International Center for Scholars, Washington, DC, 1983. http://www.wilsoncenter. org/sites/default/files/125.Party%20Opposition.Valenzuela%20%2526%20 Valenzuela.pdf.

Volkens, Andrea. "Quantifying the Election Programmes: Coding Procedures and Controls." In *Mapping Policy Preferences: Estimates for Parties, Electors, and Governments, 1945–1998*, edited by Ian Budge, Hans Dieter Klingemann, Andrea Volkens, Judith Bara, and Eric Tanenbaum, 93–109. Oxford: Oxford University Press, 2001.

Wall, Frank. Interview by Sean McGraw. Dublin, December 2007.

Walsh, Dick. *The Party: Inside Fianna Fáil.* Dublin: Gill and Macmillan, 1986.

Walsh, James A. *People and Place: A Census Atlas of the Republic of Ireland.* Maynooth, County Kildare: National Institute for Regional and Spatial Analysis, National University of Ireland, Maynooth, 2007.

Weeks, Liam. "Appendix 4: The Irish Electoral System." In *How Ireland Voted 2007: The Full Story of Ireland's General Election*, edited by Michael Gallagher and Michael Marsh, 246–47: Basingstoke, Hampshire: Palgrave Macmillan, 2008.

Weeks, Liam. "We Don't Like to Party: Explaining the Significance of Independents in Irish Political Life." Paper presented at the First Annual International Conference of Minor Parties, Independent Politicians, Voter Associations, and Political Associations in Politics, Institute of Local Government Studies, University of Birmingham, November 29–December 1, 2007.

Weeks, Liam, and Alistair Clark, eds. "Minor Parties in Irish Political Life." Special issue, *Irish Political Studies* 25, no. 4 (2010).

Weeks, Liam, and Aodh Quinlivan. *All Politics Is Local.* Cork: Collins, 2009.

Whyte, J. H. "Ireland: Politics without Social Bases." In *Electoral Behaviour: A Comparative Handbook*, edited by Richard Rose, 619–51. New York: Free Press, 1974.

World Bank. World DataBank. http://databank.worldbank.org/data/home.aspx.

World Values Survey. Surveys for 1981, 1990, and 1999. http://www.worldvalues survey.org.

Index

Note: Page numbers in italics refer to figures and tables.